D0078439

The Constitution and Economic Regulation

The Constitution and Economic Regulation

Objective Theory and Critical Commentary

Michael Conant

Transaction Publishers

New Brunswick (U.S.A.) and London (U.K.)

Library of Congress Catalog Number: 2008007307
ISBN: 978-1-4128-0774-6
Printed in the United States of America

Library of Congress Cataloging-in-Publication Data

Conant, Michael.
    The constitution and economic regulation : objective theory and critical commentary / Michael Conant.
            p. cm.
    Rev. ed. of: The constitution and the economy. University of Oklahoma
        Press, 1991.
    Includes bibliographical references and index.
    ISBN 978-1-4128-0774-6
    1. Economic liberties (U.S. Constitution) 2. Industrial laws and
legislation—United States. 3. Trade regulation—United States.
    4. Interstate commerce—Law and legislation—United States. I. Conant,
Michael. Constitution and the economy. II. Title.

KF1600.C54 2008
343.73'07—dc22   2008007307

Contents

Preface

Constitution and Economic Regulation

This study is a major revision and expansion of nine chapters in my 1991 book, *The Constitution and the Economy*. The key additions are, first, an emphasis on the epistemology of overrulings by the Supreme Court of earlier Supreme Court Opinions that had violated the textual meanings of the Constitution. The second new emphasis is on mistaken appeal briefs that centered on the wrong constitutional clauses as measured by the facts of the litigation. This aspect reinforces the framework of my earlier edition that criticizes the misinterpretation of constitutional language as measured by original meanings. The judicial creation of substantive due process, for example, was in direct violation of the historical proof that the due process clauses were limited to fair procedure. The third new emphasis is on those cases where the Supreme Court majority seems to have ignored trial court findings of fact and, in error, stated contrary facts. In all of the chapters, the notes have been revised to include the applicable books and articles since 1990.

Chapter 1 is an economic approach to constitutional structure and functions. The main addition to Chapter 1 is the appendix entitled "Amending the Amendment Clause." Most scholars who have written about the clause have failed to stress its extreme anti-majoritarian character. This appendix explains the issue of the power of those states with the least population to have two chances to block amendments: once in the Senate and the second upon voting for ratification.

The objective theory of interpretation in Chapter 2 utilizes the method of textual analysis of constitutional language, emphasizing text in its social context. It has been adopted by Justice Antonin Scalia in his book, *A Matter of Interpretation* (1997), an explanation of his decision process in the Supreme Court. This methodology is conservative in that it points to the Amendment Clause of Article 5 as the only way for change in constitutional language. This approach views the canons of documentary construction as the first step in constitutional interpretation. Law students must be informed that in law the noun "construction" is derived from the verb "to construe."

The appendix to Chapter 2 is entitled "Epistemology of Overruling." It explains the uncertainty in constitutional law, especially of 5 to 4 Supreme Court decisions, and the need to correct earlier errors by the Court. The quotations from the definitive dissenting opinions of Justice Oliver Wendell Holmes, Jr. are certified as the correct interpretations in cases where the majority opinions were later overruled as violating the textual meaning of the applicable constitutional clauses.

Chapter 3 concerns judicial review of legislation. Special emphasis is on the presumption of legality of national substantive laws. In contrast, the judicial enforcement of constitutional limitations on government receives the highest status.

Chapter 4, on the Commerce Clause, had demonstrated the plenary power in Congress to regulate all private transactions in the nation. The latter part of the chapter has been rewritten and expanded to present additional quotations from cases after 1935. As these cases overruled earlier decisions that had limited the federal regulatory power over commerce, they merely restored the textual meaning of the commerce clause. The constitutional text had made the issue of regulation one for the federal and state legislatures, not the judiciary.

Chapter 5 concerns the complex issue of whether the Congress may regulate transactions by states and their agencies. The basic presumption against such regulation is the primary test of federalism.

The appendix to Chapter 6 on the Law Merchant presents extended information on treatises that were available to men at the Constitutional Convention and to others about the time of *Swift v. Tyson.* The first was Charles Molloy's 1769 study of maritime commercial law that emphasizes the origins as part of the law of nations. The second is Justice Joseph Story's *Commentaries on the Law of Bills of Exchange* (1843), which integrates the English and American law.

The appendix to Chapter 7 on the Privileges or Immunities Clause reviews the English constitutional foundations to the U.S. Bill of Rights and such rights in early state constitutions. The first issue reports a critique of Chief Justice John Marshall's opinion in *Baron v. Baltimore,* that none of the Bill of Rights was a constraint on state governments. This is followed by a review of the compelling evidence that the majority of members in the 39th Congress proposed the 14th Amendment to make the states subject to the Bill of Rights.

Chapter 8 on the due process clauses has been almost doubled in length. The first section that presents the proof that process was a synonym for procedure is largely unchanged. There is additional reasoning that "liberty" had a limited textual meaning of freedom from imprisonment. The judicial creation of the erroneous concept of substantive due process is summarized more critically. The final third of the chapter reviews the series of overrulings that corrected the creation of liberty of contract.

Chapter 9 is a new chapter reporting on the judicial bias against labor unions with the courts erroneous use of the antitrust laws and substantive due process.

This is followed by a survey of overrulings by the Supreme Court beginning in 1939. Sections 6 and 20 of the Clayton Act are printed as the first step to assist labor unions. The function of the Norris-La Guardia Act to reinforce the Clayton Act is also reviewed.

Chapter 10 is a greatly enlarged study of the Equal Protection Clause as applied to ethnic caste systems. The key application to African-Americans did not mean that the clause protected only one group. The entire chapter has been rewritten in greater detail. Starting with the section, "Plessy was Error," a much larger and detailed analysis explains this violation of the textual meaning of equal protection.

Introduction

Economic Analysis and the Law

This study utilizes basic economics analysis as a technique to comment critically on the original meanings and the interpretations of those clauses of the Constitution that have particular bearing on the economy. Many of the conclusions are markedly different from those of the Supreme Court and earlier commentators. The view presented here is that the Commerce Clause and the Equal Protection Clause, if they had been construed consistently with their comprehensive original meanings, would have given much greater protection against state laws that impaired free markets. On the other hand, most of the final determination of economic policy for the nation was vested in Congress. To the extent that special interests could buy congressional favor for their anti-competitive activities, free markets could be impaired within the constitutional constraints as interpreted by the court. Many of these cases are criticized here for their failure to recognize the incorporation of the British antimonopoly tradition in the Ninth Amendment or their failure to recognize equal protection of the laws as incorporated into the Fifth Amendment.

This chapter summarizes for the non-economist the basic economic concepts used in the critical analysis of the Constitution and its interpretations by the courts. Some readers may find this chapter too brief. They are urged to read the first few chapters of a basic text on law and economics or to study the articles cited in the notes to this chapter.[1] It is most important to observe that the economic approach to law is only a partial one. It cannot solve all of the problems of public choice related to the economy let alone the other multiple social problems of a society.[2]

Economic policy can be understood only if one divides the issues into three main categories: (1) microeconomics, resource allocation in the productive processes; (2) macroeconomics, national income analysis and monetary policy; and (3) distribution of income. While governmental policies in any of these three areas can have effects in the other areas, it is impossible to engage in rigorous analysis without determining effects in the primary area first. For example, attempts to use microeconomic solutions for macroeconomic problems are foredoomed to failure. The macroeconomic problem of the economic depression of the 1930's resulted in Congress adopting microeconomic policies approving price-fixing in the National Industrial Recovery Act and the Agricultural Adjustment Act. As economists predicted, the monopoly pricing aggravated the national income problem.

Policy issues primarily concerned with the distribution of income are of a class where economic analysis is of least use. The ultimate distribution of income is the result of redistribution of income pursuant to legislative policy.[3] The major policy issues are philosophical rather than economic. Redistribution of income through taxation and spending can have negative effects on the economy, however, if taxation reaches a level that it impairs incentives to produce goods and services. But the basic issues of whether to adopt a marginal increase in taxes for public schools, subsidized health care for the poor or welfare payments for dependent children are philosophical.

The primary standard of microeconomic policy is efficiency. Knight defines efficiency as the ratio between useful output and total input in any production process.[4] Useful output has meaning only because it has value in the marketplace. Modern welfare economics defines efficiency in terms of Pareto superiority.[5] Taking the distribution of wealth and income as given for purposes of this microeconomic analysis, an efficient allocation of resources is one in which value is maximized. A Pareto superior transaction is one that makes at least one person better off and no other person worse off. Each person is assumed to be the best judge of his own welfare. If he enters a transaction that leaves no one worse off, he is presumed to increase total value.

If there is no situation where a Pareto superior shift can be made, then the state of affairs is Pareto optimal. This approach to maximizing value has the advantage that it does not require interpersonal comparisons of utility. It has the disadvantage that it is generally not useful as a guide for the adoption of regulatory statutes. Most statutes are designed to make some set of persons better off, but there are usually some others upon whom the impact is negative.

A less restrictive definition of efficiency is that of Kaldor-Hicks, which is adopted by most economists. Kaldor-Hicks efficiency exists if in moving to a potentially Pareto superior state, the parties could compensate anyone who is made worse off. If the compensation is actually paid, the transaction becomes Pareto superior. But in large numbers of situations, measurement of harm to third parties and the transaction costs of negotiating payment make it infeasible to compensate third parties. Thus a move toward freer trade, such as a reduction in the protected price for sugar, is Kaldor-Hicks efficient since it lowers the sugar price for all consumers closer to the cost of efficient sugar cane producers. This is true even if there is no compensation to the formerly protected, higher-cost sugar beet growers who had to shift to a less profitable crop and scrap some specialized farm machinery.

There are two general classes of cases for not compensating losers even if the amount of loss is subject to reasonable estimation. Where the regulatory statute is designed to correct a market failure, there is no reason to compensate losers. If antitrust laws are enforced against a cartel, the public gains and those who had restrained trade lose. If a regulated industry such as airline transport had blocked entry of new firms, deregulation that fostered entry and lowered rates for consumers would have negative effects on income of former monopolists.

There is also no logical reason for compensation if the transaction costs of administering compensation would be greater than the losses of those disadvantaged. Transaction costs include search costs. The problem is especially severe where there is involuntary exchange. If political activists cause an ordinance to be passed allowing loud speakers in a public park, they and those who like political speeches gain. Those who can no longer enjoy a quiet park are an indeterminate number and the correct compensation for any one of them is not subject to reasonable estimation.

Productive efficiency within firms and among firms exists when any given level of output is produced with the least cost combination of inputs.[6] Presuming inputs can be obtained in effectively competitive markets, efficiency is obtained by minimizing long-run average costs. If such condition is met, there is no possible shift in resource use within firms or between firms that would create greater output. If competitive prices prevail, there is incentive in all firms to achieve productive efficiency. Thus, competitive markets are said to have, through the bidding of buyers and sellers in input and output markets, an automatic allocation of resources that is efficient. This automaticity is sometimes labeled an "invisible hand."

Minimizing long-run average costs has the effect of determining the optimum sizes of plants and firms in relation to the sizes of markets in which they operate.[7] Before 1940, for example, because of the relatively low labor costs and the fact that a significant proportion of the working class and the unemployed had no automobiles, the optimum size urban grocery store was small and within walking distance of most of its customers. The postwar economic expansion with its rising labor costs, economies of large-scale purchasing, and a great majority of customers with autos resulted in the low-cost retail food store being very large and accompanied by a parking lot. The economic terminology for the reduction of average costs of production with larger size of plant or firm is economies of scale. The corollary is diseconomies of scale, in which average costs rise because costs of coordination exceed any economies resulting from larger size. This same terminology can be applied to the costs of government. The very large bureaucracy of the United States government and the lack of coordination in control of expenditures has caused many persons to decry its diseconomies of large scale.

Statutory controls of the economy are justifiable in economic theory if they are designed to remedy market failures and thereby increase efficiency. If statutes are passed to interfere with markets and create market inefficiencies for the benefit of special interest groups, they are to be condemned under the standards of normative microeconomics. There are four main classes of market failure: monopoly, externalities, public goods, and informational asymmetry.

Monopoly may occur in many aspects. A single firm may control the output of a product or the supply of an input of production. Where the number of firms in a market is few, they may combine to form a monopoly in a product market or an input market. Since monopoly raises prices above competitive levels by curtailing supplies, it makes for inefficiencies. The antitrust laws are designed to replace monopoly with competition where this is possible. In some instances, economies of scale in relation to the size of market are such that a monopoly is the least-cost firm. Structural monopolies such as water, electric, and local telephone utilities are examples. Statutory regulation to control monopoly pricing by such firms has received judicial approval at least since *Munn v. Illinois*.[8] Another class of monopolies that is promoted by federal statutes enacted pursuant to a specific power in Article I, Section 8 of the Constitution includes patents and copyrights. Monopolies for a limited time period are designed to promote invention and creative written works.

Externalities are the second class of market failures. While free exchange in a market is voluntary and increases value to the parties, some transactions or production processes have effects on third parties that are involuntary and sometimes harmful. A negative or harmful externality imposes costs on third parties without their consent. Pollution of streams or air by a production process is the most common example. The action of a factory can impose involuntary costs on those downstream or within the air pollution area. The costs imposed on any particular third party may be small in any single year but cumulative. The damage is hard to prove and litigation costs for an action in the tort of nuisance may be very high. The lack of a feasible remedy can be thought of as either a market failure or a judicial failure. The solution is statutory regulation that forces the firm to pay the total social cost of its production by forcing it to expend funds to reduce the level of pollution. While total elimination of pollution in an industrial nation might bring most factory production to a halt, there is some optimal level of pollution consistent with continued benefits of most productive processes.[9]

Public goods are the third class of items making for market failure. A public good has two primary characteristics. First is the fact of non-rivalous consumption. Consumption of the good or service by one person leaves it equally available to others. Second, the cost of excluding non-payers from the good or service is so high that no private enterprise will supply the good. Paving city streets is a key example. If one householder on a block were to pay for paving it, all other householders on the block could use it for free. Hence the term free rider. The cost of administering tollgates is so great that no private enterpriser could undertake the paving profitably. Consequently, only government with the power of taxation is able to successfully create public goods. The police and national defense are other common examples of public goods. Protection available to one citizen protects all others from the same harm. It is not possible to exclude those who would refuse to pay if payment were voluntary from those receiving the benefits of the service.

Asymmetric information is the fourth class of market failure. Sellers very often know much more about the quality of goods than buyers, and buyers may not even have enough knowledge to ask the right questions in the ordinary bargain in the market. This fact rebuts the presumption of the law of contract that sane adults are equal bargainers. If sellers know significantly more about a good or service, or vice versa, there is material information asymmetry in the market. In some cases, this asymmetry is corrected by market forces as sellers offer express warranties of quality in order to meet the competition of rivals. In other cases, the market fails to evoke express warranties to offset information asymmetries. Statutory intervention was necessary to correct the market failure. The Uniform Commercial Code, following the earlier model in the Uniform Sales Act, imposes implied warranties of quality and fitness for purpose upon sellers of goods. Similar statutes to induce more nearly optimal exchange are found in state statutes requiring termite inspection paid for by sellers of houses. In a key case under the commerce clause, an 1838 statute remedied asymmetry of information between owners of ships and passengers on inland waters by requiring licensing and safety inspection of ships.[10]

One important emphasis in this study is that litigation costs are analogous to transaction costs. If legal principles and rules are clearly and precisely defined by the Supreme Court when they are first construed on appeal, litigation and its costs should be minimized. The bar will have meaningful standards for advising clients and trial courts will have clear bases for granting demurrers to frivolous actions. In contrast, if legal principles or rules have a high degree of uncertainty because they lack definable standards, the number of legal actions filed and litigation costs will be much greater. There are many examples of this uncertainty phenomenon in constitutional law. One outstanding example in the economic sector, as treated in detail in Chapter 8, was the judicial creation of substantive due process. The happenstance of judicial appointments led to the five-man majority that joined in the erroneous opinion in *Lochner v. New York*.[11] Trial courts, relying on this opinion, heard hundreds of cases concerning the reasonableness of statutes regulating the economy. The period from 1905 to 1937 came to be known as the *Lochner* era. The impossibility of definable standards of reasonableness in what was essentially a legislative issue led to other five-man erroneous decisions in the Supreme Court such as *Adkins v. Childrens Hospital*.[12] This in turn promoted additional litigation challenging the many statutes enacted to remedy asserted market failures in an expanding industrial economy.

Notes

1. See Richard Posner, *Economic Analysis of Law*, 3d ed., (Boston: Little Brown, 1986); Richard Cooter and Thomas Ulen, *Law and Economics* (Glenview, IL: Scott Foreman, 1988); Werner Hirsch, *Law and Economics* (New York: Academic Press, 1979); A. M. Polinsky, *An Introduction to Law and Economics,* 2d ed., (Boston: Little Brown, 1989).
2. See Frank Knight, *The Economic Organization,* 3-4 (New York: Harper & Row, 1951); Kenneth Arrow, *Social Choice and Individual Values,* 2d ed., (New York: Wiley, 1963).
3. Harold Hochman and George Peterson, eds., *Redistribution through Public Choice* (New York: Columbia University Press, 1974).
4. Knight, *supra* note 2, at 10.
5. See Jules Coleman, *Economics and the Law: A Critical Review of the Foundations of the Economic Approach to Law,* 94 Ethics 649 (1984).
6. In technical economic language, the value of the marginal product of each factor is equal to its price in every use. Since the price of the factor is competitively determined, any disequilibrium is caused by differences in marginal physical productivities. In such a case, it is more efficient to switch some of the input from a firm with lower marginal productivity to one with higher marginal productivity. The operation of competitive bidding for inputs in free markets automatically should result in each firm minimizing the long-run average cost of producing any given output.
7. See George Stigler, *The Economics of Scale,* in *The Organization of Industry,* 71 (Homewood, IL, Richard Irwin, 1968); Stigler, *The Division of Labor is Limited by the Extent of the Market, Id.* at 129.
8. 94 U.S. 113 (1877).
9. See William Baxter, *People or Penguins: The Case for Optimal Pollution* (New York: Columbia University Press, 1974).
10. *The Daniel Ball,* 77 U.S. (10 Wall.) 557 (1871).
11. 196 U.S. 45 (1905).
12. 261 U.S. 525 (1925), *overruled* in *West Coast Hotel Co. v. Parrish,* 300 U.S. 379 (1937).

1

Constitutional Structure and Functions

A national constitution is primarily a political document whose main function is to create a structure of government and a set of limitations on government to protect individual rights.[1] From an economic viewpoint, citizens with freedom to create a republican form of government are allocating resources to acquire that protection of life, liberty, and property necessary for long-term peaceful existence. Absent government, persons might spend most of their time defending themselves, their families, and their meager assets. Government with a monopoly on physical force is the most efficient means of obtaining a general peaceful environment so that most citizens can produce goods and services other than defense. Government is thus a machine with a set of processes which allows collective action in a free society.[2]

Clear economies of scale exist in government as the means to control human aggression. The larger the geographic area under common governmental control, the less likely it is that a tribe or nation will have to engage in war with neighboring tribes or nations. The urge to extend the realm of peace through law and the finding of the means to do it are clearly as old and as enduring as the urge to fight.[3] In 1437, for example, the Florentines went to war with Lucca.[4] The modern unification of Italy under a single government leads many to forget the centuries of wars between the city states.[5] The potential for violent conflict between the thirteen former English colonies was greatly reduced by replacing the Articles of Confederation with a national Constitution that created a single free trade area and allocated the military force to the national government.[6]

From an economic viewpoint, the constitutional principles of government can be seen as a set of given goals or constraints. The economic issue is how to allocate human and other resources in order to achieve these goals with efficiency, a minimum cost. In this context, the primary cost must be defined in terms of social conflict, the breaking down of political institutions. Consequently, efficient government is firstly that which fosters long-term social stability. Such a system concentrates social policy differences in institutions that function well in resolving them peacefully, usually legislatures. While legislative processes

1

may be inefficient in procedures, their responsiveness to the electorate makes them the most efficient social institutions to resolve social conflict.

Revolution and civil war are evidence of inefficiency of key operative institutions of government in resolving social conflict. The *Dred Scott*[7] case is an outstanding example. The judiciary attempted to usurp the resolution of the major political conflict of the time, the issue of whether slavery should be expanded into the western territories. The issue had been tentatively settled by the Congress in the Missouri Compromise,[8] which the Court in *Dred Scott* held unconstitutional.[9] The majority decision was one significant factor that desta-bilized social relations on an issue that had been partially settled. The Court could have avoided the constitutional issue and ruled on the narrower one of whether the "voluntary" return of Scott to Missouri precluded a challenge to his status.[10] Instead the majority adopted a view that aggravated the controversy that led eventually to civil war.

The Constitution of the United States is held to be basic and superior law because it is derived from the people themselves through the process of ratifica-tion. This is immediately apparent from the Preamble which begins, "We the people of the United States, in order to form a more perfect union . . ."[11] Chief Justice John Marshall pointed out that the Constitutional Convention created a mere proposal to be submitted to the conventions of delegates in each of the states for ratification. He concluded: "The government of the Union . . . is emphatically, and truly, a government of the people. In form and in substance, it emanates from them. Its powers are granted by them, and are to be exercised directly on them, and for their benefit."[12]

The key clauses of a constitution are general principles of government. They differ from the narrow rules of liability found in most of the common law and statutes, both in their magnitude of generality and their function of creating a structure for public law. Nevertheless, it is error to presume that most constitutional principles were wholly designed in the convention. The origin of many is evolutionary as is the common law and most rules enacted into statutes.[13] The vesting of all national legislative powers in the Congress, for example, derives from the British parliamentary supremacy over the king, incorporated in the Bill of Rights of 1689.[14] This was the result of centuries of conflict to establish effective representative government.[15] As to civil rights, the British Habeas Corpus Act of 1679[16] was the result of a long fight against arbitrary imprisonment.[17] Even though the act was not operative in the colonies, every former colonist in America claimed the benefit of this principle, whether incorporated in a written state constitution or not. This was reconfirmed by the Ninth Amendment.

In economic terms, votes needed to get law enacted can be viewed as costs. The Constitution of the United States differs from statute law in its higher costs of enactment and amendment.[18] The general principles creating a representative government and a set of civil rights were not to be easily withdrawn, even by a majority of the populace. The majority could be affected by some hysteria of the time, fostered by fanatic leaders. The costs of amendment must be high in order to prevent amendment in response to hysteria. This does not prevent legislative adjustment to social change. The general principles that make up the main clauses of the Constitution do not need change in language to govern a changing society. The broad national power to regulate commerce, for example, does not need amendment to encompass all the new methods of commerce and any negative externalities such methods might create.[19]

Representative government is much less costly than pure democracy in which political issues are always submitted to the entire electorate. The information costs of explaining all political issues to every citizen, especially those with little education, would be so large that the society would reject pure democracy. Representatives, on the other hand, develop special skills in policy formation and are thus the least-cost method of government that is responsible to the citizens. As to election of representatives, there are at least three arguments supporting universal suffrage.[20] Denial of the franchise to any groups gives opportunity to those in power to redistribute income from disenfranchised persons to themselves. Such redistribution has social costs and the effect on the disenfranchised is to provoke protest and even rebellion. Secondly, general elections are the least-cost way for policy makers to learn majority preferences. Thirdly, the larger the electorate, the more difficult it is for groups of voters to form coalitions to do harm to specific minorities.

Economics of Federalism

A workable division of legislative power between the national and state governments was essential to long-term survival of the union.[21] Madison noted that states' rights were protected in part by the fact that the national government was one of limited powers. He stated that "its jurisdiction extends to certain enumerated objects only, and leaves to the several States a residuary and inviolable sovereignty over all other objects."[22] He later compared the numbers of powers. "The powers delegated by the proposed Constitution to the federal government are few and defined. Those which are to remain in the State governments are numerous and indefinite."[23]

Although the national government is one of enumerated powers, some of these are the basic essentials of government. Powers of taxation, spending, war, and regulation of private commerce are stated as general principles, not narrow legal rules. They are meaningful only if broadly construed. In order to insure broad construction the draftsmen inserted the "sweeping" clause, giving Congress the power "to make all laws which shall be necessary and proper for carrying into execution the foregoing powers, and all other powers vested by this Constitution in the government of the United States, or in any department or office thereof."[24] As Madison said, "Without the substance of this power, the whole Constitution would be a dead letter."[25] The opponents of the Constitution, in their opposition to ratification, repeatedly charged that the clause amounted to an unlimited grant of power to Congress.[26] As to the effect on the breadth of the enumerated powers, they correctly interpreted the meaning of the language. So long as a regulatory statute could be subsumed under an enumerated power and did not violate a constitutional limitation, it was valid.

The primary economic issues of federalism concern economies and diseconomies of scale. Certain of the national powers in Article I, Section 8, are exclusive because the character of the activities is national in scope, and they are more efficiently executed on a national level. The war powers, the power to coin money, to establish post offices, to establish uniform laws of bankruptcy and to regulate commerce among the several states are examples.[27] The exclusive national bankruptcy power, for example, was adopted because some state laws prior to union had created havens for dishonest debtors. Those states "created an ignoble array of legislative schemes for the defeat of creditors and the invasion of contractual obligations."[28] The national power to regulate the interstate segment of commerce among the several states is exclusive because conflicting state regulations of any single transaction between parties in different states could greatly impede commerce.

Some governmental powers are shared by the nation and the states in the sense that they may possibly be exercised by either one but not both at the same time. Delegates to the convention of 1787 quickly realized that efficient government could not function if national and state laws on the same subject conflicted and proposed a congressional veto of state laws.[29] The eventual solution was to transfer this resolution to the judiciary by adoption of the supremacy clause.[30] A prominent example of shared power has been the regulation of local commerce that affects more states than one. In almost all cases, the Supreme Court has given broad application to federal preemption under the supremacy clause.[31] In one narrow area where the Court deviated from this principle, there has been costly promotion of much litigation. In *Parker v. Brown,*[32] the Court expressly noted conflict between the Sherman Antitrust Act and a state statute giving regulatory approval of cartel pricing of raisins. Yet it upheld the state policy, partly on grounds that there also existed a congressional policy to aid distressed agriculture. The state action defense to the antitrust laws developed thereafter without thorough consideration by the Court of the scope of the supremacy clause.

Concurrent powers, those which may be exercised by the nation and the states at the same time, are best illustrated by taxation and spending. In the fiscal area, the competitive concept of federalism that prevailed for about one hundred years from the 1830s to the 1930s has given way to a dominant concept of cooperative federalism. National grants in aid to the states for numerous welfare purposes are a prime example.[33] While the states have been unable or unwilling to tax themselves for all these local activities, the federal government has become a major source of finance. The chief objection to cooperative federalism is that it fosters continuing enlargement of national power and expanded national bureaucracy. The superior taxing power and borrowing power of the national government means that the Congress is the dominant force and the state legislatures submissive to directions from Washington.

Diseconomies of scale are a significant result of national subsidy and control of local government functions.[34] Public school education, for example, has largely been under the control of local school districts. Local interests insist on continued local control because they fear bureaucratic centralized management of schools. But local financing, especially in the poorer states, has been difficult. Persons voting in local elections to increase school taxes internalize the costs and may underinvest in education in terms of its long-run benefits.[35] They do not internalize national grants in aid and therefore may give political support for such aid. The creation of the U.S. Department of Education superimposed an additional layer of governmental administration whose cost must be added to the total social cost of public education.[36]

As to shared or concurrent powers, absent economies of scale, the Tiebout hypothesis is that local government will be a more efficient provider of services than the national government.[37] Public choice is greatly enhanced when services are provided locally because municipalities and even states have much less monopoly power as providers than does the national government. If persons dislike the mix of taxes and services in one town or state, they may move to another so long as they can earn a living in the second. This citizen mobility should cause localities and states to compete with one another for productive citizens by responding to consumer demand with the desired mix of services. Only imperfect information and imperfect mobility should limit the practical effect of the Tiebout hypothesis.

One of the key economic effects of federalism is interstate externalities. The issue is the incentive each state has to improve its income position by imposing costs on residents of other states.[38] States export costs by taxation or regulation the incidence of which is borne by those in other states.[39] They import benefits by attracting investors through tax benefits and other public services. The Supreme Court has power under the Commerce Clause and the Equal Protection Clause to prevent such interstate discrimination. It has exercised this power to invalidate taxes on non-resident consumers and tariffs on state imports. It has sometimes failed to invalidate state statutes whose effect is an export of taxation. In *Commonweath Edison Co. v. Montana*,[40] the Court failed to see that a state's 30 percent severance tax on coal would have its main impact on out-of-state consumers. The Court's failure to meet the issue of the incidence of the taxation distorts resource allocation from true comparative advantage and in effect upholds interstate taxation.

Economics of Separated Powers

The separation of governmental powers into legislative, executive, and judicial, together with a set of checks and balances, has the political objective of preventing monopolization of the coercive power of the state.[41] Separated powers promote rival interests in the branches and avoid the collusion that could lead to totalitarian control.[42] The costs of collusion increase with the increase in the number of people necessary to make it effective. A majority of the legislature may succumb to the hysteria of an era and pass totalitarian legislation, but if the executive avows that such laws are unconstitutional and refuses to execute them, tyranny may be forestalled. Even if the executive should carry out such laws, the judiciary may refuse to use its sanctions for noncompliance and also, under the habeas corpus principle, order the release of those who have been detained. As Justice Louis Brandeis observed, the doctrine of separated powers was adopted "not to promote efficiency but to preclude the exercise of arbitrary power. The purpose was, not to avoid friction, but, by means of the inevitable friction incident to the distribution of the governmental powers among three departments, to save the people from autocracy."[43]

Separated powers are effective only if the officers of the three departments are independent of one another.[44] The first essential of independence is that persons holding office in one department do not owe their tenure to the will or preferences of persons in another of the branches.[45] Thus, under the United States Constitution, the president and members of Congress are continued in office or not at the will of the electorate at general elections.[46] And the federal judges hold office during good behavior, and their compensation may not be reduced.[47] The second essential of independence is that officials in one department may not concurrently hold office in either of the other two departments,[48] and may not usurp or encroach upon the powers which the Constitution clearly assigns to another department.[49]

While checks and balances of governmental powers are said to impair government efficiency, another argument hypothesizes that separated powers are merely an example of the division of labor. Locke observed that while a legislature may be in session for only a short time each year, the execution of laws requires continuous activity throughout the year.[50] Furthermore, the representative character of a legislature makes it too large and also too slow to carry out the executive function.[51] Many of the founding fathers commented on this phenomenon.[52] Justice James Wilson contrasted legislative and executive methods as follows:

> In planning, forming, and arranging laws, deliberation is always becoming, and always useful. But in the active scenes of government, there are emergencies, in which the man, as in other cases, the woman, who deliberates, is lost. Secrecy may be equally necessary as despatch. But, can either secrecy or despatch be expected, when, to every enterprise and to every step in the progress of every enterprise, mutual communication, mutual consultation, and mutual agreement among men, perhaps of discordant views, of discordant tempers and of discordant interests, are indispensably necessary? How much time will be consumed! and when it is consumed; how little business will be done! . . . If, on the other hand, the executive power of government

is placed in the hands of one person, who is to direct all the subordinate officers of the department, is there not reason to expect, in his plans and conduct, promptitude, activity, firmness, consistency, and energy?[53]

Alexander Hamilton emphasized that, unlike the contesting legislature, efficiency in the executive required that it be vested in a single person. "It is essential to the protection of the community against foreign attacks; it is not less essential to the steady administration of laws, to the protection of property against those irregular and high-handed combinations which sometimes interrupt the ordinary course of justice, to the security of liberty against enterprises and assaults of ambition, of faction, and of anarchy."[54] He concluded: "Decision, activity, secrecy, and despatch will generally characterize the proceedings of one man in a much more eminent degree than the proceedings of any greater number; and in proportion as the number is increased, these qualities will be diminished."[55]

An efficient judiciary is one with maximum independence from the other two branches.[56] Strict separation is necessary for pursuit of the ideal of deliberative objectivity, especially in the enforcement of constitutional limitations against the legislature and executive. The effectiveness of the judicial bar to arbitrary and oppressive government can be guaranteed only by a judiciary that is free from executive or legislative control.[57] In the classic statement of Lord Coke: "No man may be a judge in his own cause."[58] Neither the legislature which has exercised the sovereign law-making power in enacting a statute nor the executive officers charged with enforcing a statute may sit in judgment of a defendant charged with violating the statute. For both the legislature and executive, in their efforts to govern, have a vested and therefore biased interest in unlimited statutory enforcement.[59] They cannot be impartial judges of the constitutional limitations on their own acts.[60] Only an independent judiciary can perform this function.

The doctrine of the separation of powers is a general constitutional principle and was not conceived as rigid.[61] It has exceptions. While the legislature is granted exclusive law-making power,[62] efficient government makes it necessary for secondary legislative power to be delegated to executive agencies.[63] The legislative power is general and prospective.[64] While the primary legislative function of setting general rules is assigned to the legislature, there are many instances where it would be highly inefficient and perhaps impossible for the legislature to set all the detailed secondary rules. Rate regulation is a prime example. In order to remedy the market failure of monopoly, statutes regulating maximum rates or prices were adopted.[65] The legislature would be making an inefficient allocation of its time if it spent thousands of hours setting individual rates for a railroad or an electric utility. In fact, the legislature may lack the technical skill to set the rates. Instead, the legislature is basically a duty-assigning body that delegates to a specialized administrative agency the power to do such acts as are necessary to achieve the results required by the statute.[66]

Legislative bodies have high transaction costs. The cost to a legislator of acting when the public is sharply divided on the need for and scope of proposed legislation may be the loss of one's seat. If the legislature passes a very general statute and leaves the executive to fill in the substance, some of these costs may be avoided. The degree of generality in statutes may become very great as factions in a legislature compromise by adopting indefinite, general language.[67] There are other instances where complexity makes detailed legislation impossible. When the legislature lacks the skill to construct a multifaceted statutory remedy, for example, it must leave the detailed rules to the executive.[68] Furthermore, dynamic changes may make it essential that some detailed rules be under constant change. It can be argued that the Necessary-and-Proper Clause of the Constitution gives Congress explicit authority to delegate secondary legislative functions.[69]

The primary negative criticism of the delegation of legislative powers is that the elected representatives shirk their responsibilities and, by general language, shift most of the legislative function to non-elected appointees in the executive branch. Only in a few extreme cases has the Supreme Court invalidated statutes on the ground that the primary legislative power is non-delegable. Two cases arose under the National Industrial Recovery Act of 1933,[70] where the president approved codes of "fair competition" designed by representatives of labor and management.[71] Under vague standards, the statute largely delegated legislative power to private persons to engage in monopoly pricing, thereby aggravating market failure. In the *Schecter* case, Chief Justice Charles E. Hughes writing for a unanimous Court, held the statute void and stated: "The Congress is not permitted to abdicate or to transfer to others the essential legislative functions with which it is thus vested. . . . Congress cannot delegate legislative powers to the President to exercise an unfettered discretion to make whatever laws he thinks may be needed or advisable for the rehabilitation and expansion of trade or industry."[72]

This bar to the delegation of primary legislative functions has not survived. Vague and indeterminate legislative standards have been upheld, although the background of the doctrine of nondelegation has in a few instances caused narrow construction of delegated power.[73] Justice William Rehnquist, in dissent, has urged broader application of the nondelegation doctrine.[74] In fact, the Supreme Court approval of almost unlimited delegation of primary legislative power has encouraged Congress to ignore its duties to create definable, limited standards of regulation. In many fields, the drafting of more precise standards would not have a high cost. Substantive regulations in many fields, with the exception of price controls, require only that the congressional staff assemble sufficient data from interested parties so that the issues can be detailed to the elected Congress. If coalitions cannot be formed to achieve the majority needed to adopt rigorous regulatory language, the principle of separated powers dictates that regulation should not become law. Politicians facing a demand for legislative remedies do not want to face the cost of taking clearly identifiable stands on the controversial political and economic issues of the day. The issue is whether, under representative government, they have the power to pass vague laws that enable executive employees to make general public policies for the nation.[75]

In order to offset the great legislative power delegated to administrative agencies, Congress in recent years has often adopted a method to recover control, the legislative veto. Congress enacts legislation with an express condition that the executive may enact regulations if one or both houses of Congress do not veto it. Under the statute, proposed regulations are submitted to Congress. Under some statutes, one or both houses of Congress may by resolution veto them. Under other statutes, the regulations gain the force of law only after one or both houses approves them.

The transaction costs in Congress of reviewing for approval or disapproval of many separate regulations adopted over time to effectuate a single statute should be much greater than the costs of negotiating a single detailed and precise statute without later veto of regulations. The use of the legislative veto illustrates that Congress is capable of considering the detailed application of some legislation. As to those statutes, the majority have chosen not to do so at the time of passing the statute, probably to avoid the political costs of enactment.

While the legislative veto had been upheld in the lower courts,[76] it had been attacked by the commentators.[77] Until 1983, the Supreme Court had avoided the issue.[78] Then, in *Immigration and Naturalization Service v. Chadha*,[79] the Court, in very general language, held that congressional veto unconstitutional. Under the statute, the suspension of deportation of an alien by the executive had to be reported to Congress. In this case, the House of Representatives passed a resolution vetoing the decision of the attorney general to suspend the deportation of Chadha. Under the statute, the resolution was not treated as "legislation" and it was not sent to the Senate or the president. The Court held that the resolution was legislation and the failure to submit it to the president violated the Presentment Clause.[80] It also violated the bicameral requirement and the separation of governmental powers.[81] The case is illustrative of the relatively high costs in congressional time of reviewing individual deportations as opposed to the public benefits from allocation of legislative time to statutes having broad effects on the public welfare.

While *Chadha* concerned congressional review of one deportation and thus seemed a replication of a long executive proceeding, the invalidation of the legislative veto had been followed in other areas. In two summary affirmances, the Court disapproved the veto. The first applied to the regulation of natural gas pricing by the Federal Energy Regulatory Commission.[82] The second applied to rulemaking by the Federal Trade Commission.[83]

Constitutional Limitations

The second main function of the national Constitution is to guarantee the civil rights of persons within the United States by express limitations on the powers of national and state governments. The idea of protecting individual liberties in the Anglo American legal system has a long history that goes back at least to Magna Carta.[84] Given the totalitarian dictatorships in most of the world, both in the past and in the present, the idea of representative government that effectively limits the powers of those delegated the authority to govern is the most fundamental concept of human liberty. Protection of individuals from oppression by agents of government must be considered the primary function of government in a free society and the allocation of governing power merely subservient to it. In fact, the separation of powers in government, with a set of checks and balances, was designed to protect individuals from arbitrary and unjust treatment by governmental officials.

The enforcement of constitutional limitations by judicial review is treated in Chapter 3. The last four chapters of this study are devoted to the economic implications of express constitutional limitations. Chapters 7 through 10 are devoted to the three clauses of Section 1 of the Fourteenth Amendment: privileges or immunities, due process, and equal protection. There are also express limitations on the taxing power and on barriers to international trade. The Supreme Court has held in addition that there are also implied constitutional limitations. As noted in Chapter 4, the plenary power in Congress to regulate commerce among the several states carries the implication that the states may not regulate parts of that commerce. Transactions between parties in different states may not be regulated by the conflicting statutes of the two states because such state regulation would bring interstate commerce to a halt.

Some express constitutional limitations, such as those enforcing procedural protections for the accused in criminal cases, present only two-sided controversies between citizens and government. Others are more complex. Substantive constitutional limitations may be invoked in controversies between private factions in which one special interest gets legislation enacted that is detrimental to other persons. This is especially true of the equal protection clause. Economic interest groups have subsidized legislators and thereby bought special legislation for their control of the supply of some goods or service in the market.[85] Such statutes bar the entry of rivals into the market and result in the market failure of monopoly. Supply of the resource of product is reduced and prices are increased to all users. Challenges to such legislation usually do not originate with the state but rather with other suppliers that are barred from the market. The economic history of the Constitution is full of examples. *Gibbons v. Ogden*[86] concerned a long-term state grant of monopoly to one steamboat operator. The *Slaughter-House Cases*[87] concerned a state grant of monopoly to a small group of New Orleans butchers. Numerous other examples under the Equal Protection Clause are reviewed in Chapter 10. In these cases, judicial intervention to curtail legislative grants of monopoly is clearly appropriate.

In fact, one of the earliest precedents in English constitutional law for enforcing constitutional limitations concerned a Crown grant of monopoly. In *Dr.*

Bonham's Case[88] a letters patent from King Henry VIII to the Royal College of Physicians in London granted the college the power to impose fines on persons practicing medicine in London who had not been admitted to practice by the college. The college further claimed the right to govern the professional conduct of all physicians in London and implement its rules, if necessary, by fines and imprisonment. The letters patent in this case had been confirmed by statute.[89] This statute was in derogation of the common law precedents against Crown grants of monopoly in the ordinary trades or professions.

Dr. Thomas Bonham, a medical graduate of Cambridge University, was cited by the college for practicing medicine in London without their certificate. He was fined and, when he persisted, he was imprisoned for seven days. Bonham brought a tort action for false imprisonment against the leading members of the Royal College of Physicians. Chief Justice Coke held for Bonham and asserted five arguments to support his view. The one that is important here was that since the college was to receive one-half of all fines, the members were both parties to the cause of action and judges therein.[90] The lack of fundamental fairness in procedure was a denial of the due process of the law. In dictum, Coke asserted that "when an Act of Parliament is against common right and reason, or repugnant, or impossible to be performed, the common law will control it and adjudge such Act to be void."[91] Thus one of the earliest pronouncements on judicial enforcement of constitutional limitations was this application of Coke's strong views against governmental grants of monopoly power.[92]

There is space here for only one illustrative example of how the courts have in many areas given decreased enforcement of constitutional limitations when applied to economic activity. The relation of the First Amendment to commercial expression, especially advertising, shows the judicial failure to comprehend the significance of information systems to the efficient functioning of markets. Hayek long ago pointed out the importance of prices in free markets as signals for decision making in resource allocation.[93]

The economic theory of perfect competition presumes perfect and costless information in all parties to transactions and to those who consider transactions and reject them.[94] This theoretical ideal of efficient markets, those which maximize welfare under any given distribution of assets and income, is the objective of the free market system. In the real world, access to information is imperfect and search for information has costs.[95] Thus, imperfect information makes for imperfect competition. Fully rational economic decisions are impossible because of the presence of uncertainty about factual aspects of the subject matter of transactions.[96] In this sense, the subject matter includes not only the price and quality characteristics of one seller or buyer but also the same facts about the offers of all rival sellers or buyers. Uncertainty about current facts in a market thus makes for disutility on the part of those lacking information. If the flow of factual information about goods and services can be improved, efficiency of markets will be improved.

A key impediment to effective competition is asymmetric information of sellers and buyers. For most goods and services, sellers are specialists in the item and buyers are not. Buyers who must act in ignorance of significant facts about the item or its market are unlikely to make purchase decisions that maximize utility. Furthermore, buyer ignorance increases the risk that false advertising will provoke transactions and not be detected. From the viewpoint of economics, any activity that makes for more symmetrical access to information increases competition. Thus, informative advertising reduces ignorance on the part of buyers concerning the price and quality of goods and services and thereby contributes to the efficiency of markets. Statutes that bar informational advertising from the mails, such as that for contraception, impede efficiency.[97]

Supreme Court opinions on abridging freedom of speech and of the press are notable for their lack of rigor. The most fundamental distinction in the topic is often ignored. This is the dichotomy between protection of the *content* of speech and publications on the one hand, and the necessary regulation of time, place, and manner of speaking and distributing publications on the other.[98] It is clear that the underlying purpose of these sections of the First Amendment was to protect *content* of expressions.[99] Leading commentators have pointed out that most speech is subject to regulation of time, place, and manner.[100] The Congress of the United States has rules prohibiting speech when the speaker has granted the floor to another member.[101] Courts have large sets of rules regulating what may be spoken and admitted as evidence and the order in which persons may speak.[102]

The failure of the Supreme Court to begin analysis of each case concerning freedom of speech with a finding of whether it concerns content or not have caused confusion in the Court's discussion of its own earlier opinions and left lower courts without clear guidelines for decision making. This has caused especially severe problems in the field of commercial speech and publications. The leading early cases holding that commercial speech and publication were not protected by the first amendment concerned only time, place, or manner. *Valentine v. Chrestensen*[103] upheld a New York City ordinance prohibiting distribution of commercial advertising materials in the streets. Chrestensen had printed handbills advertising tours of a former U.S. Navy submarine that he exhibited for profit and distributed them in the streets. There was no assertion that the content, true statements concerning legal events, if distributed by mail or at gatherings on private property, would not have been protected from abridgement by the First Amendment. The Court had previously upheld the constitutional right peacefully to distribute handbills with political content on public ways.[104] In *Chrestensen*, Justice Roberts noted that while the state may regulate distribution of political matter on the streets, they may not unduly burden or proscribe it. He then concluded: "We are equally clear that the Constitution imposes no such restraint on government as respects purely commercial advertising."[105] The inference from this statement that commercial expression had no constitutional protection was misinterpreted as applying to content and was subject to attack. In 1959, Justice Douglas asserted that the *Chrestensen* "ruling was casual, almost offhand. And it has not survived reflection."[106]

The Court adopted its reasoning in *Chrestensen* in another case concerning time, place, and manner of commercial speech and publications. In *Breard v. Alexandria*,[107] the Court upheld an ordinance prohibiting door-to-door selling as applied to persons selling magazine subscriptions. The commercial aspect was emphasized because eight years earlier the Court had voided an ordinance that prohibited door-to-door distribution of printed matter as applied to free publications of Jehovah's Witnesses.[108] The Court recently invalidated an ordinance that limited door-to-door solicitation to the hours 9 a.m. to 5 p.m. as applied to political canvassing.[109] The distinction between political and commercial solicitation had no logical basis. Both disturb the solitude of the thinking householder and should be subject to statutory prohibition. There seems to be a denial of equal protection of the laws to commercial solicitors.

Later courts, not observing that *Chrestensen* was concerned only with time, place, and manner, felt they had to distinguish cases concerning content of publication from *Chrestensen*. In *New York Times v. Sullivan*,[110] the Court reversed a judgment for defamation as applied to a paid advertisement containing political criticism. The Court found it necessary to conclude that a paid advertisement soliciting funds for a civil rights group was not a commercial advertisement in the sense in which "commercial" was used in *Chrestensen*.[111] Given the political content of the advertisement, the profit motive of the newspaper was not relevant.

The second fundamental issue relating to commercial speech and publications is whether the original meaning of the First Amendment applies to it at all. While the context of the adoption of the amendment was to protect political expression, the unqualified language is not limited to political issues. Even Meikeljohn, whose early writing centered on the political function of free expression, conceded that the amendment protected expression in the form of literature, philosophy, education, and science.[112] The protection must extend to both informative expression of facts and opinions. In practice, the borderline between political or scientific expression and commercial expression is not easy to determine. In *Bigelow v. Virginia*,[113] the Court upheld the right to advertise when the advertisement contained factual material of clear public interest. A Virginia statute barring publication to encourage or prompt the procuring of an abortion was held invalid as to advertisements in a Virginia newspaper by a New York City abortion referral service. Persons in need of an abortion could learn of the difference in law between New York and Virginia.[114]

Those who would limit the protection of the First Amendment to political expression would protect a consumer's journal that advocated new statutes regulating a particular industry with market failure or deregulating an industry where existing special-interest statutes promoted monopoly pricing.[115] Such a printed article, advocating deregulation of prescription drug pricing, might contain a survey of the many different prices on specific drugs found in the pharmacies of a given city. If this publication is protected by freedom of the press as political, can there be a logical reason not to protect dissemination of the raw data, price advertisements by druggists for prescription drugs? This was the issue in *Virginia State Board of Pharmacy v. Virginia Citizens Consumer Council, Inc.*[116] The plaintiffs attacked a Virginia statute that prohibited the advertising of prices for prescription drugs because lack of effective competitive increased prices. The Court first held that the First Amendment right to expression could be asserted by the recipients of the information.[117] Next, the Court set aside the purported ruling of the *Chrestensen* case that there was no protection for commercial speech. The Court recognized that *Chrestensen* concerned only the manner of distributing the advertising.[118] It held that speech which does no more than propose a commercial transaction was entitled to First Amendment protection.[119] If one of the objectives of free expression is individual self-fulfillment, then relief for the least educated and disabled citizens form high drug prices through dissemination of price information furthers that objective.[120] The society has a strong interest in the free flow of commercial information. There is little point in forcing sellers to frame their advertisements as political comments in order to free them from legislative suppression. Furthermore, "no line between publicly 'interesting' or 'important' commercial advertising and the opposite kind could ever be drawn."[121]

The breadth of the constitutional protection for advertising is illustrated by the cases concerning advertising by attorneys.[122] *Zauderer v. Office of Disciplinary Counsel*[123] reviewed the law on the topic. The Court invalidated rules that forbade soliciting clients through advertisements containing information or advice regarding specific legal problems.[124] In *Zauderer,* discipline of an attorney was upheld for misleading advertising when the ads failed to reveal that clients would be liable for litigation costs even if their lawsuits were unsuccessful.[125] The one case barring a class of truthful expression by attorneys was *Ohralik v. Ohio State Bar Association,* [126] where the Court upheld a ban on direct, in person solicitation of clients because of the likelihood of overreaching and undue influence. Here again, the Court failed to note that this was a regulation of time, place, and manner of speech and not of content. The Court did note that physically approaching a potential client was conduct, not expression, and that the regulation was primarily one of conduct.[127]

The failure of the Court to make a clear preliminary distinction between free speech and publication cases that do not concern content, but rather concern time, place, and manner of expression, has continued to cause confusion. *Pacific Gas & Elec. v. P.U.C. of California*[128] is a recent example concerning place. The utilities commission ordered the utility to enclose a newsletter of a public interest group in its billing envelopes. The content of the newsletter was political and clearly protected by the First Amendment. The Court held the utility commission order to be an impermissible burden on the utility. The issue was solely one of place and manner, and the Court had earlier upheld the right of a utility to include political matter with its bills.[129] The order here gave access only to those who disagreed with the utility and might provoke the utility to stop expressing its views, thus reducing the free flow of information and ideas.[130] The place, namely the envelope, forced the utility to associate with speech of other private parties with which it disagreed. This was an unreasonable regulation, quite different from the surgeon general's warning that the government requires on cigarette packages. The latter does not abridge free expression because it requires the truthful factual findings on health be distributed in order to make the assertions of the seller not misleading.[131]

The issues of freedom of speech and publications in regulated industries are complex. In an industry where a regulatory commission controls prices or rates and costs, every expenditure is conduct subject to regulation. When the expenditure is for the purpose of publishing information or opinions, conduct and expression are joint acts. In *First National Bank of Boston v. Bellotte*,[132] the Court invalidated a state statute that prohibited expenditures to influence voters on taxation of income, property, or transactions. The statute applied to banks and other regulated industries. Such political expression was at the heart of the concern of the First Amendment.[133] The content will be protected even when published by a corporation.[134] Three of the four dissenters felt that regulating expenditures on issues that did not directly concern the corporation, such as personal income taxation, was well within the regulation of conduct necessary to protect shareholders.[135]

The issue of whether the protection of the content of expressions extended to commercial advertising by a firm with regulated costs was presented in *Central Hudson Gas v. Public Service Commission of N.Y.*[136] The state commission extended a policy begun during the oil shortage of 1973 to prohibit promotional advertising by electrical utilities. The ban did not apply to institutional and informational advertising and was adopted as part of a national policy to conserve energy. The Supreme Court held the ban to violate the First Amendment. It easily could have distinguished *Virginia Pharmacy Board* because the industry here was one of regulated cost structure and the ban was only on non-informational advertising. While noting the state grant of monopoly, the Court failed to discuss the issue of regulating conduct (costs) that was related to expression in regulated industries. The Court did reiterate its distinction between commercial speech, which is subject to regulation for deception, and other types of speech. The Court adopted a four-part analysis.[137] First, commercial speech is protected only if it concerns lawful activity and is not misleading. Second, there must be a substantial governmental interest in regulation. Third, the regulation must directly advance the governmental interest. Fourth, regulation must not be more extensive than is necessary to serve that interest.

Here it was clear that the expressions related to lawful conduct and were not deceptive. The Court found that monopoly in the service area did not reduce the value of commercial advertising, but it appears to have forgotten that informational advertising had not been banned by the commission.[138] The state interests were energy conservation and inequities caused by failure to base the utilities' rates on marginal cost.[139] The former was found advanced by the commission order while the latter was not. As to the fourth test, the commission order was found to be more extensive than necessary to promote conservation.[140]

Justice William Rehnquist, the sole dissenter, recognized that the case primarily concerned economic regulation and that the issues of free expression were subordinate.[141] He failed, however, to explain the distinction between regulating conduct that has secondary effects on expression and direct suppression of speech or press. In this case, economic policy strongly supported curtailing conduct, advertising expenditures, and an emphasis on this aspect should have justified the regulation.

The issue of commercial advertising in regulated industries was again litigated in *Posadas De Puerto Rico Assoc. v. Tourism Co.*[142] Casino gambling as a regulated industry was much different from the electric utilities in *Central Hudson* since casino cost structures were not subject to regulation. By a 5 to 4 decision, the Court upheld the facial constitutionality of a Puerto Rico statute that prohibited advertising of the licensed casinos to the public in Puerto Rico but permitted such advertising outside Puerto Rico. The Court's application of the four-step test of commercial speech in *Central Hudson* illustrates the arbitrary character of the second test, the substantiality of the asserted governmental interest.[143] The legislature's interest in protecting the health, safety, and welfare of its citizens can be found in any statute regulating expression. Here the harmful effects on Puerto Ricans from casino gambling are not harmful when applied to tourists. Justice Brennan, in dissent, points out that the legislative legalization of casino gambling is a determination that it will not have "serious harmful effects" on Puerto Ricans.[144] The Court also found that the third and fourth tests of *Central Hudson* were satisfied. The restrictions prevented the increase in demand that would result from local advertising and they were not more extensive then necessary.

The Court made the additional argument that since the legislature could have prohibited casino gambling, it was permissible to take the lesser step of reducing demand through restrictions on advertising.[145] This again confuses regulation of conduct with regulation of expression. Control of gambling is control of conduct, exercised by many legislatures, while control of expression is a distinct activity protected by the First Amendment.[146] This is just one more example of the fallacious reasoning based on the view that "abridge" in the First Amendment applies differently to truthful commercial expression than it does to other truthful expression.

Justice Stevens' dissent emphasized the issue of unequal treatment under the First Amendment.[147] If there was a constitutional right to advertise this legal activity, could the state validly deny the information to one specific group of citizens? The discriminatory ban on advertising was a system of prior restraint with standards that were hopelessly vague and unpredictable.

Conclusion

The economics of information explains why maximizing the factual information in actors in a market increases the likelihood of maximizing utility, the measure of total welfare. The First Amendment, in barring abridgement of freedom of speech and of the press, was designed to protect dissemination of truthful facts and opinions on all the controversial issues in the society. In effectively competitive markets, the bids of sellers and buyers are the information signals that enable the economy to function efficiently. The underlying facts of the market contest are analogous to the facts asserted by politicians in their arenas. Governmental restriction on the dissemination of truthful facts in either arena invades the core protection of the First Amendment.

The Supreme Court mistakenly relegated factual advertising to second-class protection in cases concerning time, place, and manner of expression. Even though the Court later recognized that these early cases did not concern content, it continues to assert that commercial speech is entitled to less protection than other varieties of speech. There is no logical basis for this when applied to truthful speech. On the other hand, false or misleading advertising, like libel, is not a class of communication subject to constitutional protection. As to truthful advertising, it is time for the Court to recognize that it is part of that general class of expression that government may not abridge.

Appendix to Chapter 1:
Amending the Amendment Clause

A key structural element of the Constitution is the Amendment Clause. There exists a large historical literature on the Amendment Clause in Article 5 of the Constitution and much of it concerns imperfections.[148] Fundamental law that creates the governmental structure for a nation and defines limitations on government that are the basic civil rights of persons should not be easily amended. Intense conflict of opinion about issues in a society may lead to hysteria against a social minority; that is the wrong time to rush to amendment. On the other hand, the Amendment Clause should not set approval conditions so severe that changes which are desired by most citizens can be easily blocked by political minorities. A prime example was the Court's 1875 failure to apply the clear textual meaning of the Equal Protection Clause; it denied women's right to vote.[149] This ruling was finally reversed by the Nineteenth Amendment in 1920.

The framers of the Constitution realized that changing economic and social conditions would foster a need to modify fundamental law. The few amendments that have been ratified is the primary evidence that the political barriers to amendment are too high. The Bill of Rights and the three amendments following the Civil War were overwhelmingly approved. The fact that the people of the nation have been able to secure ratification of only fourteen additional amendments is strong evidence of the overwhelming political barriers to amendments. In fact, the entire industrial revolution took place with the accompanying great rise in per capita income, but the needed amendment to the Commerce Clause to overrule *Hammer v. Dagenhart*[150] and limit child labor failed to be ratified.[151] Likewise, the Supreme Court's creation of constitutional liberty of contract in *Lockner v. New York*[152] and other opinions barring labor legislation were not reversed by amendment.

The unfortunate fact is that most proposals for amendment that are drafted by members of Congress are sent to committees of the House or Senate and are buried there.[153] They never even reach a vote of the entire House or Senate. A prime example is the House Joint Resolution 300 of May 19, 1939 that was introduced by Congressman Emanuel Celler and referred to the Judiciary Committee. This proposal was designed to correct the misconstruction of the Fourteenth Amendment by the Supreme Court. The first section would have corrected the Court's misinterpretations of the constitutional privileges or immunities clause:

> Section 1. No State shall make or enforce any law or adopt or enfoce any constitution which shall abridge the privileges or immunities of citizens of the Unived States. Such privileges and immunities shall include, among others, the free establishment and free exercise of religion, freedom of speech, freedom of the press, the right of peaceful assembly, the right to petition the Government for a redress of grievances, and the right freely to enjoy life, liberty, and property.[154]

This section was designed to make the substantive clauses in the Bill of Rights enforceable against the states by force of the privileges or immunities clauses. One objective was to correct the Supreme Court's fallacious use of substantive due process to make the First Amendment effective against the states.[155]

Section 2 of the Joint Resolution restated all of the procedural protection in the Bill of Rights and would have made them enforceable against the states. This was designed to correct a long series of Supreme Court opinions that had held that the due process clause of the Fourteenth Amendment did not incorporate the individual procedural protections of the Bill of Rights. The immediate provocation for this section may have been the 1937 decision in *Palko v. Connecticut*[156] in which the Fifth Amendment immunity from double jeopardy was held not to apply to the states. The resolution here preceded the famous 5 to 4 decision in *Adamson v. California*[157] of 1947 by eight years. In that case, the majority held the Fifth Amendment immunity from self-incrimination was not incorporated in the due process clause of the Fourteenth Amendment. The comprehensive dissent of Justice Black was later vindicated when *Adamson* was overruled.[158] Justice Black's later dissent, in *Giswold v. Connecticut*[159] was a valid response to the Court majority opinion that usurped the amending power to create a constitutional right of privacy.

It seems clear that the non-majoritarian aspects of the Amendment Clause that appear first in approval of a proposed amendment by two-thirds vote of the Senate and second in ratification requirement of three-fourths of the states are cumulative in creating political barriers to amendment. Most citizens may not realize the severity of the non-majoritarian character of the Senate. Each state has two U.S. senators. But in the year 2000, the six largest states had a combined population of 114.4 million while the six least-populated states had a combined census of 4 million. The requirement in Article 5 for approval by a two-thirds vote of the Senate can be viewed as a high wall for social movements to climb before issues can meet the ultimate contest for ratification.

The conclusion here is that Article V should be amended to terminate the requirement for a senate vote on amendment proposals. This would leave the vote on proposals entirely in the House of Representatives, the majoritarian branch of the Congress. This amendment would leave ratification as the only non-majoritarian constraint on amendment. The key question is whether two-thirds of the senate would vote to give up its power over amendment proposals. If not, the severe imperfections in the amendment process may have no remedy. It would seem that a great popular movement would be necessary to convince the Senate that the present two non-majoritarian barriers to amendment are too many.

If the Senate vote were terminated, the question then would be whether the required vote of two-thirds of the members of the House should be continued or should the vote be reduced to a smaller majority. One must hypothesize situations where the two major political parties are in disagreement over the proposal for an amendment. Would a reduction of the required House vote to 60 percent or to 55 percent foster proposals to turn narrow regulatory statutes into constitutional principles? If that could be anticipated, the two-thirds vote for approval should be the retained requirement.

The ratification by three-fourths of the states, though non-majoritarians because of the radical population differences between states, is much less likely to be viewed by citizens as subject to amendment. This ultimate requirement for change is viewed by most thoughtful citizens as the fundamental protection of civil rights of persons. Consequently, the only possible amendment of ratification would be an additional alternative of securing the consent of three quarters of the voters. This added alternative would be majoritarian with a 75 percent approval requirement. Such a vote could be confined to the same time as congressional elections in order to attract the highest number of citizens to the polls.

Professor Dow points out that the only method for adding the alternative ratification process of a super-majority of voters is by pursuing the current amendment process.[160] As to the plain meaning of Article 5, Dow cites the established legal maxim of documentary construction: *expression unius est exclusion alterius.* The expression of one concept is the exclusion of another. Article 5 must be understood as exclusive because the structure of government established by the Constitution depends upon its exclusivity. Consequently, Dow asserts that we must reject the proposals of Amar[161] and Ackerman[162] that constitutional amendment by majority vote in an election should bypass the language that was ratified in Article 5.

Notes

1. See Charles H. McIlwain, *Constitutionalism: Ancient and Modern,* ch. I (Ithaca, NY: Cornell Univ. Press, 1947); Thomas C. Grey, *Constitutionalism: An Analytical Framework,* in *Constitutionalism,* Nomos 20, 189 (J. Pennock and J. Chapman, eds., 1979).
2. See James Buchanan and Gordon Tullock, *The Calculus of Consent 13* (Ann Arbor: Univ. of Michigan Press, 1962).
3. E. Adamson Hoebel, *The Law of Primitive Man* 330 (Cambridge: Harvard Univ. Press, 1954).
4. Niccolo Machiavelli, *History of Florence* 240 (C. W. Colby, ed. 1901). See generally, Ferdinand Schevill, *History of Florence* (New York: Frederick Unger, 1936).
5. See George M. Trevelyan, *Garibaldi and the Thousand* (London: Longmans Green, 1909).
6. M. Farrand, 1 *Records of the Federal Convention of 1787,* 19,166 (1911)   [Hereinafter cited as Farrand].
7. *Scott v. Sandford,* 60 U.S. (19 How.) 393 (1857). See Don E. Fehrenbacher, *The Dred Scott Case: Its Significance in American Law and Politics* (New York: Oxford Univ. Press, 1978); Charles Warren, *The Supreme Court in United States History,* ch. 26 (1926).
8. 3 Stat. 545-48 (1820).
9. *Scott,* 60 U.S. at 452.
10. See *Strader v. Graham,* 51 U.S. (10 How.) 82 (1850).
11. U.S. Const. Preamble.
12. *McCulloch v. Maryland,* 17 U.S. (4 Wheat.) 316, 404 (1819).
13. Friedrich A. Hayek, "Law, *Legislation and Liberty,* I," *Rules and Order,* 134-36 (Chicago: Univ. of Chicago Press, 1973).
14. I, Will and Mary, sess. 2, c. 2. (1689).
15. See Richard L. Perry and John C. Cooper, *Sources of our Liberties* 245-50 (Chicago: American Bar Foundation, 1959).
16. 31 Car. 2., c. 2 (1679); 56 Geo. III, c. 100 (1816).
17. See William F. Duker, *A Constitutional History of Habeas Corpus* (Westport, Conn.: Greenwoord Press, 1980); Perry and Cooper, *supra* note 15, at 189-203; Albert V. Dicey, *Introduction to the Study of the Law of the Constitution,* 209-33 (7th ed., 1908).
18. See Richard Posner, *Economic Analysis of Law,* 581-82 (Boston: Little Brown, 3d ed. 1986).
19. The Commerce Clause is reviewed in Chapter 4.
20. Posner, *supra* note 18, at 582.

21. See Harry Scheiber, *Federalism and the Constitution: The Original Understanding, in American Law and the Constitutional Order: Historical Perspectives* 85-98. L. Friedman and H. Scheiber eds. (1978).
22. *Federalist* 39, at 262. (E. Borne, ed. 1947) [cited hereinafter as Federalist]. "This government is acknowledged by all, to be one of enumerated powers." *McCulloch v. Maryland,* 17 U.S. (4 Wheat.) 316, 404 (1819).
23. *Federalist* 45, at 319.
24. U.S. Const., Art. I, § 8, Cl. 18.
25. *Federalist* 44, at 308. For comments of Hamilton, see *Federalist* 33, at 211-13.
26. Forrest McDonald, *Novus Ordo Seclorum* 267 (Chicago: Univ. of Chicago Press, 1985) citing Herbert J. Storing, ed., *Complete Anti-Federalist,* II: 58, 118, 159-60, 366; III: 36, 202.-3; IV: 36; VI: 35 (1981).
27. Express prohibition on states exercising some of these exclusive federal powers, but not all of them, are stated in U.S. Const., Art. I, § 10.
28. *Home Building and Loan Ass'n v. Blaisdell,* 290 U.S. 398, 427 (1934), per Chief Justice Hughes.
29. Farrand I: 21, 250, 318, 337, 438, 447; II: 440, 589; III: 24, 56, 65, 73, 112.
30. U.S. Const., Art. VI, Cl. 2. See *Federalist* 33, at 214-15.
31. *Hines v. Davidowitz,* 312 U.S. 52 (1941); *Rice v. Santa Fe Elevator Co.,* 331 U.S. 218 (1947); *Pennsylvania v. Nelson,* 350 U.S. 497 (1956).
32. 317 U.S. 341 (1943). See Michael Conant, *The Supremacy Clause and State Economic Controls,* 10 Hastings Con. L. Q. 255, 269-74 (1983).
33. Federal grants to state and local governments in 1986 totaled $112.6 billion. U.S. Dept. of Commerce, Bureau of the Census, *Federal Expenditures by State for Fiscal Year* 1986, 2. (1987).
34. See Gordon Tullock, *Federalism: Problems of Scale,* 6 Public Choice 19 (1969).
35. See Gary Becker, *Human Capital,* 2nd ed. (Chicago: Univ. of Chicago Press, 1975).
36. Federal expenditures for elementary, secondary, and vocational education rose from $2.5 billion in 1969 to $7.8 billion in 1986. U.S. Office of Management and Budget, *Historical Tables: Budget of the United States Government,* table 3.3 (1987).
37. Charles M. Tiebout, *A Pure Theory of Local Expenditures,* 64 J. Pol. Econ. 416 (1956).
38. Susan Rose-Ackerman, *Does Federalism Matter?* 89 J. Pol. Econ. 152. (1981).
39. See Posner, *Economic Analysis, supra* note 18, ch. 26.
40. 453 U.S. 609 (1981). See Stephen Williams, *Severance Taxes and Federalism,* 53 U. Colo. L. Rev. 281 (1982.).
41. See M. J. C. Vile, *Constitutionalism and the Separation of Powers* ; (Indianapolis: Liberty Fund, 2d ed. 1998); William B. Gwyn, *The Meaning of the Separation of Powers* (New Orleans: Tulane Univ. Press, 1965); Malcolm Sharp, The Classical American Doctrine of "the Separation of Powers, 2 U. Chi. L. Rev. 38 5 (1935); Benjamin Wright, *The Origins of the Separation of Powers in America,* 13 Economica 169 (1933).
42. *Federalist* 48, quoting Thomas Jefferson, *Notes on the State of Virginia,* 195; Federalist 50. See Charles Fried, *Saying What the Law Is* 49-77 (Cambridge: Harvard Univ. Press, 2004); M. Elizabeth Magill, *The Real Separation in Separation of Powers Law,* 86 Va. L. Rev. 1127 (2000).
43. *Myers v. United States,* 272 U.S. 52, 293 (1926).
44. "James Wilson, one of the framers of the Constitution and a Justice of this court, in one of his law lectures said that the independence of each department required that its proceedings 'should be free from the remotest influence, direct or indirect,

of either of the other two powers.'" Andrews, *The Works of James Wilson* (1896), vol. 1, p. 367. And the importance of such independence was similarly recognized by Mr. Justice Story when he said that in reference to each other neither of the departments "ought to possess, directly or indirectly, an overruling influence in the administration of their respective powers." *I. Story on the Constitution* (4th ed.), Sec. 530. To the same effect, the *Federalist* (Madison) No. 48." *O'Donoghue v. United States,* 289 U.S. 516, 530-31 (1933).

45. *Humphrey's Ex's v. United States,* 295 U.S. 6oz (1935), holding that the president may not at his will and in violation, of statute remove a member of Federal Trade Commission, since FTC members perform subsidiary legislative functions.

46. U.S. Const. Art. I, § 2-5, and Amend. XVII; Art. II, § 1, and Amend. XII. Each house shall be the Judge of the Elections, Returns, and Qualifications of its own Members. Article I, Section 5.

47. U.S. Const., Art. III, § I.

48. U.S. Const., Art. I, § 6.

49. The legislature may not usurp the executive or judicial powers. *Springer v. Philippine Islands,* 277 U.S. 189 (1928); *Kilbourn v. Thompson,* Io3 U.S. 168 (1881). The executive may not usurp the legislative or judicial powers. *Youngstown Sheet and Tube Co. v. Sawyer.* 343 U.S. 579 (1952); *In Re Yamashita,* 327 U.S. I (1946). The judiciary may not usurp legislative or executive powers. *United States v. National City Lines,* 334 U.S., 588-89 (1948); *National City Bank of New York v. Republic of China,* 348 U.S. 356, 358 (1955).

50. John Locke, *The Second Treatise of Government,* § 144, at 74 (J. W. Gough ed., 1956).

51. *Id.,* 1160, at 82.

52. See Arthur S. Miller, *An Inquiry in the Relevance of the Intentions of the Founding Fathers,* 27 Ark. L. Rev. 583, 588 (1973).

53. Jame Wilson, *Works of James Wilson,* 294, 296, R. McCloskey ed., (Cambridge: Harvard Univ. Press, 1967).

54. *Federalist* 70, at book II, 49.

55. *Id.* at 50.

56. Effective separation of powers in England is said to date from the passage of a statute making judges removable from office only by impeachment by Parliament for misconduct. 12 Will. 3, c. 2 (1701). See Reginald Parker, *Historic Basis of Administrative Law,* 12 Rutgers L. Rev. 449, 450 (1958).

57. *O'Donoghue v. United States,* 289 U.S. 516, 531-34 (1933); *Evans v. Gore,* 253 U.S. 245, 248-53 (1920). "The complete independence of the courts of justice is peculiarly essential in a limited constitution." Hamilton in *Federalist* 78, at ioo (Bourne ed., 1947).

58. For citations and discussions see Edward S. Corwin, *The "Higher Law" Background of American Constitutional Law,* 42 Harv. L. Rev. 365, 370 (1929). See Lowell B. Mason, *Language of Dissent* 303 (Cleveland: World Publishing, 1959); Raoul Berger, *Removal of Judicial Functions from Federal Trade Commission to a Trade Court,* 59 Mich. L. Rev. 199, 204-6 (1960).

59. "[B]ias from strong and sincere conviction as to public policy may operate as a more serious disqualification than pecuniary interest." Great Britain, *Report of the Committee on Ministers' Powers* (Cmd. 4060, 1932). "Unlike a judge, who is theoretically neutral about government programs, an administrator often has an affirmative program to carry out; he often has a mission, a purpose, a policy." Professor Davis, in Report of the Special Subcommittee on Legislative Oversight of the House Committee on Interstate and Foreign

Commerce, *Independent Regulatory Commissions,* H. R. 2.711, 85th Cong. 2d Sess., 1959, p. 78. See Frank E. Cooper, *The Executive Department of Government and the Rule of Law,* 59 Mich. L. Rev. 515, 517-18 (1961).

60. "From a body which had even a partial agency in passing bad laws, we could rarely expect a disposition to temper and moderate them in the application. The same spirit which had operated in making them would be too apt to influence their construction; still less could it be expected that men who had infringed the Constitution in the character of legislators would be disposed to repair the breach in that of Judges." Hamilton in *Federalist* 81, at 121.

61. *Federalist* 47, at book I, 330.

62. U.S. Const., Art. I,

63. John B. Cheadle, *The Delegation of Legislative Functions,* 27 Yale L. J. 842, 897 (1918).

64. Legislation involves the creation or extinction of general classes of rights or immunities for all persons who engage in the action treated by the particular laws. See *Dash v. Van Kleeck,* 7 Johns (N. Y. Ch.) 477, 502. (1811), per Kent, C. J.; *San Diego Land & Town Co. v. Jasper,* 189 U.S. 439, 440 (1903), per Holmes, J.; *Prentis v. Atlantic Coast Line,* 2 1 1 U.S. 210, 226 (1908), per Holmes, J.

65. *Munn v. Illinois,* 94 U.S. 113 (1877).

66. *Kendall v. United States,* 37 U.S. (12 Pet.) 524, 610 (1838).

67. See Edward H. Levi, *An Introduction to Legal Reasoning* 31 (1948); Arthur S. Miller, *Statutory Language and the Purposive Use of Ambiguity,* 42. Va. L. Rev. 23 (1956).

68. "Congress legislated on the subject as far as was reasonably practicable, and from the necessities of the case was compelled to leave to executive officers the duty of bringing about the result pointed out by the statute. To deny the power of Congress to delegate such a duty would, in effect, amount but to declaring that the plenary power vested in Congress to regulate foreign commerce could not be efficaciously exerted." *Buttfield v. Stranahan,* 192 U.S. 470, 496 (1904). See F. Goodnow, *Principles of Administrative Law of the United States* 324 (1905); Ernst Freund, *Standards of American Legislation* 301 (1917); Marvin B. Rosenberry, *Administrative Law and the Constitution,* 23 Am. Pol. Sci. Rev. 3.2, 35 (1929).

69. *Hampton. v. United States,* 2.76 U.S. 394, 404-6 (1928), holding delegating power to president to adjust tariffs to equalize costs of production is constitutional.

70. 48 Stat. 195 (1933).

71. *Panama Refining Co. v. Ryan,* 293 U.S. 388 (1935); *Schechter Poultry Co. v. United States,* 2.95 U.S. 495 (1935).

72. 2.95 U.S. at 529, 537-38.

73. *Industrial Union Department v. American Petroleum Institute,* 448 U.S. 607 (1980).

74. *American Textile Manufacturers Institute v. Donavan,* 452 U.S. 490, 543-48 (1981).

75. See Henry J. Friendly, *The Federal Administrative Agencies* (Cambridge: Harvard Univ. Press, 1962).

76. *United States v. Atkins,* 556 F. zd 1028, 1058-71 (Ct. Cl. 1977) (per curiam), cert. denied, 434 U.S. 1009 (1978).

77. Harold Bruff and Ernest Gelhorn, *Congressional Control of Administrative Regulation,* 90 Harv. L. Rev. 1369 (1977); H. Lee Watson, Congress Steps Out, *63* Calif. L. Rev. 983 (1975).

78. *Buckley v. Valeo,* 424 U.S. I, 140n (1976).

79. 462 U.S. 919 (1983). For critical comments, see Laurence Tribe, *Constitutional Choices* 66-83 (1985); E. Donald Elliot, *INS v. Chadha: The Administrative Constitution, the Constitution and the Legislative Veto,* 1983 Sup. Ct. Rev. 125; Peter L. Strauss, *Was There a Baby in the Bathwater?* 1983 Duke L. J. 789; Laurence Tribe, *The Legislative Veto Decision,* 21 Harv. J. Legis. 1 (1984).
80. U.S. Const., Art. I, § 7, Cl. 2, 3.
81. *Id.,* Art. I, § 1 and 7, Cl. 2.
82. *Process Gas Consumers Group v. Consumers Energy Council of America,* 463 U.S. 1216 (1983).
83. *U.S. Senate v. F.T.C.,* 463 U.S. 1216 (1983).
84. See A. E. Dick Howard, *The Road from Runnymede* (Charlottesville: Univ. of Virginia Press, 1968).
85. See George Stigler, *Theory of Economic Regulation, infra* note 115.
86. 22, U.S. (9 Wheat.) 1 (1824).
87. 83 U.S. (16 Wall.) 36 (1873).
88. 8 Co. 114a, 77 Eng. Rep. 646 (C. P. 161o). See Dudley McGovney, *The British Origin of Judicial Review of Legislation,* 93 U. Pa. L. Rev. I (1944); Theodore Plucknett, *Bonham's Case and Judicial Review,* 40 Harv. L. Rev. 30 (1926).
89. 14 & 15 Hen. 8, c. 5 (1523); I Mary, 2d sess. c. 9 (1553).
90. See *Tumey v. Ohio,* 273 U.S. 510 (1927).
91. 8 Co. 114a, 118a, 77 Eng. Rep. 646, 652.
92. Donald O. Wagner, *Coke and the Rise of Economic Liberalism,* 6 Econ. Hist. Rev. 30 (1935).
93. Friedrich Hayek, *The Use of Knowledge in Society,* 35 Am. Econ. Rev. 519 (1945).
94. See Frank Knight, *Risk, Uncertainty, and Profit,* ch. 7 (1921); Ronald H. Coase, *The Market for Goods and the Market for Ideas,* 4 Amer. Econ. Rev., Papers and Proceedings, (1974).
95. See George Stigler, *The Economics of Information,* 69 J. Pol. Econ. 2,13 (1961), reprinted in G Stigler, *The Organization of Industry* 171 (1968).
96. See Ejan MacKay, *Economics of Information and Law,* ch. 5 (1982).
97. See *Bolger v. Youngs Drug Products Corp.,* 463 U.S. 60 (1983).
98. This distinction has been noted and thoroughly explained by the commentators. See, e.g., Geoffrey Stone, *Restrictions of Speech Because of Its Content,* 46 U. Chi. L. Rev. 81 (1978).
99. See George Anastaplo, *The Constitutionalist,* ch. 5 (Dallas: Southern Methodist Univ. Press, 1971).
100. See Alexander Meiklejohn, *Political Freedom* 25 (1948).
101.   See Alexander Meiklejohn, *The First Amendment Is an Absolute,* 1961 Sup. Ct. Rev. 245, 261.
102. See Vern Countryman, "Advertising Is Speech," in A. Hyman and M. Johnson, eds., *Advertising and Free Speech* 35, 39 (1977)
103. 316 U.S. 52, (1942).
104. *Schneider v. State (Town of Irvington),* 308 U.S. 147 (1939).
105. 316 U.S. at 54.
106. *Cammarano v. United States,* 358 U.S. 498, 514 (1959) (concurring opinion).
107. 341 U.S. 622 (1951).
108. *Martin v. City of Struthers,* 319 U.S. 141 (1943). The Court also invalidated a license tax as applied to the sales of religious books by Jehovah's Witnesses. *Murdock v. Pennsylvania,* 319 U.S. 105 (1943).
109. *City of Watseka v. Illinois Public Action Council,* 107 S. Ct. 919 (1987).

110. 376 U.S. 254 (1964).
111. *Id.* at 266.
112. Meiklejohn, *First Amendment, supra* note 101, at 257.
113. 421 U.S. 809 (1975).
114. *Id.* at 822.
115. On the efforts of firms to secure legislative protection from competition, see George Stigler, *The Theory of Economic Regulation,* 2. Bell J. Econ. & Mgmt. Sci. 3 (1971); Richard Posner, *Theories of Economic Regulation,* 5 Bell J. Econ. & Mgmt. Sci. 335 (1974).
116. 425 U.S. 748 (1976). See Thomas W. Merrill, *First Amendment Protection for Commercial Advertising,* 44 U. Chi. L. Rev. 2.05 (1976); Martin H. Redish, *First Amendment in the Marketplace: Commercial Speech and the Values of Free Expression,* 39 Geo. Wash. L. Rev. 429, 452-58 (1971).
117. "If there is a right to advertise, there is a reciprocal right to receive the advertising, and it may be asserted by these appellees." 425 U.S. 757. See *Thornhill v. Alabama,* 310 U.S. 88, 102. (1940).
118. *Virginia State Board of Pharmacy,* 425 U.S. at 760.
119. *Id.* at 762.
120. *Id.* at 763.
121. *Id.* at 765. See Alex Kozinski & Stuart Banner, *Who's Afraid of Commercial Speech,* 76 Va. L. Rev. 627, 631 (1990).
122. See in re R. M. J., 455 U.S. 191 (1982); *Bates v. State Bar of Arizona,* 433 U.S. 350 (1977).
123. 471 U.S. 626 (1985).
124. 471 U.S. at 639-41.
125. *Id.* at 650-53.
126. 436 U.S. 447 (1978).
127. *Id.* at 545. On the necessary distinction between speech and conduct, see Cox v. Louisiana, 379 U.S. 559 (1965), and especially the dissent of Justice Hugo Black. *Id.* at 581. Compare Laurence Tribe, 2 *American Constitutional Law,* ch. 12 (3rd ed. 2000).
128. 475 U.S. I (1986).
129. *Consolidated Edison Co. v. Public Service Comm'n of New York,* 447 U.S. 530 (1980).
130. *Pacific Gas & Electric* 475 U.S. at 14.
131. See *Banzhof v. F.C.C.,* 405 F.2d 1082 (D.C. Cir. 1968), cert. denied sub nom. *Tobacco Institute, Inc. v. F.C.C.,* 396 U.S. 842 (1969). On the fairness doctrine, see *Red Lion Broadcasting Co. v. F.C.C.* 395 U.S. 367 (1969); Benno Schmidt, *Freedom of the Press v. Public Access* 166 (1976).
132. 425 U.S. 765 (1978).
133. *Id.* at 776, citing *Thornhill v. Alabama,* 310 U.S. 88, 101-2 (1940).
134. 425 U.S. at 784. See Victor Brudney, *Business Corporations and Stockholders' Rights under the First Amendment,* 91 Yale L. J. 235 (1981).
135. 435 U.S. 802-22.
136. 447 U.S. 557 (1980).
137. *Id.* at 566.
138. *Id.* at 566-68.
139. *Id.* at *568-69.*
140. *Id.* at 569-73.
141. *Id.* at 583.
142. 478 U.S. 328 (1986).

143. *Id.* at 341-42.
144. *Id.* at 352-53.
145. *Id.* at 346.
146. *Id.* at 354, n.4 (Brennan, dissenting).
147. *Id.* at 359-63.
148. See Sanford Levinson, ed., *Responding to Imperfection: The Theory and Practice of Constitutional Amendment* 3-11 (Princeton: Princeton Univ. Press, 1995); David E. Kyvig, *Explicit and Authentic Acts: Amending the U.S. Constitution 1776-1995* (Lawrence: Univ. of Kansas Press, 1996); Donald S. Lutz, *Toward a Theory of Constitutional Amendment,* 88 Amer. Pol. Sci. Rev. 355 (1994).
149. *Minor v. Happersett*, 88 U.S. (21 Wall.) 162 (1875). See Elizabeth Frost-Knappman and Kathryn Cullen-DuPont, *Women's Suffrage in America* (New York: Facts on File, 2005).
150. 247 U.S. 251 (1918), overruled, *United States v. Darby,* 312 U.S. 100 (1941).
151. See Chapter 4, notes 149 and 150, and accompanying text.
152. 198 U.S. 45 (1905). See Chapter 8, notes 77 to 85 and accompanying text.
153. John R. Vile, *Encyclopedia of Constitutional Amendments, Proposed Amendments, and Amending Issues, 1789-2002,* 3 Vols, 2nd ed. (Santa Barbara, CA: ABC-CLIO, 2003).
154. U.S. Cong., House, H. J. Resolution 300 (76th Cong., 1st Sess., May 19, 1939).
155. *Gitlow v. New York,* 268 U.S. 652, 666 (1925; *Stromberg v. California,* 283 U.S. 359 (1931); *Near v. Minnesota,* 283 U.S. 697 (1931). See Charles Warren, *The New Liberty Under the Fourteenth Amendment,* 139 Harv. L. Rev. 431 (1926); Klaus H. Heberle, *From Gilow to Near: Judicial 'Amendment' by Absent-Minded Incrementalism,* 34 J. of Politics 458 (1972).
156. 302 U.S. 319 (1937), overruled, *Benton v. Maryland,* 395 U.S. 784 (1969).
157. 332 U.S. 46 (1947), overruled, *Malloy v. Hogan,* 378 U.S. 1, 6 (1964).
158. 332 U.S. at 68-123.
159. 381 U.S. 479, 522 (1965).
160. David R. Dow, *When Words Mean What We Believe They Say: The Case of Article V,* 76 Iowa Law Review 1 (1990).
161. Akhil Reed Amar, *The Consent of the Governed,* 94 Colum. L. Rev. 457 (1994).
162. Bruce Ackerman, "Higher Lawmaking," in Sanford Levinson, ed., *Responding to Imperfection*, *supra* note 148, at 63.

2

Objective Theory of Interpretation:
Textual Analysis in Social Context

Constitutional theory matters, not just to scholars, but to the entire community.[1] The constitutional theory or theories adopted by justices on the Supreme Court of the United States fix their approach to decision making. The substantive methodology that is adopted determines the scope of judicial discretion in real cases that in turn can be determinant of the decisions.

This chapter begins with an explanation of the necessary rejection of *stare decisis* in constitutional cases in the Supreme Court. This is followed by a demonstration that the search for subjective intent of the framers and ratifiers, a popular slogan of some political conservatives, is an impossibility. The conclusion is not that judicial discretion in the highest court is unlimited. Instead, the textual analysis of this chapter presents an objective theory of interpretation that is based on original meanings of constitutional language.[2] These are the meanings to reasonably educated readers at time of adoption. Textual analysis first requires application of the canons of documentary construction, and, if needed, evidence of total social context that facilitates the search for purposes. The methodology presented by Justice Joseph Story in 1833 is shown to be just as relevant and applicable today as it was then.

The primary constitutional principles underlying a rational and rigorous theory of constitutional interpretation are the separation of governmental powers and the reservation of the amending power to the people in Article 5. The Supreme Court is an appointed elite, and under the present system of judicial review, its majority of five can hold any statute unconstitutional. But the people did not ratify a constitution that provided for maximum governance by the judiciary. The scope and breadth of judicial discretion in the Court when interpreting the principles incorporated in the more general constitutional clauses must be determined by the Court in the frame of its own counter-majoritarian character.

All legislative and judicial officers take the same oath to support the Constitution.[3] The legislature, as initiator of law, must be given the presumption of acting in good faith to write laws. The judiciary must frame its interpretation in this light. The discretion in the Court when invalidating a statute as unconstitutional must be exercised with clear recognition of the presumption of constitutionality.[4]

The first principle of interpretation is the rejection of a strong or binding version of *stare decisis* by the Supreme Court when interpreting the Constitution. This rejection is unique because the strong version of *stare decisis* applies to all statutory interpretation,[5] including that in the Supreme Court, and it applies to constitutional interpretation in lower courts.[6] The rejection of binding precedent in interpretation of the Constitution by the highest court arises directly from the superior status of constitutions. The Constitution is supreme law because it is derived from the people themselves through their ratification of proposals adopted at a Constitutional Convention.[7] No constitutional decisions of the Supreme Court, or of any other court, have been submitted to the people for ratification.

A workable system of constitutional interpretation requires the Supreme Court to give dominant status only to that which the people have ratified, not what a majority of justices may have said about a particular constitutional clause in some earlier decision concerning a specific and narrow fact situation. As Justice Felix Frankfurter said in *Graves v. New York,* "The ultimate touchstone of constitutionality is the Constitution itself and not what we have said about it."[8] An erroneous constitutional interpretation by the Supreme Court cannot become a binding precedent on that Court in later similar cases. Such application of *stare decisis* would allow judicial error to amend the Constitution. If, for example, the erroneous decision in *Hammer v. Dagenhart*[9] were binding precedent, the necessary federal regulation of national economic problems would be impossible. As Senator Garrett Davis said in 1866, when the *Dred Scott*[10] decision was argued to be controlling law, "This is not a Government of precedents; it was never intended to be; and there cannot be any more dangerous principle established in our government than that precedents shall make Constitutional law."[11] Justice William O. Douglas, in language similar to Justice Peter Daniel has concluded: "A judge looking at a constitutional decision may have compulsions to revere past history and accept what was once written. But he remembers above all else that it is the Constitution which he swore to support and defend, not the gloss which his predecessors may have put on it."[12]

A second reason for the highest court to reject *stare decisis* in constitutional cases is that the people do not stand ready to amend the broad language of the Constitution just because the majority of electors think one case was wrongly decided. Amendment was designed to be a costly, time-consuming process.[13] And broad, general language is difficult to amend while still retaining most of the same meaning in the clause. For this reason, the highest court has adopted an efficient method to correct what it considers errors in its earlier constitutional interpretations. It exercises its power to overrule them in subsequent similar cases. And the methodology of overruling is the exact opposite of *stare decisis.*

The contrast between correcting errors in statutory interpretation and in constitutional interpretation was stated by Justice Louis Brandeis:

> *Stare decisis* is usually the wise policy, because in most matters it is more important that the applicable canon of law be settled than that it be settled right. . . . This is commonly true even where the error is a matter of serious concern, provided correction can be had by legislation. But in cases involving the Federal Constitution, where correction through legislative action is practically impossible, this Court has often overruled its earlier decisions. The Court bows to the lessons of experience and the force of better reasoning, recognizing that the process of trial and error, so fruitful in the physical sciences, is appropriate also in the judicial function.[14]

In effect, a constitutional decision is law only if it is correct. Chief Justice Roger Taney noted this in observing that the majority of the Supreme Court had refused to follow his earlier interpretations:

> After such opinions, judicially delivered, I had supposed that question to be settled, so far as any question upon the construction of the Constitution ought to be regarded as closed by the decision of this court. I do not, however, object to the revision of it, and am quite willing that it be regarded hereafter as the law of this court, that its opinion upon the construction of the Constitution is always open to discussion when it is supposed to have been founded in error, and that its judicial authority should hereafter depend altogether on the force of the reasoning by which it is supported.[15]

The best authority for the canon that the Supreme Court has the power and the duty to reject *stare decisis* and overrule its earlier constitutional decisions which it considers erroneous is the fact that it has done so in over 170 cases.[16] The exact figure cannot be stated because some overrulings are not explicit, and legal historians disagree on the real effect of some implied overrulings. *Erie R.R. Co. v. Tompkins*,[17] for example, expressly and mistakenly overruled only the interstate law merchant case of *Swift v. Tyson*,[18] but it impliedly overruled a large group of Supreme Court cases that had erroneously created federal common law in many areas. The true significance of these figures can be realized only if one knows how high courts try to avoid admitting their own clear errors.[19] If two cases have many identical facts but the later court can find one material fact which is different, that court will likely distinguish the two cases and avoid the issue of direct conflict in law. Consequently, each overruling in the highest court comes only after a clear admission that the cases cannot be distinguished. They are essentially identical in reference to the constitutional issue before the court. Rejecting *stare decisis* as not apposite, the highest court is bound to point out its error and correct it.

Rejection of Intent of Framers

The modern definition of intent is, in its true subjective sense, the thoughts that were in the minds of the persons who spoke or who drafted or approved a document. Search for subjective intent in this sense is an impossibility. No one knows the thoughts of each person at the Constitutional Convention and at the ratifying conventions that turned the proposed document into law.[20] Some commentators assert that statements by leaders at the convention imply the subjective intent of a silent majority on any given topic.[21] This speculation has no basis in fact. The framers probably had varying and conflicting intents. The convention of 1787 was deliberately closed to all outsiders and no official report made on the speeches in order to bar the influence of statements of leaders on the interpretation of the final document. This was later emphasized by James Madison: "As a guide in expounding and applying the provisions of the Constitution, the debates and incidental decisions of the Convention can have no authoritative character."[22] Since no official record of proceedings of the framers was made, none could be sent to the ratifying conventions. Those who voted for ratification voted for the language in the text, not the unknown subjective thoughts of fifty-five framers. The predominance of the text also applies to the amendments. As Justice Horace Gray noted, "Doubtless the intention of the Congress which framed and of the states which adopted [the Fourteenth] Amendment of the Constitution must be sought in the words of the Amendment; and the debates in Congress are not admissible as evidence to control the meaning of those words."[23]

The background for those who drafted and ratified the Constitution in 1787 were the common-law canons of documentary construction. While the idea of intent had some ambiguity at that time, it was not used in the subjective sense because lawyers knew that searching for the thoughts of writers of documents was impossible. The emphasis was on the language itself and evidence of generally accepted meanings. Thus, John Powell wrote in 1790 that contract was not concerned with "internal sentiments" but only with the "external expressions" of the parties.[25] The "intent" of the maker was to be found in the meaning of the document in common understanding of English. This view of common-law contract has been restated for modern times by Judge Learned Hand:

> A contract has, strictly speaking, nothing to do with the personal, or individual intent of the parties. A contract is an obligation attached by the mere force of law to certain acts of the parties, usually words, which ordinarily accompany and represent a known intent. If, however, it were proved by twenty bishops that either party, when he used the words, intended something else than the usual meaning which the law imposes upon them, he would still be held, unless there were some mutual mistake, or something else of the sort.[26]

The eighteenth-century courts recognized that interpretation of statutes presented the same impossibility in finding subjective intent in interpreting statutes.[27] Absent total expressed consensus on the meaning of the words, there is no such thing as collective intent. Committee reports and legislative record may show the intent of a few legislators except that some of those may have been misstating their views. One or more may have been totally against a statute and still have signed a report in favor of it because the language had been so weakened in committee that its effect would be minimal. The economics of regulation hypothesizes that, regardless of their subjective evaluation, many legislators' votes can be purchased in money or future power.[28] Congressmen may feel totally opposed to tobacco growers and their cancerous product or to milk cartels that exploit the consumers but, for a large gift, they vote in favor of subsidies to the special interests.[29] Perhaps the most important reason that search for intent of legislators about the scope of statutory language is impossible is that most of them have none. The majority are not sponsors of the particular bill and have time to give it only superficial thought. They take the advice of party leaders in voting or trade for votes on bills they sponsor by agreeing to vote on bills sponsored by others. A modern statement of the interpretive issue was made by Justice Robert Jackson: "For us to undertake to reconstruct an enactment from legislative history is merely to involve the Court in political controversies which are quite proper in the enactment of a bill but should have no place in its interpretation."[30]

The delegates to the Constitutional Convention and the ratifying conventions acted in the framework of the existing canons of construction to interpret English charters and statutes.[31] None of these canons provided for the impossible search for subjective intent.[32] The emphasis was on the intrinsic meaning of the language and the extant methods of statutory construction. Those who attended the ratifying conventions were mere agents of the people as a whole. The intentions of the majority of people were to ratify the stated language of the Constitution, not what was in the many differing minds of their agents, nor the conflicting views voiced by the minority who spoke at the ratifying conventions. The expectations of the legal community and others familiar with the legislative process was that the broad constitutional clauses would be interpreted beginning with textual analysis that applied the canons of documentary construction. Supreme Court opinions would give lower courts and the people a more detailed understanding of the intrinsic meaning of constitutional language as of date of adoption.

Objective Textual Interpretation

To most scholars, the constitutional language itself and methods for finding its most general meaning at time of adoption are the first and dominant elements of a theory of interpretation.[33] The integrity of the constitutional text must be the starting point.[34] The Committee of Detail at the Constitutional Convention of 1787 worked long and laboriously to refine an internally consistent document which would be subject to the extant canons of documentary construction.[35] As to the prime importance of the language itself, Chief Justice Charles E. Hughes quotes Chief Justice Roger Taney:

> In expounding the Constitution of the United States, every word must have its due force, and appropriate meaning; for it is evident from the whole instrument, that no word was unnecessarily used, or needlessly added. The many discussions which have taken place upon the construction of the Constitution, have proved the correctness of this proposition; and shown the high talent, the caution, and the foresight of the illustrious men who framed it. Every word appears to have been weighed with the utmost deliberation, and its force and effect to have been fully understood.[36]

A few words and phrases in the Constitution have narrow, specific meanings determinable by the text alone. They can be employed without resort to extrinsic evidence of meaning. The age requirements for congressman and the president are examples.[37] But the important contested clauses of the Constitution contain general principles to allocate governing power and to delineate the civil rights of persons.[38] Such general clauses require interpretation. Some phrases use common words of the English language of the time, such as "commerce among the several states."[39] Others are technical legal terms, such as "privilege of the writ of habeas corpus."[40] In either case, scope and breadth of the language is subject to debate. How one uses extrinsic evidence to determine textual meaning is often helped by canons of documentary construction. The leading authorities on eighteenth-century construction of documents were Thomas Rutherforth and Matthew Bacon.[41] Their work was a prime source for Justice Joseph Story's long chapter, "Canons of Construction," in his *Commentaries*.[42] The following discussion is based on those canons.

Justice Story cited three Supreme Court decisions which held that construction must be contemporary with the document.[43] In effect, he was reiterating the canon that the changing meanings of words over time cannot be allowed to amend the Constitution. He explained the scope of this canon as follows:

> Contemporary construction is properly resorted to, to illustrate, and confirm the text, to explain a doubtful phrase, or to expound an obscure clause; and in proportion to the uniformity and universality of that construction, and the known ability and talents of those, by whom it was given, is the credit, to which it is entitled. It can never abrogate the text; it can never fritter away its obvious sense; it can never narrow down its true limitations; it can never enlarge its natural boundaries.[44]

One primary source that defined usage of the English language for the colonists in America was Samuel Johnson's dictionary.[45]

Commentators today who assert that eighteenth century construction makes us slaves of a bygone age do not understand the broad general scope of national powers and civil rights embodied in the principles that the language incorporates. Textual analysis in Chapter 4 demonstrates that "commerce among the several states" vested a plenary power in Congress to regulate every transaction in the United States. Textual analysis also shows that "due process of law" meant required or appropriate procedure, not the actual procedure of 1791, but whatever procedure the current judges consider required for full and fair hearing in criminal and civil actions.[46] The broad principles in the Constitution are words of general classification. The actual facts or events falling in any class in 1789 or 1791 have no affect on and put no limit on those that fall in the same class today. Selling microchip computers is a valid example of commerce, and *Miranda*[47] warnings are a valid example of modern canons necessary to enforce the privilege against self-incrimination.

The only principled method of construing a written constitution is an objective theory of documentary interpretation. It is based on the meaning of language to reasonably educated readers of the time, not the unknown intents of the writers. Objective interpretation was best described by Justice Oliver Wendell Holmes:

> What happens is this. Even the whole document is found to have a certain play in the joints when its words are translated into things by parol evidence, as they have to be. It does not disclose one meaning conclusively according to the laws of language. Thereupon we ask, not what this man meant, but what those words would mean in the mouth of a normal speaker of English, using them in the circumstances in which they were used, and it is to the end of answering this last question that we let in evidence as to what the circumstances were. . . . We do not inquire what the legislature meant; we ask only what the statute means.[48]

Justice Story used the word "intention," but, following the usual method of the times, he clearly indicates that he is really concerned with objective textual meaning. Quoting William Blackstone, he wrote, "That the intention of a law is to be gathered from the words, the context, the subject–matter, the effects and consequences, or the reason and spirit of the law."[49] Story applies this as follows:

> In construing the constitution of the United States, we are, in the first instance, to consider, what are its nature and objects, its scope and design, as apparent from the structure of the instrument, viewed as a whole, and also viewed in its component parts. Where its words are plain, clear, and determinate, they require no interpretation; and it should, therefore, be admitted, if at all, with great caution, and only from necessity, either to escape some absurd consequence, or to guard against some fatal evil. Where the words admit of two senses, each of which is conformable to common usage, that sense is to be adopted, which, without departing from the literal import of the words, best harmonizes with the nature and objects, the scope and design of the instrument. . . . In examining the constitution, the antecedent situation of the country, and its institutions, the existence and operations of the state governments, the powers and operations of the confederation, in short all the circumstances, which had a tendency to produce, or to obstruct its formation and ratification, deserve a careful attention. Much, also, may be gathered from the contemporary history, and contemporary interpretation, to aid us in just conclusions.[50]

Story thus emphasizes that law has purposes and, for the general, ambiguous clauses of the Constitution, one may have to search the institutional context for purpose in order to determine the scope of the language.[51] As to the technical legal language in the Constitution, one must recall with Sir Henry Maine that "The Constitution of the United States is a modified version of the British Constitution; but the British Constitution which served as its original was that which was in existence between 1760 and 1787."[52] The due process clause, for example, has meaning only in terms of its developmental history that goes back to Magna Carta.[53] The privilege of the writ of habeas corpus has meaning only in light of the British Habeas Corpus Act of 1679.[54] The meaning of these technical legal terms in the late eighteenth century was known to the lawyers at the convention and those in the general public who urged ratification. Hence, one can argue that there were known meanings of both ordinary English and technical legal terms. If the scope of these meanings were in contest, current interpretation should center on the relative suitability of the various eighteenth-century meanings.

Justice Story viewed broad construction as directed by the Constitution itself. "(1) It is to be construed as a *frame* or *fundamental law* of government, established by the PEOPLE of the United States, according to their own free pleasure and sovereign will."[55] He urged reasonable interpretation. "By a reasonable interpretation, we mean, that in case the words are susceptible of two different senses, the one strict, the other more enlarged, that should be adopted which is most consonant with the apparent objects and intent of the constitution; that which will give it efficacy and force as a *government*, rather than that which will impair its operations."[56] He followed this with a series of more specific canons of construction, all of which have as much applicability today as they had when written.[57] Like all canons of construction, however, they are more difficult to apply than they are to state. The point is that controversies over the meaning of language in the text should center on these canons and the reasonableness of their application in any particular situation.

The writings of Story, Holmes, and Hand present forcible arguments that the original meaning of language is to be found under objective standards, the meaning of language to reasonably educated readers of the times. This view of constitutional construction emphasizes historical linguistics supplemented by contemporaneous canons of documentary construction. These canons assist in exploring extrinsic evidence needed in order to resolve ambiguities of general language. The judge is not a slave to these canons of construction, but rather adopts those that his or her sound reason indicates will be helpful.

A prime example, addressed in Chapter 10, is the Equal Protection Clause of the Fourteenth Amendment.[58] Evidence of possible intent of some framers from speeches at the 39th Congress indicates that it was designed solely to assure that former slaves received limited equality of treatment by the state with that afforded white citizens.[59] But the comprehensive, general language of the clause is not controlled by evidence of a limited purpose to protect Afro-Americans because construction can never abrogate the text.[60] The clause applies to all classifications of persons and firms who are discriminatorily treated differently from others who are in like circumstances.

One of the most neglected aspects of the theory of constitutional interpretation is that the language incorporates the ideals of the community.[61] In fact, the language is often so general in order to incorporate the conflicting ideals in the community. The compromises of contesting blocs of delegates at a Constitutional Convention or a legislature adopting an amendment are reached by rising to higher levels of generalization in the final language. The framers do not want to constitutionalize society's existing legal and social structure. They are people with a mission to design a better government and broader enforcement of civil rights, ideal citizen-government relationships.[62] The Equal Protection Clause of the Fourteenth Amendment is a prime example. The radical Republicans were determined to wipe out all aspects of slavery and to prevent inferior treatment of former slaves.[63] They deplored the remnants of state-sponsored racial segregation in the North and were determined to excise it. The radicals convinced the majority to adopt the most general language for the amendment, ideal behavior that incorporated absolutely equal state treatment for all persons in like circumstances. As elucidated in Chapter 10, state segregation statutes of the 1880's and 1890's were deliberate attempts to evade the clear meaning of the clause with the fiction that separate could be equal.[64] The keenly perceptive dissent of Justice John Marshall Harlan in *Plessy v. Ferguson*[65] emphasized that in racial matters the termination of a caste system mandated a color-blind Constitution.

Purpose in Modern Interpretation

The textual meaning of constitutional language, as supplemented by canons of documentary construction of the time if they are helpful in a particular case, may still leave substantial ambiguities. In such instances, it may be useful to search for the purposes in the adoption of the clause. Purpose is not a subjective concept. It is concerned with the social issues, problems, or conflicts that caused the adoption of the particular clause. As Karl Llewellyn said of statutes, language "must be read in the light of some assumed purpose."[66] Judge J. Skelly Wright argued that in the interpretation of the broad language of constitutional limitations, analysis of purposes is primary:

> A judge or scholar should begin by expounding his view of the theory and purpose behind the constitutional provision in question. . . . The proper approach for the judiciary, then, is to state "principled goals" and general canons with a comprehensiveness and degree of clarity sufficient to establish at least a very strong presumption against a range of government actions violative of the articulated purpose.[67]

The search for purpose at time of adoption requires the use of extrinsic materials, and the research of modern historians can be helpful. This was explained by Judge McCurn when he met the rare case requiring him to interpret the allocation of power in our first Constitution:

> Although interpreting the Articles of Confederation is more difficult than contemporary statutory construction because of the passage of time, the approach is the same. To determine the Articles' meaning the court must examine the Articles' language, the legislative history, the interpretations that the period's statesmen and historical experts have given the Articles, how the Articles were applied, the period's general history, and revelant secondary sources.[68]

Since key constitutional clauses incorporate very broad principles for a structure of government and delegation of powers, history of the social problems that were to be resolved by any particular clause may also be ambiguous. Nonetheless, some fundamental background facts are significant. The Articles of Confederation had not created effective government. There was a need for a national government with comprehensive power to enforce a single national economy and with a power to tax and spend for the general welfare. While there are only social facts and structural needs to explain the purposes of the congressional powers, there was substantial legal history to give light to the purposes of the procedural constitutional limitations in the Bill of Rights.[69] It is clear that there is not always one purpose that will be found for any given clause or that dissenting opinions will disappear when and if all justices follow objective interpretation. Controversy should center, however, on the original meaning of the text and its purpose.[70]

The first canon of construction in this area that must be recognized is that evidence of purpose may never be used to contradict or curtail broad constitutional language. As Chief Justice Marshall noted: "[A]lthough the spirit of an instrument, especially of a constitution, is to be respected not less than its letter, yet the spirit is to be collected chiefly from its words."[71] This has been clearly illustrated in the economic clauses of the Constitution. In Chapter 4, linguistic history of the Commerce Clause shows that the meaning was not ambiguous, and thus, search for purpose would be inappropriate. The words "nation" and "states" in the Commerce Clause most often meant groups of people with a common government. Consequently, commerce "among the several states" meant commerce among the several groups of people who formed the United States. This meant all their transactions. The fact that the primary purpose was to terminate state barriers to interstate trade could not diminish the plenary affirmative power to regulate commerce delegated to Congress by the language.[72] Another example is the dictum of Justice Samuel Miller in the *Slaughter–House Cases*[73] about the purpose of the Fourteenth Amendment. He noted that the primary purpose was to end discrimination and injustice against the ex-slaves. But his dictum erroneously suggested that the purpose would curtail the broad language of the clauses.[74] The later Supreme Courts, as shown in Chapter 10, have correctly applied the broad Equal Protection Clause to persons and firms throughout the society.

When drafting the Constitution, the framers were aware that, in the creation of a government, they could not anticipate the many future controversies that would arise concerning the meaning and purpose of any given clause. They tried to incorporate the ideals of representative government for the long-term future. As John Ely notes, they wanted to create open channels for political change.[75] This is illustrated in *United States v. Classic*,[76] where the court determined that Article I, Section 2 included the right to choose representatives in primary elections. Justice Harlan F. Stone noted: "To decide it we turn to the words of the Constitution read in their historical setting as revealing the purpose of the framers, and in search for admissible meanings of its words which, in the circumstances of their application, will effectuate those purposes."[77] He explained the latitude to be given language that is to endure for the ages:

> We may assume that the framers of the Constitution in adopting that section, did not have specifically in mind the selection and elimination of candidates for congress by the direct primary any more than they contemplated the application of the commerce clause to interstate telephone, telegraph and wireless communication which are concededly within it. But in determining whether a provision of the Constitution applies to a new subject matter, it is of little significance that it is one with which the framers were not familiar. For in setting up an enduring framework of government they undertook to carry out for the indefinite future and in all the vicissitudes of the changing affairs of men, those fundamental purposes which the instrument itself discloses. Hence we read its words, not as we read legislative codes which are subject to continuous revision with the changing course of events, but as the revelation of the great purposes which were intended to be achieved by the Constitution as a continuing instrument of government.[78]

Where the meaning of constitutional language has been contested and viewed as unclear, the results of studies that search for the social purposes of clauses may supplement legal-linguistic research in confirming original meanings. In Chapter 7, linguistic history of the terms "privileges" and "immunities" from the Charter of Virginia in 1607 to 1868 demonstrates that they were together a synonym for constitutional limitations. They supported the conclusion that the Privileges-or-Immunities Clause of the Fourteenth Amendment incorporated the Bill of Rights as effective against the states. The recent comprehensive study of Michael Curtis on the purposes of this clause reinforces these conclusions.[79] They confirm the dissenting opinion of Justice Hugo L. Black in *Adamson v. California*[80] and rebut those who would search for subjective intents of framers.

Presumptions in Constitutional Method

Some of the most difficult cases appealed to the Supreme Court present head-on conflicts between two or more constitutional clauses. In such cases, neither the text nor the historical meaning of language will assist a solution. The Court must create solutions on the basis of the total structure of constitutional law. Many of these cases fall into two large groups. The first concerns conflicts between national or state legislative power and one or more of the constitutional limitations. The second group concerns conflicts between national legislative powers and state legislative powers. The argument presented here is that these conflicts of constitutional clauses in the most difficult cases on appeal cannot result in a consistent pattern of decisions if decided on an ad hoc basis. It is therefore posited that the Court must approach constitutional conflicts in terms of the total structure of the Constitution. Out of this structure, the Court should be able to derive principles which create a set of rebuttable presumptions on the relationships between national legislative powers, state legislative powers, and constitutional limitations. These presumptions of priority of one group of constitutional clauses over another are abstract structural principles. Like scientists' theories, the principles do not by themselves solve cases. They merely create a framework of relationships which point toward solution unless some sound, reasoned policies rebut the presumptions.

As to the national legislative powers, departmental finality is argued in Chapter 3. If they are litigated, the canon of *McCulloch v. Maryland*[81] requires broad construction. The Court has held that the express constitutional limitations are also to be given broad construction. Justice David Brewer explained:

> We are not here confronted with a question of the extent of the powers of Congress but one of the limitations imposed by the Constitution on its action, and it seems to us clear that the same canon and spirit of construction must also be recognized. If powers granted are to be taken as broadly granted and as carrying with them authority to pass those acts which may be reasonably necessary to carry them into full execution; in other words, if the Constitution in its grant of powers is to be so construed that Congress shall be able to carry into full effect the powers granted, it is equally imperative that where prohibition or limitation is placed upon the power of Congress that prohibition or limitation should be enforced in its spirit and to its entirety. it would be a strange canon of construction that language granting powers is to be liberally construed and that language or restriction is to be narrowly and technically construed.[82]

Since both the national powers and limitations are to be given broad construction, no insight to priorities between them can be gained from looking at their breadth. Nonetheless, the structure of constitutional law creates a decisional presumption in favor of constitutional limitations. Denial of the civil rights of Englishmen against government led to the American Revolution. Enforcement of these rights against their new government was the primary basis for a written constitution and for adoption of the Bill of Rights. Legislative acts are primarily general substantive regulations to limit human behavior. The constitutional limitations are particular substantive and procedural prohibitions on the action of government against oppression of individual citizens. Thus, generality and constraint on freedom are the key characteristics of legislative acts while particularity and constraint on government are the key characteristics when a citizen asserts the protection of a constitutional limitation. When one considers the fundamental objective of protecting human freedom which pervaded the writing of the Constitution, presumptive priority must go to the constitutional limitations.

The presumptive priority of constitutional limitations over national legislative powers, if it had been adopted by the Supreme Court, would have pointed the direction of solution in many past cases. Though not explicitly stated, the principle was applied in *Ex Parte Milligan*[83] in 1866. The judicial conflict was between the War Powers of Article I, Section 8, and the rights to due process of law and jury trial under the Fifth and Sixth Amendments. The Court ordered the release of Milligan, a civilian who had been tried and sentenced to death in Indiana by a military commission even though the civil courts were open there. The military commission was held to be without jurisdiction so long as civil legal process was unobstructed. This principle was followed, although belatedly, in 1944, in *Ex Parte Endo,*[84] where detention without trial in a relocation camp of a U.S. citizen of Japanese ancestry whose loyalty was conceded was held illegal. The presumptive priority of constitutional limitations was not followed in 1944 in *Korematsu v. United States,*[85] a 6 to 3 decision. The Supreme Court upheld forcible evacuation of American citizens of Japanese ancestry from the western United States even though the civil courts were fully operative and there had been no declaration of martial law. The judicial contest was between the War Powers and (1) the prohibition of Bills of Attainder in Article I, Section 9; (2) the right to due process of law in the Fifth Amendment, falsely argued to incorporate equal protection; and (3) jury trial before punishment in the Sixth Amendment. Citizens who the government later conceded were loyal were banished from the states where they had homes, employment, and businesses. Banishment of citizens has been considered penal in nature in the Anglo-American and European legal systems for hundreds of years.[86] Had the courts in this case commenced their consideration with a presumption in favor of the constitutional limitations, it is unlikely the decision would have upheld the evacuation of U.S. citizens.

The necessary priority of constitutional limitations is demonstrated in by the chief substantive protection for property in the Bill of Rights, the eminent domain clause guarantee of just compensation. This final clause of the Fifth Amendment creates an immunity which is a necessary component of any social system whose economic development depends on private saving and investment. For this reason, Chief Justice Marshall was clearly wrong in his dictum that "the power to tax involves the power to destroy."[87] Many later cases have recognized that the taxing power is subject to the limitation on eminent domain.[88] And Justice Holmes stated this succinctly when he said, "the power to tax is not the power to destroy while this Court sits."[89] Similarly, rate regulation under the commerce power must have an ultimate limit in the constraint on eminent domain.[90] And the Court has held the national bankruptcy power also to be limited by the eminent domain protection.[91] A court may not deprive a mortgagee of substantial property rights solely in the interest of a mortgagor. The purpose of bankruptcy law, however, is to forgive debts. Hence, it would seem that a presumption in protecting the lender's property in them could in many instances be rebutted.

As to state legislation conflicting with national constitutional limitations, the failure of the Court to have confirmed a strong presumption in favor of the latter has also made for confusion in the decision process. The flag salute cases are a prime example. Here the conflict was between state police power and the First Amendment as incorporated into the Fourteenth. In *Minersville School Dist. v. Gobitis*,[92] a small, isolated, powerless minority proved that saluting the flag conflicted with their serious, deeply felt religious beliefs.[93] Justice Frankfurter, for the majority, noted that "A grave responsibility confronts this Court whenever in the course of litigation it must reconcile the conflicting claims of liberty and authority."[94] He then upheld the local requirement that all children must salute the flag. His view that this small and powerless minority group might protect itself through the electoral process was a legal fiction. He held that "except where the transgression of constitutional liberty is too plain for argument, personal freedom is best maintained—as long as the remedial channels of the democratic process remains open and unobstructed—where it is ingrained in a people's habits and not enforced against popular policy by the coercion of adjudicated law."[95] *Gobitis* was overruled in spite of the patriotic fervor of wartime in *West Virginia State Bd. of Educ. v. Barnette*.[96] True patriotism is not created by flag salutes. Exempting a tiny religious minority from engaging in a symbolic act would in no way cause material harm to the state. Justice Jackson, for the Court, stated the controlling canon: "The very purpose of a Bill of Rights was to withdraw certain subjects from the vicissitudes of political controversy, to place them beyond the reach of majorities and officials and to establish them as legal principles to be applied by the courts."[97] He concluded that "the test of legislation which collides with the Fourteenth Amendment, because it also collides with the principles of the First, is much more definite than the test when only the Fourteenth is involved."[98] His example of legislation involving only the Fourteenth was public utility regulation and the "rational basis" test under the due process clause. In contrast, free speech, press, assembly, and worship "are susceptible of restriction only to prevent grave and immediate danger to interests which the state may lawfully protect."[99]

The modern cases are merely examples of a continuing failure of the Court to articulate a clear presumption of constitutional limitations over state legislation. The one outstanding early example bearing on the security of transactions under capitalism is the prohibition of Article I, Section 10 that no state shall pass any law impairing the obligation of contracts. Starting in 1827 with *Ogden v. Saunders*,[100] the Court majority gave the Contracts Clause a narrow interpretation and held it to prohibit only retrospective state insolvency laws. In the leading mortgage relief case of this century, *Home Building and Loan Association v.*

Blaisdell[101] in 1934, a 5 to 4 decision again gave the Contracts Clause a narrow interpretation. The Court also failed to apply the exclusive national bankruptcy power of Article I as setting part of the mandatory framework of national powers designed to limit state laws. The leading recent case holding the state police power superior to the Contracts Clause was *City of El Paso v. Simmons.*[102] A Texas statute which materially altered the contracts rights of prior purchasers of public lands was held constitutional. In dissent, Justice Black argued that the Court did not have the power to set its own balance between a state law and the national constitutional limitation whose language was admittedly violated. He argued in vain for the supremacy of the constitutional limitations.

When one turns to the relationships between national legislative powers and state legislative powers, there are more than presumptions in favor of the federal law. Article VI, Clause 2, states an explicit mandate in favor of the national constitution and laws. Justice Holmes noted its crucial importance:

> I do not think the United States would come to an end if we lost our power to declare an Act of Congress void. I do think the Union would be imperiled if we could not make that declaration as to the laws of the several States. For one in my place sees how often a local policy prevails with those who are not trained to national views and how often action is taken that embodies what the Commerce Clause was meant to end.[103]

The Supremacy Clause of Article VI was the cement chosen by the framers to hold the nation together when state and national policies conflicted. They predicted that national supremacy would usually make for national unity while state supremacy would make for disintegration and possibly civil war. As the industrial revolution brought specialization in manufacture and national channels of marketing, most commerce affected more states than one. The mandate in the Court to protect the national commerce power and to prohibit interstate barriers to trade created a legal environment that fostered economic growth. Judicial enforcement of the constitutional prohibition on state autarchy may well have prevented the kind of trade barriers that fostered many of the wars in Europe.

The Supremacy Clause is an express rejection of the theory of dual federalism, that the national and state governments are equal sovereigns. Chief Justice Marshall declared both in *McCulloch v. Maryland*[104] and in *Gibbons v. Ogden*[105] that Article VI established the principle of national supremacy in the law. Nonetheless, a number of Supreme Court majorities for a hundred years chose to ignore Article VI and assert in the alternative that the Tenth Amendment withdrew some matters of internal police from the reach of power expressly granted to Congress. Shortly after Marshall's death this viewpoint was asserted in *New York v. Miln,*[106] which has since been overruled. The conception of a "complete, unqualified, and exclusive" police power residing in the states and limiting the power of the national government was also asserted ten years later by Chief Justice Taney in the *License cases*.[107] This doctrine of independent power in the Tenth Amendment was first used to hold a federal statute unconstitutional in 1871 in *Collector v. Day*,[108] which was also later repudiated. As noted in Chapter 4, in 1918 the Tenth Amendment was also asserted as one basis for the 5 to 4 decision nullifying the Federal Child Labor Law in *Hammer v. Dagenhart*.[109] The complete repudiation of this interpretation in the later cases has restored the mandate of national supremacy.[110] But, in spite of this relegation of the Tenth Amendment to its original and proper place in constitutional structure, the Supreme Court has failed to revive the Supremacy Clause of Article VI to its status as the prime analytical tool for every case where federal and state legislative powers conflict.

The inconsistency of the court in application of the Supremacy Clause is exemplified by the state action defense to the federal antitrust laws under the doctrine of *Parker v. Brown*.[111] This doctrine created an exception to the general principle of the Supremacy Clause that state legislation that conflicts with national law or would frustrate the scheme of a national statute must fall.[112] In spite of the quasi-constitutional status of the national antitrust laws,[113] the Court in *Parker* upheld the validity of the California Agricultural Prorate Act,[114] a state-established price-fixing program as applied to raisin growers. Justice Stone devoted the bulk of his opinion to the indisputable canon that state officers acting in a governmental regulatory capacity were immune from injunction under Section 4 of the Sherman Act.[115] His other basis of decision was state sovereignty,[116] and there he ignored the paramount position of the Supremacy Clause in issues of federalism.

As to the substance of the State Act, the Court stated, "We may assume for present purposes that the California prorate program would violate the Sherman Act if it were organized and made effective solely by virtue of a contract, combination or conspiracy of private persons, individual or corporate."[117] If the Court had used preemption analysis, the opinion would have drawn to a quick conclusion. The California statute establishing cartel pricing was in actual conflict with the Sherman Act. Injunction against state officials to enforce the Supremacy Clause was the appropriate remedy.[118]

While the Court admitted that a state cannot give immunity to "those who violate the Sherman Act by authorizing them to violate it,"[119] it held that command and supervision by the state creates an antitrust exemption. However, the Sherman Act contained no express exemption for persons and firms violating its provisions under state compulsion and supervision, and its language does not imply one.[120] Sections 1 and 2 of the Sherman Act begin with the unambiguous word "Every."[121] Section 1 has been interpreted consistently with the word "every" to hold all horizontal combinations to fix prices and other private cartels illegal per se.[122] No reasonable user of English would interpret the statutory language to imply an antitrust exemption for violators of the Sherman Act because their cartel was state imposed and administered. On the basis of mere legislative omission, the Supreme Court had no power to create one. Furthermore, the presumptions of our legal system are just the opposite. The Supremacy Clause controls the relationship between federal and state law, not unexpressed statutory intent. National statutes generally do not have supplementary clauses prohibiting conflicting state statutes because they are unnecessary. The Constitution obviates this task.

In *Parker*, there was no discussion by the Court of the language and scope of the Supremacy Clause. The state action defense was approved with full knowledge that the state law was inconsistent with, and contrary to, the mandate of competition in the Sherman Act.[123] The Court noted that there were similar federal statutes protecting agricultural prices in derogation of the Sherman Act. But this was not relevant. Congress may create such exemptions to the antitrust laws as required by political expediency. The states have no power to create exemptions for federal statutes. That is the essence of the Supremacy Clause.

Appendix to Chapter 2: Epistemology of Overruling

Epistemology is concerned with seeking long-term, sustainable truths. In the sciences, this is achieved by critics replicating other's discoveries to search for errors. Testing and retesting is the method to assure truth in individual epistemology. Law, being concerned with social interaction, is analyzed as a subset of social epistemology. It examines the spread of information and misinformation across the members of a profession. Professor Goldman, a leading authority, devotes an entire chapter to the social epistemology of law.[124] He cites Professor Akhil Reed Amar on the treatment of criminal procedure in the Fifth and Sixth Amendments.[125] As to the privilege against self-incrimination, Amar wrote: "Truth is a preeminent criminal procedure value in the Bill of Rights: most procedures were designed to protect innocent defendants from *erroneous* conviction. Especially when pressured, people may confess—or seem to confess —to crimes they did not commit."[126]

In constitutional law, the epistemological issue concerns the extent to which lower court judges, lawyers, and other careful readers can gain reliable knowledge of the scope of legal rules from majority opinions of the Supreme Court. Some scholars argue that epistemic indeterminacy reaches its maximum in constitutional law.[127] Five to four constitutional opinions of the Supreme Court in our system of judicial supremacy are the prime example of unsettled law. While all lower courts are bound by precedent to follow the majority opinions, it is argued that in constitutional cases there is no such thing as settled law. Any Supreme Court majority opinion that does not conform to the ratified textual language may eventually be overruled.[128] Even unanimous opinions of the Supreme Court may seem ambiguous, as in the school segregation cases, if they are reached by compromise that may not express the precise views of any of the justices on the scope or breadth of a constitutional clause.[129]

Constitutional law casebooks for students and histories are noted for failing to explain the basic epistemology of Supreme Court overruling of earlier opinions. Some legal historians, emphasizing judicial supremacy and a "living constitution," treat overruling as merely one lesser aspect in the progressive development of constitutional law.[130] That view rejects the more formal analysis which asserts that the original meaning of the ratified language in most constitutional clauses is largely determinable. The new overruling opinion and the past opinion which is being repudiated concern the same legal issue and are inconsistent. The new opinion on the scope of the constitutional clause in contest is held to be the legal truth in interpreting the ratified language. Consequently, the overruled opinion was in error when written. A prime example was the *Dred Scott* case. The majority opinion was in error in holding that an owner could bring a slave into Illinois and the Northwest Territories where slavery was absolutely prohibited by law and still maintain involuntary servitude.[131] The dissent of Justice Benjamin Curtis was the textually correct opinion. He might have persuaded a Court majority to join his view if only there had been a trial court opinion favoring Scott. That could have happened had this slave been able to sue while he was in the free state of Illinois instead of the actual later legal action in the slave state of Missouri. After the Civil War, *Dred Scott* was overruled by the Thirteenth and Fourteenth Amendments.[132] This is a vivid example of the legal maxim: *Leges posteriores priores contrarias abrogant.* (Later laws abrogate prior laws that are contrary to them.)

The second epistemic question of overruling is whether the earlier dissents help understanding constitutional history. Since the reasoning of the Court in the overruled case is totally rejected, the issue is what aspects of the dissents in that case would have correctly explained binding law for lower courts. The simple answer is that one must search the dissenting opinions in such cases for rationales that conform to the original meanings of constitutional clauses. A prime example, explained in Chapter 8, was *Lochner v. New York*[133] which was overruled *sub silentio* in *Bunting v. Oregon*[134] and expressly noted as overruled in later cases.[135] Unfortunately, both the majority opinion for *Lochner* and Justice Harlan's dissent adopted the fallacious guardian review of "liberty of contract" as the basis for decision. Justice Harlan only corrected the statement of facts so that it conformed to the lower court opinion. Only the dissent of Justice Holmes rejected the due process clause as a valid basis for substantive regulation, and this was not fully explained in terms of the separation of governmental powers.[136]

The principle that overruled opinions were erroneous when decided is illustrated for the Equal Protection Clause of the Fourteenth Amendment in *Plessy v. Ferguson*.[137] As explained in detail in Chapter 10, the clause did not treat social or political equality but did mandate absolute equality before the law.

The Louisiana statute that required racial segregation on trains was upheld by the Supreme Court majority even though the statute was designed to perpetuate a racial caste system. *Plessy* was finally overruled in a transportation case in 1956. Consequently, the systematic dissent of Justice John M. Harlan, observing that the true meaning of equal protection was a caste-free, color-blind society, was the correct law of the *Plessy* case.[138]

The Supreme Court's misconstruction of the Fourteenth Amendment also illustrates overruled erroneous opinions whose dissent was eventually vindicated as correct law. *Maxwell v. Dow,*[139] a 1900 opinion that was overruled in 1968, is a prime example. Maxwell had been convicted of the felony of robbery in a Utah court. He had been tried before a jury of eight persons and sentenced to eighteen years in prison. His conviction was affirmed in the Utah courts and by Justice Peckham for the majority of the U.S. Supreme Court. The issue on appeal was whether the Fourteenth Amendment incorporated the Sixth Amendment right to trial by jury, which had been construed to follow English and U.S. precedents requiring twelve jurors.

Justice Harlan, in dissent, first emphasized the original meaning of constitutional privilege or immunities of citizens of the United States.[140] He reviewed all of these limitations in the Constitution and the Bill of Rights. His conclusion that the privileges or immunities clause of the Fourteenth Amendment incorporated the Bill of Rights against the states was a precursor to the dissent of Justice Black in *Adamson v. California.*[141] Harlan's extensive historical survey of the Anglo-American constitutional right to criminal trial by a jury of twelve persons, adopted in the Sixth Amendment, was first applied to the District of Columbia and territories of the United States. Since this was a procedure case, Harlan also reasoned that the due process clause of the Fourteenth Amendment mandated incorporation of the Sixth Amendment.[142]

One of the most renowned decisions that was eventually overruled was the 5 to 4 ruling in *Adamson v. California.*[143] The majority, following the decision in *Twining v. New Jersey,*[144] held that the Fifth Amendment privilege against self-incrimination was not incorporated in the Fourteenth Amendment. Justice Black's extended dissent argued at length that the text of the Fourteenth Amendment incorporated amendments I to VIII of the Bill of Rights as effective against state governments. This led to great contests in the law journals.[145] The *Twining* and *Adamson* decisions were overruled in *Malloy v. Hogan*[146] (1964), but the Court did not adopt Justice Black's earlier view on total incorporation of amendments I to VIII into the Fourteenth. Since the *Malloy* opinion cancelled the decisions and rationales in *Twining* and *Adamson,* it is limited to its own rationale and not an adoption of Justice Black's dissent in *Adamson.*

Retired Justice Lewis F. Powell spoke on the frequency of Supreme Court overrulings.[147] He noted that during the sixteen years of the Warren court, 1953 to 1969, there were sixty-three Supreme Court overrulings. During the seventeen years of the Burger court, 1969 to 1986, there were sixty-one overrulings.

On a rough average, the Court overruled less than four cases per term. The importance of cases which are overruled varies greatly. Powell asserted that the most important overrulings of the Warren court were in *Brown v. Board of Education*.[148] These were the 1899 case of *Cumming v. Board of Education*[149] and the 1927 case of *Gong Lum v. Rice*.[150]

While Powell recognized the absolute necessity for overruling when earlier constitutional opinions were clearly wrong, he urged recognition of the non-binding constitutional precedents before the Supreme Court in other cases. He failed to emphasize the original meaning of constitutional language to the ratifiers examined in its full social context. He did quote Justice Scalia and others who urge that original meaning of constitutional language must take priority over precedent.[151]

Notes

1. See Jack N. Rakove, *Original Meanings* (New York: Alfred A. Knopf, 1996); Laurence H. Tribe, *American Constitutional La*w 30-51 (New York: Foundation Press, 3rd ed., 2000); Douglas Laycock, *Constitutional Theory Matters,* 65 Texas L. Rev. 767 (1987).

2. See H. Jefferson Powell, *Parchment Matters: A Meditation on the Constitution as Text,* 71 Iowa L. Rev. 1427 (1986); *Symposium: Textualism and the Constitution,* 66 Geo. Wash. L. Rev. 1088-1394 (1998). Compare Antonin Scalia, *A Matter of Interpretation,* 23-29, 37-41 (Princeton: Princeton Univ. Press, 1997); Martin H. Redish, *The Constitution as Political Structure* 6-10 (New York: Oxford Univ. Press, 1995).

3. U.S. Const., Art. 6, Cl. 3.

4. *Fletcher v. Peck,* 10 U.S. (6 Cranch) 87, 128 (1810); *Hylton v. United States,* 3 U.S. (3 Dallas) 171, 175 (1796). See James B. Thayer, *The Origin and Scope of the American Doctrine of Constitutional Law,* 7 Harv. L. Rev. 129 (1893).

5. Statutory rules are much narrower than constitutional principles, and the entire community relies on the first comprehensive interpretation of a statute by the highest court as a controlling precedent. Consequently, the highest court considers itself bound to follow this precedent in later similar cases. The legislature is expected to amend or replace statutes that it feels the highest court has misinterpreted. See Edward H. Levi, *Introduction to Legal Reasoning* 27-33 (Chicago: Univ. of Chicago Press, 1961).

6. *Northern Virginia Reg. Pk. Auth. v. United States Civ. Serv. Com.,* 437 Fed 1346, 1350 (4th Cir. 1971), cert. denied, 403 U.S. 936 (1971).

7. See Chapter 1, notes 11 and 12, and accompanying text.

8. *Graves v. New York,* 306 U.S. 466, 491-492 (1939), overruling *Dobbins v. Commissioners of Erie County,* 41 U.S. (16 Pet.), 435 (1842); *Collector v. Day* 78 U.S. (It Wall.) 113 (1871); *New York ex rel. Rogers v. Graves,* 299 U.S. 401 (1937); *Brush v. Commissioner,* 300 U.S. 352. (1937).

9. 247 U.S. 251 (1918), overruled in *United States v. Darby,* 312 U.S. 100 (1941).

10. *Scott v. Sandford,* 6o U.S. (19 How.) 393 (1857).

11. Congressional Globe, 39th Gong., 1st Sess., 3917 (July 19, 1866).

12. William O. Douglas, *Stare Decisis,* 49 Colum. L. Rev. 735, 736 (1949). See License Cases, 46 U.S. (5 How.) 504, 612 (1847) (Daniel, J.).

13. Only four amendments have been passed specifically to overrule Supreme Court decisions: the Eleventh to overrule *Chisholm v. Georgia,* 2 U.S. (2 Dall.) 419

(1793); the Fourteenth, Sec. 1, to overrule *Scott v. Sandford,* 60 U.S. (19 How.) *393* (1857); the Sixteenth to overrule *Pollock v. Farmers' Loan & Trust Co.,* 157 U.S. 429 (1895), 158 U.S. 601 (1895); the Twenty-sixth to overrule *Oregon v. Mitchell,* 400 U.S. 112 (1970).

14. *Burnet v. Coronado Oil & Gas Co.:* 285 U.S. *393, 406-8* (1932) (dissenting opinion), overruled in *Helvering v. Mountain Producers Corp.,* 303 U.S. 376 (1938). Other justices have reiterated this view on overruling constitutional error. Justice Reed, for the Court, held racial discrimination in party primary elections to violate the Fifteenth Amendment. In overruling *Grovey v. Townsend,* 295 U.S. 45 (1935), he commented: "In constitutional questions, where correction depends upon amendment and not upon legislative action, this Court throughout its history has freely exercised its power to reexamine the basis of its constitutional decisions. This has long been accepted practice, and this practice has continued to this day" (*Smith v. Allwright,* 321 U.S. 649, 655 [1944]). Justice Black contrasted statutory and constitutional method as follows: "I do not believe that the principle of *stare decisis* forecloses all reconsiderations of earlier decisions. In the area of constitutional law, for example, where the only alternative to action by this Court is the laborious process of constitutional amendment and where the ultimate responsibility rests with this Court, I believe reconsideration is always proper" (*Boys Markets v. Retail Clerks Union,* 398 U.S. *235, 259* [1970]).

15. Passenger Cases, 48 U.S. (7 How.) 283, 470 (1849). Two years later, Chief Justice Taney, writing for the Court, adopted the principle of rejecting constitutional *stare decisis* when he expressly overruled the decision in *The Steam-boat Thomas Jefferson,* 23 U.S. (10 Wheat.) 428 (1825). He explained the rationale of overruling:

> It is the decision in the case of *The Thomas Jefferson* which mainly embarrasses the court in the present inquiry. We are sensible of the great weight to which it is entitled. But at the same time we are convinced that, if we follow it, we follow an erroneous decision into which the court fell, when the great importance of the question as it now presents itself could not be foreseen; and the subject did not therefore receive that deliberate consideration which at this time would have been given to it by the eminent men who presided here when that case was decided. . . . And as we are convinced that the former decision was founded in error, and that the error, if not corrected, must produce serious public as well as private inconvenience and loss, it becomes our duty not to perpetuate it.

> *Genesee Chief v. Fitzhugh,* 53 U.S. (12 How.) 443, 456, 459 (1851).

16. See Albert R. Blaustein and Andrew H. Field, *"Overruling" Opinions in the Supreme Court,* 57 Mich. L Rev. 151 (1958); J. Killian and G. Costello, eds., *The Constitution of the United States of America: Analysis and Interpretation* 2245-56 (S. Doc. 103-6, 103d Cong., 1st Sess. 1996).

17. 304 U.S. 64 (1938).

18. 41 U.S. (16 Pet.) 1 (1842). See Chapter 6, which explains that *Swift* was an interstate law-merchant case, a class distinct from the common law, and was the one case that should not have been overruled.

19. Robert H. Jackson, *Decisional Law and Stare Decisis,* 30 A.B.A. J. 334 (1944).

20. Many commentators have noted the intention fallacy. For example, Charles Curtis writes: "The intention of the framers of the Constitution, even assuming we could discover what it was, when it is not adequately expressed in the Constitution, that is to say, what they meant when they did not say it, surely that has no binding force upon us. If we look behind or beyond what they set down in the document, prying into what else they wrote and what they said, anything we may find is only advisory.

They may sit in at *our* councils. There is no reason why we should eavesdrop on theirs" (*Lions under the Throne* 2 [1947]). See Thomas Cooley, *A Treatise on the Constitutional Limitations* 80-81, 6th ed. (Boston: Little Brown, 1890); Alfred Kelly, *Clio and the Court: An Illicit Love Affair*, 1965 Sup. Ct. Rev. 119; John Wofford, *The Blinding Light: The Uses of History in Constitutional Interpretation*, 31 U. Chi. L. Rev. 502 (1964); William Anderson, *The Intention of the Framers*, 49 Am. Pol. Sci. Rev. 340 (1955).

21. See Raoul Berger, *Government by Judiciary* 8-10, 402-457, (Indianapolis: Liberty Fund, 2d ed., 1997); Monaghan, *Our Perfect Constitution*, 56 N.Y.U. L. Rev. 353, 375-81 (1981). See critiques of Akhil Reed Amar, *The Bill of Rights* 193-197 (New Haven: Yale Univ. Press, 1998); Hans W. Baade, *"Original Intention": Raoul Berger's Fake Antique*, 70 N.C.L. Rev. 1523 (1992); John J. Gibbons, *Intentionalism, History, and Legitimacy*, 140 U. of Pa. L. Rev. 613, 621 (1991); Walter Murphy, *Constitutional Interpretation*, 87 Yale L. J. 1752 (1978).

22. James Madison to Thomas Ritchie, Sept. 15, 1821, in 3 Farrand 447.

23. *United States v. Wong Kim Ark*, 169 U.S. *649, 699* (1898).

24. See Jefferson Powell, *The Original Understanding of Original Intent*, 98 Harv. L. Rev. 885, 894-96 (1985).

25. John Powell, *Essay Upon the Law of Contracts and Agreements* 372-73 (London: J. Johnson, 1790).

26. *Hotchkiss v. National City Bank of New York*, 200 F. 287, 293 (S. D. N. Y., 1911).

27. See Powell, *Original Understanding, supra* note 24, at 897-902.

28. See George Stigler, *The Theory of Economic Regulation*, 5 Bell J. Econ. & Mgmnt. Sci. 335 (1974).

29. Henry Adams reports the following comment of his time about congressmen: "You can't use tact with a congressman! A congressman is a hog! You must take a stick and hit him on the snout!" in H. Adams, *The Education of Henry Adams: An Autobiography,* 261 (Boston: Houghton Mifflin, 1918).

30. *Schwegmann Bros. v. Calvert Distillers Corp.*, 341 U.S. *384, 396* (1951).

31. See citations in Powell, *supra* note 24, at 903-13.

32. See Gordon S. Wood, *The Creation of the American Republic,* 524-43 (1969).

33. See Rakove, *Original Meanings supra,* note 1 at ch. 11; Robert Bork, *Neutral Principles and Some First Amendment Problems*, 47 Ind. L. J. 1, 8 (1971); Hans Linde, *Judges, Critics, and the Realist Tradition*, 8 Yale L. J. 227, 254 (1972); John Ely, *The Wages of Crying Wolf*, 83 Yale L. J. 920, 949 (1973); Douglas Laycock, *Taking Constitutions Seriously*, 59 Texas L. Rev. 343 (1981); Henry P. Monaghan, *Our Perfect Constitution*, 56 N. Y. U. L. Rev. 353 (1981); J. Clifford Wallace, *The Jurisprudence of Judicial Restraint*, 50 Geo. Wash L. Rev. 1 (1981); James B. White, *Law as Language*, 60 Texas L. Rev. 415 (1982); Robert Nagel, *Interpretation and Importance in Constitutional Law*, in *Liberal Democracy*, Nomos 25, 181, J. Pennock and J. Chapman, eds. (1983). See generally, Learned Hand, *How Far Is a Judge Free in Rendering a Decision? The Spirit of Liberty* 103, 2d ed. (1953).

34. Hugo Black, *A Constitutional Faith* 1 (New York: Alfred A. Knopf, 1968); Richard Epstein, *Takings*, Ch. 3 (Cambridge: Harvard Univ. Press, 1985); M. Merrill, *Constitutional Interpretation: The Obligation to Respect the Text*, in *Perspectives of Law* 260, Roscoe Pound et al., eds. (1964). See generally, Leslie F. Goldstein, *In Defense of the Text* (Savage, MD: Roman & Littlefield, 1991).

35. See Max Farrand, *The Framing of the Constitution of the United States*, Ch. 9 (New Haven: Yale Univ. Press, 1913).

36. *Wright v. United States,* 302 U.S. 583, 588 (1938), quoting *Holmes v. Jennison,* 39 U.S. (14 Pet.) 540, 570-71 (1840). See *Martin v. Hunter's Lessee,* 14 U.S. (1 Wheat.) 304, 333-34 (1816).

37. U.S. Const., Art. I, § 2. & 3; Art. II, § 1.

38. On the theory of two types of clauses, see Edward S. Corwin, *Judicial Review in Action,* 74 U. Pa. L. Rev. 639, 659-60 (1926); Monaghan, *Our Perfect Constitution, supra,* note 33, at 361-67.

39. U.S. Const., Art. I, § § 8.

40. U.S. Const., Art. I, § § 9.

41. Thomas Rutherforth, 2 *Institutes of Natural Law,* Ch. 7 (Cambridge: J. Bentham 1756); Matthew Bacon, *A New Abridgement of The Laws of England* 3rd ed. (London: A. Strahan, 1768).

42. Joseph Story, 1 *Commentaries on the Constitution of the United States,* Ch. 5 (Boston: Hilliard Gray, 1833) [hereinafter cited as Story].

43. *Stuart v. Laird* 5 U.S. (1 Cranch.) 299, 309 (1803); *Martin v. Hunter's Lessee* 14 U.S. (1 Wheat.) 304 (1816); *Cohens v. Virginia,* 19 U.S. (6 Wheat.) 264, 418-21 (1821).

44. Story, I: 390.

45. Samuel Johnson, *Dictionary of the English Language,* 1755 (Reprint: New York, AMS Press, 1967). See Henry Hitchings, *Dr. Johnson's Dictionary: The Extraordinary Story of the Book that Defined the World* (London: John Murray, 2005).

46. See Chapter 8 on the distinction between expanded procedural protections to meet the needs of a changing society and the illegitimate creation of substantive due process.

47. *Miranda v. Arizona,* 384 U.S. 436 *(1966).*

48. Oliver W. Holmes, "Theory of Legal Interpretation," in *Collected Legal Papers,* 203, 204, 207 (New York: Harcourt Brace, 1920).

49. Story, I: 383.

50. Story, I: 387.

51. Story, I: 404. As to recognition of controlling contextual factors, see Ernest M. Jones, *System Approaches to Socio-economic Problems Confronting Governments: an Appraisal* 18 J. of Public Law 21, 32-37 (1969); Michael Conant, *Systems Analysis in the Appellate Decisionmaking Process,* 24 Rutgers L. Rev. 293, 317 (1970).

52. Henry Maine, *Popular Government* 253 (London: Murray, 1886); A. E. Dick Howard, *The Road from Runnymede* 99-112 (Charlottesville: Univ. Press of Virginia, 1968).

53. William S. McKechnie, *Magna Carta,* 2nd edition, Ch. 39 (Glasgow: Maclehose, 1914). See Edward Corwin, *Liberty Against Government* 23-59 (Baton Rouge: Louisiana, Univ. Press, 1948); Roscoe Pound, *The Development of Constitutional Guarantees of Liberty* 55-81 (New Haven: Yale Univ. Press, 1957); C. Ellis Stevens, *Sources of the Constitution of the United States* (New York: Macmillan, 1894).

54. See Chapter 1, notes 16 and 17.

55. Story, I: *393.* See Richard Posner, *Economics, Politics and the Reading of Statutes and the Constitution,* 49 U. of Chi. L. Rev. 263, 282 (1982).

56. Story, I: 404.

57. The rules of interpretation, which Justice Story explains in detail, are stated here in summary form:

    1. Where the power is granted in general terms, the power is to be construed as coextensive with the terms, unless some clear restriction upon it is deducible from the context.

2. A power given in general terms is not to be restricted to particular cases merely because it may be susceptible of abuse, and if abused, may lead to mischievous consequences.

3. On the other hand, a rule of equal importance is not to enlarge the construction of a given power beyond the fair scope of its terms merely because the restriction is inconvenient, impolitic, or even mischievous.

4. No construction of a given power is to be allowed which plainly defeats or impairs its avowed objects. Where a power is remedial in its nature, it should be construed liberally.

5. In the interpretation of a power, all the ordinary and appropriate means to execute it are to be deemed a part of the power itself.

6. In the interpretation of the Constitution, there is no solid objection to implied powers.

7. Exclusive delegation of power to the federal government would only exist in three cases: where the Constitution in express terms granted an exclusive authority to the Union; where it granted in one instance an authority to the Union and in another prohibited the states from exercising the like authority; and where it granted an authority to the Union in which similar authority in the states would be absolutely and totally *contradictory* and *repugnant.*

8. In order to ascertain how far an affirmative or negative provision excludes others or implies others, we must look to the nature of the provision, the subject matter, the objects, and the scope of the instrument.

9. The natural import of a single clause is not to be narrowed so as to exclude implied powers resulting from its character simply because there is another clause, which enumerates certain powers, which might otherwise be deemed implied powers within its scope.

10. Every word employed in the Constitution is to be expounded in its plain, obvious, and common sense, unless the context furnishes some ground to control qualify or enlarge it.

11. Define words in reference to the context, and shape the particular meaning so as to make it fit that of the connecting words and agree with the subject matter.

12. Where clearly technical words are used, the technical meaning is to be applied to them, unless it is repelled by the context.

13. It is not a correct rule of interpretation to construe the same word in the same sense wherever it occurs in the same instrument.

14. A constitution of government does not, and cannot, from its nature, depend in any great degree upon more verbal criticism, or upon the import of single words. Story, I: 407-41.

58. U.S. Const., Amendment 14, § § 1. See Ch. 10.

59. See Berger, *Government by Judiciary, supra* note 21, Ch. 10.

60. See *supra* note 44 and accompanying text. See *Yick Wo v. Hopkins,* 118 U.S. 356 (1886) (a city regulation that was applied only to Chinese laundries violated the Equal Protection Clause).

61. See Levi, *supra* note 5, at 58. A significant counterexample is the implied recognition of slavery in the Constitution of 1787.

62. J. Skelly Wright, *Professor Bickel, The Scholarly Tradition and the Supreme Court,* 84 Harv. L. Rev. 769, 784-85 (1971).

63. See Alexander M. Bickel, *The Original Understanding and the Segregation Decision,* 69 Harv. L. Rev. 1(1955).

64. See Ch. 10.

65. 163 U.S. 537, 559 (1896), overruled in *Gayle v. Browder,* 352 U.S. 903 (1956).
66. Karl Llewellyn, *The Common Law Tradition,* 374 (Boston: Little Brown, 1960).
67. Wright, *supra* note 62, at *785-786.* See John Wofford, *The Blinding Light,* 31 U. Chi. L. Rev. 502, 425-427 (1964).
68. *Oneida Indian Nation of N.Y. v. State of N.Y.,* 649 F. Supp. 420, 427 (N. D. N. Y., 1986).
69. See Richard Perry and John Cooper, *Sources of Our Liberties* (Chicago: American Bar Foundation, 1952); Stevens, *Sources of the Constitution, supra* note 53, Ch. 6 (1894).
70. As Judge Wright noted: "Naturally there will be differences over purposes and underlying political theories of the various constitutional protections. But they will be reasoned differences, subject to argument. Judicial decisions of which we disapprove can best be challenged on their merits, and in a wholly reasonable manner. Arguments over purposes and theories will be healthy, aiding both judges and the political officials who appoint them" (Wright, *supra* note 62, at 786-87).
71. Sturges v. Crowninshield, 17 U.S. (4 Wheat.) 122, 202 (1819).
72. Compare Raoul Berger, *Federalism,* Ch. 6 (Norman: Univ. of Oklahoma Press, 1987).
73. 83 U.S. (16 Wall.) 36 (1873).
74. "We doubt very much whether any action of a state not directed by way of discrimination against the negroes as a class, or on account of their race, will ever be held to come within the purview of this provision." *(Id.* at 81).
75. John H. Ely, *Democracy and Distrust: A Theory of Judicial Review,* Chs. 4 and 5 (Cambridge: Harvard Univ. Press, 1980).
76. 313 U.S. 299.
77. *Id.* at 317-18.
78. *Id.* at 315-16.
79. Michael Curtis, *No State Shall Abridge,* Chs. 1 and 2. (Durham: Duke Univ. Press, 1986). See Howard J. Graham, *The Early Antislavery Backgrounds of the Fourteenth Amendment,* 1950 Wis. L. Rev. 479, 610, reprinted in H. J. Graham, *Everyman's Constitution,* Ch. 4 (1968); Robert J. Kaczorowski, *The Politics of Judicial Interpretation* (Dobbs Ferry: Oceana Publications, 1985); Alfred Kelly, *Clio and the Court,* 1965 Sup. Ct. Rev. 119, 132-34; Tinsley Yarbrough, *The Fourteenth Amendment and Incorporation,* 30 U. Miami L. Rev. 2.31 (1976).
80. 332 U.S. *46,* 68-123 (1947). See Charles Fairman, *Does the Fourteenth Amendment Incorporate the Bill of Rights?* 2 Stan. L. Rev. 5 (1949). Compare William W. Crosskey, *Charles Fairman "Legislative History" and the Constitutional Limitations on State Authority,* 22. U. Chi. L. Rev. i (1954).
81. 17 U.S. (4 Wheat.) 316 (1819).
82. *Fairbank v. United States,* 181 U.S. 283, 288-89 (1901) (stamp tax on foreign bills of lading held a tax on exports violating art. I, § 9).
83. 71 U.S. (4 Wall.) 2. (1866).
84. 323 U.S. 283 (1944).
85. 323 U.S. 214 (1944). See Jacobus J. ten Broek, Edward Barnhart and Floyd Matson, *Prejudice, War and the Constitution,* Ch. 6 (Berkeley: Univ. of California Press, 1968).
86. Emer de Vattel, *Law of Nations,* bk. 1, sec. 228, Chitty ed. (Philadelphia: T. & J. Johnson, 1870). See, e.g., *Rex v. Lewis,* 168 Eng. Rep. 1308 (1932); *People v. Baum,* 251 Mich. 187, 231 N.W. 95 (1930).
87. *McCulloch v. Maryland,* 17 U.S. (4 Wheat.) 316, 429 (1819).

88. See *Acker v. C. I. R.* 258 F. 2d 568, 577 (6th Cir. 1958).
89. *Panhandle Oil Co. v. State of Mississippi ex rel. Knox,* 277 U.S. 218, 223 (1928) (dissenting opinion), overruled, *Alabama v. King & Boozer,* 314 U.S. I (1941).
90. *Baltimore & Ohio R. Co. v. United States,* 345 U.S. 146 (1953).
91. *Louisville Joint Stock Land Bank v. Radford,* 295 U.S. 555 (1935).
92. 310 U.S. 586 (1940).
93. See Exodus, 20:4-5.
94. 310 U.S. at 591.
95. *Id.* at 599 (footnote omitted).
96. 319 U.S. 624 (1943).
97. *Id.* at 638.
98. *Id.* at 639.*Id.*
99. *Id.*
100. 25 U.S. (12 Wheat.) 213 (1827). This was the only constitutional case in which Chief Justice Marshall dissented.
101. 290 U.S. 398 (1934).
102. 379 U.S. 497 (1965).
103. Holmes, *Collected Legal Papers,* supra note 48, at 295-96.
104. 17 U.S. (4 Wheat.) 316, *436* (1819).
105. 22 U.S. (9 Wheat.) 1, 210-11 (1824).
105.   36 U.S. (11 Pet.) 1oz, 139 (1837), overruled, *Edwards v. California,* 314 U.S. 160 (1941).
107.   46 U.S. (5 How.) 504 (1847).
108.   78 U.S. (11 Wall.) 113, 124 (1870), overruled, *Graves v. New York ex rel. O'Keefe,* 306 U.S. 466 (1939).
109.   247 U.S. 251 (1918), overruled, *United States v. Darby,* 314 U.S. 100 (1941)
110.   *Id.* at 12, 3-24.
111. 317 U.S. 341 (1943).
112. *Ray v. Atlantic Richfield Co.,* 435 U.S. 151 (1978); *Jones v. Rath Packing Co.,* 430 U.S. 519 (1977); *Florida Lime & Avocado Growers, Inc. v. Paul,* 373 U.S. 132 (1963); *Hines v. Davidowitz,* 312 U.S. 52 (1941).
113. The revered status of the antitrust laws was explained by Justice Thurgood Marshall:

Antitrust laws in general, and the Sherman Act in particular, are the Magna Carta of free enterprise. They are as important to the preservation of economic freedom and our free-enterprise system as the Bill of Rights is to the protection of our fundamental personal freedoms. And the freedom guaranteed each and every business, no matter how small, is the freedom to complete, to assert with vigor, imagination, devotion, and ingenuity whatever economic muscle it can muster. Implicit in such freedom is the notion that it cannot be foreclosed with respect to one sector of the economy because certain private citizens or groups believe that such foreclosure might promote greater competition in a more important sector of the economy.

United States v. Topco Associates, Inc., 405 U.S. 596, 610 (1972).
114. 1933 Cal. Stat., ch. 754, amended by 1935 Cal. Stat., chs. 471, 743; 1938 Extra Sess., ch. 6; 1939 Cal. Stat., chs. 363, 548, 894; 1941 Cal. Stat., chs. 603, 1150, 1186 (current version at Cal. Agric. Code SS 59641-662 [West 1968]).
115. "We find nothing in the language of the Sherman Act or in its history which suggests that its purpose was to restrain a state or its officers or agents from activities directed by legislature." *(Parker,* 317 U.S. at 350-51).

116. "In a dual system of government in which, under the Constitution, the states are sovereign, save only as Congress may constitutionally subtract from ... their authority, an unexpressed purpose to nullify a state's control over its officers and agents is not lightly to be attributed to Congress" *(Id.* at 351).
117. *Parker,* 317 U.S. at 350.
118. See *supra* note 92.
119. *Parker,* 317 U.S. at 351.
120. On the presumptions against antitrust exemptions, see *Group Life & Health Ins. Co. v. Royal Drug Co.,* 440 U.S. 205, 231 (1979). See also *Carnation Co. v. Pacific Westbound Conf.,* 383 U.S. 213, 217-18 (1966), *modified, 383* U.S. *932* (1966); California v. Federal Power Comm'n, 369 U.S. 482, 485 (1962).
121. "Sec. 1. Every contract, combination in the form of trust or otherwise, or conspiracy, in restraint of trade or commerce among the several States, or with foreign nations is hereby declared to be illegal" (15 U.S. C. S [1976]).
    "Sec. 2. Every person who shall monopolize, or attempt to monopolize, or combine or conspire with any other person or persons, to monopolize any part of the trade or commerce among the several states, or with foreign nations, shall be deemed guilty of a felony" (15 U.S.C., § 2. [1976]).
122. See, e.g., *Catalano, Inc. v. Target Sales, Inc.,* 446 U.S. 643 (1980); *United States v. Topco Assocs., Inc.,* 405 U.S. 596 (1972); *United States v. Socony-Vacuum Oil Co.,* 310 U.S. 150 (1940); *United States v. Trenton Potteries Co.,* 273 U.S. 392. (192.7). In light of the unswerving application of the per se illegality rule in price fixing cases both before and after *Appalachian Coals, Inc. v. United States,* 288 U.S. 344 (1933), that case must be considered a depression aberration and without value as precedent.
123. See *Parker,* 317 U.S. at 367-68.
124. Alvin I. Goldman, *Knowledge in a Social World* 272-314 (New York: Oxford Univ. Press, 1999).
125. Akhil Reed Amar, *The Constitution and Criminal Procedure: First Principles* (New Haven: Yale Univ. Press, 1997).
126. *Id.* at 84.
127. Ken Kress, *A Preface to Epistemological Indeterminacy,* 85 Nw L. Rev. 134, 138 (1990).
128. See Albert R. Blaustein and Andrew H. Field, *Overruling Opinions in the Supreme Court,* 57 Mich. L. Rev. 151 (1958).
129. *Brown v. Board of Education,* 347 U.S. 483 (1954).
130. See G. Edward White, *The Constitution and the New Deal* (Cambridge: Harvard Univ. Press, 2000) at 307:
    The vast majority of the significant provisions of the constitutional text have no fixed or finite meaning. Therefore, the only fundamental lodestar in constitutional interpretation is conformity to the principles of democratic theory, which requires deference in many cases, as well as aggressive scrutiny, against a backdrop of normal deference, in a few. Given the causal significance of human power holding in modern societies, the only way to check potential tyranny or arbitrariness in judges is to make them accountable to a political philosophy that treats all human contributions as potentially deserving of equal concern and respect. Thus, judicial creativity is not checked by the Constitution, "the law," or any permanent metaprinciples undergirding those entities, but by conforming to the foundational values of democratic theory.

131. *Scott v. Sanford,* 60 U.S. (19 How.) 393 (1857).
132. U.S. Const., Amend. 13.

133. 198 U.S. 45 (1905).
134. 243 U.S. 426 (1917). See statement concluding *sub silentio* overruling of *Lochner* by Chief Justice Taft in *Adkins v. Children's Hospital*, 261 U.S. 525, 528 (1923).
135. *Ferguson v. Skrupa*, 372 U.S. 726, 730 (1963).
136. *Lochner*, 198 U.S. at 75-76.
137. 163 U.S. 537 (1896) overruled, *Gayle v. Browder*, 352 U.S. 903 (1956).
138. *Plessy*, 163 U.S. at 559. See Harvey Fireside, *Separate and Unequal: Homer Plessy and the Supreme Court Decision that Legalized Racism* (New York: Carroll & Graf Publishers, 2004).
139. 176 U.S. 581 (1900), overruled, *Duncan v. Louisiana*, 391 U.S. 145, 148 (1968).
140. 176 U.S. at 605.
141. 332 U.S. 46, 68-123 (1947). The majority opinion was overruled in *Malloy v. Hogan*, 378 U.S. 1, 6 (1964).
142. 176 U.S. at 613.
143. 332 U.S. 46, 68-123 (1947).
144. 211 U.S. 78 (1908).
145.   See Charles Fairman, Does the Fourteenth Amendment Incorporate the Bill of Rights? *The Original Understanding*, 2 Stanford L. Rev. 5 (1949); William W. Crosskey, *Charles Fairman "Legislation History" and the Constitutional Limitations on State Authority*, 22 Univ. of Chicago L. Rev. I (1954); Charles Fairman, *A Reply to Professor Crosskey*, 22 Univ. of Chicago L. Rev. 144 (1954).
146. 378 U.S. I, 6 (1964).
147. Lewis F. Powell, *Stare Decisis and Judicial Restraint*, 47 Wash. & Lee L. Rev. 281 (1990).
148. 347 U.S. 483 (1954).
149. 175 U.S. 528 (1899).
150. 101 U.S. 78 (1927).
151. *South Carolina v. Gathers*, 490 U.S. 805, 823 (1989) (Scalia, J., dissenting); Charles Cooper, *Stare Decisis: Precedent and Principle in Constitutional Adjudication*, 73 Cornell L. Rev. 401 (1988).

3

Judicial Review of Legislation: Scope and Limits

Judicial review is defined as the final determination by the courts in a litigated case of the constitutionality of state and national executive or legislative actions.[1] It is thus not a power in the courts that exists generally to review acts of state or national officers or legislatures, but is restricted to a case of which the particular court has jurisdiction. The question of constitutionality must be put in issue so that it must be determined by the court as part of its obligation to dispose of the case according to law. This chapter centers on judicial review of the national legislative powers.

Economic analysis poses the question of which aspects of judicial review are efficient methods of facilitating effective representative government and also protecting civil rights of persons.[2] From this viewpoint, judicial review of the scope and breadth of delegated legislative powers is very different from judicial review to enforce constitutional limitations. A statute that imposes taxes or regulates commerce is of a different class from a bill of attainder or a law regulating the content of newspapers. The first class is concerned with exercising powers delegated by the people solely to the legislature while the second class is concerned with invasion of civil rights of individuals by officials in any department of government. Since the legislature and the executive have strong biases toward political objectives, only the independent judiciary has an incentive toward impartiality in enforcing civil rights. Thus, judicial review may be the only efficient method of enforcing constitutional limitations. In contrast, judicial finality in reviewing the scope and breadth of delegated legislative powers is not efficient.

The legislature is a democratic institution designed to absorb political pressures and to resolve the major social conflicts of the society. Legislative finality on the scope and meaning of the constitutional language in the delegated powers is the only efficient method to resolve social conflict through elected representatives. The appointed elite of the judiciary are not a democratic institution and were not created to resolve major legislative issues. The Supreme Court has little ability to respond to political attack by a majority or significant minority of citizens because it is not structured as a political institution.

This distinction is demonstrated in the literature attacking judicial review as being undemocratic.[3] The Anglo-American constitutional system has a tradition going back to Magna Carta for judicial enforcement of constitutional limitations against the executive that was expanded in the U.S. Bill of Rights to be effective against the legislature.[4] Judicial protection of individual rights from legislative oppression has seldom been termed undemocratic. It was only when the Due Process Clause was, without foundation in the constitutional text, converted from a protection of individual procedural rights into a general enforcement of freedom of contract that it was subject to public attack.[5] In 1789, there was no Anglo-American tradition for judicial review of the scope and breadth of legislative powers, and this is the main area for the modern charge of undemocratic judicial review. The English constitutional tradition of legislative supremacy was the starting point for the framers.[6] Judicial review of legislation that is not challenged as invading civil rights must be found in facts or arguments that rebut the English tradition.

In the national government, judicial review of legislative powers was and is attacked as undemocratic because the appointed judiciary has a veto over the elected Congress for all statutes of enough social importance to be litigated.[7] The public has expressed great dissatisfaction with judicial review of substantive legislation of Congress since the early 1900s. Justice Frankfurter, before his appointment to the Court, wrote to President Roosevelt in 1937 as follows:

> Dissatisfaction with a few isolated judicial decisions would never have given rise to deep and widespread disquietude concerning the relation of the Supreme Court to the national welfare. *With accumulating disregard of its own settled canons of constitutional construction,* the Supreme Court for about a quarter of a century has distorted the power of judicial review into a revision of legislative policy, thereby usurping powers belonging to the Congress and to the legislatures of the several states, always by a divided court and always over the protest of its most distinguished members. With increasing frequency a majority of the Court have not hesitated to exercise a negative power on any legislation, state or federal, which does not conform to their own economic notions.[8]

Forty years earlier, Justice Holmes spoke of similar extra-constitutional decisions as unconscious expressions of extreme laissez-faire judicial bias:

> When socialism first began to be talked about, the comfortable classes of the community were a good deal frightened. I suspect this fear has influenced judicial action both here and in England, yet it is certain that it is not a conscious factor in the decisions to which I refer. I think that something similar has led people who no longer hope to control the legislatures to look to the courts as expounders of the Constitutions, and that in some courts new principles have been discovered outside the bodies of

those instruments, which may be generalized into the acceptance of the economic doctrines which prevailed about fifty years ago.[9]

A conservative Supreme Court majority imposed their laissez-faire biases on the nation.[10] Beginning in the 1870's and extending to 1937, the Supreme Court constricted the scope of the Commerce Clause to a fraction of its original plenary meaning.[11] Starting about 1890, the Supreme Court adopted, without Constitutional basis, the concept of substantive due process.[12] The Court used its commerce limitations and due process creation to hold unconstitutional large numbers of statutes designed to remedy market failures, especially in the field of labor relations.[13] Since these statutes had represented the majority will for regulated expansion of industrial society, the Court's misinterpretations became a great counter-majoritarian force.

The primary historical conclusion of this chapter is that the judiciary was never delegated power to review the constitutionality of substantive acts of Congress enacted pursuant to Article I except those challenged as violating specific constitutional limitations. It will be shown that the decision on judicial review of Chief Justice Marshall in *Marbury v. Madison*[14] was precedent only for the construction of Article III, the subject matter of that case. His statements on the general nature of judicial review, which have been adopted as binding law to this day, were unnecessary to the decision.[15] His simplistic view of a self-applying constitution with no uncertainties about the meaning of language and a self-evident function of judicial review assumed as a premise the conclusion he intended to reach. Leading modern scholars have objected to Marshall's generalizations.[16] They should not have been binding on lower courts as the law on judicial review of the general legislative powers since *Marbury* did not concern Article I.

Under the American system of separated powers, judicial review of legislation can be justified as constitutional only on three bases: textual, historical, or structural.[17] Before explaining these bases, it is important to note that the issue is one of jurisdiction: in what classes of cases does the constitutional text, history, or structure require or permit the courts to exercise judicial review? It is essential to distinguish this issue from the issue of what methodology the Court may utilize after taking jurisdiction. The scope of constitutional doctrines and the issue of conflict between constitutional clauses in a particular fact situation are in the area of methodology of decision making and not our concern here.

The textual basis of judicial review is also historical. It is concerned with the connotation of language as of date of adoption. The changing meaning of words in the English language over time is not supposed to amend the Constitution.[18] If maritime law, for example, included the law merchant in 1789, it should be included today.[19] Connotation, however, does not mean denotation. Many constitutional clauses enact broad principles. It will be shown that in 1789 "commerce" included all transactions. Its same connotation today includes the sale of computers even though computers were unknown in 1789. Furthermore, the common use of language at time of adoption cannot be determined in the abstract. Evidence of context is needed to give language meaning. To the extent that language in the Constitution was borrowed from English charters and statutes, the meaning of those writings in the late eighteenth century may be significant aids in determining constitutional meanings. Absent a textual basis, there may still be historical bases of judicial review. As noted, the Constitution of the United States was not created in a historical vacuum. Judicial review in England of executive actions had been established only after a long, hard-fought battle, eventually leading to the statute known as the English Bill of Rights of 1689. The most significant aspect of this history is that it pertained to constitutional limitations on the executive. But, any historical argument for judicial review of legislation that invades civil rights must be found in the peculiar history and structure of the American Constitution.

Structural bases for some aspects of judicial review may exist even though not specified in the text or derived from English constitutional history.[20] The issue is what areas of judicial review are necessarily implied by constitutional structure. The separation of governmental powers is the most important structural element. One key issue is whether this separation creates three co-equal departments so that each of them has final say on the constitutionality of actions delegated to it. This is known as departmental review or the tripartite theory of review. On another level, the separation of powers between the national and state governments is the prime structural element in determining the constitutionality of national laws not enacted pursuant to Article I and openly usurping residual powers of the states.

Review of State Laws: Umpiring the Federal System

There is a textual basis for judicial review of state laws challenged in litigation as conflicting with national laws or the Constitution.[21] While most contests between the nation and the states are settled politically on the floors of Congress, a few of them lead to litigation and must be decided by the courts. The provision for judicial review to enforce the supremacy of national law over state law is in Article VI, Clause 2:

> This Constitution, and the Laws of the United States which shall be made in Pursuance thereof; and all Treaties made, or which shall be made, under the Authority of the United States, shall be the supreme Law of the Land; and the Judges of every State shall be bound thereby, any Thing in the Constitution or Laws of any State to the Contrary notwithstanding.[22]

State judges are expressly bound by this national law, "anything in the Constitution or Laws of any State to the Contrary notwithstanding." This final phrase was necessary because in addition to their oath pursuant to Article VI, Clause

3[23] to support the national constitution, they take oaths to support state constitutions and laws. Judges of the United States courts are different. They take only the oath to support the national constitution and laws. Hence, the general supremacy language of Article VI, Clause 2 is sufficient to bind them to give primacy to the national law over state law in any litigation where such an issue is tested.

The initial proposal in the Constitutional Convention was for a congressional negative of unconstitutional state laws. The sixth resolution of Randolph of Virginia at the opening of the convention moved that the national legislature have power "to negative all laws passed by the several States, contravening in the opinion of the National Legislature the articles of the Union."[24] One objective was to give Congress the opportunity to negative acts of state legislatures before the date that they became effective. Since the original resolution dealt only with constitutionality and not conflict between national and state law, Pinkney later moved that Congress have "authority to negative all [state] laws which they should judge to be improper."[25] This indeterminate language was debated and the proposal was defeated.[26] Continuous review by the Congress of state laws as they were passed was not an efficient form of control. Most state laws would conform to the national constitution and review of these would not be an efficient use of the time of congressmen.

Having rejected the congressional negative, the framers began drafting a supremacy clause directed at the judiciary. The original version of the Supremacy Clause provided only for the priority of national laws and treaties over state laws and did not specify constitutions.[27] Luther Martin, the draftsman, said it contemplated the supremacy of state constitutions over national statutes and treaties.[28] The Committee of Detail remedied this by adding "the constitutions of the states" to the final "notwithstanding" clause.[29] Subsequently, the convention adopted without further debate the final version that preceded "Laws of the United States" with "This Constitution."[30] It was thus clear that the entire convention saw the necessity of resolving conflict between state laws and the Constitution and the need for national supremacy.

A federal system requires a final umpire to resolve conflicts between state and national laws and constitutions. The final umpire of the federal system is the Supreme Court of the United States. Local biases of state supreme courts cannot be allowed to stand as law if the mandate of the Supremacy Clause is to prevail.

The Supremacy Clause plus the comprehensive appellate jurisdiction vested in the Supreme Court in Article III, Section 2 confirm the national judicial review of state court judgments on national law.[31] The judicial power extends to all cases arising under the Constitution, Laws, and treaties of the United States. For cases other than in the Supreme Court's original jurisdiction, the Court has general appellate jurisdiction. The language does not limit these cases to those arising in national courts. Consequently, issues arising under the national constitution and laws that have been litigated in the state courts are subject to the appellate jurisdiction of the Supreme Court. The 25th Section of the Judiciary Act of 1789[32] was designed to implement this appellate jurisdiction of the Supreme Court over state courts. Section 25 enacted that a final judgment in the highest court of a state might be reexamined and reversed or affirmed in the Supreme Court if the judgment held a statute or treaty of the United States unconstitutional or if it upheld a statute or an authority exercised under a state against a charge that it violated the federal constitution, statutes, or treaties.

The constitutionality of this section was tested and upheld by the Supreme Court in *Martin v. Hunter's Lessee.*[33] The case concerned thousands of acres of rich timber and tobacco lands in Virginia which had belonged to Lord Fairfax. The State of Virginia, under claim of having confiscated the estates during the Revolution in 1777, granted title to a part of the land in 1789 to David Hunter. Hunter brought an action in the state court to eject Martin, who held title under the will of Lord Fairfax. Martin argued in defense that the Treaty of Peace and Jay's Treaty of 1795 confirmed the titles of British subjects to land in America. The trial court and the Virginia Court of Appeals held against Martin and upheld Hunter's claim to title from the state. The Supreme Court of the United States, having granted review on a writ of error pursuant to Section 25 of the Judiciary Act, reversed this decision in 1813 and upheld the superior status of federal treaties.[34] The Virginia Court of Appeals refused to comply with the mandate of the Supreme Court, its view being that the Supreme Court had no appellate jurisdiction over state courts, and thus it considered Section 25 to be unconstitutional. This refusal was brought before the Supreme Court in 1815.

Justice Story gave the opinion of the Court since Chief Justice Marshall had disqualified himself because of financial interest in the Fairfax estates. In holding Section 25 to be constitutional, he rejected the Virginia contention of state sovereignty. He began by noting that the Constitution of the United States was created by the people themselves. The powers in the federal government could be broader than that vested by the several peoples in their state governments. To the extent that these powers conflicted, Article VI clearly indicated that the people of the United States wished to limit state sovereignty.

The Constitution could be implemented to create a national government only if the enumerated powers were construed broadly. Justice Story held that, since Article III extends the judicial power to all cases arising under the Constitution, laws or treaties of the United States, there must be power in Congress to give the courts appellate jurisdiction over these matters. The language of Article III does not limit these cases to those originating in federal courts. Consequently, the fact that a federal issue arises in the state courts rather than the lower federal courts is no ground to limit this appellate jurisdiction. In fact, the underlying issue is one of equal protection of the laws. Uniform interpretation of the national Constitution, laws, and treaties could be enforced only if judgments of all courts where such issues arose were subject to appeal to the single Supreme Court of the United States. The constitutional language demonstrated that the framers clearly recognized that the unity of the nation depended on the supremacy of the national constitution and laws over any state legislation that conflict with them.

Legal scholars have disputed the meaning of the word "pursuance" in the Supremacy Clause. Crosskey, quoting Dr. Johnson's 1755 *Dictionary*, says the term most commonly meant "done in consequence or prosecution of anything."[35] Bickel concurs, stating that pursuance of the Constitution meant "that the statutes must carry the outer indicia of validity lent them by enactment in accordance with the constitutional forms."[36] From this view of pursuance, and in light of the necessary and proper clause,[37] any act of Congress that could possibly carry out one of the enumerated powers and is duly enacted should preempt conflicting state law.

National Laws Violating Constitutional Limitations

Historical analysis confirms the existence of the one area of judicial review that until recently has received the least comment as a separate class. That area is federal statutes that are challenged as being in violation of the constitutional limitations. The function of constitutional limitations is exactly the opposite of the substantive clauses that delegate governing power. The function is to prohibit government officials in any department from depriving any person of specified rights or privileges. In fact, the first Supreme Court ruling on constitutionality of national legislation concerned the limitation on direct taxation.[38]

The national constitutional limitations begin with Article 1, Section 9 which protects the privilege of the writ of habeas corpus, and prohibits bills of attainder and ex post facto laws. The remainder of the national constitutional limitations are found primarily in Amendments I to X, XIII to XV, XIX, and XXIV. While most of the constitutional limitations are procedural, some of them are substantive. Amendments I to IV, XIII, XV, XIX, and XXI are primarily substantive.

The judicial function of enforcing constitutional limitations in all three departments of government is not spelled out expressly in the Constitution. Nonetheless, its historical development from Magna Carta to the time of the Constitutional Convention, confirms that it was the legal context in which the Constitution and especially the Bill of Rights were written. The idea of civil rights developed in England as protection of the individual against the Crown and is known there as the "Rule of Law."[39] Dicey notes that as a part of the English Constitution, it includes under one expression at least three distinct though kindred conceptions: "We mean in the first place, that no man is punishable or can be lawfully made to suffer in body or goods except for a distinct breach of law established in the ordinary legal manner before the ordinary courts of the land."[40] The second is that not only is no person above the law, but every person, regardless of rank, is subject to the ordinary law and the jurisdiction of the ordinary courts. The third is that the general principles of the Constitution are the result of judicial decisions determining the rights of private persons in particular cases brought before the courts.[41]

Thus, one sees the whole idea of civil rights of persons developing either out of court decisions, statutes, or the great charters, culminating in the English Bill of Rights of 1689. Article 13 thereof mandates "That excessive bail ought not to be required nor excessive fines imposed nor cruel and unusual punishments inflicted."[42] As Dicey points out, these and other constitutional constraints are supplemented by the conventions of the Constitution, a body of constitutional and political ethics.[43] Under these conventions, the Parliament, though supreme, would never pass legislation to invade those civil rights that have become part of the English Constitution.

The civil rights of English citizens and the tradition of judicial enforcement of those rights was brought to the American colonies by the settlers. Most of the colonial charters actually recited the colonist rights to the "liberties of Englishmen."[44] As the struggle developed against oppressive legislation passed by Parliament, the colonists started looking to the courts to enjoin what they considered violations of their constitutional rights. The most famous was the Writs of Assistance Case of 1761.[45] These general warrants enabled royal officers to search any house or ship, force entry and seize goods at will. James Otis, relying on the opinion of Lord Coke in *Bonham's Case*,[46] challenged the validity of the writs under the English Constitution.[47] While Otis was unsuccessful, his argument is characterized as the firing of the opening gun in the American Revolution.[48]

The colonists continued to demand these rights against the Crown before the revolution and against their state governments during and after the revolution. For example, the privileges and immunities of citizens in Article IV of the Articles of Confederation were primarily those of the English Constitution. This fact is clearly seen in the first committee draft of July 12, 1776, in which Clause VI read: "The Inhabitants of each Colony shall henceforth always have the same Rights, Liberties, Privileges, Immunities and Advantages, in the other Colonies, which the said Inhabitants now have, in all Cases whatever, except in those provided for by the next following Article."[49] Since this language was written before most states had adopted constitutions, the phrase "which the said inhabitants now have" had to refer to the English constitutional limitations. In other words, the Declaration of Independence discarded those parts of the English Constitution that imposed a framework of government but not the constitutional rights of Englishmen that the colonists had for so long argued were theirs.

The original Constitution did contain some constitutional limitations, such as Article I, Sections 9 and 10, but it did not contain a bill of rights. When the issue of a proposed declaration of civil rights was raised near the end of the Constitutional Convention, it was voted down. The debates indicate that some delegates felt that the civil rights of Englishmen against government, which they argued were theirs, did not need enumeration.[50] But the national government was arguably novel and, unlike the states, might not have inherited the English limitations.When the subsequent demand for an express bill of rights became so great that it was a condition of ratification, Madison promised to introduce the proposals for amendment in the first congress.[51] The adoption of the Bill of Rights did more than codify existing civil rights. Enumeration of some of them in absolute form, such as the first amendment, made them more comprehensive than they were in the English Constitution.[52]

A key function of codifying and ratifying the U.S. Bill of Rights was to rebut the English presumption of legislative supremacy and thus to impose constitutional limitations on both the executive and the legislative branches. Madison, in proposing the national Bill of Rights, noted the great differences between the English and U.S. constitutions. He observed, "it may not be thought necessary to provide limits for the legislative power in that country, yet a different opinion prevails in the United States. The people of many States have thought it necessary to raise barriers against power in all forms and departments of Government. . . . It therefore must be leveled against the legislative, for it is the most powerful, and most likely to be abused, because it is under the least control."[53]

It is submitted that the broad jurisdictional clause of Article III, Section 2 of the Constitution, extending the judicial power "to all cases, in Law and Equity, arising under this Constitution," was specifically designed to protect the constitutional limitations. Such cases might arise in the absence of any act of Congress. If, for example, a U.S. Marshall incarcerated a citizen without trial, legal action is based directly on rights defined in the Constitution. It is clear that this same tradition of civil liberties extends to acts of Congress which attempt to impose any similar infringement of civil rights. As Madison declared when introducing the Bill of Rights to the First Congress: "If they are incorporated into the Constitution, independent tribunals of justice will consider themselves in a peculiar manner the guardians of those rights; they will be an impenetrable bulwark against every assumption of power in the Legislature or Executive; they will be naturally led to resist every encroachment upon rights expressly stipulated for in the Constitution by the declaration of rights."[54] Jefferson, who was a leading opponent of general judicial review, expressly supported judicial enforcement of the Bill of Rights.[55] James Wilson, Samuel Adams, John Hancock, Patrick Henry, Richard Henry Lee and others also stated this view.[56]

Comprehensive judicial review of the acts of Congress, while not provided in the substantive sense, is effective procedurally under the Bill of Rights. Under the Fifth Amendment, the general procedural limitation is that one may not be deprived of life, liberty, or property without due process of law.[57] This rule applies to all three branches of government. All national procedural statutes are subject to judicial review on the challenge that they violate due process by failing to provide full and fair hearing pursuant to established law. Any substantive act of Congress also can be challenged on the limited procedural ground that the constitutional or statutory requirements for enacting a statute have not been fully met.[58]

In concluding that judicial review of national laws challenged as violating constitutional limitations is clearly founded in the history and structure of the Constitution, one can conclude likewise that the paramount function of judicial review is to guard against governmental infringement of individual liberties secured by the Constitution.[59] In light of this emphasis, it is useful to reconsider *Marbury v. Madison.*[60] After asserting the general power of judicial review in the Supreme Court, Chief Justice Marshall presented illustrations, all of which are constitutional limitations. They are (1) "no tax or duty shall be laid on articles exported from any state," (2) "No bill of attainder or ex post facto law shall be passed," and (3) "no person shall be convicted of treason unless on the testimony of two witnesses of the same overt act, or on confession in open court."[61] One can only hypothesize that Marshall might have adopted a rationale that was less than a general power of judicial review if counsel had argued a more limited power of judicial self-defense plus securing constitutional limitations.

One final issue emerges about this limited or partial judicial review. Most of the state precedents before 1789 allegedly supporting a general power of judicial review, even if they survive the charge of being spurious,[62] are cases concerning constitutional limitations.[63] They are as follows: *Case of Josiah Philips*[64] (bill of attainder), *Holmes v. Walton*[65] (right to jury of twelve persons), *Commonwealth v. Caton*[66] (legislative pardon; separation of powers), *Rutgers v. Waddington*[67] (state statute violated national treaty of peace), *Symsbury Case*[68] (legislature was highest judicial tribunal; hence, no judicial review), *Trevett v. Weeden*[69] (denial of jury trial in criminal case), *Bayard v. Singleton*[70] (denial of jury trial in common law action to recover real property). None of these cases support a *general* power of judicial review in the highest appeals court of a state. *Rutgers v. Waddington*[71] was the only civil action upholding judicial review and not concerned with a traditional constitutional limitation. In this case, a state statute was held to violate a national treaty. It merely supports the supremacy of national law over state law. At most, these state cases illustrate limited judicial review of alleged violations of constitutional limitations.

National Laws Regulating the Judicial Function

Judicial review of congressional acts regulating the judicial function, while not expressly stated in the text of the Constitution, is clearly implied by the text and also is founded on the structure and historical background of the Constitution. The first basis is textual. As noted, the Bill of Rights provides for judicial review of all national procedural laws under the due process clause of the Fifth Amendment.[72] Amendments Five through Eight are procedural and are clearly directed at the judiciary for enforcement. The due process clause, requiring full hearing and fair procedure according to established law, requires the judiciary to rule on whether statutes setting judicial procedures violate that standard.

The second basis of judicial review of statutes regulating the judiciary is structural and is based on the separation of powers. Under Article III, the entire judicial power is vested in the "Supreme Court and in such inferior Courts as the Congress may from time to time ordain and establish."[73] Statutes regulating this function, including those on federal jurisdiction, must conform to Article III. The final determination of this conformity must rest with the Supreme Court, the authoritative head of the judicial branch. As Elbridge Gerry said of the judiciary at the Constitutional Convention, "They will have a sufficient check against encroachment on their own department by their exposition of the laws, which involved a power of deciding on their Constitutionality."[74] This is an application of the theory of departmental review, that each of the three branches is co-equal and has final say on the scope of constitutional powers vested in it. This application of judicial review is known as "judicial self defense."[75]

Under the above rule, the Supreme Court in *Marbury v. Madison*[76] correctly assumed jurisdiction to pass on the constitutionality of Section 13 of the Judiciary Act of l789.[77] The power of the Congress to add to the original jurisdiction of the Supreme Court was clearly an issue under Article III, Section 2. Leading constitutional historians have severely criticized the decision in *Marbury.*[78] Since the decision on the merits has no bearing on the more general issue of judicial review, it will not receive comment here.

The primary issue of *Marbury* was not the scope of judicial review, but whether the executive could defy the law, and most of the opinion is devoted to the latter topic.[79] Here it is important to note that Marshall's generalizations on the Court's power of judicial review were *obiter dicta* and erroneous.[80] The correct principle of judicial review of *Marbury* is the narrower one stated above, that under departmental review the Court has final say on the meaning of Article III. Marshall's general statements that, under a written constitution, the judiciary must determine all constitutional controversies appealed to it are not consistent with his earlier language in the opinion. He noted that, under the separation of governmental powers, the political acts of the president and executive officers acting for him are not subject to judicial review.[81] Just as the Court refuses to hear clearly political controversies, it could and should refuse to hear constitutional challenges to substantive acts of Congress except for claims of violation of civil rights.

Marshall adopted the generalizations of Hamilton in *Federalist* No. 78.[82] But Hamilton's political generalizations were not law, and, in this case they were clearly misleading.[83] One can hypothesize why Hamilton made these statements. The key public fear about the Constitution was that it put too much power in the legislature.[84] Hamilton, whose anti-democratic proposals had been rejected at the Constitutional Convention,[85] was writing a political tract to urge ratification. He decided to assuage public fear by declaring the existence of a general judicial control over possible legislative excesses. Hence, he presented judicial review of all acts of Congress that are litigated as a necessary result of a written constitution. While asserting this general judicial supremacy, he also asserts disingenuously in the very same paper that the judiciary will always be the *least dangerous* department of government.[86] Many judges and scholars, who should know better, put great weight on all of the *Federalist.* But, careful discrimination is required.[87] While many, perhaps most, *Federalist* papers are useful analyses, some of them are exaggerations and a few are totally misleading.[88]

Choper points out that congressional regulation of judicial authority has from the earliest days been a matter for judicial review.[89] Under the separation of powers, the Congress may not impose non-judicial functions on the courts or subject judicial determinations to executive revision. In *Hayburn's Case,*[90] three different circuit courts, on which five of the six Supreme Court justices sat, held that they could not perform the executive function of ruling on the validity and amount of veterans' pension claims. On the other hand, the Court has approved statutes creating legislative courts so long as their decisions are reviewable in a U.S. Court of Appeals.[91] Recently, however, the Court held a congressional grant of general jurisdiction to legislative courts under the bankruptcy act to be unconstitutional.[92]

National Substantive Laws Enacted Pursuant to Article I

Neither constitutional text, nor its history, nor its structure provides support for judicial review of congressional statutes enacted pursuant to the delegated powers of Article I. On the contrary, the history and structure of the Constitution point to legislative finality on the scope and breadth of such statutes so long as they do not also contain violations of the express constitutional limitations. Most authorities assert that there is no textual basis for judicial review of national substantive laws. It is not explicitly mentioned in the Constitution and cannot be reasonably inferred from Article III, which is merely jurisdictional.[93] Its exclusion by the framers when they expressly provided for judicial review of state legislation in Article VI is a strong indication that no general power of judicial review of national laws was to be inferred from the document.

Legal historians point out that there was no settled public opinion at the time on whether general judicial review was implied.[94] While Hamilton wrote of judicial review in broadest terms, both Madison and Jefferson opposed a general power of judicial review of acts of Congress. Madison, who clearly supported judicial review to enforce the Bill of Rights voiced strong objection at the Convention to general judicial review. The original proposal of the Committee of Detail on the jurisdiction of the Supreme Court was firstly for "cases arising under laws passed by the Legislature of the United States."[95] On August 27, 1787, Dr. Johnson moved to insert the words "this Constitution and the" before the word "laws."[96] Madison reports his reaction:

> Mr. Madison doubted whether it was not going too far to extend the jurisdiction of
> the Court generally to cases arising Under the Constitution, & whether it ought not

to be limited to cases of a Judiciary nature. The right of expounding the Constitution in cases not of this nature ought not to be given to that Department.

The motion of Docr. Johnson was agreed to neo-con: it being generally supposed that the jurisdiction given was constructively limited to cases of a Judiciary nature.[97]

"Cases of a judiciary nature" is nowhere defined. He could have meant arising under the judicial function, judicial self-defense. He could also have meant to include enforcing the Bill of Rights and other constitutional limitations, as was the historical judicial function of the British courts. He surely was voicing opposition to general judicial review of legislation, a practice unknown to British or American legal history. On possible judicial refusal to enforce legislative acts, Madison wrote in 1788, "This makes the Judiciary Department paramount in Fact to the Legislature, which was never intended and can never be proper."[98] In the first Congress, discussing the question of granting to the President the power of removal, Madison stated:

> I beg to know upon what principle it can be contended that any one department draws from the Constitution greater power than another, in marking out the limits of the powers of the several departments. The Constitution is the charter of the people in the government; it specifies certain great powers as absolutely granted, and marks out the departments to exercise them. If the constitutional boundary of either be brought into question, I do not see that any one of these independent departments has more right than another to declare their sentiments on that point.[99]

Jefferson, who also supported judicial review to enforce the Bill of Rights, strongly opposed the generalizations of Chief Justice Marshall in *Marbury v. Madison* concerning judicial review. He wrote:

> That instrument [the Constitution] meant that its co-ordinate branches should be checks on each other. But the opinion which gives the Judges the right to decide what laws are constitutional, and what not, not only for themselves in their own sphere of action, but for the Legislative and Executive also in their spheres, would make the Judiciary a despotic branch.[100]

The inference from constitutional structure of legislative finality on legislative powers is supported by the comments of James Wilson at the Constitutional Convention. In supporting the view that the judiciary should share with the executive in the veto power, he recognized that the Supreme Court could hold unconstitutional statutes regulating the judiciary but implied that the Court could not invalidate statutes enacted pursuant to Article I:

> It had been said that the Judges, as expositors of the Laws would have an opportunity of defending *their* constitutional rights. There was weight to this observation; but this power of the Judges did not go far enough. Laws may be unjust, may be unwise, may be dangerous, may be destructive; and yet not be so unconstitutional as to justify the Judges in refusing to give them effect.[101]

The framers did not include language providing for general judicial review of substantive Acts of Congress because that would have been inconsistent with the historical context of English legislative supremacy and with the basic separation of governmental powers. "The Constitution of the United States is a modified version of the British Constitution, but the British Constitution which served as its original was that which was in existence between 1760 and 1787."[102] The British Constitution in existence during the years of the Federal Convention was dominated by the English Bill of Rights of 1689 which established parliamentary supremacy.[103] This fact was the basic framework of government in Blackstone's *Commentaries*, the leading law book in the colonies.[104] The idea of legislative supremacy, as borrowed from the writings of John Locke, had great influence in the American colonies.[105] While the framers of the Constitution were concerned with limiting possible abuses of legislative supremacy, it is not consistent with this background to infer from the nature of the Constitution that they had adopted as a remedy the judicial supremacy for all acts of Congress that were litigated. The historical presumption in favor of legislative supremacy was rebutted for constitutional limitations and judicial self-defense but not for substantive acts of Congress.

The basic structural characteristic of the Constitution was the separation of governmental powers.[106] In this context, those sections of the Constitution vesting substantive governing power in one department of government were not expressly subject to a general veto by another department. Such veto would make the separation of powers a hollow gesture. Yet, a general veto power in the judiciary for all acts of Congress that were litigated was the rationalization that Chief Justice Marshall adopted in *Marbury v. Madison*.[107] The more reasonable inference from separated powers is that each co-equal department was to make its own final determination on the breadth of the affirmative governing powers vested in it by the people. As has been noted, this is labeled *departmental review*.[108] Bickel concludes that the requirement of Article VI, Clause 3 for officials of all three departments of government to take oaths to support the Constitution means that each department is to construe with finality the performance of its own peculiar functions.[109] A leading constitutional historian has pointed to the application of departmental review in the executive,[110] and it is easily illustrated in the legislative branch. Article I, and especially Section 8 of that Article, for example, delegates broad legislative powers to the Congress. The members of Congress, following their oaths of office to support the Constitution, are rightly presumed to conform to their oaths. Since both constitutions and statutes must be expounded in written language that contains some level of uncertainty of meaning, Congressmen are just as qualified as justices to assess the scope of both and determine the constitutionality of powers vested in them. As Justice Holmes admonishes, "it must be remembered that legislatures are ultimate guardians of the liberties and welfare of the people in quite as great a degree as the courts."[111]

Given the overwhelming power in the judiciary when it assumes the prerogative of final review of substantive powers of the legislature, it is not surprising
that persons of such diverse views as President Jackson and President Lincoln
should make statements in opposition. In his veto message of July 10, 1832,
Jackson supported co-equal departmental review:

> The Congress, the Executive, and the Court must each for itself be guided by its
> own opinion of the Constitution. Each public officer who takes an oath to support
> the Constitution swears that he will support it as he understands it, and not as it is
> understood by others. . . . The opinion of the judges has no more authority over
> Congress than the opinion of Congress has over the judges, and on that point the
> president is independent of both. The authority of the Supreme Court must not,
> therefore, be permitted to control the Congress or the Executive when acting in their
> legislative capacities, but to have only such influence as the force of their reasoning
> may deserve.[112]

President Lincoln, in his first inaugural address, sought to limit the impact
of the *Dred Scott* case.[113] Though he conceded that the nation must accept the
decision as it applied to the particular parties, he challenged its finality for the
other branches of government. He spoke: "[I]f the policy of the Government
upon vital questions affecting the whole people is to be irrevocably fixed by
decisions of the Supreme Court, the instant they are made in ordinary litigation
between parties in personal actions, the people will have ceased to be their own
rulers, having to that extent practically resigned their Government into the hands
of that eminent tribunal."[114]

The idea of a general veto power in the Supreme Court over all substantive
laws enacted by Congress that are litigated is further repudiated by another
structural element—the character of representative government created in the
Constitution. The Congress is a representative body, responsible to the people at
every general election. If the majority of voters should conclude that a national
statute exceeds the delegated powers of Congress, it may within the next two
years vote out of office those Congressmen who supported such enactment. The
judiciary, in contrast, is an appointed elite with lifetime tenure. If the Supreme
Court should hold a national law unconstitutional that the overwhelming majority of citizens view as clearly within a delegated power of Congress, there is no
remedy short of impeachment. One must conclude that the theory of electively
responsible government would rank legislative finality of substantive legislative powers over review by the appointed judiciary. A rejection of any general
veto power in the appointed judiciary is further reinforced by the fact that the
Constitutional Convention voted down a proposed Council of Revision with
veto power over Congress that was to contain "a convenient number" of the
national judiciary.[115]

The conclusion that judicial review of the constitutionality of national
substantive statutes was not adopted in the Constitution has effect not only in

the Supreme Court, but in all lower courts, both national and state courts. This conclusion means that Section 25 of the Judiciary Act of 1789,[116] allowing appeal to the Supreme Court for specified classes of state and national constitutional issues decided in state courts, should have been divided by the Court into two groups. As to national laws, judicial review of the issues should have applied only to procedural statutes and those substantive statutes challenged as violating constitutional limitations. Since the state courts, like the national, had no power to rule on the constitutionality of all other national substantive laws, appeals from unwarranted assumption of jurisdiction in such cases should have resulted in summary orders of dismissal of the action.

Recent scholarship points to the conclusion that Chief Justice Marshall did not consider his generalizations about judicial review in *Marbury* to apply to legislative acts of Congress under its delegated powers in Article I.[117] The idea of legislative finality for decisions concerning the scope and breadth of delegated powers is reasonably inferred from Marshall's opinion in *McCulloch v. Maryland*.[118] One key issue was the constitutionality of the congressional act creating the second bank of the United States. The particular question was whether the creation of a nationally chartered banking corporation was valid in the absence of an express power in the Constitution. In upholding the constitutionality of the second bank, Chief Justice Marshall made a structural analysis based on the concept of implied powers.[119] Even before his discussion of the "necessary-and-proper clause" he found that workable government could function only if Congress could choose the most efficient means to execute its express powers.[120] Marshall gave the following primarily structural explanation of the existence of broad, implied legislative power:

> A constitution, to contain an accurate detail of all the subdivisions of which its great powers will admit, and of all the means by which they may be carried into execution, would partake of the prolixity of a legal code, and could scarcely be embraced by the human mind. It would probably never be understood by the public. Its nature, therefore, requires, that only its great outlines should be marked, its important objects designated, and the minor ingredients which composed those objects be deduced from the nature of the objects themselves. That this idea was entertained by the framers of the American Constitution, is not only to be inferred from the nature of the instrument, but from the language. Why else were some of the limitations, found in the ninth section of the first article, introduced? It is also, in some degree, warranted by their having omitted to use any restrictive term which might prevent its receiving a fair and just interpretation. In considering this question, then, we must never forget, that it is a constitution we are expounding.[121]

Like Hamilton in *Federalist* 33, Marshall minimized the significance of the necessary-and-proper clause.[122] In answering the argument that the world "necessary" precluded implementing the fiscal powers by incorporating a national bank, Marshall stated:

The subject is the execution of those great powers on which the welfare of a nation essentially depends. It must have been the intention of those who gave these powers, to insure, as far as human prudence could insure, their beneficial execution. This could not be done by confining the choice of means to such narrow limits as not to leave it in the power of Congress to adopt any which might be appropriate, and which were conducive to the end. This provision is made in a constitution intended to endure for ages to come, and, consequently, to be adapted to the various crises of human affairs.[123]

* * *

We admit, as all must admit, that the powers of the government are limited, and that its limits are not to be transcended. But we think the sound construction of the Constitution must allow to the national legislature that discretion, with respect to the means by which the powers it confers are to be carried into execution, which will enable that body to perform the high duties assigned to it, in the manner most beneficial to the people. Let the end be legitimate, let it be within the scope of the Constitution, and all means which are appropriate, which are plainly adapted to that end, which are not prohibited, but consist with the letter and spirit of the Constitution are constitutional.[124]

The implication of *McCulloch* is that the final word on implementation of express powers in the legislature is left to the legislature. This is only a short step from saying that the scope and breadth of legislative powers were to be determined with finality by the Congress. Marshall did not go so far as to assert the departmental theory of judicial review. If he had done so, it would have been consistent with the holding of *Marbury,* which concerned judicial self-defense, but not with his *obiter dicta* in that case on the general character of judicial review.

What of the highly unlikely situation that Congress should enact a statute that is openly and obviously not pursuant to any of the powers enumerated in the Constitution? Examples would be a national wills act or a national statute defining negligence for local vehicular torts.[125] Such national statute could be in direct conflict with existing state statutes and common-law rules on these topics. Where such a statute is beyond reasonable doubt outside the subject matter of any enumerated power, the Supreme Court would hold it ineffective under the Supremacy Clause and would uphold conflicting state law under the Tenth Amendment.[126] This principle must be strictly construed.[127] Holding a national statute ineffective under the Supremacy Clause technically does not make it void.[128] If the decision that held it ineffective is later overruled by the Court, the statute again becomes legally effective.[129]

Criticism of Judicial Review

Most of the critics of judicial review have failed to distinguish its application to constitutional limitations from its application to delegated powers. As a result, they tend to make generalizations for or against its continuance. Professor Commager, after reviewing the Court's misuse of judicial review between 1870 and 1937, suggested that the only way to end such abuse of power was to terminate judicial review.[130] He felt that legislative supremacy, even with extremist statutes enacted in time of national crisis, would be less detrimental to society than were the abuses by the Court majority under judicial review. His view was that judicial review leads inevitably to judicial legislation and that, consequently, judicial review is destructive of a true separation of governmental powers. The school of legal realists, concerned with the social and economic background of judges and their effects on decision making, dealt very harshly with the whole notion of judicial objectivity.[131] They felt that bias was unavoidable. Commager preferred the biases of the majority of the elected Congress to the biases of the appointed elite on the Supreme Court. He felt that the congress was basically conservative and would seldom deliberately attempt to evade the clear language of the Constitutional limitations. Consequently, he was prepared to place his trust in a majority of Congress to respect civil liberties as opposed to placing his trust in a majority of the Supreme Court.

The proponents of judicial review marshal many defenses against the charge of its undemocratic character.[132] They argue that the misuse of judicial review by some Supreme Court majorities through abuse of judicial discretion should be remedied by techniques to prevent recurrence of abuses, not the total termination of this vital judicial check on possible legislative tyranny. They further argue that abuses of judicial discretion before 1937 have taught present and future justices a lesson, so that future excesses are much less likely. The essential effect of terminating all judicial review, it is argued, would be the termination of all constitutional limitations. These clauses were specifically designed to prevent a duly elected majority of the legislature from oppressing minorities. The judiciary was given life tenure so that they would act fearlessly to enforce constitutional limitations against the public's unbridled passions of the moment that may result in the passage of oppressive legislation.

Mr. Justice Cardozo spoke of judicial review as a vital background factor affecting legislatures in their consideration of proposed laws:

The utility of an external power restraining the legislative judgment is not to be measured by counting the occasions of its exercise. The great ideals of liberty and equality are preserved against the assaults of opportunism, the expediency of the passing hour, the erosion of small encroachments, the scorn and derision of those who have no patience with general principles, by enshrining them in constitutions, and consecrating to the task of their protection a body of defenders. By conscious or subconscious influence, the presence of this restraining power, aloof in the background, but none the less always in reserve, tends to stabilize and rationalize the legislative judgment, to infuse it with the glow of principle, to hold the standard aloft and visible for those who must run the race and keep the faith. . . . The restraining power of the judiciary does not manifest its chief worth in the few cases in which the legislature has gone beyond the lines that mark the limits of discretion. Rather shall we find its chief worth in making vocal and audible the ideals that might otherwise be silenced, in giving them continuity of life and of expression, in guiding and directing choice within the limits where choice ranges. This function should preserve to the courts the power that now belongs to them, if only the power is exercised with insight into social values, and with suppleness of adaptation to changing social needs.[133]

There is a counterargument that judicial review cannot save a nation bent on destroying its freedoms and that the judiciary should not be assigned the impossible duty of ultimate savior. Judge Learned Hand has argued for limits on judicial review in the Supreme Court even in cases concerning constitutional limitations:

> And so to sum up, I believe that for by far the greater part of their work it is a condition upon the success of our system that the judges should be independent; and I do not believe that their independence should be impaired because of their constitutional function. But the price of this immunity, I insist, is that they should not have the last word in those basic conflicts of "right and wrong—between whose endless jar justice resides." You may ask what then will become of the fundamental principles of equity and fair play which our constitutions enshrine; and whether I seriously believe that unsupported they will serve merely as counsels of moderation. I do not think that anyone can say what will be left of those principles; I do not know whether they will serve only as counsels; but this much I think I do know—that a society so riven that the spirit of moderation is gone, no court *can* save; that a society where that spirit flourishes, no court *need* save; that in a society which evades its responsibility by thrusting upon courts the nurture of that spirit, that spirit in the end will perish.[134]

History has shown that when the tide of opinion favors suppression of political minorities, the Supreme Court majority will many times find a way of upholding oppressive statutes.[135] If the Court does resist the oppression and orders protection for a minority, its order may be ignored. Such was the case when the Supreme Court held unconstitutional certain Georgia statutes depriving the Cherokee Indians of their lands in that state.[136] It is thus clear that the willing cooperation of all three departments of government is the prime prerequisite for effective judicial review in order to enforce constitutional limitations.

The general judicial review of congressional legislation that prevails today was founded on the *obiter dicta* of Chief Justice Marshall in *Marbury v. Madison.*[137] While scholars have pointed to the holding of *Marbury* as a case of judicial self-defense that does not support Marshall's generalizations, the courts have not recognized this elementary fact. There seems small likelihood that the Supreme Court will soon recognize legislative finality for federal statutes not challenged under constitutional limitations. The development of general judicial review after the Civil War and up to the present time makes it an established institution.[138] There is no present movement to restore national legislative finality through constitutional amendment.[139] Since 1937, the court has recognized very broad powers in Congress under the taxation and commerce clauses.[140] This removes any urgency to restore federal legislative finality. Should a swing of the judicial pendulum result in the return to the narrow interpretations like those in the decades just before 1937, a movement for constitutional amendment could arise.

Notes

1. Muskrat v. United States, 219 U.S. 346 (1911); Massachusetts v. Mellon, 262 U.S. 447 (1923). See Leonard Levy, *Judicial Review and the Supreme Court,* 1-41 (New York: Harper & Row, 1967).
2. For an analysis of the literature on justice and efficiency, see Richard Posner, *The Economics of Justice,* 13-115 (Cambridge: Harvard Univ. Press, 1983).
3. The literature is reviewed in John Agresto, *The Supreme Court and Constitutional Democracy* (Ithaca, NY: Cornell Univ. Press, 1984); Clifton McCleskey, *Judicial Review in a Democracy,* 3 Houston L. Rev. 354 (1966). See Janet S. Lindgren, *Beyond Cases,* Wis. L. Rev. 583, 585-91 (1983).
4. See William McKecknie, *Magna Carta,* ch. 39 (2d ed., Glasgow: J. Maclehose, 1914). See *infra* note 53 and accompanying text.
5. On the violation of textual construction in the creation of substantive due process, see Chapter 8.
6. Donald Lutz, *The Origins of American Constitutionalism,* 92-95, 105-6 (Baton Rouge: Louisiana State Univ. Press, 1988); Albert Dicey, *Introduction to the Study of the Law of the Constitution* (7th ed., London: Macmillan 1908); E. Wade and G. Phillips, *Constitutional Law,* ch. 4 (6th ed., London: Longmans, 1960).
7. See Charles G. Haines, *The American Doctrine of Judicial Supremacy,* 17-28 (New York: Russel and Russel, 1959); Robert Jackson, *The Struggle for Judicial Supremacy,* ch. 10 (New York: Alfred Knopf, 1941); Henry Commager, *Majority Rule and Minority Rights* (New York: Oxford Univ. Press, 1943).
8. *Roosevelt and Frankfurter* 384, Max Freedman, ed., (Boston: Little Brown, 1967) (emphasis added). Frankfurter's charge of usurpation must be read in light of his earlier attack on those who had asserted that all judicial review was usurpation. Frankfurter, *A Note on Advisory Opinions,* 37 Harv. L. Rev. tool, 1003, n. 4 (1924). See Walton Hamilton and Douglas Adair, *The Power to Govern,* ch. 7 (New York: W. W. Norton, 1938).
9. Oliver W. Holmes, *The Path of the Law* (1897), reprinted in *Collected Legal Papers* 167, 184 (New York: Harcourt Brace, 1920).
10. Benjamin Twiss, *Lawyers and the Constitution* 168-70, 196-97 (Princeton: Princeton Univ. Press, 1942.); Felix Cohen, *Field Theory and Judicial Logic*, 59 Yale L. J. 238, 244-45 (1950).
11. See Chapter 4.
12. See Chapter 8.
13. See Leonard Levy, ed., *American Constitutional Law* 130 (New York: Harper & Row, 1966).
14. 5 U.S. (1 Cranch) 137 (1803).
15. "It is emphatically the province and duty of the judicial department to say what the law is. Those who apply the rule to particular cases must of necessity expound and interpret that rule. If two laws conflict with each other, the courts must decide on the operation of each. So if a law be in opposition to the Constitution; if both the law and the Constitution apply to a particular case, so that the court must either decide that case conformably to the law, disregarding the Constitution; or conformably to the Constitution, disregarding the law; the court must determine which of these conflicting rules governs the case. This is of the very essence of judicial duty."
    Id. at 177-78. See William Nelson, *The Eighteenth-Century Background of John Marshall's Constitutional Jurisprudence,* 76 Mich. L. Rev. 893 (1978).

16. Alexander Bickel, *The Least Dangerous Branch,* 1-14 (Indianapolis: Bobbs Merrill, 1962); Robert McCloskey, *The American Supreme Court,* 40-43 (Chicago: Univ. of Chicago Press, 4th ed., 2005); Learned Hand, *The Bill of Rights* 3-6 (Cambridge: Harvard Univ. Press, 1958); Thomas Powell, *Vagaries and Varieties in Constitutional Interpretation* 12-23 (1956); Henry Commager, *Majority Rule and Minority Rights* (New York: Oxford Univ. Press, 1943); James Thayer, *The Origin and Scope of the American Doctrine of Constitutional Law,* 7 Harv. L. Rev. 129 (1893).

17. See Philip Bobbit, *Constitutional Fate* 7 (New York: Oxford Univ. Press, 1982). This assumes, of course, that the appointed elite of the judiciary have limited interpretive functions and are not empowered to impose extra-constitutional moral standards on the elected legislature. Compare Michael Perry, *The Constitution, the Courts and Human Rights* (New Haven: Yale Univ. Press, 1982).

18. The power to amend the Constitution is reserved to the people in Article V. See Appendix to Chapter 1.

19. See Chapter 6.

20. See *Crandall v. Nevada,* 73 U.S. (6 Wall.) 35, 44 (1868) (structure of national polity includes the right of citizens to travel unimpeded from state to state); Charles Black, *Structure and Relationship in Constitutional Law* (Baton Rouge: Louisiana State Univ. Press, 1969).

21. For a detailed analysis of the supremacy clause as mandating national judicial review of state laws, see Charles Black, *The People and the Court,* ch. 5 (New York: Macmillan, 1960); William Crosskey, 2 *Politics and the Constitution in the History of the United States,* 984-90 (Chicago: Univ. of Chicago Press, 1953).

22. U.S. Constitution, article VI.

23. "The Senators and Representatives before mentioned, and the Members of the several State Legislatures, and all executive and judicial Officers, both of the United States and of the several States, shall be bound by Oath or Affirmation, to support this Constitution; but no religious Test shall ever be required as a Qualification to any Office of public Trust under the United States" (U.S. Const., article VI, cl. 3.

24. Max Farrand, 1 *The Records of the Federal Convention of 1787,* 21 (New Haven: Yale Univ. Press, 1911) [cited hereinafter as Farrand]. This resolution received unanimous assent. *Id.* 54.

25. Farrand, I: 164.

26. *Id.* at 168. The vote was 7 to 3 with one delegation divided.

27. "That the legislative acts of the United States, made by virtue and in pursuance of the articles of union, and all treaties made and ratified under authority of the United States, shall be the supreme law of the respective states, so far as those acts or treaties shall relate to the said states or their citizens, and that the judiciaries of the several states shall be bound thereby in their decisions, any thing in the respective laws of the individual states to the contrary notwithstanding" *Id.* at II: 28-29.

28. *Id.* at III: 286-87.

29. *Id.* at II: 183.

30. *Id.* at II: 381-82.

31. "Section 2. [I] The judicial Power shall extend to all Cases, in Law and Equity, arising under this Constitution, the Laws of the United States, and Treaties made, or which shall be made, under their authority; . . . [2] In all Cases affecting Ambas-

sadors, other public Ministers and Consuls, and those in which a State shall be a Party, the supreme Court shall have original Jurisdiction. In all other Cases before mentioned, the supreme Court shall have appellate Jurisdiction, both as to Law and Fact, with such Exceptions, and under such Regulations as the Congress shall make" (U.S. Const., Art. III).

32. 1 Stat. 85-88 (1789).
33. 14 U.S. (I Wheat.) 304 (1816). See *Cohens v. Virginia,* 19 U.S. (6 Wheat.) 264 (1821). See generally, G. Edward White, *The Marshall Court and Cultural Change, 1815-35,* Vol. 3-4 of *History of the Supreme Court of the United States,* 495-524 (New York: Macmillan, 1988); Charles Warren, 1 *The Supreme Court in United States History,* 442-53, 547-64 (Boston: Little Brown, 1926). See modern application in *Cooper v. Aaron,* 358 U.S. 1 (1958) (governor and legislature of Arkansas bound by Supreme Court decision forbidding enforced racial segregation in public schools).
34. *Fairfax's Devisee v. Hunter's Lessee,* 11 U.S. (7 Cranch) 603 (1812).
35. Crosskey, II, *supra* note 21, at 991-93. See the similar view of Chief Justice Taney in *Ableman v. Booth,* 62 U.S. (21 How.) 506, 520 (1858).
36. Bickel, *supra* note 16, at 9. A few members of the ratifying conventions spoke of "pursuant" in a narrower sense as a synonym of "consistent with," but none of these suggested that the Supreme Court would review the scope and breadth of the affirmative governing powers delegated to Congress. Furthermore, they did not pretend objective linguistic analysis. These delegates made persuasive speeches deliberately minimizing the scope of national power in order to induce other reluctant delegates to support ratification. See *infra,* notes 83 to 88.
37. U.S. Const., Art. I, sec. 8, par. 18.
38. *Hylton v. United States,* 3 U.S. (3 Dallas) 171 (1796), holding a carriage tax valid against attack under Article I, sec. 9, Cl. 4.
39. Dicey, *Law of the Constitution, supra* note 6, at chs. 4-7.
40. *Id.* at 183.
41. *Id.* at 189, 191.
42. see Lois G. Schwoerer, *The Declaration of Rights, 1689,* 297 (Baltimore: John Hopkins Univ. Press, 1981).
43. Dicey, *supra* note 6, at chs. 14 and 15.
44. A. E. Dick Howard, *The Road from Runnymede,* ch. 1 (Charlottesville: Univ. Press of Virginia, 1968); Arthur Sutherland, *Constitutionalism in America,* ch. 8 (New York: Blaisdell, 1965); Robert Perry and John Cooper, eds., *Sources of Our Liberties* (Chicago: American Bar Foundation, 1959); Roscoe Pound, *The Development of Constitutional Guarantees of Liberty* (New Haven: Yale Univ. Press, 1957).
45. *Case of the Writs of Assistance,* Quincey's Report 51-57 (Mass. 1761).
46. 8 Coke's Reports 107, 77 Eng. Rep. 638 (1610). See George Smith, *Dr. Bonham's Case and the Modern Significance of Lord Coke's Influence,* 41 Wash. L. Rev. 297 (1966).
47. "As to Acts of Parliament. An Act against the Constitution is void; an act against natural equity is void; and if an act of Parliament should be made, in the very words of this petition, it would be void. The executive Courts must pass such acts into disuse. 8 Rep. 118 from Viner. *Reason or the common law to control an act of Parliament"* (John Adams, 2 *The Works of John Adams,* 522 [C. F. Adams, ed. 1850]).
48. See Edward S. Corwin, *Liberty against Government,* 39 (Baton Rouge: Louisiana Univ. Press, 1948).

49. *Journals of the Continental Congress* 546, 547 (reprint 1906). Article VII of the first draft reads as follows: "The Inhabitants of each Colony shall enjoy all the Rights, Liberties, Privileges, Immunities, and Advantages, in Trade, Navigation, and Commerce, in any other Colony, and in going to and from the same from and to any Part of the World, which the Natives of such Colony . . . enjoy."

50. Farrand, II: 582, 587-88; III, 143-44, 161-62 (Rev. ed. 1937).

51. See Leslie Dunbar, *James Madison and the Ninth Amendment*, 42 Va. L. Rev. 627 (1956).

52. See C. Ellis Stevens, *Sources of the Constitution of the United States,* ch. 8 (New York: Macmillan, 1894); Robert Rutland, *The Birth of the Bill of Rights*, chs. 1 and 2 (Chapel Hill: Univ. of N.C. Press, 1955).

53. *Annals of Congress,* 1, 454 (1834). See Zechariah Chafee, *How Human Rights Got into the Constitution,* 19-21 (Boston: Boston Univ. Press, 1952).

54. *Annals of Congress,* 1, 457 (1834).

55. T. Jefferson, 5 *Writings of Thomas Jefferson,* 80-81 (P. Ford, ed., 1895). See Samuel Krislov, *Jefferson and Judicial Review,* 9 J. Pub. L. 374 (1960).

56. Charles Warren, *Congress, The Constitution and the Supreme Court,* 91-93 (1925). Justice James Wilson contrasted British legislative supremacy with the United States Constitution as follows:

In the United States, the legislative authority is subjected to another control, beside that arising from natural and revealed law; it is subjected to the control arising from the constitution. From the constitution, the legislative department, as well as every other part of government, derives it power: by the constitution, the legislative, as well as every department, must be directed; of the constitution, no alteration by the legislature can be made or authorized. In our system of jurisprudence, these positions appear to be incontrovertible. The constitution is the supreme law of the land: to that supreme law every other power must be inferiour and subordinate.

J. Wilson, 1 *Works of James Wilson,* 329, R. McCloskey, ed., (Cambridge: Harvard Univ. Press, 1967).

57. U.S. Const., Amend. V.

58. *Field v. Clark,* 143 U.S. 649 (1892). See William Van Alstyne, *A Critical Guide to Marbury v. Madison,* 1969 Duke L. J. 1, 20.

59. See Jesse Choper, *Judicial Review and the National Political Process* 64 (Chicago: Univ. of Chicago Press, 1980).

60. 5 U.S. (1 Cranch) 137 (1803).

61. *Id.* at 179.

62. See Leonard Levy, ed., *Judicial Review and the Supreme Court* 8-10 (New York: Harper & Row, 1967).

63. See Haines, *The American Doctrine of Judicial Supremacy, supra* note 7 at 88-121. Since many of these cases are not found in official reports, the citations will be to Haines.

64. Jesse Turner, *A Phantom Precedent,* 48 Am. L. Rev. 321 (1914). See Haines, *supra* note 7 at 89.

65. Austin Scott, *Holmes v. Walton, the New Jersey Precedent,* 4 Am. Hist. Rev. 456 (1899). See Haines, *supra* note 7, at 92; Crosskey, II, *supra* note 21, at 948-52.

66. 4 Call. (Va.) 5 (1782).

67. (1784) in *Select Cases of the Mayor's Court of New York City* 302. (R. Morris, ed., 1935). See Julius Goebel, 1 *The Law Practice of Alexander Hamilton: Documents and Commentary* 415 (New York: Columbia Univ. Press, 1964).

68. Kirby (Conn.) 444-53 (1785).
69. James Varnum, *The Case, Trevett Against Weeder* (Providence: John Carter, 1787). See Haines, *supra* note 7, at 105.
70. Martin (N .C.) 42, 178.
71. See *supra* note 63. See *Ware v. Hylton,* 3 U.S. (3 Dallas) 198 (1796), explaining the later supremacy of treaties over state laws under Article VI, Clause 2 of the Constitution.
72. U.S. Const., Amend. V.
73. U.S. Const., Art. III.
74. Farrand, I: 97.
75. See Corwin, *The Supreme Court and Unconstitutional Laws of Congress,* 4 Mich. L. Rev. 616, 620 (1906); Louis Boudin, 1 *Government by Judiciary,* 114 (New York: W. Goodwin, 1932); Crosskey, II, *supra* note 21, at 1002-7.
76. 5 U.S. (Cranch) 137 (1803). See Robert Clinton, M*arbury v. Madison* and *Judicial Review* (Lawrence: Univ. of Kansas Press, 1989).
77. 1 Stat. 81, Sec. 13 (1789). See *United States v. Lawrence,* 3 U.S. (3 Dallas) 42 (1795). See generally, Albert Beveridge, 3 *The Life of John Marshall,* ch. 3 (Boston: Houghton Mifflin, 1919); George Haskins and Herbert Johnson, *Foundations of Power, John Marshall, 1801-1815, History of the Supreme Court of the United States,* Vol. 11, part 1, ch. 6 (New York: Macmillan 1981).
78. See Edward Corwin, *The Doctrine of Judicial Review* 4-10 (1914); Crosskey, II, *supra* note at 1035-46; William Van Alstyne, *A Critical Guide to Marbury v. Madison,* 1969 Duke L. J. 1; Susan Bloch and Marva Marcus, *John Marshall's Selective Use of History in Marbury v. Madison,* 1986 Wis. L. Rev. 301.
79. See William Nelson, *The Eighteenth-Century Background of John Marshall's Constitutional Jurisprudence,* 76 Mich. L. Rev. 893, 936-42. (1978).
80. See Boudin, I, *supra* note 75 at 230-33; Van Alstyne, *supra* note 78 at 34.
81. 5 U.S. (1 Cranch) at 165-66.
82. "The interpretation of the laws is the proper and peculiar province of the courts. A constitution is, in fact, and must be regarded by the judges, as a fundamental law. It therefore belongs to them to ascertain its meaning, as well as the meaning of any particular act proceeding from the legislative body. If there should happen to be an irreconcilable variance between the two, that which has the superior obligation and validity ought, of course, to be preferred; or, in other words, the Constitution ought to be preferred to the statute, the intention of the people to the intention of their agents" Federalist 78, book 2, at 101 (Bourne ed., 1947). See Nelson, *supra* note 15, at 937.
83. See James Smith, *The Spirit of American Government* 73-85 (New York: Macmillan, 1911); William Trickert, *Judicial Dispensation from Congressional Statutes,* 41 Am. L. Rev. 65, 83 (1907).
84. At the convention, Madison said: "Experience in all the States had evinced a powerful tendency in the Legislature to absorb all power into its vortex. This was the real source of danger to the American Constitutions; & suggested the necessity of giving every defensive authority to the other departments that was consistent with republican principles" (Farrand, 11: 74).
85. The leading historian of the Constitutional Convention commented: "Hamilton was out of touch with the situation. He was aristocratic rather than democratic, and while his ideas may have been excellent, they were too radical for the convention and found but little support" (Farrand, *The Framing of the Constitution of the United States 197* [1913]). See Jared Sparks, 3 *The Life of Gouverneur Morris,* 260-62 (Gray and Brown, 1832).

86. Federalist 78, supra note 82, at 99. Hamilton reiterated: "It proves incontestably that the judiciary is beyond comparison the weakest of the three departments of power" (*Id.*) See Bickel, *supra* note 16.

87. An objective theory of constitutional interpretation precludes taking comments on the Constitution at face value. The legal context and circumstances under which constitutional language was adopted does not include subsequent comments on the language itself. See Oliver W. Holmes, *Theory of Legal Interpretation* (1899), reprinted in *Collected Legal Papers* 203, 204, 207 (1920); Jacobus ten Broek, *Admissibility and Use by the United States Superior Court of Extrinsic Aids in Constitutional Construction*, 26 Calif. L. Rev. 287 (1938).

88. See, e.g., Hamilton's minimization of the significance of the supremacy clause of Article VI, CI. 2. in *Federalist* 33, at 214-15 (Bourne ed., 1947). See generally, George Billias, *The Federalists* (Lexington: D. C. Heath, 1970).

89. Jesse Choper, *Judicial Review and the National Political Process,* ch. 6 (Chicago: Univ. of Chicago Press 1980).

90. 2 U.S. (2 Dallas) 409 (1792). See *Keller v. Potomac Electric Power Co.*, 261 U.S. 428 (1923).

91. *American Insurance Co. v. Canter,* 26 U.S. (1 Peters) 511 (1828); *Lockerty V. Phillips,* 319 U.S. 182. (1943).

92. *Northern Pipeline Const. Co. v. Marathon Pipe Line Co.,* 458 U.S. 50 (1982).

93. Robert Jackson, *The Supreme Court in the American System of Government* 22 (Cambridge: Harvard Univ. Press, 1955); Bickel, *supra* note 16, at 5-6; Crosskey, II, *supra* note 21, at 983; Hand, *supra* note 16, at 10.

94. See William Nelson, *Changing Conceptions of Judicial Review,* 120 U. Pa. L. Rev. 1166 (1972).

95. Farrand, II: 186. Except for omitting the Constitution, the proposed jurisdictional clause was limited to classes of cases and controversies similar to those that were eventually ratified in Article III, Section 2. The language indicates a general understanding of following the English practice of limiting courts to actual adversary litigation.

96. Farrand, II: 430.

97. *Id.* It seems clear that "cases of a judiciary nature" did not refer to the "case-or-controversy" rule, barring advisory opinions. See *supra* note 95.

98. Madison on Jefferson's Draft of a Constitution for Virginia, 6 *Papers of Thomas Jefferson,* 315, Boyd ed., (Princeton: Princeton Univ. Press, 1955). See William Miller, *Cases of a Judiciary Nature,* 8 St. Louis U. Pub. L. Rev. 47 (1989).

99. *Annals of Congress,* 1, 520 (1834). One day earlier, Madison had emphasized the same point: "The legislative powers are vested in Congress, and are to be exercised by them uncontrolled by any other department, except the constitution has qualified it otherwise. The constitution has qualified the legislative power, by authorizing the President to object to any act it may pass, requiring, in this case, two-thirds of both Houses to concur in making a law; but still the absolute legislative power is vested in the Congress with this qualification alone" (*Id.* at 481). See George Anastaplo, *The Constitutionalist* 54-65 (Dallas: Southern Methodist Univ. Press, 1971).

100. Jefferson to Mrs. Adams, Sept. 11, 1804, 8 *Writings of Thomas Jefferson,* 311 (Ford ed. 1897). See Donald Morgan, *Congress and the Constitution* 71-82 (Cambridge: Harvard Univ. Press, 1966).

101. Farrand, 11: 73 (emphasis added).

102. Henry Maine, *Popular Government* 253 (London: Murray, 1886). The Constitution must be interpreted as a unified whole within the English constitutional and common-law legal environment of its adoption. *Ex Parte Grossman,* 267 U.S. 87, 108-9 (1925); *United States v. Wong Kim Ark,* 169 U.S. 649, 668-72 (1898). See the comments of Justice Henry Baldwin, *Origin and Nature of the Constitution and Government of the United States* 9 L. Ed. 869, 893-94 (1837).

103. See Dicey, *Law of the Constitution, supra* note 6 at ch. 1. Charles McIlwain, *The High Court of Parliament and Its Supremacy,* ch. 5 (New Haven: Yale Univ. Press, 1910). Concerning the presumption that the same legal system would stay in force in the former colonies until changed by affirmative law, see *Blankard v. Galdy,* 91 Eng. Rep. 356, 357 (1693).

104. William Blackstone, *Commentaries on the Laws of England,* 49-52 (1st Am. ed. 1771-72.). See Crosskey, II, *supra* note 21 at 1326 n. 3; Nolan, *Sir William Blackstone and the New Republic,* 51 N.Y.U. Rev. 731 (1976).

105. See Crosskey, II, *supra* note 21, at 1325, n. 25; Donald Lutz, *The Origins of American Constitutionalism* 92-95 (Baton Rouge: Louisiana State Univ. Press, 1988).

106. See Arthur Vanderbilt, *The Doctrine of the Separation of Powers and its Present-Day Significance* (Lincoln: Univ. of Nebraska Press, 1953); Malcolm Sharp, *The Classical American Doctrine of "The Separation of Powers,"* 2 U. of Chi. L. Rev. 385 (1935).

107. 5 U.S. (1 Cranch) 137 (1803).

108. See Edward Corwin, *Court over Constitution* 6-7, 69-73 (Princeton: Princeton Univ. Press, 1938); Learned Hand, *The Bill of Rights* 4 (Cambridge: Harvard Univ. Press, 1958).

109. Rejecting Chief Justice Marshall's statements in Marbury v. Madison, Bickel asserts:

> Far from supporting Marshall, the oath is perhaps the strongest textual argument against him. For it would seem to obligate each of these officers, in the performance of his own function, to support the Constitution. . . . [I]t may be deduced that everyone is to construe the Constitution with finality insofar as it addresses itself to the performance of his own peculiar function. Surely the language lends itself more readily to this interpretation than to Marshall's apparent conclusion, that everyone's oath to support the Constitution is qualified by the judiciary's oath to do the same, and that every official of government is sworn to support the Constitution as the judges, in pursuance of the same oath, have construed it, rather than as his own conscience may dictate.

Bickel, *supra* note 16 at 8. This critique adopts the views of J. Gibson in *Eakin v. Raub,* 12 S.&R. 330, 353 (Pa. 1825) (dissent).

110. "The President acting in his executive capacity may yield to the opinion of the Court and accept its decisions as practically a part of the Constitution; but under the theory of the separation of powers he is not under strict technical constitutional obligation. He too can interpret the Constitution. . . . The President is no more bound by an unconstitutional law than is the Court. Johnson refused to be bound by the Tenure of Office Act, though it was passed by a two-thirds vote over his veto. No one probably would deny now that in so refusing he was within his constitutional power," Andrew McLaughlin, *The Courts, the Constitution and Parties 60-61* (Chicago: Univ. of Chicago Press, 1912).

111. *M. K. & T. Ry. Co. V. May,* 194 U.S. 267, 270 (1904). See J. Thayer, *John Marshall* 98 (New York: Houghton Mifflin, 1904).

112. *Messages and Papers of the Presidents,* II, 581-82 (J.D. Richardson, ed. 1897).

113. *Scott V. Sandford,* 60 U.S. (19 How.) 393 (1857).

114. *Messages and Papers of the Presidents, supra,* note 112, at VI, 9.

115. See Crosskey, II, *supra* note 21 at 1013-18.

116. 1 Stat. 85-88 (1789). See Crosskey, II, supra note 21 at 1029-35.

117. Morgan, *supra* note 100, at 82-89.

118. 17 U.S. (4 Wheat.) 316 (1819).

119. See Black, *Structure and Relationship, supra* note 20 at 14.

120. Walter Smith, *Economic Aspects of the Second Bank of the United States,* ch. 12 (Cambridge: Harvard Univ. Press, 1953).

121. McCulloch, 17 U.S. at 407.

122. See *Federalist* 33 at 212-13 (Bourne ed. 1947). Hamilton, in a structural analysis wrote that the clause is "only declaratory of a truth which would have resulted by necessary and unavoidable implication from the very act of constituting a federal government, and vesting it with certain specified powers. . . . The declaration itself, though it may be chargeable with tautology, or redundancy, is at least perfectly harmless" (*Id.*).

123. McCulloch, 17 U.S. at 415.

124. *Id.* at 411.

125. See the similar examples of Hamilton in *Federalist* 33 at 213-14 (Bourne ed., 1947).

126. U.S. Const., Amend. 10.

127. On the presumptions in favor of national regulation and against the Tenth Amendment, see *Hodel v. Virginia Surface Min. and Reclam. Ass'n,* 452 U.S. 264, 266-67 (1981); *United States v. Darby,* 312 U.S. 100, 123-24 (1941). On the general presumption of constitutionality and the proof that should be needed to rebut it, see Thayer, *supra* note 16.

128. "Marshall's opinion in *Marbury v. Madison* satisfactorily explained judicial refusal to give effect, in litigation before a court, to a governmental act inconsistent with the Constitution, but not why such a determination of unconstitutionality binds the other branches of the government. This power, which is the essential element of judicial review of constitutionality, is difficult to reconcile with the theory of the judiciary as a coordinate branch of government, which is so clearly the theory of the Constitution of the United States and of all the State constitutions. No attempt at reconciliation has ever satisfactorily met Mr. Justice Gibson's analysis in *Eakin v. Raub* (12 S. & R. 330, 334 et seq. [Pa. 1825])." Frank Strong, *Judicial Review: A Tri-Dimensional Concept of Administrative-Constitutional Law,* 69 W.Va. L. Rev. III, 118-19 (1967). See Stanley Kutler, *John Bannister Gibson,* 14 J. Pub. Law 181 (1965); William Meigs, *The Relation of the Judiciary to the Constitution,* ch. 10 (New York: Neale Pub., 1919).

129. *West Coast Hotel Co. v. Parrish* (300 U.S. 379), overruling *Adkins v. Children's Hospital* (261 U.S. 525) made the District of Columbia minimum-wage law of the latter case again valid and enforceable. 39 *Opinions of the Atty. Gen.* 22 (1937). See Oliver Field, *The Effect of an Unconstitutional Statute* (Minneaplis: Univ. of Minnesota Press, 1935).

130. Commager, *supra* note 7.

131. See, e.g., Jerome Frank, *Law and the Modern Mind* (New York: Brentanos, 1930).

132. See Black, *People and the Court, supra* note 21; Rostow, *The Democratic Character of Judicial Review,* 56 Harv. L. Rev. 193 (1952).

133. Benjamin Cardozo, *The Nature of the Judicial Process* 92-94 (New Haven: Yale Univ. Press, 1921).
134. Learned Hand, *The Spirit of Liberty* 164, 2d ed., (New York: A. Knopf, 1953).
135. See *Dennis v. United States,* 341 U.S. 494 (1951); *Korematsu v. United States,* 323 U.S. 214 (1944).
136. *Worcester v. Georgia,* 31 U.S. (6 Pet.) 515 (1832). See Warren, *Supreme Court, supra* note 33, ch. 19 (1926).
137. 5 U.S. (1 Cranch) 137 (1803).
138. See Christopher Wolfe, *The Rise of Modern Judicial Review* (New York: Basic Books, 1986).
139. For an argument for termination of judicial review of legislation, see Charles Haines, *Judicial Review of Acts of Congress and the Need for Constitutional Reform,* 45 Yale L. J. 816, 852-56 (1936).
140. *United States v. Sanchez,* 340 U.S. 42 (1950); *Wickard v. Filburn,* 317 U.S. 111 (1942).

4

Commerce Clause: Textual Meaning and Judicial Misconstruction

The Commerce Clause is a prime example of delegated legislative powers whose final interpretation under departmental review should have been in the Congress. Article I, Section 8, Clause 3 states: "The Congress shall have power . . . to regulate commerce with foreign nations, and among the several states, and with the Indian tribes."[1] The economic test is the effectiveness of this language in creating efficient nationwide markets unimpeded by state barriers to trade and governed by uniform congressional regulation to remedy market failures. In 1789, most transactions were local and without effect on national commerce, though another substantial amount moved between states going to and from ocean ports. Over two hundred years, economic development, especially in transportation and communications, has given most transactions some national impact. Consequently, most state regulation of commerce has national impact, and if restrictive, will reduce efficiency in the national market.

The evidence presented in this chapter will show that the original meaning of the commerce clause delegated to Congress a plenary power to regulate all private transactions in the nation. In order to prevent state barriers to trade and conflicting state regulations of transactions between states, the national power over interstate and foreign commerce had to be exclusive. The national power over intrastate trade was to be shared with the states, and any conflicts were to be resolved by the Supremacy Clause. The extent to which this power would be used was left to the political arena, the Congress. Citizens expected their elected representatives, not the appointed elite, the Supreme Court majority, to determine when national regulations would be the most effective.

The Commerce Clause must be assessed in relation to the prohibitions on state tax of exports and imports in Article 1, Section 10, Clause 2.[2] The legal historians argue that the language and background of this clause demonstrate that it was designed to enforce a national free-trade area by barring all duties on interstate or foreign trade.[3] The Supreme Court, however, has construed this clause to apply only to foreign imports.[4] Consequently, the Commerce Clause stands alone as a prohibition on customs duties between states.[5]

Mercantilist Background

Before the American Revolution, the colonies were part of the internal free trade area of the British empire.[6] But, on the international level, the political-economic outlook was still one of mercantilism. The strength of the nation was believed to be tied to maximizing exports and minimizing imports. The accumulation of precious metals was thought necessary for the needed increased supply of money that enabled the increased number of transactions characteristic of economic growth. The political economy of the period from 1600 to 1800 centered in a spirit of nationalism that led to interminable conflicts of the European powers.[7] A nominal peace was only a state of undeclared hostility. Under these conditions, the economic nationalism of the mercantile system is more easily understood.

The spirit of mercantilism was still dominant when the Revolution made each of the thirteen colonies a sovereign nation. Although Adam Smith's *Wealth of Nations*[8] had been published in 1776, its arguments on the benefits of free trade had not become politically significant by 1787. Thus, leading historians could label the economic issues of the constitutional convention a "debate among mercantilists."[9] An influential leading document illustrative of this is Alexander Hamilton's *Report on Manufactures*,[10] of which Tench Coxe was a probably co-author. Among the barriers to international trade, the report recommended duties high enough to prohibit import of foreign articles that were rivals of domestic ones, prohibitions on the export of materials of manufacture, bounties, premiums, statutory encouragement of new inventions, and laws facilitating transportation.

It is not surprising that merchant groups in most states sought legislative barriers to trade when the colonies became independent. And since the Articles of Confederation did not contain a national commerce power, a likely outcome of prevailing ideology was mercantilist enactments in the separate states. Justice Robert Jackson noted the result:

> When victory relieved the Colonies from the pressure for solidarity that war had exerted, a drift toward anarchy and commercial warfare between states began. "* * * each state would legislate according to its estimate of its own interests, the importance of its own products, and the local advantages or disadvantages of its position in a political or commercial view." This came "to threaten at once the peace and safety of the Union." Story, The Constitution, §§ 259, 260. . . . The sole purpose for which Virginia initiated the movement which ultimately produced the Constitution was "to take into consideration the trade of the United States; to examine the relative situations and trade of the said states; to consider how far a uniform system in their commercial regulation may be necessary to their common interest and their permanent harmony" and for that purpose the General Assembly of Virginia in January of 1786 names commissioners and proposed their meeting with those from other states.[11]

Representatives of only five states met at Annapolis in September, 1786.[12] Their conclusion was that they alone could not remedy the problem. Consequently, they recommended that a convention be called to review and to revise the Articles of Confederation. Pursuant to this resolution, the Continental Congress requested all of the states to send delegates to Philadelphia in May, 1787.[13]

The Virginia delegation was led by Washington, Madison, and Randolph. Since Virginia was largely responsible for the calling of the convention, they had prepared a series of resolutions that became the basis for initial discussions. These were read by Randolph at the opening of the convention of 1787.[14] Part of the sixth resolution stated that the national legislature should be empowered "to legislate in all cases to which the separate states are incompetent, or in which the harmony of the United States may be interrupted by the exercise of individual legislation."[15] This resolution was passed by the convention.[16]

There was very little discussion of the domestic commerce power in the Constitutional Convention. Paterson of New Jersey presented a plan that included a power in Congress "to pass acts for the regulation of trade and commerce as well with foreign nations as with each other."[17] The Committee of Detail reported on August 6 with proposed language that was much broader. It gave the legislature power "to regulate commerce with foreign nations, and among the several states."[18] The language, "with the Indian tribes" was added later.

Historians assert that the purpose of the broad power to regulate domestic commerce must be found in all of the prior problems it was designed to remedy. Keeping in mind the canon of construction that the Constitution must be read as an integrated whole, Robert Stern, a leading historian of federal jurisdiction, wrote in 1934:

> The history and proceedings of the Convention and of the ratifying conventions in the states indicate that the purpose of the commerce clause was to give the Federal Government as much control over commercial transactions as was and would in the future be essential to the general welfare of the union, and there is no suggestion that this power was to be limited to control over movement. The framers of the Constitution would have been exceedingly surprised if they had thought that by the language employed to accomplish that purpose—"commerce among the several states"—they had so restricted the national power as to create a union incapable of dealing with a commercial condition even more serious than the one that had brought them together. They were acutely conscious that they were preparing an instrument for the ages, not a document adapted only for the exigencies of the time.[19]

Textual Meaning of Language

The word "commerce" in 1789, like today, had many meanings. The issue is which meaning was adopted in a national constitution to enable the legislature to remedy the many problems of trade and state regulation of trade that previously existed. The narrow definition of commerce as trade in goods was used in the context of marketing merchandise. But the lawyers who drafted the Commerce

Clause as fundamental law for the nation could not have had such a narrow conception. The context of their dealing with commerce was in commercial litigation. The commercial law, also known as the law merchant, comprehended all transactions for money and in barter.[20] The English and American law reports in the second half of the eighteenth century contained many commercial cases concerning transactions for shipping and insurance services[21] and transactions in legal rights such as bills of exchange and promissory notes.[22]

Legal historians present massive evidence that the idea of general commerce included all gainful activity.[23] This would mean all transactions in agriculture, manufacturing, transportation, and finance, among others. Among the many treatises illustrating this point is Anderson's four-volume history of commerce.[24] A significant part of this study concerns service transactions in the shipping trade. Tench Coxe, noted economist and delegate to the Annapolis Convention, wrote "The commerce of America, including our exports, imports, shipping, manufactures, and fisheries, may properly be considered as forming one interest."[25] Alexander Hamilton wrote in *The Federalist* of marine transport services as "an ACTIVE COMMERCE in our own bottoms."[26]

Chief Justice John Marshall noted in *Gibbons v. Ogden* that the verb "to regulate" in the eighteenth century was a synonym for the verb "to govern."[27] Regulation included both promotion through subsidy or limitations, including total prohibition.

In the eighteenth century, the preposition "among" had more than one meaning also. In a few contexts, it was used as a synonym for between. In "treaties among nations" and "hostilities among nations," among was substituted for between in the context of nations as governments.[28] But in most other contexts, between and among were not synonyms. At the Constitutional Convention, the Committee of Stile would surely have adopted the words "between states" if they had meant from one territory into another.[29] "Among" would not have been used in an interterritorial sense when territories were contiguous because it would not have been idiomatic English. The adopted constitutional language was not the narrower subset, "commerce between the several states" or its synonym, interstate commerce.

The most common use of "among" in the eighteenth century was "intermingled with" or "in the midst of."[30] It made idiomatic sense when applied to groups of persons but none when applied to contiguous territories. In 1824, Chief Justice Marshall noted in *Gibbons* that "among" in the Commerce Clause meant "intermingled with."[31] It seems easier to understand when one uses "in the midst of."

The final step is to determine which of the three main uses of the word "state" in the eighteenth century made idiomatic sense with the word "among."[32] As just noted, the territorial sense of state does not fit. This is in contrast to Article IV, where "state" preceded by the preposition "in" could be interpreted in a territorial sense. Second, "state" as a government does not make sense in the

Commerce Clause. The thrust of Article I, Section 8 is not the governance of intergovernmental relations but of the citizens as a whole.

The idiomatic use of "state" in the eighteenth century, like the word "nation" in the same clause, must be determined here in the context of the word "commerce." The third and most common use of "state" in eighteenth-century England and the new U.S.A. was as a synonym for "nation," a group of people with a common government.[33] Article I, Section 2, for example, provides that "representatives and directs taxes shall be apportioned *among the several states* . . . according to *their respective numbers*."[34] It is this collective use of the noun "state" that makes idiomatic sense with "among." This is reinforced by the evidence that the phrase "several states" was a collective term used to refer to the states as a unified group.[35] Commerce in the midst of the several groups of peoples forming the United States meant all commerce in which they engaged. That would include both interstate and intrastate. The conclusion is that by ratifying this clause, the people vested in Congress a plenary power to regulate all commercial transactions of the people of the United States. Thus, it is not surprising that Tench Coxe spoke of one of the measures of the Convention of 1787 as "the establishment of a national legislature with complete powers over commerce and navigation."[36]

The Congressional view of the plenary power over commerce is confirmed by the first Congress in passing the Coasting Act of September 1, 1789.[37] The Congressmen, many of whom were leaders at the Constitutional Convention, adopted a statute licensing vessels "destined from district to district, or to the bank or whale fisheries." This would include both interstate and intrastate travel on the coasts and navigable rivers of the United States. It is notable that this early statute, enacted pursuant to the commerce clause, licensed persons engaging in transactions for the sale of transport services. The first Congress, like the later Supreme Court in *Gibbons,* viewed commerce as not limited to transactions in goods.

The effect of the Coasting Act was to require a national license even if a ship owner was going to operate only between ports in one state. Thus, there was general acceptance at the time of this regulation of intrastate commerce. The constitutionality of the statute was not challenged.

Early Cases

The early cases indicate the broad scope of the language, "regulate commerce among the several states." In *United States v. William,*[38] upholding the constitutionality of the Embargo Act of 1807, the issue concerned the scope of the power to regulate foreign commerce. In holding that the power to regulate included the power to prohibit entirely, Judge John Davis wrote, "the power to regulate commerce is not to be confined to the adoption of measures, exclusively beneficial to commerce itself, or tending to its advancement; but, in our national system, as in all modern sovereignties, it is also to be considered as an instrument for other purposes of general policy and interest."[39] Noting that the congressional power over foreign commerce was exclusive, Judge Davis went on to speak of those objects that require national regulation:

> Commerce is one of those objects. The care, protection, management and control, of this great national concern, is, in my opinion, vested by the Constitution, in the Congress of the United States, and this power is sovereign, relative to commercial intercourse qualified by the limitations and restrictions expressed in that instrument.[40]

In 1820, Chief Justice Marshall, on circuit, had to face the issue of whether shipping or navigation was part of commerce. In *Wilson v. United States,*[41] the issues were whether statutory duties on imports and tonnage applied to foreign privateers and whether a statutory prohibition on bringing Negroes into ports where states barred their entry applied to colored seamen. In holding that, under the Commerce Clause, ships as well as their cargoes may be regulated, Marshall noted that such laws had never been questioned. He stated, "From the adoption of the Constitution, till this time, the universal sense of America has been, that the word 'commerce,' as used in that instrument, is to be considered a generic term, comprehending navigation."[42]

In the 1823 case of *Elkinson v. Deliesseline,*[43] Justice William Johnson, on circuit, held that the power in Congress to regulate foreign commerce and the interstate part of commerce among the several states was exclusive. An 1822 statute of South Carolina provided that free Negro seamen brought into that state from any other state or foreign port should be seized and jailed until the ship departed the state. If the captain of the ship failed to pay the expenses of such detention, the free seamen were to be declared slaves and sold. While the action for writ of habeas corpus concerned a British subject, a free Negro seaman in foreign trade, Justice Johnson held the entire South Carolina statute to violate the Commerce Clause. He rejected the state's argument that it had concurrent power over interstate and foreign commerce. Johnson, a noted Jeffersonian, wrote:

> The right of the general government to regulate commerce with the sister states and foreign nations is a paramount and exclusive right; and this conclusion we arrive at, whether we examine it with reference to the words of the constitution, or the nature of the grant. That this has been the received and universal construction from the first day of the organization of the general government is unquestionable; and the right admits not of a question any more than the fact. In the Constitution of the United States, the most wonderful instrument ever drawn by the hand of man, there is a comprehension and precision that is unparalleled.[44]

Steamboat Monopoly

The series of cases that arose over the New York state steamboat monopoly provided major additions to the interpretation of the Commerce Clause. The original grant in 1798 by the New York legislature to Livingston and Fulton was an exclusive right to navigate the waters of the state with steam-propelled vessels.[45] This grant probably came under an exception to the British constitutional tradition against governmental grants of monopoly in the ordinary trades.[46] This exception was designed to promote invention and innovation of a new technique and, thus, was not in the ordinary trades. But exceptions to the antimonopoly tradition were, under the precedents, to be limited in time. Only short-term monopolies were held to benefit the public by fostering innovation. Thus, when the monopoly of Livingston and Fulton was renewed and extended in 1808 for another thirty years, its validity under the constitutional principles brought from England became questionable.

New York enforced the steamboat monopoly both against local vessels and those in interstate commerce. This resulted in retaliatory statutes by New Jersey, Connecticut, and Ohio.[47] If the New York and New Jersey grants of monopoly to rival steamboat companies on the Hudson River had been enforced, steamboat travel between those two states would have had to cease. The greatest public outcry, however, was from New York customers of the monopoly. This provoked New York firms to enter the steamboat business on the Hudson River without securing a license from the monopolists.

The intrastate enforceability of the steamboat monopoly was tested in the New York courts in 1811 in *Livingston v. Van Ingen*.[48] The action was for injunction to restrain Van Ingen and associates from operating a steamboat on the Hudson River between New York and Albany. The defendants had failed to obtain a license under the Federal Coasting Act of 1793[49] even though that statute applied to navigable rivers. Consequently, they did not allege conflict with a national statute. Chancellor Lansing avoided ruling on the Commerce Clause. He denied the injunction because it violated the natural right of all citizens to free navigation of the waters of the state.[50] The Court of Errors reversed Chancellor Lansing. Since all persons were free to navigate the waters of New York by every power other than steam, no fundamental principle of government was violated. Furthermore, Chief Justice James Kent ruled that the state monopoly had not violated Commerce Clause in its dormant state. Kent held a broad view of state power over intrastate commerce. "All the internal commerce of the state by land and water remains entirely, and I may say, exclusively, within the scope of its original sovereignty."[51] In 1825, in another intrastate steamboat case subsequent to *Gibbons,* Kent's view of the exclusive state power over intrastate commerce was overruled by the New York court.[52]

The application of the New York steamboat monopoly to interstate commerce was held invalid in *Gibbons v. Ogden*.[53] Ogden had an assignment from Livingston and Fulton to operate steamboats from New York to New Jersey. Gibbons was licensed to engage in the coasting trade under the Federal Coasting Act of 1793 and entered the shipping trade in competition with Ogden. Ogden secured an injunction against Gibbons in the New York courts for violation of his monopoly. Chancellor Kent, sitting as trial judge, treated the decision in the *Van Ingen* case as controlling.[54] He held that a federal coasting license, being a mere permission to operate, did not override the New York statute. This was affirmed in the highest court of New York[55] and appeal was taken to the Supreme Court of the United States.

The Supreme Court reversed the New York decision and held the state monopoly to violate the Commerce Clause. The first issue was whether commerce included the sale of transport services, navigation. Given the long-standing acceptance of statutes regulating navigation, the Embargo Act and the Coasting Acts, together with lower federal court decisions upholding their constitutionality, it is surprising this issue was seriously argued. Chief Justice Marshall held navigation to be an integral part of commerce, following his earlier opinion in *Wilson v. United States.*[56] "Commerce, undoubtedly, is traffic, but it is something more, —it is intercourse. It describes the commercial intercourse between nations and parts of nations, in all its branches, and is regulated by prescribing rules for carrying on that intercourse."[57] He concluded, "All America understands, and has uniformly understood, the word 'commerce' to comprehend navigation. It was so understood, and must have been so understood when the constitution was framed."[58]

The second issue was the meaning of "regulate commerce among the several states." Marshall noted that "among" meant "intermingled with" and that "to regulate" meant "to govern."[59] But he defined the phrase "among the several states" somewhat differently from what the modern historians say it meant in 1789. This was because he failed to recognize that the most common meaning of state had changed by 1824. Marshall used state to mean a territory, not a group of people with a common government.

Marshall defined commerce among the several states as "commerce which concerns more states than one."[60] In modern terms, this is interstate commerce plus that part of intrastate commerce that affects other states. While the facts of the case concerned commerce between states, Marshall's opinion centered on defining the breadth of the phrase. He excluded from national power only that commerce which was completely internal to one state and which did not affect other states. In Marshall's language:

> Commerce among the states cannot stop at the external boundary-line of each state, but may be introduced into the interior. . . . The genius and character of the whole government seem to be, that its action is to be applied to all the external concerns of the nation, and to those internal concerns which affect the states generally; but not to those which are completely within a particular state, which do not affect other states, and with which it is not necessary to interfere for the purpose of executing some of the general powers of the government.[61]

Marshall could have confined his opinion to those facts demonstrating the New York attempt to regulate commerce between states (interstate) and ruled that regulation of this sector of commerce among the several states was delegated exclusively to the national government.[62] Had he done this, his negative implication would have been that the New York decision in the *Van Ingen* case was valid law because it applied to ports within one state. Marshall did not want to do this. The Coasting Act of 1793 expressly applied to transport between custom districts and between ports within one district.[63] Marshall needed the fact of this statute to state a rule broad enough to imply that the decision in the *Van Ingen* case was wrong. Hence, he stated, "the sole question is, can a state regulate commerce with foreign nations and among the states, while Congress is regulating it?"[64] He could answer the question with a rule that applied to interstate and intrastate transport on the coasts and the navigable rivers that ran to the coasts.

In conclusion, Marshall held that the Commerce Clause and the Supremacy Clause combined vested in the national government the power to preempt regulation of commerce among the several states.[65] The Coasting Act, under which Gibbons was licensed, was treated as a significant national regulation of commerce. It was held to preempt the New York grant of monopoly to Ogden's assignors to navigate the coastal waters of New York.

Justice Johnson, concurring, had a broader view of "commerce among the several states" than did the Chief Justice.[66] Following his opinion in *Elkinson v. Deliesseline,*[67] he in effect stated that the Constitution delegated to Congress a plenary power to regulate commerce. He further viewed the power in Congress to be exclusive. "It can reside but in one potentate; and hence, the grant of this power carries with it the whole subject, leaving nothing for the state to act upon."[68] Under this view, the Federal Coasting Act was not relevant. The national commerce power had ousted the state commerce power. Johnson noted, however, that state health and safety laws applied to goods arriving by ship would not be regulations of commerce and thus would not conflict with an exclusive power in Congress to regulate commerce.[69] Likewise, he viewed the state laws supplying or fostering ferries and turnpikes not to be regulations of commerce.[70]

The application of the national commerce power to intrastate commerce was confirmed by the highest appeals court of New York in holding the steamboat monopoly invalid even in local operation. *North River Steamboat Co. v. Livingston*[71] applied the national preemptive rule of *Gibbons* to navigation between ports within New York. The Chancellor had originally denied an injunction against operation of a steamboat competing with the monopoly between New York City and Troy even though he viewed the commerce power as limited to interstate commerce.[72] His reason was that, under the facts of this case, the boat had stopped en route in Jersey City and thus was for a short time in interstate commerce. By petition and affidavits, plaintiff asserted that the stops in New Jersey were not *bona fide*. The Chancellor then issued an injunction against direct trips from New York to Troy but denied an injunction for trips when there was a stop in another state.[73]

Upon appeal, the Court of Errors reversed the order for injunction against intrastate voyages and affirmed the denial of injunction against interstate voyages. The court held that the rule of *Gibbons v. Ogden* necessarily applied to intrastate commerce. If ships arriving from other states could make numerous stops in the state of New York under the rule of *Gibbons,* enforcing the monopoly only against local carriers with no interstate stops in their routes would foster the unequal treatment in commerce that the Commerce Clause was designed to prevent.

There were more fundamental reasons for applying the Coasting Act to intrastate voyages. The court held that the constitutional language vested a plenary power in Congress to regulate all commerce. Chief Justice John Savage noted the original meaning of the language:

> It was the thought that commerce among the States meant among the people of the states; that this commerce was internal as related to the Government of the U.S. and its citizens, and as contradistinguished from foreign commerce. It was at that time supposed that the Constitution intended to guaranty to the citizens of the Whole U.S. an equality of commercial rights and privileges.[74]

Pursuant to this broad commerce power, Congress adopted in the Coasting Act of 1793[75] a direct application to intrastate commerce. The act was to apply to ships operating between different districts in different states, between different districts in the same state, and between different places in the same district, on the seacoast or on a navigable river. Given the competition of carriers from many states for this trade, even intrastate trips involved commerce that concerned more states than one. Such trade would not come under Chief Justice Marshall's narrow exception in *Gibbons* for purely internal commerce that did not affect other states.

Limiting State Regulation

In *Brown v. Maryland,*[76] the Supreme Court reaffirmed the Constitution as the protector of free markets. Maryland had passed a license tax of $50 on importers or wholesalers before they could sell at wholesale goods brought into the state. The statute was held unconstitutional on two grounds. Even though it was an importers' license, it was held as a tax on foreign imports while they were still in their original packages. It violated Article 1, Section 10, the prohibition on state duties on imports and exports.[77] It also violated the Commerce Clause since it regulated foreign and interstate commerce. As to the commerce power, Chief Justice Marshall wrote:

> The power is coextensive with the subject on which it acts, and cannot be stopped at the external boundary of a state, but must enter its interior . . . . Congress has a right, not only to authorize importation, but to authorize the importer to sell.[78]

The next test of the scope of the Commerce Clause was in 1829 in *Willson v. Black Bird Creek Marsh Company.*[79] This case explained the operation of the shared national and state powers over intrastate commerce. Chief Justice Marshall sustained a Delaware statute that authorized landowners to build a dam that blocked navigation on a small, navigable tidal creek that ran into the Delaware River. The defendant's sloop broke and injured the dam. While the defendant was licensed under the Federal Coasting Act, this fact was not relevant because no transport between ports on the coast or navigable rivers was involved. The "dormant" Commerce Clause would not override this type of state regulation of local, intrastate commerce. But Marshall's dictum noted that Congress could have passed a valid statute concerning small, navigable creeks and the national statute would have preempted that of Delaware.[80] In this case, the Court used cost-benefit analysis. The clear economic benefits from draining marshes greatly outweighed the smaller losses of those forced to terminate navigation. In modern legal terminology, the state burden imposed on commerce among the several states was not undue.

In the first commerce case of the Taney era, a sharply divided Supreme Court had to define the borderline between the police power of the states and the national commerce power. In *New York v. Miln,*[81] a New York statute of 1824 required the master of each ship arriving from another country or another state to file a report to the mayor of New York containing a set of facts on each passenger debarking. The second section allowed the mayor to require each master to give bond of $300 for each foreign passenger to protect the city from the cost of maintenance of those who were destitute. The action was to recover a statutory penalty of $75 per person for 100 passengers for whom the master filed no report. Justice Philip Barbour, writing for five of the seven justices, held that the statute was not a regulation of commerce in violation of the Commerce Clause but a valid exercise of the state's police power.[82] He further stated that even if the statute were considered a commercial regulation, it did not violate the Commerce Clause because Congress had not acted on the topic.[83] In fact Congress had recognized the state police power in a 1799 law requiring customs officers to aid in the enforcement of state quarantine and health laws.[84]

Justice Joseph Story dissented in the *Miln* case. While admitting that states have the power to pass health, quarantine, and poor laws, he denied that they have the power to "trench upon the authority of Congress in its power to regulate commerce."[85] Since the statute required bond in dollars and regulated masters of ships before they landed, Story found this to be either a regulation of foreign commerce or of commerce with other states, depending on the origin of the ship. Story, citing *Gibbons,* was of the view that the power to regulate foreign and interstate commerce was delegated exclusively to the national government. Story was subsequently vindicated. In *Henderson v. New York,*[86] the state requirement of bond for persons arriving from foreign ports was held unconstitutional. In

Edwards v. California,[87] a state barrier to the entry of indigent persons was held to violate the Commerce Clause. *New York v. Miln* was overruled.

In the *License Cases* of 1847,[88] the Supreme Court again had to fix a borderline between the local police power of the states and the dormant national commerce power. With six justices delivering separate opinions, the Court upheld statutes of three states regulating and taxing the intrastate sale of alcoholic liquors. In the New Hampshire case, the approved tax was levied on alcoholic beverages from other states still in their original packages, apparently rejecting the general rule of *Brown v. Maryland*.[89] Since the regulations and taxes were on goods that had become part of intrastate commerce and there was no conflicting federal statute, the decision was not inconsistent with earlier cases. Chief Justice Roger Taney's statements on the concurrent national and state power over commerce are not a reversal of earlier law if read, as they should be, to apply to intrastate commerce.[90]

In the *Passenger Cases*[91] of 1849, with eight justices writing separate opinions, the Court held unconstitutional state statutes imposing a tax per passenger on operators of ships bringing immigrants to their ports. This was an attempt at direct taxation of foreign commerce and thus violated the Commerce Clause.

Except for *New York v. Miln*, which was later overruled, the Supreme Court had created a consistent pattern of cases before 1850. Exclusive national power over foreign and interstate (between states) commerce and a concurrent national and state power over intrastate commerce was an efficient division of powers. But the many opinions in the *License* and *Passenger* cases left the legal community unsure of this law. The *obiter dictum* of *Cooley v. Board of Wardens*[92] was an attempt to state a general rule. The law of the *Cooley* case is affected by an Act of Congress of 1789[93] providing that ship pilots in the bays and harbors of the United States be regulated by existing state law and state law enacted in the future until Congress provide otherwise. The Pennsylvania statute required pilots on all vessels entering and leaving the state's ports. They would be in interstate or foreign commerce. Any master refusing a pilot still had to pay one-half the pilotage fee. As Chief Justice Marshall noted in *Gibbons v. Ogden*,[94] this is a Congressional adoption of state law passed before 1789 because Congress may not delegate the exclusive portion of its commerce power to the states. Since the Pennsylvania law was passed in 1803, another rule was needed. The Court held that for state pilot statutes passed after 1789, the Act of Congress was a designation that the commerce power was not exclusive on this topic. Justice Benjamin Curtis, in upholding the constitutionality of the Pennsylvania statute undertook to categorize the statutes. He wrote "Whatever subjects of this power are in their nature national, or admit of only one uniform system, or plan of regulation, may justly be said to be of such a nature as to require exclusive legislation by Congress."[95] This broad statement of principle is too general to be useful guidance to counsel in any particular controversy. While some commentators hailed it as reconciling the law, the rule of the case in allowing state regulation of interstate and foreign commerce was inconsistent with prior law. Justices John McLean and James Wayne dissented.

Transportation Cases

It was only in the area of transportation that the Supreme Court continued a broad construction of the commerce power as applicable to intrastate commerce. Even though the Court adopted the limiting phrase "interstate commerce" as a synonym for commerce among the several states, local activities affecting interstate transportation were held subject to federal regulation. A key decision was the *Daniel Ball*.[96] Congress exercised its plenary power to regulate commerce in a statute designed to remedy the market failure of asymmetric information about safety between owners of and passengers on steamboats. An Act of 1838 required licenses and safety inspection of all ships on inland navigable waters. In spite of the fact that the *Daniel Ball* operated entirely in Michigan, the Supreme Court held it subject to the statute because part of the merchandise transported by her originated in or was destined to other states. This broad construction of the commerce power was applied to railroads after the passage of the Interstate Commerce Act of 1887.[97] The principle that commerce among the several states extended to local acts directly affecting the movement of goods between states was explicitly embodied in the *Minnesota Rate Cases*[98] and the *Shreveport Case*.[99] Local rates could be regulated by Congress because of their competitive relation to interstate rates[100] and their general effect upon railroad revenues.[101] Local trains were subject to federal safety appliance legislation because of the danger to interstate traffic on the same lines if they went unregulated.[102] Maximum hours were validly prescribed for employees engaged in local work connected with the movement of interstate trains.[103]

The Supreme Court also upheld federal statutes prohibiting the transportation between states of some types of goods and persons though it felt compelled to rationalize such prohibitions on the basis of harmful effects or moral pestilence of the subject matter.[104] Most of these were criminal statutes. Among them were the Lottery Act,[105] the Pure Food and Drug Act,[106] the Mann Act,[107] the Adamson Act,[108] the Bill of Lading Act,[109] the Motor Vehicle Theft Act,[110] and the Animal Industry Act.[111] The Court also upheld federal regulation of local stockyards and grain exchanges who business affected transactions throughout the country.[112]

Judicial Reduction of the Commerce Power

Starting in 1869 and accelerating toward the turn of the century, the Supreme Court majority rendered a series of opinions that reduced the national commerce power to substantially less than its original meaning. Like the prior transition of the word "state" from a group of people to a territory, none of the reinterpretations noted here was founded on eighteenth century meanings. Allowing changes in common usage of words to amend the Constitution is more than just a violation of canons of documentary construction. It violates Article 5, which reserves the amending power to the people. Key opinions during this period did not fit the structural and commercial realities of an integrated industrial economy. It is not surprising that starting in 1937 most of these cases were overruled, expressly or impliedly, though again without reference to the original meaning of the commerce clause.

Two ideologies were prominent in American society after the Civil War that were inconsistent with continuance of the early broad construction of the national commerce power. The ideology of laissez-faire recognized no exceptions in terms of market failures and thus viewed the American industrial revolution of the time as best nurtured without legal controls.[113] The ideology of states rights, as one element of the effort to heal the social wounds of the Civil War, became an additional instrument in the arsenal of the business attorneys to attack national regulation. One would expect these ideologies to underlie arguments in the Congress since the legislative branch of government is where conflicting viewpoints are to be aired and resolved. But, if commercial regulation passed Congress over the opposition of the business community, it was because the majority of citizens had supported the regulation. It was not expected that the appointed elite that formed the Supreme Court majority would be so overcome with the ideologies of the times that they would misconstrue constitutional language in order to veto Congress. A likely factor may have been deficient government briefs that failed to argue the original plenary meaning of the Commerce Clause.

The reduction of the commerce power began in 1869 with a limit of the term "commerce" in *Paul v. Virginia*,[114] which in 1944 was overruled. The Court upheld a Virginia statute requiring bonds of foreign insurance corporations up to $50,000. This effectively barred their entry and promoted local monopolies. One basis for the decision was Justice Stephen Field's assertion that insurance contracts "are not articles of commerce in any proper meaning of the word . . . Such contracts are not inter-state transactions, though the parties may be domiciled in different states."[115] The opinion was factually false and contrary to the explanation of Marshall in *Gibbons* that all transactions (intercourse), including those for services, were part of commerce.[116]

In 1870, the Court rejected the attempt by Congress to assert its plenary power over commerce to regulate the quality of goods in transactions. A federal statute made it a misdemeanor to sell illuminating oils that were flammable at less than 110 degrees. The economics of this regulation is explainable in the asymmetric information of sellers and buyers and was most efficient at the national level. But in *United States v. Dewitt*[117] the statute was held unconstitutional as applied to intrastate commerce. Ignoring the view of Marshall in *Gibbons* that commerce among the several states had to extend into the interior of the states, Chief Justice Samuel Chase in effect denied that local commerce could affect other states. He asserted that the Commerce Clause implied "a virtual denial of any power to interfere with the internal trade and business of the separate states."[118]

A key shift in interpretation of the word "among" occurred in the *Case of the State Freight Tax*.[119] The Court correctly invalidated a state tonnage tax as applied to interstate cargo. The importance to the Commerce Clause is that this case contained the Court's first authoritative limitation on the word "among." The Court used "between" as a synonym for "among" in this context, a misinterpretation of the ratified language. As a result of the Court's adoption of "between," the Commerce Clause was limited to interstate commerce in the territorial sense, a mere subset of the original textual meaning.

This total exclusion of intrastate commerce from the congressional power was reiterated in 1879 in the *Trademark Cases*.[120] In the Trademark Act of 1870, Congress had exercised what they considered their plenary power to regulate commerce by enacting a general statute for registration and enforcement of trademarks. This was another regulation founded in the economics of information and most efficient at the national level. Identifying the origin of articles and protection against "passing off" enables consumers to know the producer and attach quality valuations.[121] Following the *Freight-Tax* ruling, Justice Samuel Miller invalidated the statute. He wrote "Commerce among the several States means commerce between the individual citizens of different States."[122] All application of the Trademark Act was held unconstitutional because separation of the interstate application from the intrastate application was not possible.

Another major shift in language that further reduced the meaning of "commerce" arose from later courts' misunderstanding of *Kidd v. Pearson*.[123] An Iowa statute of 1884 prohibited the manufacture of intoxicating liquors except for medicinal or similar purposes. The law was held constitutional against a distiller whose total output was to be shipped to other states. Justice Lucius Lamar stated, "No distinction is more popular to the common mind, or more clearly expressed in economic literature, than that between manufactures and commerce. Manufacture is transformation—the fashioning of raw materials into a change of form for use."[124] Lamar distinguished the physical manufacture of goods from their sale, which is part of commerce. He held in effect that state control of the physical manufacture of a dangerous substance was within the police power of the state. Later courts incorrectly cited *Kidd v. Pearson* as holding that sale of goods by manufacturers was not commerce.

The effect of this set of cases was that "among" and "commerce" were completely redefined. Commerce among the several states was reduced to mean transport between states.[125] This was a fraction of Chief Justice Marshall's "commerce which concerns more states than one." The effect of the shifts in language was to limit the commerce power to inter-state movements and those few local activities found to be part of the "stream of interstate commerce" or to have a direct effect on interstate commerce.

Some of the earliest applications of the new, narrow interpretation of the Commerce Clause were to frustrate the initial fifteen years of the Sherman Antitrust Act[126] except as applied to interstate railroads. The act was designed to remedy the market failure of monopoly. The Jurisdiction Llause of the Sherman Act, "commerce among the several states" was borrowed directly from the Commerce Clause. Section 1 applied to agreements in restraint of trade. In *United States v. E. C. Knight Co.,*[127] a suit to enjoin agreements to combine almost all the sugar refiners in the United States into one company was dismissed even though the complaint centered on restraint of trade in sales. Although most of the sugar was eventually shipped to other states, the local manufacture of sugar was held not to be commerce. This was an erroneous extension of the rule of *Kidd v. Pearson.* In *Knight,* sales transactions by sugar refiners were held exempt from antitrust because they were found to have only "indirect" effects on interstate commerce.[128] The powerful and persuasive dissent of Justice John M. Harlan emphasized the plenary power of Congress over commerce as applied to make national restraints of trade illegal.[129] It was only in 1911 in *Standard Oil Co. v. United States*[130] that the narrow jurisdictional concept of the *Knight* case was overruled.

Antitrust law had been revived in 1905 in *Swift & Co. v. United States.*[131] The trial court had issued an injunction against defendants' violation of the Sherman Antitrust Act. Meatpackers in six major cities had engaged in price-fixing combinations whereby their agents were ordered not to bid against one another to purchase livestock. Their combination also extended to the sale of fresh meats. Justice Oliver Wendell Holmes, for a unanimous Court, affirmed the trial court and explained the impact of commerce clause:

> . . . [C]ommerce among the states is not a technical legal conception but a practical one, drawn from the course of business. When cattle are sent for sale from a place in one state, with the expectation that they will end their transit, after purchase, in another, and when in effect they do so, with only the interruption necessary to find a purchaser at the stock yards, and when this is a typical, constantly recurring course, the current thus existing is a current of commerce among the states, and the purchase of the cattle is a part and incident of such commerce.[132]

The opinion of Justice Holmes in *Swift* had a long-run impact on later statutes and opinions on interstate transactions concerning stockyards and the futures market for grain.[133]

The laissez-faire bias of the Court majority had its greatest impact in invalidating congressional acts designed to protect employees. The view of the public and the majority of Congress that there were market failures in labor relations requiring legislative action was vetoed by five or six members of the Court. Surprisingly, some of these vetoes even occurred in the interstate railroad industry. One railroad case concerned workmen's compensation for injury. The economic basis for statutes requiring such compensation is to force firms to internalize the costs of an externality that arises from the production process.[134] In the first *Employers' Liability Cases,*[135] a 5 to 4 decision invalidated a federal statute making common carriers between the several states liable for injury or death of any employee resulting from negligence of another employee or defects in equipment or tracks. The Court ruled that "any employee" could include local rail shop workers who were not in interstate transport. Narrowly interpreting the Commerce Clause, the Court held that the statute wrongfully applied to local workers. It further held that interstate employees and intrastate employees were so interblended that the entire statute was unconstitutional. Justice Holmes dissented, stating: "The phrase 'every common carrier engaged in trade or commerce' may be construed to mean 'while engaged in trade or commerce' without violence to the habits of English speech, and to govern all that follows."[136]

Congress responded and retreated by passing a similar statute applying only to interstate employees of common carriers,[137] which was held constitutional.[138] In 1939, after the Court had adopted more comprehensive interpretations of commerce, Congress rewrote the railroad employees liability act to include all employees.[139] In holding this act constitutional, the Court overruled the 1908 decision and upheld Holmes's dissent.[140]

The leading case invalidating federal labor legislation concerned national uniformity in prohibiting child labor. The economic rationale for regulation was not only the market's failure to protect the health of children. In an industrial economy, where income levels are high enough so that child labor is not necessary for survival, laws prohibiting child labor force parents to keep children in school. The economic effect is to prevent underinvestment in education so that children will acquire the knowledge and skills needed for this highest possible lifetime productivity and income.[141]

The most negatively criticized case was *Hammer v. Dagenhart*,[142] a 5 to 4 decision in which the Federal Child Labor Act of 1916[143] was held unconstitutional. The act was drafted in terms of interstate transport because the Court's opinions had reduced the commerce power to that. It prohibited the shipment in interstate commerce of manufactured articles from factories in which children under fourteen years old were employed in production; children ages fourteen to sixteen were limited to eight hours work per day. Citing the Tenth Amendment, Justice William Day erroneously held that the regulation of labor transactions of manufacturers, a key aspect of cost structures, was reserved to the states. Since the input and output transactions of manufacturers are clearly commerce, Day was in error when he asserted that commerce begins by "actual delivery to a common carrier for transportation."[144] Consequently, Day mistakenly stated that the congressional power to prohibit interstate commerce was limited to articles in themselves harmful or deleterious, such as lottery tickets, impure food and drugs, and prostitutes. This ruling left child labor legislation effective only in those states that had enacted it. The opinion barred child labor products from interstate regulation. Congress could not regulate such shipments because it would invade the power of the states. Other states could not bar the entry of such products because that would invade the power of Congress.

Justice Holmes dissented and was later totally vindicated by the overruling of *Dagenhart*. He explained that the comprehensive power delegated to Congress to regulate commerce should not be usurped by the judiciary:

The notion that prohibition is any less prohibition when applied to things now thought evil I do not understand. But if there is any matter upon which civilized countries have agreed—far more unanimously than they have with regard to intoxicants and some other matters over which this country is now emotionally aroused—it is the evil of premature and excessive child labor. I should have thought that if we were to introduce our own moral conceptions where in my opinion they do not belong, this was preeminently a case for upholding the exercise of all its powers by the United States. . . .

Under the Constitution such commerce belongs not to the States but to Congress to regulate. It may carry out its views of public policy whatever indirect effect they may have upon the activities of the States. Instead of being encountered by a prohibitive tariff at her boundaries the State encounters the public policy of the United States which it is for Congress to express. The public policy of the United States is shaped with a view to the benefit of the nation as a whole. . . . The national welfare as understood by Congress may require a different attitude within its sphere from that of some self-seeking State. It seems to me entirely constitutional for Congress to enforce its understanding by all the means at its command.[145]

The Court also frustrated an attempt to control child labor through taxation. In *Bailey v. Drexel Furniture Co.,*[146] the Child Labor Tax Law of 1919 was held unconstitutional. This statute had assessed a 10 percent tax on profits of firms employing children under 14 years of age. This too was ruled an indirect method of governing local manufacture. The unreal distinction between transactions of manufacturers and commerce in these cases inhibited Congress from passing effective labor legislation for another fifteen years.

The economic depression of the 1930's brought new public demands for federal remedies. The resulting National Industrial Recovery Act of 1933[147] provided for industry to create codes of self-regulation of output, prices, wages, and hours of work. They became operative upon approval of the president of the United States. Economists who were critical of the statute knew that these particular controls were foredoomed attempts at microeconomic solutions for macroeconomic problems of deflation and unemployment. Since they created exceptions to the Sherman Act and promoted monopoly pricing, they would accentuate the depression rather than affect a partial remedy.

Two constitutional issues were raised by the NIRA litigation. The first was a valid charge of violation of the separation of governmental powers. The second charge was a violation of a narrowly defined scope of the federal commerce power. The Court also upheld this attack in a few key cases, but this narrow definition of commerce was subsequently rejected by the Court.

Section 9(c) of the NIRA authorized the president to prohibit the transportation in interstate commerce of petroleum or petroleum products produced in violation of state law. In *Panama Refining Co. v. Ryan,*[148] in 1935 these output controls in the oil industry were held to be an unconstitutional delegation of legislative power to the executive department because the indefinite standards in the federal statute put no controls on the administration. In *Schechter Poultry Corp. v. United States*,[149] concerning the sale of chickens in New York, the Court unanimously struck down the main sections of the statute on the same ground; Justice Cardozo, who concurred, described it as "delegation running riot." As a second ground, the Court held the particular application in the Poultry Code in New York was outside the power of Congress under the Commerce Clause. It found the effects on interstate commerce to be indirect and that, under the Tenth Amendment, control of such matters was reserved to the states.

Three weeks before the *Schechter* decision the Court, by a 5 to 4 decision, had invalidated the Railroad Retirement Act of 1934.[150] The act had established compulsory retirement and pension systems for railroad employees. The majority held that the statute had purely social ends and no direct relation to interstate commerce. As a result, Congress had to take a new statutory approach to railroad retirement.[151]

Following the *Schechter* case, the Congress attempted a few selective controls in particular industries. The Bituminous Coal Conservation Act of 1935[152] had two major operative control regulations. Part II created and authorized the National Bituminous Coal Commission to regulate prices at which that grade of coal was sold in interstate commerce.[153] Part III gave miners the right to organize unions and to bargain collectively. It also created a labor board to set minimum wages and maximum hours for that set of coal miners when coal output was to be shipped in interstate commerce. In *Carter v. Carter Coal Company*,[154] by a 5 to 4 decision, the majority held that the two parts of the statute were inseparable. They held the entire statute was unconstitutional on the ground that mining preceded commerce and that input transactions of mining firms had only indirect effect upon interstate commerce. This part of the Act was deemed invalid also on the ground of unlimited delegation of legislative power.

Justice Cardozo dissented and insisted that the two parts of the statute were separable. As to Part III, he viewed any suits premature because regulations of labor were not yet in operation. In his positive view of Part II, Cardozo wrote:

> I am satisfied that the Act is within the power of the central government in so far as it provides for minimum and maximum prices upon sales of bituminous coal in the transactions of interstate commerce and in those of intrastate commerce where interstate commerce is directly or intimately affected. . . . To regulate the price for such transactions is to regulate commerce itself, and not alone its antecedent conditions or its ultimate consequences. The very act of sale is limited and governed. Prices in interstate transactions may not be regulated by the states. They must therefore be subject to the power of the nation unless they are to be withdrawn altogether from governmental supervision.[155]

Restoration of the Commerce Power

The Supreme Court's frustration of the congressional attempts to regulate business and labor relations in a time of economic crisis led President Roosevelt in 1937 to call for legislation of "reorganize the judicial branch."[156] The so-called court-packing plan was to increase the size of federal courts by allowing new additional appointments whenever an incumbent judge reached voluntary retirement age and refused to retire. At that time, six of the nine members of the Supreme Court were past the voluntary retirement age. Coincidentally with this proposal, which was ultimately rejected, the Supreme Court majority shifted. The four conservative justices with biases against governmental regulation of business began to retire.[157] President Roosevelt replaced them with liberal justices and this was the primary reason that the restrictive interpretations of the Commerce Clause and other constitutional constraints on the regulation of business came to an end.

The Supreme Court initiated its return to broad construction of the commerce clause in 1937 with *N.L.R.B. v. Jones & Laughlin Steel Corp.,*[158] a 5 to 4 decision. The National Labor Relations Act of 1935[159] defined the term commerce as "trade, traffic, commerce, transportation, or communication among the several states. . . ." It defined "affecting commerce" as "in commerce, or burdening or obstructing commerce or the free flow of commerce, or having led or tending to lead to a labor dispute burdening or obstructing commerce or the free flow of commerce." Section 7 protected employees rights to self-organization and to bargain collectively through representatives of their own choosing. Section 8 described unfair and discriminatory labor practice by employers. Section 10 empowered the NLRB to prevent unfair labor practices affecting commerce. It was clear that the economic objective was to reduce the transaction costs of negotiating long-term relational contracts between employers and workers.[160]

Chief Justice Charles E. Hughes, for the majority, upheld the constitutionality of the act and its application to Jones & Laughlin. The firm's giant Aliquippa Plant was part of a highly integrated production process. Major inputs consisted of coal and iron shipped from other states to Pennsylvania. Its steel output was shipped to many states across the nation. Hughes explicitly rejected the narrow reasoning of the *Schechter and Carter* cases on the meaning of commerce. He wrote:

> Giving full weight to respondent's contention with respect to a break in the complete continuity of the "stream of commerce" by reason of respondent's manufacturing operations, the fact remains that the stoppage of those operations by industrial strife would have a most serious effect upon interstate commerce. In view of respondent's far-flung activities, it is idle to say that the effect would be indirect or remote. It is obvious that it would be immediate and might be catastrophic. We are asked to shut our eyes to the plainest facts of our national life and to deal with the question of direct and indirect effects in an intellectual vacuum. . . . We have often said that interstate commerce itself is a practical conception. It is equally true that interfer-

ences with that commerce must be appraised by a judgment that does not ignore actual experience.[161]

In the next two years, the Court reaffirmed the application of the Labor Relations Act to intrastate producers.[162]

In *United States v. Darby*[163] in 1941, Justice Harlan F. Stone, for a unanimous Supreme Court, upheld the constitutionality of the Fair Labor Standards Act of 1938.[164] The act prohibited interstate shipment of manufactures where the producer violated the prescribed minimum wages or maximum hours.[165] The act was enforced by individual employee suits for back wages or suits by the secretary of labor seeking an injunction as well as back wages. Darby cut lumber at his Georgia sawmill and sold to customers in other states. He paid less than the legal minimum wage. Since the statutory language was limited to interstate transactions, Justice Stone chose not to explain the full scope of "commerce among the several states." He wrote as follows:

> The power of Congress over interstate commerce "is complete in itself, may be exercised to its utmost extent, and acknowledges no limitations other than are prescribed in the Constitution." *Gibbons v. Ogden.* That power can neither be enlarged nor diminished by the exercise or non-exercise of state power. Congress, following its own conception of public policy concerning the restrictions which may appropriately be imposed on interstate commerce, is free to exclude from the commerce articles whose use in the states for which they are destined it may conceive to be injurious to the public health, morals or welfare, even though the state has not sought to regulate their use. . . .
>
> *Hammer v. Dagenhart* has not been followed. The distinction on which the decision was rested that Congressional power to prohibit interstate commerce is limited to articles which in themselves have some harmful or deleterious property—a distinction which was novel when made and unsupported by any provision of the Constitution—has long since been abandoned. The thesis of the opinion that the motive of the prohibition or its effect to control in some measure the use or production within the states of the article thus excluded from the commerce can operate to deprive the regulation of its constitutional authority has long since ceased to have force.
>
> The conclusion is inescapable that *Hammer v. Dagenhart,* was a departure from the principles which have prevailed in the interpretation of the Commerce Clause both before and since the decision and that such vitality, as a precedent, as it then had has long since been exhausted. It should be and now is overruled. . . .
>
> So far as *Carter v. Carter Coal Co.* is inconsistent with this conclusion, its doctrine is limited in principle by the decisions under the Sherman Act and the National Labor Relations Act, which we have cited and which we follow.[166]

Justice Stone concluded by noting the relation to the Commerce Clause of the necessary and proper clause and of the Tenth Amendment. As to the former, Congress "may choose the means reasonably adapted to the attainment of the permitted end, even though they involve control of intrastate activities."[167] As to the latter, the Tenth Amendment "states but a truism that all is retained which has not been surrendered."[168] The Fair Labor Standards Act was subsequently held applicable to employees in various occupations in intrastate commerce.[169]

Agriculture cases approving monopoly pricing through regulation demonstrated the most comprehensive federal governance of purely local commerce. The fact that price elasticity of demand for farm output is very low meant that farm income could be materially raised by controlling supply.[170] This was achieved through acreage controls and marketing orders limiting domestic sales. In *United States v. Rock Royal Cooperative, Inc.*,[171] the Court upheld milk marketing orders under the Agricultural Adjustment Act of 1935. In *Wickard v. Filburn*,[172] the Court upheld wheat marketing quotas under the Agricultural Adjustment Act of 1938. The decision sustained the allocation of quotas even to crops which were fed to livestock on the same farm. Justice Robert Jackson concluded that "even if appellee's activity be local and though it may not be regarded as commerce, it may still whatever its nature, be reached by Congress if it exerts a substantial economic effect on interstate commerce, and this irrespective of whether such effect is what might at some earlier time have been defined as 'direct' or 'indirect.'"[173] Critics labeled this case *Filburn's* aggregation doctrine, combining all wheat farmers who fed part of their crops to livestock. Nevertheless, the case was highly contested because the facts lacked the key element of commerce—transactions.

Restoration of the broad application of federal power to regulate local commerce was also seen in litigation under the antitrust laws. In *United States v. South-Eastern Underwriters Ass'n.*,[174] in 1944, the Court overruled *Paul v. Virginia* and held insurance contracts, each of which is made in a single state, to be a part of commerce. Justice Hugo L. Black, renowned for emphasizing the control position of ratified constitutional language, cited *Gibbons* and wrote:

> Ordinarily courts do not construe words used in the Constitution so as to give them a meaning more narrow than one which they had in the common parlance of the times in which the Constitution was written. To hold that the word "commerce" as used in the Commerce Clause does not include a business such as insurance would do just that. Whatever other meanings "commerce" may have included in 1787, the dictionaries, encyclopedias, and other books of the period show that it included trade: business in which persons bought and sold, bargained and contracted. And this meaning has persisted to modern times.[175]

Black referred to Chief Justice Marshall's statement in *Gibbons* that commerce is among the several states when it "concerns more states than one" or when it will "affect the people of more states than one."[176]

In *Mandeville Island Farms Co. v. American Crystal Sugar Co.*,[177] in 1948, the Sherman Act was held applicable to an agreement among processors in a single state to fix prices paid farmers in the same state for their sugar beets, on the ground that these fixed input prices would inevitably affect the processors' output prices in interstate commerce. Justice Wiley Rutledge, speaking of the line between federal and state power over commerce states, "the essence of the affectation doctrine was that the exact location of this line made no difference, if the forbidden effects flowed across it to the injury of interstate commerce or to the hindrance or defeat of congressional policy regarding it."[178] In the *Women's Sportswear Case*[179] of 1949, the Sherman Act was applied to price-fixing combinations of manufacturers in a single city who dealt only with local jobbers, who in turn shipped the goods in commerce. Justice Jackson remarked, "If it is interstate commerce that feels the pinch, it does not matter how local the operation which applies the squeeze."[180]

Later litigation affirming the broad scope of the Commerce Clause has been under the Civil Rights Act of 1964.[181] The Act guaranteed equal enjoyment of the goods, services, and accommodations of business establishments serving the public without discrimination on the ground of race, color, religion, or national origin. In *Heart of Atlanta Motel, Inc. v. United States,*[182] the constitutionality of the act in reference to hotels and motels was upheld. The statutory language was limited to enterprises having a direct and substantial relation to the interstate flow of goods and people. Justice Tom Clark wrote: "The power of Congress to promote interstate commerce also includes the power to regulate the local incidents thereof, including local activities in both the States of origin and destination, which might have a substantial and harmful effect upon that commerce."[183] In *Katzenbach v. McClung,*[184] the section of the 1964 act pertaining to restaurants was also upheld. The decision was based on the fact that in one year the restaurant purchased $69,683 of meat from a local supplier who had procured it from outside the state.

The modern interpretation of the Commerce Clause has in effect returned the clause to its original meaning—a plenary power to regulate American commerce. Thus, Justice John P. Stevens asserted, "Today, there should be universal agreement on the proposition that Congress has ample power to regulate the terms and conditions of employment throughout the economy."[185] Citing *Gibbons v. Ogden,*[186] he further stated "Neither the Tenth Amendment, nor any other provision of the Constitution, affords any support for . . . judicially constructed limitation on the scope of the federal power granted to Congress by the Commerce Clause."[187] In spite of the fact that the Court may continue to use the limiting phrase "interstate" commerce—all local transactions are found to affect that commerce. The so-called "dormant commerce clause" is merely a recognition of the exclusivity of the plenary power in Congress.[188]

The commerce power has come full circle. The original eighteenth-century meaning of the Commerce Clause was a plenary power in Congress to regulate all transactions in the economy. After more than a century of being ignored by the Supreme Court majority, the original meaning has been restored by the Court as official. This conclusion is not impaired by the 1995 opinion in *United States v. Lopez,*[189] where Congress unsuccessfully attempted to use the commerce power to regulate noncommercial activity. The Gun-Free School

Zones Act of 1990 made it a national crime for any individual knowingly to possess a firearm within 1000 feet of the grounds of a school. Lopez, a senior at San Antonio High School, carried a concealed handgun and five bullets to school. State criminal charges were dismissed when Lopez was charged under the federal act. The Supreme Court, by a vote of 5 to 4, affirmed dismissal of the federal action. Justice Rehnquist, for the majority, noted that the act "neither regulates a commercial activity nor contains a requirement that the possession be connected in any way to interstate commerce."[190] Noncommercial intrastate crimes are twice remote from an estimable substantial affect upon commerce.

Conclusion

Most constitutional histories fail to emphasize the epistemological importance of Supreme Court constitutional overrulings. Law students, social scientists, and even lawyers who have never litigated a constitutional issue need the explanation or reminder that overrulings declare earlier majority opinions were invalid when issued. The social consequences of some Court overrulings have been to terminate grave injustice. A large number of trial courts and lower appeals courts, bound by *stare decisis*, were obliged to follow the earlier majority opinions which were later nullified by the Supreme Court. The outstanding example under the Commerce Clause was *Hammer v. Dagenhart* (1918) which was overruled in *United States v. Darby* (1941). The positive effect of the *Darby* ruling was to recognize the dissent of Justice Holmes in *Hammer* as the only valid law of that older case. Meanwhile, hundreds of thousands of twelve-year-old children from poor families were taken out of school and put to work for long hours per day in reliance on the invalid rule of *Hammer.* The public outcry against both child labor and the majority decision in *Hammer* fostered a demand for Congress to pass a Child Labor Amendment to the Constitution. While almost succeeding, the proposal did not secure ratification by three-fourths of the states.

The Commerce Clause opinions of the Court can be viewed as having a close relation to those creating substantive due process, which is critically analyzed in Chapter 8. The laissez-faire bias of conservative members of the Court and the bias against the working class of some of them led to majority opinions that violated the ratified language of the Constitution. Justice Holmes dissented from this group of majority opinions that held business regulation, the statutory protection of workers' rights to organize and join unions, and minimum wage laws to be unconstitutional. This study has demonstrated the fundamental validity of Holmes' dissents as confirmed when those cases were later overruled. Holmes was concerned with the original meaning of constitutional language even when he failed to present a full analysis of the meaning of the words in some relevant clauses.

Notes

1. U.S. Const., Art. I, § 8, Cl. 3.
2. U.S. Const., Art. I, § 10, Cl. 2: "No State shall, without the Consent of the Congress, lay an Imposts or Duties on Imports or Exports, except what may be absolutely necessary for executing its inspection Laws: and the net Produce of all Duties and Imposts, laid by an State on Imports or Exports, shall be for the Use of the Treasury of the United States; and all such Laws shall be subject to the Revision and Control of the Congress."
3. William W. Crosskey, 1 *Politics and the Constitution in the History of the United States,* 295-323 (Chicago: Univ. of Chicago Press, 1953). [hereafter cited as Crosskey]
4. *Woodruff v. Parham,* 75 U.S. (8 Wall.) 123, (1868).
5. *Baldwin v. G.A.F. Seelig, Inc.,* 294 U.S. 511 (1935). See John B. Sholley, *The Negative Implications of the Commerce Clause,* 3 Univ. of Chi. L. Rev. 556 (1936).
6. Lawrence H. Gipson, 3 *The British Empire before the American Revolution,* 291-94 (New York: Alfred Knopf, Rev. ed., 1960).
7. Gustav Schmoller, *The Mercantile System and Its Historical Significance,* 69 (Reprint, New York: A. M. Kelley, 1967). On the economics of colonial dependency under mercantilism, see Joseph Dorfman, 1 *The Economic Mind in American Civilization, 1606-1865,* 135-141 (New York: Viking Press, 1946).
8. Adam Smith, *An Inquiry into the Nature and Causes of the Wealth of Nations,* (1776) (Oxford England: Clarendon Press, reprint 1869).
9. Walton Hamilton and Douglass Adair, *The Power to Govern,* ch. 5 (New York: W.W. Norton, 1937). See Forrest McDonald, *Novus Ordo Seclorum,* ch. 4 (Lawrence, Kansas: Univ. of Kansas Press, 1985).
10. U.S. Cong., *Am. State Papers,* Class III, *Finance,* I, 123, 135-37 (1832).
11. *Hood & Sons v. DuMond,* 336 U.S. 525, 533 (1949), citing U.S. Cong., *Documents, Formation of the Union,* 12 H. Doc., 69th Cong., 1st Sess., 38 (1927). See Wiley Rutledge, *A Declaration of Legal Faith,* 25-26 (Lawrence: Univ. of Kansas Press, 1947).
12. The report of the Annapolis meeting is reprinted in J. Elliot, 1 *Debates in the Several State Conventions on the Adoption of the Federal Constitution,* 116-119 (1836).
13. *Id.* at 119-20.
14. Max Farrand, ed., 1 *Records of the Federal Convention of 1787,* 20-23 (New Haven, CT: Yale Univ. Press, 1911). [Hereafter cited as Farrand].
15. Farrand, I: 21.
16. *Id.* at I: 54.
17. *Id.* at I: 243.
18. Farrand, Vol 2: 181.
19. Robert Stern, *That Commerce which Concerns More States Than One,* 47 Harv. Rev. 1335, 1344-45 (1934).
20. George Caines, *An Enquiry into the Law Merchant of the United States; or Lex Mercatoria Americana, on Several Heads of Commercial Importance* (New York: Isaac Collins, 1802); Charles Molloy. *De Jure Maritimo Et Navali: Or a Treatise of Affairs Maritime, and of Commerce,* 2 volumes (London: T. Waller, 9th ed. 1769).
21. See, e.g., *Luke v. Lyde,* 2 Burr. 882, 97 Eng. Rep. 611 (K.B. 1759); *Pelly v. Company of the Royal Exchange Assurance,* 1 Burr. 341, 97 Eng. Rep. 342 (K.B. 1757).
22. A commerce dictionary of the era devoted twenty-three pages to examples of different types of bills of exchange. Malachy Postlethwayt, *The Universal Dictionary*

of Trade and Commerce (London: W. Straham, 1774). See James M. Holden, The History of Negotiable Instruments in English Law, c. 5 (London: Univ. of London, Athlone Press, 1955).

23. Crosskey, supra note 3, at 3-186; Hamilton and Adair, Power to Govern, supra note 9, at 42-53.

24. Adam Anderson, Historical and Chronological Deduction of the Origin of Commerce (London: J. Walter, 1787).

25. Tench Coxe, A View of the United States of America, 7 (London: J. Johnson, 1794).

26. Alexander Hamilton, The Federalist, No. XI, 71 (Bourne ed., 1947).

27. 22 U.S. (9 Wheat.) 1, 196 (1814).

28. See Hamilton, Federalist VI, 35; VII, 42 (Bourne ed., 1947).

29. The Committee of Stile did not alter the language adopted by the Committee of Detail. Farrand II: 595.

30. Crosskey, supra note 3, at 50-55.

31. Gibbons v. Ogden, 22 U.S. (9 Wheat.) 1, 194.

32. Madison, in discussing whether the Constitution was adopted as a compact of the states, noted the different uses of the word "states":

   It is indeed true that the term "states" is sometimes used in a vague sense, and sometimes in different senses, according to the subject to which it is applied. Thus it sometimes means the separate sections of territory occupied by the political societies within each; sometimes the particular governments established by those societies; sometimes those societies as organized into those particular governments; and lastly, it means the people composing those political societies, in their highest sovereign capacity. Although it might be wished that the perfection of language admitted less diversity in the signification of the same words, yet little convenience is produced by it, where the true sense can be collected with certainty from the different applications. In the present instance, whatever different construction of the term "states," in the Resolution, may have been entertained, all will at least concur in the last mentioned; because in that sense the Constitution was submitted to the "states"; in that sense the "states" ratified it; and in that sense of the term "states," they are consequently parties to the compact from which the powers of the federal government result.

   James Madison, Report on the Virginia Resolutions, in 4 Debates of the Several State Conventions on the Adoption of the Federal Constitution, 547 (Jonathan Elliot ed., 1836).

33. See sources cited in Crosskey, supra note 3, at 55-69 and 1267-74. Crosskey cites a number of dictionaries, including Samuel Johnson, Dictionary of the English Language. (1775) (Reprint: New York: AMS Press, 1967). Noting "state" as a group of persons and not citing any use of the term as a territory. It was common parlance of the times to say "I am of Vermont" or "I belong to Vermont." Id. at 57-58. See Joseph Story, 1 Commentaries on the Constitution of the United States, § 208 (Boston: Hillard, Gray, 1833).

34. U.S. Const., Art. 1, Sec. 2 (emphasis added).

35. Wilfred J. Ritz, Rewriting the History of the Judicial Act of 1789, 83-86 (Norman: Univ. of Oklahoma Press, 1990).

36. Coxe, View of the United States, supra note 25, at 32-33.

37. An Act for Registering and Clearing Vessels, Regulating the Coasting Trade, and for other purposes, 1st Cong. Sess. 1, ch. 11, Sept. 1, 1789, 1 Stat. 55.

38. 28 Fed. Cas. 614 (No. 16,700) (D. Mass. 1808). See George L. Haskins and Herbert A. Johnson, Foundations of Power: John Marshall, 1801-15, Vol. 2, History of the

Supreme Court of the United States, 305-307 (New York: MacMillian, 1981). On the politics of the embargo see Alfred H. Kelly, Winifred A. Harbison, and Herman Belz, *The American Constitution: Its Origins and Development,* 150-153 (New York: Norton, 6th ed., 1983).

39. 28 Fed. Cas. At 621.
40. *Id.* at 620-21.
41. 30 Fed. Cas. 239 (no. 17, 846) (C.C. Va. 1820).
42. *Id.* at 243.
43. *8 Fed.* Cas. 493 (no. 4,366) (C.C.S.C. 1823). See Donald Morgan, *Justice William Johnson: The First Dissenter,* 192-202 (Columbia, SC: Univ. of South Carolina Press, 1954).
44. 8 Fed. Cas. at 495.
45. Albert J. Beveridge, 4 *The Life of John Marshall,* 398-405 (Boston: Houghton Mifflin, 1919), describing the original grant of monopoly and its renewals.
46. Harold G. Fox, *Monopolies and Patents* 57 (Toronto: Univ. of Toronto Legal Studies, 1947). The British constitutional tradition is founded in the *Case of Monopolies,* 11 Coke 84, 77 Eng. Rep. 1260 (K.B. 1602) and the Statute of Monopolies, 21 Jac. 1, Ch. 3 (1624). On the antimonopoly tradition in America, see Chapter 7.
47. Beveridge, *supra* note 45, at 403-405; George L. Haskins, *Marshall and the Commerce Clause of the Constitution,* in *Chief Justice John Marshall: A Reappraisal,* 145-47, W. Jones, ed. (Ithaca: Cornell Univ. Press, 1956).
48. 9 Johns. 507 (N.Y. 1812).
49. An Act for enrolling and licensing ships or vessels to be employed in the coasting trade and fisheries, and for regulating the same, 2d Cong., Sess. 2, ch. 8, Feb. 18, 1793, 1 Stat. 305.
50. *Livingston,* 9 Johns. at 514-21.
51. 9 Johns. at 578.
52. *North River Steamboat Co. v. Livingston,* 3 Cowen 713 (N.Y. 1825), citing *Gibbons v. Ogden,* 22 U.S. (9 Wheat.) 1 (1824).
53. 22 U.S. (9 Wheat.) 1 (1824). See G. Edward White, *The Marshall Court and Cultural Change,* 1815-35, Vol. 3-4 *History of the Supreme Court of the United States,* 568-86 (New York: Macmillan Co., 1988); Maurice G. Baxter, *Steamboat Monopoly: Gibbons v. Ogden, 1824* (New York: A. Knopf, 1972); Charles Warren, 1 *The Supreme Court in United States History,* 587-632 (Boston: Little Brown, 1926). [Hereafter cited as Warren].
54. *Ogden v. Gibbons,* 4 Johns. ch. 150 (N.Y. 1819).
55. *Gibbons v. Ogden,* 17 Johns. 488 (N.Y. 1820). See Thomas Campbell, *Chancellor Kent, Chief Justice Marshall and the Steamboat Cases,* 25 Syracuse L. Rev. 497, 513 (1974).
56. 30 Fed. Cas. 239 (no. 17, 846) (C.C. Va. 1820).
57. *Gibbons,* 22 U.S. at 189-90.
58. *Id.* at 190.
59. *Id.* at 194, 196.
60. *Id.* at 194.
61. *Id.* at 194-195.
62. Marshall devotes many pages to a demonstration that the power of Congress over foreign and interstate commerce is exclusive. *Id.* at 197-209.
63. The statute applied to ships or vessels "found trading between district and district, or between different places in the same district." Coasting Act of 1793, Sec. 6, 1 Stat. 307.
64. *Gibbons,* 22 U.S. at 200.

65. *Id.* at 221.
66. *Id.* at 222.
67. 8 Fed. Cas. 493 (no. 4, 366) (C.C. S.C. 1823).
68. 22 U.S. at 227.
69. *Id.* at 235.
70. See Albert Abel, *Commerce Regulation before Gibbons v. Ogden,* 25 N. C. L. Rev. 121 (1947).
71. 3 Cowen 713 (N.Y. 1825).
72. *North River Steamboat Co. v. Livingston,* 1 Hopkins Ch. 149 (N.Y. 1824).
73. 3 Cowen at 714-715.
74. 3 Cowen at 752.
75. 1 Stat. 305 (1793)
76. 25 U.S. (12 Wheat.) 419 (1827). See the application of the original package doctrine in *Leisy v. Hardin,* 135 U.S. 100 (1890).
77. U.S. Const. Art. I, § 10, Cl. 2. See *supra* note 2.
78. 25 U.S. at 446-47. In *Woodruff v. Parham,* 75 U.S. (8 Wall.) 123 (1869), the original package doctrine was held inapplicable to interstate commerce. It was in effect overruled for foreign commerce in *Michelin Tire Co. v. Wages,* 423 U.S. 276 (1976), *overruling Low v. Austin,* 80 U.S. (13 Wall.) 29 (1872).
79. 27 U.S. (2 Pet.) 245 (1829).
80. *Id.* at 252.
81. 36 U.S. (11 Pet.) 102 (1837), See Carl B. Swisher, *The Taney Period 1836-64, Vol. 5, History of the Supreme Court of the United States,* 360-65 (New York: Macmillan, 1974).
82. 36 U.S. at 139.
83. *Id.* at 138.
84. An Act Respecting Quarantine and Health Laws, ch. 12, Feb. 25, 1799, 1 Stat. 619.
85. 36 U.S. at 156.
86. 92 U.S. 259 (1876).
87. 314 U.S. 160 (1941).
88. 46 U.S. (5 How.) 504 (1847), See Swisher, *supra* note 81, at 370-77.
89. 25 U.S. (12 Wheat.) 419 (1827).
90. 46 U.S. at 579. See Felix Frankfurter, *The Commerce Clause under Marshall, Taney and Waite* 51-53 (Chapel Hill: Univ. of North Carolina Press, 1937).
91. 48 U.S. (7 How.) 28 (1849). See Swisher, *supra* note 81, at 382-91; Warren, *supra* note 53, at II, 174-181.
92. 53 U.S. (12 How.) 299 (1851). See Swisher, *supra* note 81, at 404-6.
93. 1 Stat. 54 (1789).
94. *Gibbons,* 22 U.S. 1, 207-8 (1824).
95. 53 U.S. at 319.
96. 77 U.S. (10 Wall.)556 (1871). See Louis C. Hunter, *Steamboats on the Western Rivers,* ch. 13 (Cambridge: Harvard Univ. Press, 1949).
97. 24 Stat. 379 (1887).
98. 230 U.S. 352 (1913).
99. *Houston, E. & W. Texas Railway V. United States,* 234 U.S. 342 (1914).
100. *Id.* at 358-59.
101. *Railroad Com'n of Wisconsin v. Chicago, B. & Q. R. R.,* 257 U.S. 563 (1922).
102. *Southern Ry. v. United States,* 222 U.S. 20 (1911).
103. *Baltimore & Ohio R. R. v. ICC,* 221 U.S. 612 (1911).

104. Edward S. Corwin, *Congress' Power to Prohibit Commerce*, 18 Cornell L. Q. 477 (1933).

105. *Champion v. Ames*, 188 U.S. 321 (1903). On the fine opinion by Justice John M. Harlan, explaining the scope of the Commerce Clause, see James W. Ely Jr., *The Chief Justiceship of Melville W. Fuller 1885-1910*, 139-40 (Columbia, SC: Univ. of South Carolina Press, 1995).

106. *Hipolite Egg Co. v. United States*, 220 U.S. 45 (1911).

107. *Hoke v. United States*, 227 U.S. 308 (1913). See Michael Conant, *Federalism, the Mann Act, and the Imperative to Decriminalize Prostitution*, 5 Cornell J. of Law and Pub. Policy 99 (1996).

108. *Wilson v. New*, 243 U.S. 332 (1917).

109. *United States v. Ferger*, 250 U.S. 199 (1919).

110. *Brooks v. United States*, 267 U.S. 432 (1925).

111. *Thornton v. United States*, 271 U.S. 414 (1926).

112. See notes 131 to 140 *infra*, and accompanying text.

113. See Benjamin R. Twiss, *Lawyers and the Constitution* 18-92 (Princeton, NJ: Princeton Univ. Press, 1942); John R. Tucker, *The Congressional Power over Interstate Commerce*, 11 A.B.A. Rep 260 (1888).

114. 75 U.S. (8 Wall.) 168, 183 (1869), *overruled in United States v. South Eastern Underwriters Ass'n*, 332 U.S. 533 (1944).

115. 75 U.S. (8 Wall.) at 183. See contrary view of Justice Holmes in *Fidelity & Deposit Co. of Md. v. Tafoya*, 270 U.S. 426, 434 (1926).

116. 22 U.S. (9 Wheat.) 1, 195-196 (1824).

117. 76 U.S. (9 Wall.) 41 (1870). On market failure based on consumer ignorance and the costs of search, see Ejan MacKay, *Economics of Information and Law*, 107-15, 150-52, (Boston: Kluwer-Nijhoff, 1982).

118. 76 U.S. at 44.

119. 82 U.S. (15 Wall.) 232 (1873).

120. 100 U.S. 82 (1878). Since there have been no constitutional challenges to the intrastate application of twentieth-century U.S. trademark statutes, the Supreme Court has not had an opportunity to overrule the 1878 decision.

121. See Richard A. Posner, *Economic Analysis of Law* 37-38 (Boston: Little Brown, 3d ed. 1986); Conant, *Multiple Trademarks and Oligopoly Power*, 1 Industrial Org. Rev. 115 (1973).

122. 100 U.S. at 96.

123. 128 U.S. 1 (1888).

124. *Id.* at 20.

125. See Robert Stern, *That Commerce Which Concerns More States Than One*, 47 Harv. L. Rev. 1335, 1348 (1934):

The use of the convenient phrase "interstate commerce" instead of the words of the Constitution has unfortunately tended to cause the connotation of "intermingling" in the phrase "commerce among the states" to be neglected, and the element of interstate movement to be over-emphasized. Thus, the impression is often given that the commerce power of Congress is dependent upon the existence of movement *between* the states. But the Constitution says "among", rather than "between", and the difference between the two words is ignored if the commerce power is limited to the control of acts affecting movement across state lines.

126. 26 Stat. 209 (1890), 15 U.S.C.A. § 1 (1997).

127. 156 U.S. 1 (1895). See Twiss, *Lawyers and the Constitution, supra* note 113, ch.9.

128. 156 U.S. at 16.

129. *Id.* at 33-44. See Loren P. Beth, *John Marshall Harlan: The Last Whig Justice* 195 (Lexington, KY: Univ. of Kentucky Press, 1992).
130. 221 U.S. 1, 68-69 (1911).
131. 196 U.S. 375 (1905). The Sherman Act had been applied to direct restraints on shipping goods between states. *Addyston Pipe & Steel Co. v. United States,* 175 U.S. 211 (1899).
132. 196 U.S. at 399. See David Gordon, *Swift & Co. v. United States: The Beef Trust and the Stream of Commerce Doctrine,* 28 Amer. J. of Legal Hist. 244 (1984).
133. *Strafford v. Wallace,* 258 U.S. 495 (1922), upholding the Packers and Stockyards Act, 42 Stat. 159 (1921); *Chicago Board of Trade v. Olsen,* 262 U.S. 1 (1923), upholding the Grain Futures Act of 1922, 42 Stat. 998 (1922); *Tagg Bros. & Moorhead v. United States,* 280 U.S. 420, 439 (1930), upholding application of the Packers and Stockyards Act.
134. See Posner, *Economic Analysis, supra* note 121, at 235.
135. *Howard v. Illinois C.R. Co.,* 20 7 U.S. 463 (1908). See 34 Stat. 232 (1906).
136. 207 U.S. at 541.
137. 35 Stat. 65 (1908).
138. *Second Employers' Liability Cases,* 223 U.S. 1 (1912).
139. 53 Stat. 1404 (1939), 45 U.S.C.A. § 51 (1986).
140. *Southern Pacific Co. v. Gileo,* 351 U.S. 493 (1956); *Reed v. Pennsylvania R. Co.,* 351 U.S. 502 (1956).
141. See Posner, *Economic Analysis, supra* note 121, at 137-43; Gary Becker, *Human Capital* (New York: National Bureau of Economic Research, 2d ed. 1975).
142. 247 U.S. 251 (1918), *overruled in United States v. Darby,* 312 U.S. 100, 116-17. See critique by Edward S. Corwin, *Twilight of the Supreme Court,* 26-37 (New Haven: Yale Univ. Press, 1934). For a description of the failed attempt to secure ratification of a Child Labor Amendment to the Constitution, see Carl B. Swisher, *American Constitutional Development,* 729-732 (Boston: Houghton-Mifflin Co., 2d ed. 1954); Clement E. Vose, *Constitutional Change: Amendment Politics and Supreme Court Litigation Since 1900,* 247-252 (Lexington: D.D. Heath, 1972).
143. 39 Stat. 675 (1916). See Stephen Wood, *Constitutional Politics in the Progressive Era: Child Labor and the Law* (Chicago: Univ. of Chicago Press, 1968); Hugh D. Hindman, *Child Labor: An American History* (Armonk, NY: M. E. Sharpe, 2002).
144. 247 U.S. at 272.
145. 247 U.S. at 280-281. The weight of scholarly opinion supported the Holmes dissent. See Alexander M. Bickel, *The Judiciary and Responsible Government 1910-21, Part One, History of the Supreme Court of the United States,* Vol. 9, 450-58 (New York: Macmillan Pub. Co., 1984); Stephen B. Wood, *Politics in the Progressive Era: Child Labor and the Law, supra* note 150.
146. 259 U.S. 20 (1920). On the broad power of Congress to use taxation as a method of regulation, see *McCray v. United States,* 195 U.S. 27 (1904).
147. 48 Stat. 195 (1933). See Peter H. Irons, *The New Deal Lawyers,* 17-57 (Princeton: Princeton Univ. Press, 1982); Robert Stern, *The Commerce Clause and the National Economy,* 59 Harv. L. Rev. 645, 883 (1946).
148. 293 U.S. 388 (1935). See Irons, *New Deal Lawyers, supra* note 147, at 58-74.
149. 295 U.S. 495 (1935); Cardozo concurs at *Id.* 553. See Irons, *New Deal Lawyers, supra* note 147, at 86-107.
150. *Railroad Retirement Board v. Alton R. Co.,* 295 U.S. 330 (1935).
151. See Leonard Lecht, *Experience under Railway Labor Legislation,* 123-31 (New York: Columbia Univ. Press, 1955).

152. 49 Stat. 991 (1935). See James P. Johnson, *The Politics of Soft Coal,* 217-238 (Urbana: Univ. of Illinois Press, 1979).

153. Ralph Baker, *The National Bituminous Coal Commission* (Baltimore: Johns Hopkins Press, 1941).

154. 298 U.S. 238 (1936), *overruled in effect* on delegation issue in *Sunshine Coal Co. v. Adkins,* 310 U.S. 381 (1940), and on commerce issue in *United States v. Darby,* 312 U.S. 100, 118 (1941). See Robert H. Jackson, *The Struggle for Judicial Supremacy,* 153-165 (New York: Alfred A. Knopf, 1941).

155. 298 U.S. at 325-327.

156. House Doc. 142, 75th Cong., 1st Sess. (1937). See Marian C. McKenna, *Franklin Roosevelt and the Great Constitutional War: the Court-Packing Crisis of 1937* (New York: Fordham Univ. Press, 2002); Maxwell H. Bloomfield, *Peaceful Revolution: Constitutional Change and American Culture from Progressivism to the New Deal* (Cambridge: Harvard Univ. Press, 2000); William E. Leuchtenburg, *The Supreme Court Reborn,* 132-162 (New York, Oxford Univ. Press, 1995).

157. Justice Van Devanter retired in June 1937 and Justice Sutherland retired in January 1938. Justice Butler was too ill to hear cases in the 1939 term and died in November, 1939. Justice McReynolds retired in February 1941. See Barry Cushman, *Rethinking the New Deal Court,* 208 (New York: Oxford Univ. Press, 1998); G. Edward White, *The Constitution and the New Deal,* 295-298 (Cambridge: Harvard Univ. Press, 2000).

158. 301 U.S. 1 (1937). See Irons, *New Deal Lawyers, supra* note 147, at 281-288. Richard C. Cortner, *The Jones & Laughlin Case* (New York: Knopf, 1970).

159. 49 Stat. 449 (1935), 29 U.S.C.A. §§ 151-169 (1998). See Irons, *New Deal Lawyers, supra* note 147, at 226-253; Richard C. Cortner, *The Wagner Act Cases,* 72-88 (Knoxville: Univ. of Tennessee Press, 1964); Edward S. Corwin, *Court Over Constitution,* 123-128 (Princeton: Princeton Univ. Press, 1938).

160. See Posner, *Economic Analysis, supra* note 121, at 302-5.

161. 301 U.S. at 41-42.

162. *Santa Cruz Fruit Packing Co. v. N.L.R.B.,* 303 U.S. 453 (1938) (NLRA applicable to processors of agricultural products grown in a single state but shipped in interstate commerce); *N.L.R.B. v. Fainblatt,* 306 U.S. 601 (1939) (NLRA applicable to New Jersey manufacturer whose input materials and products were delivered and picked up by a New York marketer).

163. 312 U.S. 100 (1941). See Alpheus T. Mason, *Harlan Fiske Stone: Pillar of Law,* 551-555 (New York: Viking Press, 1956). As to the usual irrelevance of legislative motive of Congress when exercising its delegated powers under Article 1, Section 8, see Laurence H. Tribe, 1 *American Constitutional Law,* 802-804 (New York: Foundation Press, 3d ed. 2000).

164. 52 Stat. 1060 (1938), 29 U.S.C.A., §§ 201-219 (1998).

165. See David Card and Alan B. Kruger, *Myth and Measurement: The New Economics of the Minimum Wage* (Princeton: Princeton Univ. Press, 1995); James B. Rebitzer. *The Consequences of Minimum Wage Laws: Some New Theoretical Ideas* (Cambridge, MA: National Bureau of Economic Research, 1991).

166. 312 U.S. at 114-117, 123.

167. 312 U.S. at 121.

168. *Id.* at 124. On the Tenth Amendment, See Edward S. Corwin, *The Commerce Power versus States Rights,* 115-172 (Princeton: Princeton Univ. Press, 1936).

169. *Kirschbaum v. Walling,* 316 U.S. 517 (1942) (FLSA applicable to local building employees where building tenanted by firms in interstate commerce); *Martino v. Michigan Window Cleaning Co.,* 327 U.S. 173 (1946) (FLSA applicable to watch-

men and window cleaners employed by local independent contractor to work in factories producing for commerce); *Warren-Bradshaw Drilling Co. v. Hall,* 317 U.S. 88 (1942) (FLSA Applicable to employees of firm that drilled oil wells in only one state); *Mabee v. White Plains Publishing Co.,* 327 U.S. 178 (1946) (FLSA applicable to employees of newspaper that shipped only fifty-five copies to other states).

170. D. Gale Johnson, *Farm Commodity Programs,* 31 (Washington, D.C.: American Enterprise Institute, 1973). See French, *Fruit and Vegetable Marketing Orders,* 64 Am. J. Agr. Econ. 916 (1982).

171. *307* U.S. 533 (1939) (regulations of sales by dairy farmers to local dealers who later resold in interstate commerce). See *United States v. Wrightwood Dairy Co.,* 315 U.S. 110 (1942).

172. *317* U.S. 111 (1942). See Cushman, *Rethinking the New Deal Court, supra* note 164, at 212-224; Jim Chen, "The Story of Wickard v. Filburn: Agriculture, Aggregation, and Congressional Power over Commerce," in Michael C. Dorf, *Constitutional Law Stories,* 69-118 (New York: Foundation Press, 2004).

173. *317* U.S at 125. See United States v. Haley Jr., 358 U.S. 644 (1959) (forty acres of wheat, withdrawn from 60 million acres in national market, was not too small for federal regulation).

174. 322 U.S. 533 (1944) *overruling Paul v. Virginia,* 75 U.S. (8 Wall.) 168, 183 (1869). See *supra* notes 114 and 115 and accompanying text.

175. 322 U.S. at 539.

176. *Id.* at 551-52.

177. 334 U.S. 219 (1948).

178. *Id.* at 232.

179. *United States v. Women's Sportswear Manufacturers Ass'n,* 336 U.S. 460 (1949).

180. *Id.* 464.

181. *78 Stat.* 241, 243 (1964), 42 U.S.C.A. § 2000a (2003).

182. 379 U.S. 241 (1964).

183. Id. at 258.

184. 379 U.S. 294 (1964).

185. *E.E.O.C. v. Wyoming,* 460 U.S. 226, 248 (1983).

186. 22 U.S. (9 Wheat.) 1, 196-197 (1824).

187. 460 U.S. at 248-249.

188. As Justice Stone explained in *Southern Pacific Co. v. Arizona,* 325 U.S. 761, 769 (1945): "For a hundred years it has been accepted constitutional doctrine that the commerce clause, without the aid of Congressional legislation, thus affords some protection from state legislation inimical to the national commerce, and that in such cases, where Congress has not acted, this Court, and not the state legislature, is under the commerce clause the final arbiter of the competing demands of state and national interests." See Martin H. Redish, The Constitution as Political Structure, Ch. 3 (New York: Oxford Univ. Press, 1995): Norman R. Williams, *Why Congress may not "overrule" the Dormant Commerce Clause,* 53 UCLA L. Rev. 1 (2005).

189. 514 U.S. 549 (1995). See Michael Conant, *Constitutional Structure and Purposes: Critical Commentary,* 111-126 (Westport, CT: Greenwood Press, 2001); Steven G. Calabresi, *A Government of Limited and Enumerated Powers: In Defense of United States v. Lopez,* 94 Mich. L. Rev. 752 (1995).

190. 514 U.S. at 551. *See United States v. Morrison.* 529 U.S. 598 (2000) (invalidation of the noncommercial federal Violence Against Women Act); David L. Shapiro, *Federalism: A Dialogue* 141 (1995); Deborah Jones Merritt, *The Fuzzy Logic of Federalism,* 46 Case W. Res. L. Rev. 685, 693 (1996).

5

Commerce Clause:
Federalism and the Regulation
of State Transactions

The extent to which the national commerce power is to apply to transactions of states and their municipalities raises particular issues of federalism and intergovernmental immunities. The plenary power in Congress to regulate commerce among the several states was adopted in a historical context of regulating transactions between private persons or firms or any of them.[1] A corollary is that the structure of federalism creates a presumption against national regulation of transactions of the states and their agencies. But the presumption should be rebuttable when states act like proprietors. It will be shown that state proprietary transactions are so like private transactions that nondiscriminatory regulation of these transactions in order to remedy market failures fits logically and functionally into efficient national markets. In contrast, state purchase of goods and services to be used in executing internal governmental functions do not require national regulation and may lose efficiency as a result of such regulation.

Since the monopoly power of the national government to tax and to regulate markets far exceeds the power in any state, there is a great potential for national law to supersede state law entirely. Nationally organized business associations, farmers' groups, and trade unions, may find it more feasible and less costly to "buy" legislation from the Congress than from fifty state legislatures in their efforts to gain or maintain monopoly profits.[2] The issue here is the extent of state immunities when such statutes are extended to control state transactions. The extreme case would be a federal statute regulating the wages that states may pay their governors, cabinet members, legislators, and judges.

This chapter centers on the national commerce power and possible state immunities as illustrated by *Garcia v. San Antonio Metro. Transit Auth.*,[3] which overruled *National League of Cities v. Usery*.[4] Both of these cases concerned wage transactions between state agencies and their employees.

115

State transactions like those treated here must be distinguished from state regulation of private commerce. Conflicting national and state regulation of private commerce raises issues under the Supremacy Clause.[5] Such issues were recently illustrated in *Federal Energy Regulatory COM's v. Mississippi*.[6] There the Court held that the national government may set mandatory regulatory standards for electric utilities and, if states choose to regulate such utilities, their regulations must follow the national standards.[7] The issue was one of national preemption. It was not like national regulation of state transactions in the market, which raises issues of the structure of federalism but not the particular federalism issue raised in preemption.

Structural issues, such as federalism and separated powers, are not treated explicitly in the Constitution. When such issues are litigated, the Supreme Court often tries to reframe them as issues of individual rights governed by express constitutional limitations.[8] The federal structure of the U.S. Constitution with enumerated national powers and residual powers in the states is emphasized by the truism that is the Tenth Amendment.[9] It is not useful to label this as state sovereignty acting as a restraint on federal power.[10] There is merely a division of powers between two coordinate governments. The presumption arising from federalism is that the national and state governments are distinct entities and each will administer its own governmental offices. If, for example, Congress enacted a statute requiring all potential state and municipal employees to take and pass U.S. civil service examinations as a precondition to state employment, most commentators would label it unconstitutional.

There has not been much litigation over congressional invasion of the internal administration of state governments because Congress, being composed of representatives of the states, has generally refrained from such incurrences.[11] Chief Justice Samuel Chase noted that "the Constitution, in all its provisions, looks to an indestructible union, composed of indestructible states."[12] As Madison had observed, "The federal and State governments are in fact but different agents and trustees of the people, constituted with different powers, and designed for different purposes."[13]

The one pertinent example of federal invasion of state internal administration was *Coyle v. Smith*.[14] The national statute admitting Oklahoma as a state had an express condition that the capital remain fixed for a stated period and that no state funds be appropriated for building a capital. The statute was held unconstitutional on the ground that it invalidated "essentially and peculiarly state powers."[15] The structure of state government, so long as it meets the requirement of a republican form of government, is peculiarly a state issue.[16] Thus, the size of state legislative bodies, and the number and terms of office of state executives, are presumed to be independent of congressional control. The further issue, raised in *Garcia* and *National League of Cities*, is whether internal employment policies of the states are subject to federal control.

A key issue, contested in *Garcia*, was whether the judiciary has a part in enforcing federalism by declaring federal statutes that invade the residual powers of the states to be unconstitutional. As noted, historically, the answer to this issue of judicial review is affirmative.[17] It was a key basis of persuading the public to support ratification.[18] In Chapter 2, it was argued that the final determination of the scope and breadth of the enumerated powers in Article I was vested in Congress. Here the limit of that power is tested. When congressional acts under the tax or commerce power are asserted directly against the states as governments, the issue is one of federalism subject to judicial review. The scope of the commerce power when applied to transactions of private persons and firms should be determined finally by Congress. But attempts of Congress to extend the commerce power to state transactions puts in contest issues of the federal structure of government, ultimately a judicial issue.

National regulation of state transactions presents a potential conflict between an enumerated power of Article I and the residual power of the states under federalism to administer their own governments. The fact that one constitutional clause is stated expressly and the other is implicit in constitutional structure, the very nature of federalism, should not determine any given case.[19] The Supreme Court must resolve the potential conflict by setting the borderlines between the two. Since the Commerce Clause was adopted in the context of regulating private transactions, one might expect the commerce power to be extended only to state transactions that were like private ones, proprietary transactions. On the other hand, state transactions for the administration of government should be immune from national regulation to enforce the principle of federalism. This distinction is the basis of the following critical analysis.

State Proprietary Transactions

The distinction between governmental and proprietary transactions has been controversial.[20] When the function of a state agency centers on commercial or proprietary transactions, both this function and the input transactions of the agency, such as employment relations, are subject to national regulation. While the Supreme Court prefers to use the negative classification of those activities that are not traditional governmental functions, it seems that the one clear class is proprietary functions. An activity is proprietary when the function centers on buying or selling goods or services. While the state agencies often operate at a loss so that the purchasers receive a partial subsidy, the goods or services do not fall in the economic class "public goods." They can be supplied by private firms, and each consumer can purchase the amount of service he desires without conferring benefits on others.

The leading precedent on national regulation of state proprietary services was *United States v. California*.[21] A railroad operated by California in commerce among the several states was held subject to national safety statutes. Although the activity was clearly proprietary, Justice Harlan Stone wrote, "[W]e think it unimportant to say whether the state conducts its railroad in its `sovereign' or in its `private' capacity."[22] Instead, he emphasized that the plenary power in Congress to regulate commerce applied to all the activities of an intrastate carrier operating in interstate commerce, even if owned by a state.

Proprietary activities of states were held subject to national taxation in *New York v. United States*.[23] There a non-discriminatory federal tax on sellers of bottled mineral waters was applied to New York and its immunity was denied. Justice Felix Frankfurter, for the Court, held that denial of state immunity because the activities were proprietary was too narrow a characterization. He held that states were subject to all non-discriminatory federal taxes except those that would tax states as states.[24] He exempted functions that were uniquely governmental like the statehouse and the states' tax income. In *Garcia*, Justice Blackmun writes that the *New York* case abandoned the distinction between governmental and proprietary functions.[25] This seems to overstate the case. Frankfurter cited state proprietary cases as one class of those subject to non-discriminatory federal taxes.[26]

The leading recent case concerning state proprietary transactions is *United Tramps. Union v. Long Island R. Co.*[27] The railroad, primarily a commuter carrier that also carried freight from Long Island to New York, was owned by an agency of New York. The Supreme Court held that the railroad was subject to the federal Railway Labor Act that permitted collective bargaining as opposed to New York law that prohibited strikes by public employees.[28] The railroad, founded in 1834 and acquired by the Metropolitan Transportation Authority in 1966, was subsidized by the state but operated as a separate and distinct public corporation.[29] The state had maintained that, under *National League of Cities*, the national regulation impaired the ability of the State to carry out a constitutionally preserved sovereign function in violation of the Tenth Amendment. A unanimous Supreme Court held that operation of railroads in interstate commerce was not a traditional governmental function.[30] National regulation of a state-owned railroad would in no way hamper the state government's ability to fulfill its role in the Union nor endanger its "separate and independent existence."[31] National regulation of railway labor relations had been in effect since 1888. A uniform regulatory scheme was held necessary to the operation of the national rail system.

As background to *Garcia*, it is notable that three Courts of Appeal have treated public transit as a proprietary function.[32] Relying on the *Long Island* opinion, the courts held local transit authorities were subject to national regulation under the Fair Labor Standards Act. In *Kramer v. New Castle Area Transit Authority*,[33] the Court emphasized the finding that local mass transit was not a traditional governmental function. Rather, they have historically been owned and operated by private companies. The recent socialization of most local transit was held not to alter "historical reality." In *Ale wine v. City Council of Augusta, Ga.*,[34] the Court cited this reasoning in the *Kramer* case.[35] It noted that both the commuter railroad in the *Long Island* case and local buses in Augusta carried commuters for payment. Selling transport service was held not a traditional governmental function. In *Dove v. Chattanooga Area Regional Transportation Authority,*[36] the Court also cited and followed *Kramer.*[37] Quoting the *Long Island* case, the Court noted "there is no justification for a rule which would allow the States, by acquiring functions previously performed by the private sector, to erode federal authority in areas traditionally subject to federal statutory regulations."[38]

The concept of proprietary functions was elaborated in two recent cases concerning the Commerce Clause.[39] In essence, the Supreme Court held that state proprietary activities could not be challenged under the Commerce Clause as a burden on commerce among the several states. This view is of course consistent with the view that proprietary activities are subject to national regulation and can be curbed or totally banned by Congress.

Hughes v. Alexandria Scrap Corp.[40] is the modern authority that state proprietary activity may not be challenged as a burden on interstate commerce. The main problem with the case is that the state action in question was in fact not proprietary. A Maryland state subsidy for delivering abandoned automobiles to a licensed processor discriminated against out-of-state processors.[41] Justice Powell, missing a key distinction of economics,[42] treated the subsidy as a state purchase.[43] Having erroneously held Maryland the equivalent to a private participant in the market, the Court held that Maryland as "purchaser" could have offered the subsidies only to domestic processors.[44] The derelict autos were found to have remained in the state, not because of trade barriers, but in response to market forces. "Nothing in the purposes animating the Commerce Clause prohibits a State, in the absence of congressional action, from participating in the market and exercising the right to favor its own citizens over others."[45]

While the facts of the *Alexandria Scrap* case did not concern proprietary state action, the principle announced was clearly correct. This is illustrated by *Reeves v. Stake.*[46] South Dakota had engaged in the proprietary activity of operating a cement plant for over fifty years. The plant had been built to assure users in South Dakota of a supply of cement in times of shortages. In 1978, a time of construction boom, the state cement commission reaffirmed its policy of supplying all local customers first. Reeves, a Wyoming customer of the plant, was informed that the South Dakota state cement plant could not continue to fill Reeves' orders, and Reeves sued for an injunction which the district court granted. After two appeals,[47] the Supreme Court upheld the South Dakota policies on the basis of *Alexandria Scrap.*[48] The state as market participant could not be found to burden commerce in violation of the Commerce Clause. As Professor Tribe had noted,[49] the dormant Commerce Clause was a limitation only on the regulatory and taxing actions taken by states in their sovereign capacity. The court noted, however, that state proprietary activities may be, and often are, subjected to the same national regulation that is imposed on private market participants.[50] The South Dakota plant, together with all other cement plants in the United States, could be subjected to a Congressional allocation statute. Absent such statute, each producer was free to choose its own customers.

State Governmental Transactions

In terms of economic efficiency, the services of states and municipalities can best adjust to market conditions through local control. Given different levels of economic development in different areas and some immobility of labor, both per capita income and market wage levels may vary from state to state.[51] States with lower incomes as a source of taxation may also have lower wages for unskilled and semi-skilled labor.[52] Nevertheless, powerful national unions have been able to convince a majority of both houses of Congress to extend the Fair Labor Standards Act to all government employees.[53]

The minimum-wage requirements of the law have particular application to unskilled or part-time workers, such as high school students, but they have not been the major source of litigation. Instead, the main challenge to national regulation have been in overtime requirements, as applied to workers with wages far above the minimum, including policemen, firemen, bus drivers, and others with necessarily extended work-time patterns.

Governmental transactions are concerned with the supply of public goods, those which it is not economically feasible for a citizen to provide for himself because of economies of scale and the "free rider problem."[54] The latter problem concerns uncompensated benefits conferred on others. If one citizen, in fear of criminals, hired private police to protect a sector of the city where he lived, other citizens would benefit though they would not pay.

In most cases, such public goods can be feasibly provided only by government, the one agency able to finance them by compulsory taxation. Public goods are goods the consumption of which is no rival. In contrast to private goods, where the consumption is rival, consumption of public goods by one person does not reduce the benefits received by others. The same benefits are available to all without mutual interference.[55] Taxpayers, for example, vote collectively to purchase primary education for all children in the community. There is private gain to the children and their parents. But taxpayers are also purchasing the externalities, the benefits to the general public from a literate society. The public good is a citizenry that is able to read instructions necessary to hold semi-skilled jobs and a citizenry able to read sufficiently to understand the issues of a democratic society and vote intelligently. No taxpayer could buy these public benefits by himself, and the public benefits are shared by all so that it would be inefficient to try to exclude anyone from the benefits even if this were feasible.

Maryland v. Wirtz[56] was the first case to test the extension of the Fair Labor Standards Act to state and municipal employees. The 1966 amendment applied to state hospitals, institutions, and schools.[57] In upholding the statute, Justice Harlan discussed the great breadth of the Commerce Clause without recognizing that it was adopted in the context of private transactions, not state transactions. He then asserted that "it is clear that the Federal Government, when acting within a delegated power, may override countervailing state interests whether these be described as 'governmental' or 'proprietary' in character."[58] Relying on the proprietary case of *United States v. California*,[59] Harlan stated that the Court "will not carve up the commerce power to protect enterprises indistinguishable in their effect on commerce from private business, simply because those enterprises happen to be run by the States for the benefit of their citizens."[60] Justices Douglas and Stewart dissented. Douglas asserted that "what is done here is . . . such a serious invasion of state sovereignty protected by the Tenth Amendment that is it in my view not consistent with our constitutional federalism."[61] He agreed with the dissenting judge in the district court that Congress was forcing the state either to increase taxes or curtail services. Recognizing that the Court must draw the line between the commerce power and the residual powers of the states, he concluded, "In this case the State as a sovereign power is being seriously tampered with, potentially crippled."[62]

National League of Cities v. Usery[63] overruled *Wirt* and for the first time held that the state as employer was in some activities immune from national commerce regulation. The 5 to 4 decision of the Supreme Court has received voluminous comment.[64] In the 1974 amendments to the Fair Labor Standards Act,[65] Congress extended the wages and hours provisions to all employees of states and agencies created by states except for executive, administrative, and professional personnel. Actions by a number of states and municipalities challenged the application of the amendments to "traditional" governmental functions such as fire protection, police protection, sanitation, public health, and parks and recreation. The Court invalidated the application of the amendments to traditional governmental functions. Justice William Rehnquist's opinion for the majority indicated that the decision did not rest on the scope of the Commerce Clause, but on the character of federalism.[66] While Congress clearly had a plenary power under the Commerce Clause to regulate local wages and hours of employment in private endeavor that affected other states, regulating those of state governmental employees raised issues of intergovernmental immunity.

Justice Rehnquist held that when the output functions of the state employees were traditional governmental ones, the input function of determining wages was an "undoubted attribute of state sovereignty."[67] He reviewed a number of examples where increased labor cost would materially affect governmental policies. The national policies "may substantially restructure traditional ways in which the local governments have arranged their affairs."[68] The conclusion was that the wages and hours provisions would "impermissibly interfere with the integral governmental functions"[69] of the states and their subdivisions. They would "significantly alter or displace the States' abilities to structure employer-employee relationships in such areas as fire prevention, police protection, sanitation, public health, and parks and recreation."[70] These were typical examples of public goods.

Although *National League of Cities* is obviously based on the structure of constitutional federalism, the opinion is not articulate on this primary issue. The opinion does note the states' contention that their residual powers are an affirmative limitation on delegated national powers, but there is not a full explanation of intergovernmental immunities.[71] Instead, Rehnquist introduced the issue in terms of the Tenth Amendment as an express declaration of "the constitutional policy that the Congress may not exercise power in a fashion that impairs the States' integrity or their ability to function effectively in a federal system."[72] This whole approach seems wrong or at least unnecessary since the entire federal structure was in the original Constitution.[73] The dissenting justices in *National League of Cities* correctly quoted Justice Stone's statement to discredit the argument that the Tenth Amendment created distinct policy.[74] But this did not meet the underlying issue of the scope of implied intergovernmental immunities in the federal system.

Rehnquist cited dicta from two earlier decisions that had upheld national regulation of state transactions. In *Wirtz*, the Court had noted that it had "ample power to prevent . . . the utter destruction of the State as a sovereign political entity."[75] In *Fry v. United States*,[76] the Court recognized that federalism is expressly declared in the Tenth Amendment. "The Amendment expressly declares the constitutional policy that Congress may not exercise power in a fashion that impairs the States' integrity or their ability to function effectively in a federal system."[77]

Rehnquist's use of the ambiguous term "traditional" may have misled him.[78] Time is not the correct descriptive term. Some proprietary functions, such as subways in New York, have a tradition of government operation. It is submitted that the true issue for the purposes of federalism is whether the function is necessarily governmental, whether it is a public good. In overruling *Wirtz*, the Court recognized that the public hospitals, institutions, and schools of that case were different from the fire and police departments affected by *National League of Cities*.[79] Nevertheless, both classes were non-proprietary governmental services, essential to the public as a whole. The free hospitals and institutions for the destitute or insane, in the *Wirtz* example, not only benefit those unable to purchase these services in the market. The external benefits are to all other citizens, who are protected, *inter alia*, from contagious diseases and injury or theft by insane persons.

Although the legal criteria for state immunity set by *National League of Cities* were not precise, it seems clear that its application only to "states as states" meant the internal government of states and not state regulation subject to the Supremacy Clause. Nonetheless, later court decisions demonstrated confusion on this primary distinction.

Hodel v. Virginia Surface Mining & Reclamation Ass'n[80] arose under a federal statute designed to guarantee that surface mining will be completed with least possible disturbance to the earth's surface.[81] While the states were allowed to submit reclamation plans for approval by the secretary of interior, the secretary was directed to prepare a federal program for those states failing to submit programs.[82] The lower courts[83] failed to recognize that the federal statute was a regulation of private behavior, and erroneously relying on *National League of Cities*, held key sections of the statute to violate the Tenth Amendment.

In the *Virginia Surface Mining* case, a unanimous Supreme Court reversed the district courts' holding of sections of SMCRA unconstitutional. Justice Marshall should have distinguished *National League of Cities* as inapplicable to statutes regulating private industry. Instead, he attempted to clarify the vague tests of *National League of Cities* by extracting from the opinion a three-step test for determining whether a federal statute enacted pursuant to the commerce clause violates the constitutional structure of federalism.[84]

Regulation of "States as States" seems to indicate regulation of state governmental institutions as distinguished from national regulation of individuals and corporations. But in the *Virginia Surface Mining* case, the congressional objective was to regulate private mining companies. "Indisputable attributes of state sovereignty" seems to concern policy making for or administration of internal functions of operating a state government. Power to locate the state capitol and to set wages for those employed to carry out governmental functions are the two examples cited.[85] "Directly impair the States' ability to structure integral operations in areas of traditional functions" is more complex. The Court speaks of it as Congressional displacement of state decisions that "may substantially restructure traditional ways in which the local governments have arranged their affairs."[86] The effects on state managerial decisions must be more than material. They must significantly change state operating procedures.

The final statements by the Court on the preemptive power of Congress under the Supremacy Clause should have impressed upon all lower courts and critics that *National League of Cities* did not apply to state regulation of private economic activity.[87]

Federal Energy Regulatory Commission v. Mississippi[88] (FERC) reiterated the ruling of the *Virginia Surface Mining* case. Here the Court was faced with issues of federal conditional preemption of state regulation of private economic activity. The Court upheld the constitutionality of the federal Public Utility Regulatory Policies Act of 1978 (PURPA).[89] The Act concerns regulatory policies for gas and electrical utilities. It requires state public utility commissions to "consider" the adoption and implementation of specific "rate design" and regulatory standards.[90] It prescribed procedures for considering proposed standards. Another section of PURPA encouraged cogeneration by requiring the FERC to promulgate rules in consultation with state agencies.[91]

The district court held that PURPA (1) exceeded the power of Congress under the commerce clause and (2) under *National League of Cities*, violated federalism by trenching on state sovereignty.[92] The Supreme Court unanimously reversed the trial court on the Commerce Clause issue but reversed the lower court on the federalism issue by a vote of 5 to 4. As to the latter, Justice Blackmun, for the Court, noted that "the commerce power permits Congress to preempt the States entirely in the regulation of private utilities."[93] PURPA gave the states a choice of adopting federal standards or abandoning regulation of the field altogether even though Congress had not yet adopted alternative regulation. The Court noted this was only one step beyond *Virginia Surface Mining*. Since PURPA did not regulate the "states as states" but was concerned with utility regulation, it was constitutionally determinative that PURPA did not impair the states' abilities "to structure integral operations in areas of traditional functions."[94]

The surprising aspect of the federalism part of FERC is the four dissents. Justice O'Connor in the principal dissent was primarily concerned that the federal scheme required the states to use their regulatory machinery in a fashion dictated by the national government. But she fails to see that the key explanatory point of *Virginia Surface Mining* that *National League of Cities* applies only to state transactions and not to state regulation of private economic activity.[95] She erroneously viewed PURPA as analogous to the statutory provisions in *National League of Cities*. The conditional preemption of regulation in FERC was based on the Supremacy Clause while *National League of Cities* concerned intergovernmental immunity.

One recent case approved national regulation of state transactions with an employee performing a police function and seems inconsistent with *National League of Cities*. In *Equal Employment Opportunity Commission v. Wyoming*,[96] the issue of age discrimination was treated under the Commerce Clause rather than the Fourteenth Amendment.[97] The Age Discrimination in Employment Act of 1967,[98] prohibiting discrimination on the basis of age for employees between the ages of forty and seventy, was extended in 1974 to include employees of state and local governments.[99] A supervisor for the Wyoming Game and Fish Department was involuntarily retired at age fifty-five. The supervisor filed the complaint with the EEOC which ultimately brought an action against the state. The district court dismissed the suit on the basis of the rule in *National League of Cities*.[100] The Supreme Court reversed in a 5 to 4 decision.

In applying the tests derived from the *National League of Cities*, the final one was found wanting. The first requirement, that the national statute regulate "states as states," was plainly met.[101] The second, that the national statute address an undoubted attribute of state sovereignty, was not clear. But, even assuming the second test to be met, the third was not. The Age Discrimination in Employment Act was held not to "directly impair" the State's ability to "structure integral operations in areas of traditional governmental functions."[102]

The Court concluded that the degree of federal intrusion in the *Wyoming* case was "sufficiently less serious than it was in National League of Cities so as to make unnecessary . . . to override Congress's express choice to extend its regulatory authority to the States."[103]

The small impact of the Age Discrimination Act on *Wyoming* was shown by the fact that the state could continue its mandatory retirement age if the state could demonstrate that age was a bona fide occupational qualification for a job as game warden.[104] Furthermore, unlike *National League of Cities*, in *Wyoming* there is no potential impact of the mandate of the Age Discrimination Act on the "State's ability to structure operations and set priorities over a wide range of decisions."[105] The large potential financial impact of national regulation in the former case was absent in the *Wyoming* case. The final distinction was that in *Wyoming*, there was no impairment of the state's ability to use its employment relationship with its citizens as a tool for pursuing social and economic policies beyond their immediate managerial goals.[106]

Having found application of the Age Discrimination Act to state employees to be a valid exercise of Congress's powers under the Commerce Clause, the Court held that it need not decide whether the statute could be upheld as an exercise of Congress's powers under Section 5 of the Fourteenth Amendment.[107] Critics of the opinion may find this to be an evasion of an essential issue.

The Age Discrimination Act had material impact on those able to avoid compulsory retirement and on those not promoted because of the lack of openings due to retirements. The problem is whether constitutional issues of federalism should turn on the relative size of admittedly material impacts of statutes. If the majority opinion as based on the Commerce Clause is basically unsound, then it is crucial whether the statute can be based on Section 5 of the Fourteenth Amendment. Since the statute is an amendment to the Civil Rights Act[108] and is concerned with equality of treatment for the aged, its primary purpose would seem to be to enforce the Equal Protection Clause. Any functional analysis would treat the statute as one enforcing equal protection.[109]

Chief Justice Warren Burger, for the four dissenters, also analyzed the case in terms of the three tests of *National League of Cities* as delineated in the *Virginia Surface Mining* case. As to the first, he concurred with the majority opinion that it was indisputable that the legislation was aimed at regulating states in their capacity as states.[110] As to the second, he found that the Age Discrimination Act addressed matters that were "attributes of state sovereignty."[111] Mandatory retirement laws to assure physical preparedness for game wardens were viewed as an attribute of sovereignty because parks and recreation services were identified in *National League of Cities* as traditional state activities. As to the third test, the Chief Justice disagreed completely with the majority. He felt that the federal intrusion would materially impair the ability of the state to structure integral operations. He emphasized the evidence that potentially employment costs and disability costs would increase materially.[112] He also concluded there would be non-economic hardships if the state could not hire those physically best able to do the job and had to impede promotion opportunities as upper-level, supervisory personnel refused to retire.

The majority and dissenters both adopted without question the three-step approach to *National League of Cities* that was outlined in *Hodel v. Virginia Surface Min. and Rec. Ass'n.*[113] Since the latter case was one of preemptive regulation, its statements on *National League of Cities* were dictum. One would have expected the dissenters to reject the idea that general principles of federalism can turn on detailed factual issues of financial impact of a federal regulation. The state employee in the *Wyoming* case was performing a police function, an admitted governmental regulatory activity. The dissent could have easily rested on this key distinction. If one adopts this analysis, the majority opinion in the *Wyoming* case is inconsistent with *National League of Cities.*

Lower Court Confusion

The lower federal courts also showed great uncertainty in applying *National League of Cities*. Many opinions centered on the word magic of "traditional governmental function" rather than on the impact on federalism. Justice Harry Blackmun in *Garcia* cited five cases that granted state immunity under this concept.[114] It is clear that these courts did not understand the primary distinction between state transactions and state regulation of private business. Two of them concerned municipal grants of monopoly to private firms and the possible exemption from antitrust preemption under the Supremacy Clause.[115] One concerned conflicting federal and state judicial powers and no federal regulation of states was involved.[116] Two cases granted immunity from the Fair Labor Standards Act for employment activities found to be integral government functions.[117]

Justice Blackmun in *Garcia* cited eight cases denying state immunity under *National League of Cities.*[118] Three of these cases concerned conflicts between national and state regulation and should have been governed by the supremacy clause.[119] Issues of federalism were not present. Three other cases concerned state transactions that were not uniquely governmental.[120] Two other cases concerned application of the Fair Labor Standards Act to state welfare workers.[121] Such activity was held not to be a traditional or integral function of a state, and immunity was denied.

Some of the lower-court decisions can be reconciled if one applies the primary distinction between state regulation and state transactions. The air transport cases exemplify the issue. In *Hughes Air Corp v. Public Utilities Com'n,*[122] state regulation of air transport was preempted by federal regulation. This was a simple application of the Supremacy Clause and *National League of Cities*, cited in denying immunity, should have not been mentioned. In contrast, *Meshach v. City of Cleveland*[123] concerned employment transactions, application of the Fair Labor Standards Act to employees of a municipal airport. Here the issue of federalism was correctly posed. While some critics disagree, it is within reason to find this function uniquely governmental and grant state immunity.

The San Antonio Cases

The San Antonio cases, litigated in *Garcia v. San Antonio Metro Transit Auth.*[124] concerned mandatory overtime pay under the Fair Labor Standards Act (FLSA) amendments of 1974 [125] as applied to local transit. The economic issue is the necessity of overtime in industries with two demand peak loads that do not occur in one eight hour period.[126] Because of the power of their labor unions, workers cannot be employed on a split shift where some (with less seniority) are off the payroll for four hours in midday. Given this constraint, the most efficient payroll employs some drivers more than eight hours on certain days with compensatory time off on other days.[127] The FLSA amendments required overtime pay at time and a half rates paid in cash. The budget effects on local transit, operating at a loss and surviving on taxpayer subsidies, was significant. In fact, the wage levels previously established, far above the minimum wage, had resulted from collective bargaining that took account of the often extended work day. High standard wages with compensatory time off for work beyond the eight-hour day was the bargaining result in most cities. This equilibrium compensation was upset by the imposition of mandatory overtime pay by the FLSA.[128] Established union contracts and great union power made it impossible ever to lower basic wages to offset the new high overtime pay.

Garcia brought to the Supreme Court the issue of overtime pay under FLSA for public mass transit workers. The legal background to this case was the rule of *National League of Cities* that exempted from FLSA only traditional governmental functions. San Antonio had been served from early in the century by privately owned companies. Only in 1959 was the tradition of private ownership replaced by a public authority.[129] Nonetheless, four months after *National League of Cities* was handed down, the San Antonio Transit System notified employees that it was relieved of overtime pay obligations under FLSA.[130]

In 1979, the Wages and Hours Administration of the Department of Labor issued an opinion that appellate, San Antonio Metropolitan Transit Authority's (SAMTA) operations were not constitutionally immune from FLSA under *National League of Cities*.[131] SAMTA then filed this action for declaratory judgment against the secretary of labor. Garcia and other employees also brought suit against SAMTA for overtime pay. The district court ruled twice, once before and once after the *Long Island R. Co.* decision that public mass transit was an immune traditional governmental function.[132]

In reversing the district court in a 5 to 4 decision, the Supreme Court did not take the easy course of holding transactions of local transit districts a proprietary function outside the scope of *National League of Cities* immunity.[133] Rather, the majority overruled *National League of Cities* and held that "traditional governmental functions" were not a workable standard.[134] It noted the apparently conflicting opinions of lower federal courts in trying to apply the standard.[135] It noted cases in the area of state tax immunity and the difficulty of concepts such as "essential," "usual," "traditional," or "strictly" governmental functions.[136] It was in the tax field that the Court came to reject the distinction between governmental and proprietary functions. It found that a no historical standard is also likely to be unworkable, noting the rejection of the concept "uniquely" governmental functions in the field of government tort liability.[137]

Justice Blackmun, for the majority, held that none of the distinctions in governmental functions could be "faithful to the role of federalism in a democratic society."[138] He concluded that utilizing classes such as "traditional," "integral," or "necessary" governmental functions "inevitably invites an unelected federal judiciary to make decisions about which state policies it favors and which it dislikes."[139] He, therefore, rejected as "unsound in principle and unworkable in practice" any such rule of state immunity. The Court did not deny that the federal structure of government imposes limitations on the Commerce Clause as applied to the states. But the conclusion was: "We doubt the courts ultimately can identify principled constitutional limitations over the State merely by relying on *a priori* definitions of state sovereignty."[140]

The Court found protection for that portion of sovereignty remaining in the states to be in their position in the national political process.[141] The local interests of congressmen and the equal representation in the Senate were noted. The effectiveness of the federal political process in protecting the state was illustrated by the large revenue-sharing by the national government with the states.[142] As to the specific application of FLSA to local transit, the Court found nothing destructive of state sovereignty or volatile of any constitutional provision.[143] The Congress provided substantial fiscal aid to local mass transit as it required conformity in minimum wages and overtime pay.

Justice Lewis Powell for the four dissenters, criticized the majority for overruling *National League of Cities*.[144] Justice Blackmun, who had concurred in that case, and other justices in the majority had joined in subsequent decisions that applied the tests of *National League of Cities*. In *Garcia*, they could have reversed the District Court by applying the proprietary classification of *Long Island R. Co.*, but instead they chose to overrule their own reaffirmed of the tests of federalism.

As to the Commerce Clause, Powell, like the majority, failed to recognize that the historical control was the regulation of private transactions, creating a presumption against national regulations of state transactions. As to the borderline between the commerce power and the residual powers of the states, Powell emphasized the necessity of weighing the respective interests of the states and the federal government.[145] Noting that Blackmun had concurred in *National League of Cities* in urging a balancing approach, Powell submitted that such an approach was needed to weigh the state and national powers.

Powell asserted that the majority had failed to explain how the electoral process guarantees the Congress will not impinge the residual powers of the states.[146] The majority noted the ability of the states to obtain grants in aid from the national government. But this is evidence that the states are only one of the interest groups to which Congress must respond. The negative inference could be that national taxing has increased so greatly that the states' taxing power has diminished. The people are able to control state taxing but they are demonstrably unable to stop the growth of national taxing and spending. In any case, this does not show that the political processes are sufficient to enforce constitutional limitations like the Tenth Amendment.

Powell perceived the origins and avowed purposes of the framers in designing a federal system of government. He concluded:

> The Framers believed that the separate sphere of sovereignty reserved to the States would ensure that the States would serve as an effective "counterpoise" to the power of the federal government. The States would serve this essential role because they would attract and retain the loyalty of their citizens. The roots of such loyalty, the Founders thought, were found in the objects peculiar to state government. For example, Hamilton argued that the States "regulate[e] all those personal interests and familiar concerns to which the sensibility of individuals is more immediately awake. . . ." Thus, he maintained that the people would perceive the States as "the immediate and most visible guardian of life and property," a fact which "contributes more than any other circumstance to impressing upon the minds of the people affection, esteem and reverence towards the government."[147]

Powell noted that the subsequent Supreme Court opinions have observed the narrow area of immunity carved out by *National League of Cities*.[148] He noted that case was limited to fire and police protection, sanitation, and public health—activities remote from usual commercial relations.[149] He concluded by pointing out that the facts of *Garcia* concerned only city-owned transit. Overruling *National League of Cities* was not necessary for the decision. The majority, while asserting otherwise, gave the national commerce power over the states a seemingly unlimited scope.

The commentators are in total disagreement on the soundness of *Garcia*. Some support it and draw parallels between *National League of Cities* and the *Lecher* era.[150] This is, in spite of a clear recognition that the rule of *National League of Cities*, applied only to state transactions, not those of private persons and firms. The *Lecher* analogies are combined with an argument that federalism is merely derived from constitutional structure as opposed to explicit constitutional language.[151] It is argued that this approach goes very far in cutting the Justices loose from the constraints of constitutional language. This whole framework of critique is supported by the errors of Justices Powell and O'Connor in pointing as a primary cause "the recent expansion of the commerce powers."[152] This statement is contrary to the theory of interpretation outlined in Chapter 1 of this book. There it was argued that neither the Congress nor the judiciary is vested with the constitutional power to expand any clause. Either legislative power of a given scope and breadth was delegated in the Constitution or the amendments or it does not exist. As noted in Chapter 4, the Congress was delegated in Article I the plenary power to regulate all private commerce in the U.S. The Supreme Court after 1937 restored that power; it could not validly expand it.

Other commentators have been negatively critical of *Garcia* as wrongfully curtailing the federal structure of government.[153] Of the two structural elements implicit in the Constitution separated powers has received strong judicial support but federalism has not.[154] To citizens, this may seem surprising because federalism is the only one that is restated in the Tenth Amendment and, thus, becomes an element of the Bill of Rights. Protecting federalism thus became an express constitutional limitation. Commentators support Justice Powell in citing both statements of leading framers and the historians to support this view of the original understanding.[155] Federalism was one aspect of the checks and balances designed to prevent tyranny. Constitutional amendments since 1789, especially the seventeenth, have not diminished the residual powers of the states even if they have removed some safeguards to protecting those powers.[156]

But the most important issue on which the Court split and the commentators disagree is whether the political processes perform such a safeguard to internal state government that judicial enforcement of federalism is unneeded. The issue is whether state governments, as distinct from the peoples of the states, are represented in the political process so that their internal administration will not be overrun by the Congress.

The Supreme Court has historically developed principles to determine the borderline between the powers of the national government and the states.[157] Furthermore, the assertion that the political safeguards are operative to protect state governments is just untrue. Representatives elected in the states do not represent the states as governments. Chief Justice Marshall noted long ago that the measures adopted in Congress are those of people in the states, not measures of the state governments.[158] Rather, the people are divided into factions or interest groups, asserting pressure on members of Congress to pass legislation favorable to them.[159] The economic theory of governmental regulation suggests that interest groups with money to support elections are the most powerful influence in a legislature.[160] In modern times, political action committees which represent business and labor union interests with large bankrolls have more inferior political power in Congress than do state governments.

The expected financial impact on cities of *Garcia* was so severe that immediate appeal was made to Congress for relief from the duty to pay employees in cash for overtime work. Mayor Koch of New York presented estimates of the *National League of Cities* that the total cost of compliance by all municipalities would exceed $2 billion per year.[161] Since citizens would not vote for such substantial increases, enforcing the overtime provisions of the Fair Labor

Standards Act could lead to significant decreases in services of police, fire, and transit workers. In response, Congress modified the law so that overtime could be paid by compensatory time off at a rate of one and one-half hours for each overtime hour worked.[162] Thus, the impact of *Garcia* could be reduced services but the municipalities would not have to pay overtime in cash.

Notes

1. See Chapter 4. The legal-economic analysis of this chapter is illustrated by a select set of cases concerning business regulation. For a general review of federal legislative powers and the resulting limits of state sovereignty, see Laurence H. Tribe, American Constitutional Law, chs. 3 and 5 (New York: Foundation Press, 3rd ed., 2000).
2. See George Stigler, *The Theory of Economic Regulation*, 2. Bell J. Econ. & Mgmnt. Id. 3 (1971); Sam Peltzman, *Toward a More General Theory of Regulation*, 19 J. L. & Econ. 211 (1976).
3. 469 U.S. 528 (1985).
4. 426 U.S. 833 (1976).
5. U.S. Const., art. VI, cl. 2. See *Edgar v. Mite Corp.*, 457 U.S. 624, 631 (1982), for a summary of standards for application of the Supremacy Clause.
6. 456 U.S. 742 (1982). See *Hodel v. Virginia Surface Min. & Red. Ass'n*, 452 U.S. 264, 290-93 (1981).
7. 456 U.S. at 769-71.
8. Robert Nagel, *Federalism as a Fundamental Value,* 1981 Sup. Ct. Rev. 81, 83-89. See Charles Black, *Structure and Relationship in Constitutional Law* (Louisiana State Univ. Press, 1969).
9. Justice Stone summarized the true meaning of the Tenth Amendment: "The amendment states but a truism that all is retained which has not been surrendered. There is nothing in the history of its adoption to suggest that it was more than declaratory of the relationship between the national and state governments as it had been established by the Constitution before the amendment or that its purpose was other than to allay fears that the new national government might seek to exercise powers not granted, and that the states might not be able to exercise fully their reserved powers" (*United States v. Darby*, 312 U.S. 100, 124 [1941]).
10. Andrzej Rapaczynski, *From Sovereignty to Process*, 1985 Sup. Ct. Rev. 341, 346 59. Compare Lewis Kaden, *Politics, Money and State Sovereignty*, 79 Colum. L. Rev. 847, 849-57 (1979).
11. See Herbert Wechsler, *The Political Safeguards of Federalism*, 54 Colum. L. Rev. 543, 558-60 (1954).
12. *Texas v. White*, 74 U.S. (7 Wall.) 700, 725 (1869).
13. *Federalist* 46, at 321 (E. Bourne ed. 1947).
14. 221 U.S. 559 (1911).
15. *Id.* at 565.
16. See *Baker v. Carr,* 369 U.S. 186 (1962); *Reynolds v. Sims*, 377 U.S. 533 (1964). See U.S. Const., Art. IV, § 4.
17. See Chapter 3.
18. See William Van Alstyne, *The Second Death of Federalism*, 83 Mich. L. Rev. 1709, 1729 (1985); Nagel, *supra* note 8, at 97-109.
19. See Black, *supra* note 8, at 7.
20. See generally, Michael Wells and Walter Hellerstein, *The Governmental-Proprietary Distinction in Constitutional Law,* 66 Va. L. Rev. 1073 (1980).

21. 297 U.S. 175 (1936). See *Parden v. Terminal R. Co.,* 377 U.S. 184 (1964), overruled, College Savings Bank v. Florida Prepaid Post. Edu. Expenses Bd., 527 U.S. 666, 680 (1999).
22. 297 U.S. 183.
23. 326 U.S. 572 (1946).
24. 326 U.S. 582.
25. *Garcia,* 469 U.S. at 542.
26. 326 U.S. 579.
27. 455 U.S. 678 (1982).
28. N.Y. Civ. Serv. Law, Sec. 204-14 (McKinney, 1983).
29. The Metropolitan Transportation Authority was not the alter ego of the Long Island Railroad Co. *Bujosa v. Metropolitan Transportation Auth.,* 355 N.Y.S. id 801 (N.Y. Sup. Ct. App. Div. 1974).
30. 455 U.S. 685. See *California v. Taylor,* 353 U.S. 553 (1957).
31. 455 U.S. 687. See *National League of Cities,* 426 U.S. 851, discussed infra, at note 69.
32. *Kramer v. New Castle Area Transit Authority,* 677 F. 2d 308 (3d Cir. 1982), cert. denied 459 U.S. 1146 (1983); *Alewine v. City Council of Augusta,* 699 F. 2d 1060 (11th Cir. 1983), cert. denied 470 U.S. 1027 (1985); *Dove V. Chattanooga Area Regional Trans. Authority,* 701 F. 2d 50 (6th Cir. 1983). See *Francis v. City of Tallahassee,* 424 So. 2d 61 (Fla. App. 1982).
33. 677 F.2d 308 (3d Cir. 1982), cert. denied 459 U.S. 1146 (1983).
34. 699 F. 2d 1060 (11th Cir. 1983), cert. denied 470 U.S. 1027 (1985).
35. *Id.* at 1067-68.
36. 701 F. 2d. 50 (6th Cir. 1983).
37. *Id.* at 52-53.
38. *Id.* at 53, citing *United Transportation Union v. Long Island Railroad,* 455 U.S. 678, 687 (1982).
39. *Hughes v. Alexandria Scrap Corp.,* 426 U.S. 794 (1976); *Reeves v. Stake,* 447 U.S. 429 (1980).
40. 426 U.S. 794 (1976).
41. MD. Code Ann., Art. 66 1/2, §§ 5-201 to 210 (1970), S § 11-10002 (f)(5) (supp. 1975).
42. A subsidy is a negative tax and is a technique of regulation. See Kenneth Boulding, *Economic Analysis* 155-58 (Harper 1941); Edmond Malinvaud, *Lectures on Microeconomic Theory,* 209-10 (North Holland, 1972).
43. 426 U.S. at 806, 809. Since Alexandria Scrap was not, in fact, a proprietary case, it should have been treated like other state regulatory cases. Whether the Maryland statute burdened commerce among the several states was the prime contested issue of fact. The case should not have been decided on summary judgment. *Alexandria Scrap v. Hughes,* 391 F. Supp. 46, 63 (D. Md., 1975). A trial might have established that the greater documentation required of out-of-state processors was necessary to prevent false subsidy claims by firms outside the jurisdiction of Maryland enforcement officers.
44. 426 U.S. 809.
45. *Id.* at 810. The Supreme Court also held the amended statute not to violate the Equal Protection Clause. *Id.* at 810-14.
46. 447 U.S. 429 (1980).
47. See summary, *Id.* at 433-34.
48. *Id.* at 434-436.

49. *Id.* at 437, citing Laurence Tribe, *American Constitutional Law* 336 (Foundation Press, 1978).

50. 447 U.S. 439. The Court rejected four other arguments against the state. First, the response to the charge of economic protectionism was that this was merely use of local taxation to assure a healthy building industry. Free markets did not require the state to offer the same services in neighboring states. Second, the state cement program was held not to be a hoarding of resources since cement is not a national resource. It can be produced in any state. Third, the South Dakota program did not give its suppliers of ready-mix concrete an unfair advantage in the out-of-state markets. Barring these suppliers from out-of-state markets would e the essence of protectionism. Fourth, the Court rejected the argument that since South Dakota had "replaced" the free market, it should be forced to replicate that market by selling to all buyers. The reason South Dakota had built the plant was because of market failure. Because of great fluctuations in demand, the free market failed to supply adequate cement when demand was highest.

51. In 1986 the per capita personal income in Connecticut was $18,089, and in New York $16,050; while in Mississippi it was $9,187, and in West Virginia $10,193. U.S. Dept. of Commerce, *Survey of Current Business* 24 (August 1986).

52. On the issue of whether minimum-wage laws result mainly in wage raises for lowest-income earners or mainly in unemployment, see J. Hirshleifer, *Price Theory and Applications,* 372-77 (1976).

53. See Jesse Choper, *Judicial Review and the National Political Process,* 182 (Univ. of Chicago Press, 1980).

54. See James Buchanan, *The Demand and Supply of Public Goods* (Rand McNally 1968); Richard Musgrave and Peggy Musgrave, *Public Finance in Theory and Practice,* chaps. 2 and 3 (4th ed., McGraw-Hill, 1984); Mancur Olson; *The Logic of Collective Action* (Harvard Univ. Press, 1965).

55. Musgrave and Musgrave, *supra* note 54, at 48-51.

56. 392 U.S. 183 (1968).

57. 80 Stat. 831, 832 (1966), 29 U.S.C.A. §§ 203d, 203(s)(4)(1998).

58. 392 U.S. 195.

59. 297 U.S. 175 (1936), cited at 392 U.S. 197-99.

60. *Id.* at 198-99.

61. *Id.* at 201.

62. *Id.* at 205.

63. 426 U.S. 833 (1976).

64. For citations and review of the commentaries, see Nagel, *Federalism as a Fundamental Value,* 1981 Supreme Court Rev. 81; Ronald Rotunda, *The Doctrine of Conditional Preemption and other Limitations on Tenth Amendment Restrictions,* 132 U. of Pa. L. Rev. 289, 291-95 (1984).

65. 88 Stat. 55 (1974), 29 U.S.C.A. 203(d), 203 (s)(5), 203x(v)(1998). For estimations that the increased costs or decreased state and local services resulting from the act would have its major impact on low-income citizens, see Frank Michelman, *States' Rights and States' Roles,* 86 Yale L. J. 1165, 1178-79 (1977); Laurence Tribe, *Unraveling National League of Cities,* 90 Harv. L. Rev. 1065, 1076 (1977).

66. 426 U.S. 841.

67. "We have repeatedly recognized that there are attributes to sovereignty attaching to every state government which may not be impaired by Congress, not because Congress may lack an affirmative grant of legislative authority to reach the matter, but because the Constitution prohibits it from exercising the authority in that manner" (*Id.* at 845).

68. *Id.* at 849.
69. *Id.* at 851.
70. *Id.*
71. *Id.* at 841.
72. 416 U.S. at 843, citing *Fry v. United States,* 421 U.S. 542, 547 (1975).
73. See the statement of Justice Stone in *supra* note 9.
74. 426 U.S. at 862.
75. *Wirtz,* 392 U.S. 183 (1968).
76. 421 U.S. 542. (1975).
77. *Id.* at 547.
78. Commentators have criticized the standard, "traditional governmental functions" as unworkable. D. Bruce La Pierre, *Political Safeguards of Federalism Redux,* 60 Wash. U. L. Q. 779, 956-58 (1982); Wells and Hellerstein, *supra* note 20, at 1086-87; Van Alstyne, *supra* note 18, at 1717.
79. 426 U.S. 854.
80. 452 U.S. 264 (1981). See Rotunda, *supra* note 64, at 300-4.
81. Pub. L. No. 95-87, 91 Stat. 445, codified as amended at 30 U.S.C.A. §§ 1201-1328 (1986).
82. *Id.* § 504(a), 30 U.S.C.A. § 1254 (a) (1986).
83. V*irginia Surface Mining and Reclamation Association, Inc. v. Andrus,* 483 F. Supp. 425 (W.D. Va., 1980), reversed 452. U.S. 264 (1981); *Indiana v. Andrus,* 501 F. Supp. 452 (S.D. Ind., 1980), reversed 452. U.S. 314 (1981).
84. 452 U.S. at 287-88: "[I]n order to succeed, a claim that congressional commerce power legislation is invalid under the reasoning of National League of Cities must satisfy each of three requirements. First, there must be a showing that the challenged statute regulates the 'States as States.' Second, the federal regulation must address matters that are indisputably attribute[s] of state sovereignty. And third, it must be apparent that the States' compliance with the federal law would directly impair their ability 'to structure integral operations in areas of traditional functions.'"
85. *National League of Cities v. Usery,* 426 U.S. 833, 845, citing *Coyle v. Oklahoma,* 221 U.S. 559 (1911).
86. *National League of Cities v. Usery,* 426 U.S. 833, 849.
87. 452 U.S. at 290: "[I]t is clear that the Commerce Clause empowers Congress to prohibit all-and not just inconsistent-state regulation of such activity. . . . Although such Congressional enactments obviously curtail or prohibit the States' prerogatives to make legislative choices respecting subjects the States may consider important, the Supremacy Clause permits another result. It is elementary and well settled that there can be no divided authority over interstate commerce, and that the Acts of Congress on that subject are supreme and exclusive.'"
88. 456 U.S. 742 (1982). See Rotunda, *supra* note 64, at 307-18 for a detailed analysis of this case.
89. Pub. L. No. 95-617, 92 Stat. 3117 (1978) (codified as amended in sections of 15, 16, 30, 42. and 43 U.S.C.A.).
90. PURPA, sec. 111, 16 U.S.C.A. 262 § 1 (1985); *Id.* § 113, 16 U.S.C.A. Section 2623 (2000).
91. PURPA, Section 210, 16 U.S.C.A. § 824a-3 (2000).
92. *Federal Energy Regulatory Commission,* 456 U.S. 752. The district court opinion is unreported.
93. 456 U.S. 764.
94. *Id.* at 766.
95. *Id.* at 775-80.

96. 460 U.S. 226 (1983). See Rotunda, *supra* note 64, at 319-2.1.

97. This chapter does not treat in detail the cases holding that statutes enforcing the Thirteenth, Fourteenth, and Fifteenth amendments override state power. There are no state immunities to those key civil rights. The extension of Title VII of the Civil Rights Act of 1964, 78 Stat. 253 (1964) as amended, 42. U.S.C.A. § 2000e et. seq. (2003), to states and their subdivisions, for example, was upheld in a sex-discrimination case as valid enforcement of Section 5 of the Fourteenth Amendment (*Fitzpatrick v. Bitzer,* 427 U.S. 445 [1976]). The Civil War amendments "were specifically designed as an expansion of federal power and an intrusion on state sovereignty" (*City of Rome v. United States,* 446 U.S. 151, 179 [1980]).

98. 81 Stat. 602 (1967), 29 U.S.C.A. §§ 621 et. seq. 630 (b) (1999).

99. 88 Stat. 74 (1974), 29 U.S.C.A. § 630b (1999).

100. *E.E.O.C. v. State of Wyoming,* 514 F. Supp. 595, 598-600 (D. Wyom., 1981).

101. E.E.O.C. 460 U.S. 237.

102. *Id.* at 238-39.

103. *Id.* at 239.

104. Cases on age discrimination subsequent to Wyoming have centered on whether the statutory age limit was a bona fide occupational qualification. See *E.E.O.C. v. County of Allegheny,* 705 F. 2d 679 (3d Cir. 1983); *E.E.O.C. v. County of Los Angeles,* 706 F. 2d 1039 (9th Cir., 1983), cert. denied 464 U.S. 1073 (1984); *E.E.O.C. v. U. of Texas Health Center,* 710 F.2d (1091) (5th Cir. 1983).

105. E.E.O.C. 460 U.S. at 239.

106. *Id.* at 242.

107. *Id.* at 243. The district court, citing *Penhurst State School v. Halderman,* 451 U.S. 1, 16 (1981), had held that application of the Age Discrimination Act to the states could not be justified as an exercise of Congress's power under Section 5 of the Fourteenth Amendment because Congress did not explicitly state that it had invoked that power in passing the 1972, amendments (*E.E.O.C. v. State of Wyoming,* 514 F. Supp. 596, 598-600 [D. Wyoming, 1981]). This statement seems unsound. All statutes are presumptively constitutional. *U.S. v. National Dairy Products,* 372 U.S. 29, 32 (1963). Even if Congress fails to mention a constitutional basis for a statute, the Court must uphold the statute if there is any constitutional basis for it. Had the Supreme Court found the Commerce Clause to be an inadequate basis of regulating states in this instance because of the principle of federalism, as expounded in National League of Cities, it was fully capable of upholding the statute under the Fourteenth Amendment.

108. See E.E.O.C. 460 U.S. at 229.

109. See Michael Conant, *Systems Analysis in the Appellate Decisionmaking Process,* 24 Rutgers L. Rev. 293, 317-19 (1970).

110. E.E.O.C. 460 U.S. at 252.

111. *Id.* at 252-54.

112. *Id.* at 255-56.

113. 452 U.S. 264, 287-88 (1981).

114. *Garcia,* 469 U.S. 528, 538.

115. *Gold Cross Ambulance v. Kansas City,* 538 F. Supp. 956, 967-69 (W.D.Mo., 1982.), aff'd on other grounds, 705 F. 2d 1005 (8th Cir. 1983), cert. denied 471 U.S. 1003 (1985); *Hybud Equipment Corp. v. Akron,* 654 F. 2d 1187 (6th Cir., 1981). See *Parker v. Brown,* 317 U.S. 314 (1943). For a critique of this case, see Michael Conant, *The Supremacy Clause and State Economic Controls,* 10 Hastings Con. L. Q. 255, 268-72 (1953).

116. *United States v. Best,* 573 F. 2d 1095, 1102-1103 (9th Cir. 1978).

117. *Amersbach v. Cleveland,* 598 F. 2d 1033, 1037-1038 (6th Cir. 1979) (municipal airport employees); *Enrique Molina-Estrada v. Puerto Rico Highway Authority,* 680 F. 2d 841, 845-46 (1st Cir., 1982) (irregular highway employees not entitled to overtime pay).

118. *Garcia,* 469 U.S. 528, 538-39.

119. *Oklahoma ex. rel. Derryberry v. FERC,* 494 F. Supp. 636, 657 (W.D. Okla. 1980), aff'd 661 F.2d 832 (l0th Cir. 1981), cert. denied sub nom. *Texas v. F.E.R.C.,* 457 U.S. 1105 (1982) (federal regulation of intrastate natural gas prices); *Friends of the Earth v. Carey,* 552. F. 2d. 25, 38 (2d Cir. 1977), cert. denied 434 U.S. 902. (1977) (Clean Air Act governs state regulation of traffic on public roads); *Hughes Air Corp. v. Public Utilities Com'n,* 644 F.2d 1334, 1340¬41 (9th Cir., 1981) (federal regulation of air transport overrides state regulation).

120. *Woods v. Homes and Structures of Pittsburgh, Kansas,* 489 F. Supp. 1270, 1296-97 (Kan. 1980) (issuance of local industrial development bonds held subject to federal securities regulation); *Puerto Rico Tel. Co. v. F.C.C.,* 553 F. 2d. 694, 700-01 (1st Cir, 1977) (publicly owned telephone company held subject to FCC regulation); *Public Service Co. v. FERC,* 587 F. 2d 716, 721 (5th Cir. 1979), cert. denied sub nom. *Louisiana v. F.E.R.C.,* 444 U.S. 879 (1979) (state-owned natural gas subject to federal regulation).

121. *Williams v. Eastside Mental Health Center,* 669 F. 2d. 671, 680-81 (11th Cir. 1982), cert. denied 459 U.S. 976 (1982); (not-for-profit mental-health institution is not state agency and does not perform integral state function); *Bonnette v. California Health and Welfare Agency,* 704 F. 2d. 1465, 1472. (9th Cir. 1983) (chore workers hired by state agency to perform in-home services for the disabled do not perform traditional governmental function).

122. 644 F. 2d, 1334, 1340-41 (9th Cir. 1981).

123. 598 F. 2d 1033, 1037-38 (6th Cir. 1979).

124. 469 U.S. 528 (1985).

125. Fair Labor Standards Amendments of 1974, §21b, 88 Stat. 68, 29 U.S.C. 207 n (1998).

126. J. Meyer, J. Kain, and M. Wohl, *The Urban Transportation Problem,* 88-98 (Harvard Univ. Press, 1965). Local bus and trolley companies have a morning peak-load demand from about 6:30 to 9:00 AM and an evening peak-load demand from 4:00 to 6:30 PM.

127. U.S. Cong., House Committee on Education and Labor, *Fair Labor Standards Amendments of 1973,* Hearings on H.R. 4757 and H.R. 2831, 163-67 (93d Cong. 1st sess. 1973).

128. *Id.* at 169-70.

129. 469 U.S. at 531.

130. *Id.* at 534.

131. *Id.*

132. In 1981, the district court granted SAMTA's motion for summary judgment, ruling that "local mass transit systems constitute integral operations in areas of traditional governmental functions" (469 U.S. at 535). The secretary of labor and Garcia appealed. While the appeals were pending, the Supreme Court decided *United Transportation Union v. Long Island R. Co.,* 455 U.S. 678 (1982), ruling that a state-owned commuter rail service with a private proprietary history was not a traditional governmental function and hence not immune from requirements of the Railway Labor Act under *National League of Cities.* The Supreme Court in Garcia vacated the District Court judgments and remanded them for further consideration in the light of Long Island. *Garcia v. San Antonio Met. Transit Authority,* 457 U.S.

1102. (1982). On remand, the district court refused to apply the Long Island ruling to SAMTA and adhered to its original view of constitutional immunity. *San Antonio Met. Transit Authority v. Donavan,* 557 F. Supp. 445 (W. D. Texas 1983).

133. In its first footnote, the Court cited the three courts of appeal decisions and a state appellate decision holding local mass transit to be proprietary and not immune from FLSA. 469 U.S. at 530. See *supra* note 32.

134. 469 U.S. at 539-44.

135. *Id.* at 538-39. These cases are discussed, *supra* notes 115 to 123 and accompanying text.

136. Justice Blackmun writes of "state tax immunity recognized in *Collector v. Day,*" 78 U.S. (11 Wall.) 113 (1870), cited at 469 U.S. 540. That case did not concern state-tax immunity but was the classic case concerning immunity from federal income taxation of state employees and was expressly overruled in *Graves v. New York ex rel. O'Keefe.* 306 U.S. 466, 48b (1939). The Court puts substantial weight on the obiter dicta in *Brush v. Commissioner,* 300 U.S. 352 (1937), a case concerning whether the salary of the chief engineer of New York City's water supply bureau was subject to federal income taxation. This case was overruled by Graves, as was expressly noted in the dissent (306 U.S. at 492) (McReynolds dissenting). In the *obiter dicta* of *Flint v. Stone, Tracy. Co.,* 220 U.S. 107, 172. (1911), the Supreme Court had ruled that if a private corporation supplied city water, it would be subject to a federal corporation tax. The Court stated that since a private firm could be granted a public monopoly, the supply of water was not an essential governmental function. This is erroneous since a city or state could employ a private firm to supply a public good. In *Brush, Flint* it was distinguished as dictum and the supply of water was held governmental (300 U.S. at 373). The alleged inconsistency of these two cases did not exist. Neither concerned taxation of states or their agencies. Flint was limited to federal taxation of private corporations. Brush concerned federal income taxation of individuals. Blackmun also fails to note that other cases he cites concern taxation of individuals, not state agencies. Thus, *Helvering v. Powers,* 293 U.S. 214 (1934) held that the compensation of members of boards of a state-run commuter-rail system were not immune from federal income taxation. *Herlvering v. Gebhardt* (304 U.S. 405 (1938) held that federal income-tax laws applied to salaries of employees of the Port of New York Authority.

137. Justice Blackmun cited *Indian Towing Co. v. United States,* 350 U.S. 61 (1955), cited at 469 U.S. 545 to assert that the notion of a "uniquely" governmental function is unmanageable. But the main holding of that case was that the distinction in municipal corporation law between governmental and nongovernmental is not applicable in construction of Federal Tort Claims Act. The Court in dictum stated, "all Government activity is inescapably 'uniquely governmental' in that it is performed by the government" (350 U.S. at 126). The total refusal in the federal claims context to distinguish types of activity performed by governments is no test of whether one can usefully distinguish proprietary activities of government from those that are uniquely governmental, such as policing a city or state.

138. 469 U.S. 546.

139. *Id.*

140. *Id.* at 548.

141. *Id.* at 550-51, citing J. Choper, *supra* note 53, 175-84; Wechsler, *supra* note 11.

142. *Id.* at 552- *Id.* 53.

143. *Id.* at 554.

144. *Id.* at 558-60. "I note that it does not seem to have occurred to the Court that it —an unelected majority of five Justices—today rejects almost 2.00 years of the understanding of the constitutional status of federalism" (*Id.* at 560).

145. *Id.* at 562.
146. *Id.* at 564-67.
147. *Id.* at 571.
148. *Id.* at 573-75.
149. *Id.* at 575.
150. Martha Field, *Garcia v. San Antonio Metropolitan Transit Authority,* 99 Harv. L. Rev. 84, 89-95 (1985).
151. *Id.* at 96-103.
152. *Garcia,* 469 U.S. at 572. (Powell, J., dissenting); 469 U.S. at 584-85 (O'Conner, J., dissenting).
153. See, e.g., A. E. Dick Howard, *Garcia and the Values of Federalism,* 19 Ga. L. Rev. 789 (1985).
154. On separated powers, see *Immigration and Naturalization Service v. Chadha,* 462. U.S. 919 (1983); *United States v. Nixon,* 418 U.S. 683 (1974).
155. *Garcia,* 469 U.S. at 568-70 (Powell, J., dissenting). See Roger Brooks, *Garcia, the Seventeenth Amendment, and the Role of the Supreme Court in Defending Federalism,* 10 Harv. J. L. & Pub. Pol. 189, 192-96 (1987); Van Alstyne, *supra* note 18, at 1727-31; Rapaczynski, *supra* note 10, at 380-95. Compare Choper, *supra* note 53, ch. 4.
156. See Brooks, *supra* note 155, at 199-208.
157. Zoe Baird, *State Empowerment after Garcia,* 18 Urban Lawyer 491 (1986). See authorities at 503 n. 62.
158. McCulloch v. Maryland, 17 U.S. (4 Wheat.) 316, 403 (1819).
159.   Madison, Federalist 10, at 62 (E. Bourne ed. 1947).
160.   See Stigler, *supra* note 2.
161. U.S. Cong., House Committee on Education and Labor, Hearing on the Fair Labor Standards Act 5, 7 (99th Cong., 1st Sess., 1985). See U.S. Cong., Senate Committee on Labor and Human Resources, Fair Labor Standards Amendments of 1985, Hearings (99th Cong., 1st Sess., 1985). See generally, *Overtime Work,* 109 Monthly Labor Rev. 36 (Nov. 1986).
162. Fair Labor Standards Amendments of 1985, 99 Stat. 787, 29 U.S.C.A. Section 2.07(0). See Austin Murphy and Don Nickles, *The Fair Labor Standards Act Amendments of 1985,* 37 Labor L. J. 67 (1986).

6

The Commerce Clause and the Law Merchant: Law of Nations

The purpose of the Commerce Clause has been noted as promoting national markets unimpeded by state barriers to trade and governed by uniform congressional regulation to remedy market failures. But the regulation of commerce by Congress was not its only legal control. The law merchant, a body of international commercial law, also was utilized to resolve controversies over interstate and international private transactions. This body of judge-made, customary law became part of the national law of the United States through its adoption by the federal courts in deciding commercial cases.

International and interstate commercial controversies were brought into the federal courts by both the admiralty and the diversity jurisdictions under Article III.[1] The power to make the substantive law in these areas was vested in Congress by the Commerce Clause.[2] But, absent congressional action, the federal courts still had to decide mercantile cases. They utilized the only available law on the topics, the principles, and rules of the law merchant. The mandate of the Commerce Clause for uniform law in commerce among the several states is the constitutional foundation for this federal decisional law of private transactions. While not recognized by the early courts, the theory of the Supremacy Clause[3] of Article VI mandates national preemption of this part of private commercial law. It requires in litigation of interstate and international transactions that all national and state courts follow independently determined decisions of the Supreme Court of the United States.

The functioning of domestic markets was controlled by the mandate for uniform national regulation of commerce. This was supplemented by the international regulatory function of the law merchant. The latter resulted from its customary origins. The customary behavior of merchants, acting under private incentive to minimize costs as part of maximizing profits, was the basis of mercantile law. Counsel in mercantile cases had to prove that contested customs had been in use for sufficient time that they had become accepted methods of trade before the customs were adopted by the courts as legal rules. In England, the adoption was by court decisions. In France and other major trading countries on the continent, the adoption was by statute. Consequently, the early federal courts in the United States were free to utilize either English decisions or continental codes or both in deciding mercantile litigation.

The most noted case in the American law merchant was *Swift v. Tyson*.[4] Recent studies have restored the reputation of the opinion of Justice Joseph Story as a principled application of private international law.[5] Detailed analysis of opinions before Swift will show that the decision on the commercial issues in that case was based on settled rules of the law merchant. Analysis of statutory language and early cases will show that Section 34 of the Judiciary Act of 1789[6] applied only to legal actions at common law. At the time of adoption of the Judiciary Act and in 1842, the commercial law or law merchant was not part of the common law in the narrow sense of that term. The law merchant had become part of the Common-Law System, but it was an independent branch, as were equity and maritime law. The widest sense of the rule of *Swift* as precedent should have been the refusal to apply Section 34 of the Judiciary Act to the interstate law merchant.[7]

A review of the cases will show that after the Civil War, the Supreme Court misinterpreted the Judiciary Act and the *Swift* opinion and created a federal common law. It mistakenly held many areas of local common law, such as property and torts, to be of a general nature and ruled that the federal courts were not bound by the Judiciary Act to follow state precedents on these topics. This led to forum shopping. Parties would change their state of residence in order to obtain federal diversity jurisdiction and application of the federal common law to their controversy. Great objections to the expanding federal common law were voiced by dissenting justices, legal scholars and the bar. Finally, in *Erie v. Tomkins*,[8] a common law tort case, the Supreme Court majority correctly terminated the federal common law. Unfortunately, the Court also overruled *Swift* because the appeal briefs in *Erie* failed to explain that *Swift* was a mercantile opinion and not a common-law precedent. Thus, the Court not only corrected their predecessors' past errors in creating a general federal common law; they also incorrectly eliminated the distinct classification for national customary commercial law for interstate and international transactions.

Law of Nations

Historians have demonstrated that one cannot truly understand the rule of *Swift v. Tyson* until one understands the distinct character of private international law when the Constitution and the Judiciary Act of 1789 became law.[9] Admiralty, maritime and commercial law, and the conflict of laws were a highly integrated body of law. No sharp distinctions or borderlines existed between these branches of the law of nations. Lawyers described conflict-of-laws principles as a branch of commercial law since the doctrines first arose in international commercial transactions.[10] The commercial law or law merchant was an integral part of maritime law. International contracts for the sale of goods and bills of exchange drawn on foreign merchants or financiers for payment were closely tied to maritime contracts to ship the goods by sea and to insure them.[11] In 1821, Justice Story spoke of maritime and commercial law interchangeably, noting their high degree of uniformity throughout the commercial world.

> As to commercial law. From mutual comity, from the natural tendency of maritime usages to assimilation, and from mutual convenience, if not necessity, it may reasonably be expected, that the maritime law will gradually approximate to a high degree of uniformity throughout the commercial world. This is, indeed, in every view exceedingly desirable. Europe is already, by a silent but steady course, fast approaching to that state, in which the same commercial principles will constitute a part of the public law of all its sovereignties. The unwritten commercial law of England at this moment differs in no very important particulars from the positive codes of France and Holland. Spain, Portugal, and the Italian States, the Hanseatic Confederacy, and the Powers of the North, have adopted a considerable part of the same system.[12]

The customary origin of the commercial law was a key aspect of its character.[13] It meant that courts did not, as in some areas of the common law, create descriptive categories of legal wrongs and remedies. Rather, the merchants created the patterns of customary behavior that were most efficient in marketing goods and facilitating payment, and the courts adopted rules to enforce these customs. The historical origins of this customary law precede the recognition of the law merchant by the common-law courts. The merchant courts from the fourteenth to the sixteenth centuries in the port cities and at the fairs were created by merchants for the purpose of applying established and known business practices as the standards for settling controversies.[14]

The earliest mercantile cases reported in the common-law courts also cite the proof "declared upon the customs of merchants" as the applicable law.[15] A typical declaration began "whereas by the custom of London between merchants trafficking from London into the parts beyond the seas."[16] Once a general custom had been defined and proved in a number of cases, the courts would take judicial notice of it.[17]

The customary character of commercial law was emphasized continuously by the courts into the latter part of the nineteenth century. It was best described by Chief Justice Alexander Cockburn:

> It is true that the law merchant is sometimes spoken of as a fixed body of law, forming part of the common law, and as it were coeval with it. But as a matter of legal history, this view is altogether incorrect. The law merchant thus spoken of with reference to bills of exchange and other negotiable securities, though forming part of the general body of the lex mercatoria, is of comparatively recent origin. It is neither more nor less than the usages of merchants and traders in the different departments of trade, ratified by the decisions of Courts of law, which upon such usages being proved before them, have adopted them as settled law with a view to the interests of trade and the public convenience, the Court proceeding herein on the well-known principle of law

that, with reference to transactions in the different departments of trade, Courts of law, in giving effect to the contracts and dealings of the parties, will assume that the latter have dealt with one another on the footing of any custom or usage prevailing generally in the particular department.[18]

Contract and commercial law are based on a single primary principle, enforce the reasonable expectations of parties to transactions. The objective theory of contract requires courts to enforce reasonable expectations in promises induced by the promises of promisors.[1] In contract and commercial law, however, there is a second set of expectations in parties concerning the legal framework of transactions. Agreements are made with the expectation that the established customary behavior of merchants that has been recognized as law by the courts will be applied to any controversy that arises. Risk allocation for the hundreds of market contingencies that have not been provided for in the agreement will be allocated by the courts according to customary rules. The expectation is that standing customary law is in a sense part of transactions, ready to resolve ambiguities and fill gaps in agreements of merchants.

Throughout the history of mercantile law, its customary rules of behavior were always subject to exception by express agreement of parties to a transaction. In *The Reeside*,[20] Justice Story on circuit explained the function of custom in the judicial decision process for mercantile controversies. The action was a libel under maritime law for damage to goods being shipped from New York to Boston. Story explained the priority of express promises in transactions and the use of custom as a device to construe the incomplete or ambiguous terms of an agreement that led to litigation.[21]

The dynamic character of the law merchant is its most useful trait. As more efficient methods of shipping, communication, and transacting business were developed, new customary behavior was incorporated into the law. "When a general usage has been judicially ascertained and established, it becomes part of the law merchant, which Courts of justice are bound to know and recognize."[22] Justice Bigham, in holding corporate bearer bonds to be negotiable, commented on the dynamics of the law merchant.[23]

The law merchant was brought to England from the continent and many of its rules originated in the civil law.[24] It is not surprising when in 1601 a special court was established in London to hear insurance cases, its personnel consisted of the recorder, *two doctors of civil law*, two common lawyers and eight "grave and discreet" merchants.[25]

Before 1600, mercantile cases were heard in the merchant courts.[26] Between 1600 and 1755, while mercantile cases were heard in common-law and equity courts, few of the merchant customs had been litigated sufficiently to be accepted as established legal rules.[27] Most customs still had to be proved at trial in the same manner than one proved foreign law.[28] Lord Mansfield is credited with making the great advance toward integration of merchant customs into law. His opinions incorporated the rules of the law merchant into the common-law system during his tenure as Chief Justice of Kings Bench from 1756 to 1788.[29] While the rules of mercantile law became part of the common-law system, no one spoke of them as common-law rules. There was ambiguity, however. The Common-Law system was sometimes called the general Common Law. Consequently, some courts stated that the "custom of merchants is part of the Common Law."[30] Nevertheless, lawyers and scholars who specialized in commercial law always spoke of it as distinct from the common law in the narrow sense of that term. Professor Melville Bigelow explained that this distinction continued through the nineteenth century:

> The mischief of them lies in the mistaken notion implied, that the law merchant is a sort of poor relation of the common law, or rather that it is a dependent of the common law, subject to it wherever its own language is not plain. Such instances, in other words, overlook the fact that the law merchant is an independent, parallel system of law, like equity or admiralty. The Law Merchant is not even a modification of the common law: it occupies a field over which the common law does not and never did extend.[31]

In order to understand the American law merchant and the later analysis of *Swift v. Tyson*, it is essential to emphasize that the "commercial law" was used by Justice Story in *Swift* as a synonym for law merchant or mercantile law. They were clearly synonyms at the time of the enactment of the Judiciary Act of 1789. Justice Francis Buller, in a leading case on bills of lading in 1787, spoke of the "established course among merchants" as the source of commercial law.[32] Justice James Wilson, in lectures of 1790-91, cited Mansfield in *Luke v. Lyde*,[33] the case later used by Story as authority for *Swift*, and spoke of the law of merchants as that of the commercial world.[34] And Blackstone had written that "the affairs of commerce are regulated by a law of their own, called the law merchant or *lex mercatoria*, which all nations agree in and take notice of. And in particular it is held to be part of the law of England, which decides the causes of merchants by the general rules which obtain in all commercial countries."[35]

The titles of leading treatises on commercial law both before and after *Swift* indicate the identity of commercial law and the law merchant. One of the earliest is George Caines, *An Enquiry into the Law Merchant of the United States; or Lex Mercatoria Americana, on Several Heads of Commercial Importance* (1802). The title of a textbook on commercial law by Professor Theophilus Parsons of Harvard was *Elements of Mercantile Law (1856)*.

The law merchant was not just the commercial law of the federal courts for interstate and international transactions. It was also the law adopted in state courts, when no state statute existed, to decide controversies arising in intrastate commercial transactions.[36] In 1805, Chief Justice James Kent of New York, in deciding a maritime case, said, "The *law merchant* is, however, the general law of commercial nations; and, where our own positive institutions and decisions are silent, it is to be expounded by having recourse to the usages of other nations. This has been the maxim from the time of *Rhodian* law to this day."[37] Justice John Gibson of Pennsylvania, in an action on a promissory note, stated that "equity and the commercial law perfectly agree, both being founded on principles of reason as well as convenience."[38] Chief Justice Isaac Redfield of the Vermont Supreme Court, in an action on a bill of exchange, explained the evolutionary process of the law merchant in which a growing body of reliable evidence of customary behavior developed into legal precedents.[39]

The Judiciary Act and Actions at Common Law

Section 34 of the Judiciary Act of 1789, also known as the Rules of Decision Act, read as follows: "The laws of the several states, except where the constitution, treaties or statutes of the United States shall otherwise require or provide, shall be regarded as rules of decision in trials at common law in the courts of the United States in cases where they apply."[40] Section 34 was to apply to the substantive issues, since the Process Act passed five days later governed procedure in the federal courts.[41]

Historians have presented overwhelming evidence that in 1789 the word "laws" in the phrase "laws of the several states" included both state statutory law and settled rules of state decisional law in the reports of the highest state appeals courts.[42] Even though there were no operative state supreme courts in 1789 and hence no published reports of settled state common-law rules, the Congress used general language that anticipated the creation of such specialized appeals courts and the issuance of authoritative opinions on purely local controversies. The opinions of the Supreme Court that antedated *Swift* demonstrate that the Court understood this usual contemporary meaning and was employing it.[43]

It was the misreading of both Section 34 and *Swift* that caused later courts and scholars to hold that the word laws included only state statutes. Justice Stephen Field, dissenting in *Baltimore and Ohio R. Co. v. Baugh*[44] to the Supreme Court's later unwarranted creation of a federal common law of torts, noted that only in exceptional cases was "laws" in 1789 restricted to statutes; i.e., where it was so declared or clearly indicated by context.[45] Neither of these exceptions applied to Section 34. Field illustrated the continuing usual comprehensive meaning of 'laws' by the illustration of the Fourteenth Amendment phrase "equal protection of the laws."[46] This clause does not apply only to statutes. If judges in a state in common-law decisions created one definition of negligence for white persons and a different one for African-Americans, there would be a clear violation of the clause.

The phrase "except where the Constitution, treaties or statutes of the United States shall otherwise require or provide" assists the understanding of the other terms that create the exemption of the law merchant. The Constitution vests the governing power over interstate and international commerce exclusively in the national government.[47] The power in the national judiciary in maritime and diversity cases to establish a uniform commercial law for interstate transactions by incorporating the international law merchant into a body of national case law is constitutionally based on the commerce power and on the power to utilize established conflict-of-laws rules.[48] The first issue is one of federalism. The extraterritorial commercial transactions that were the subject matter of the law merchant, as they arose in diversity cases, raised legal issues beyond the exclusive legislative authority of any single state. The application by federal courts of the traditional judicial practices of the law of nations would in no way invade that part of law reserved to the states by the structure of the Constitution and restated in the Tenth Amendment.[49] As to intrastate transactions, absent pre-emptive congressional enactments, the states were free to deviate by statute or judicial decision from the general commercial law in any manner they chose.

The objective of uniform regulation of interstate transactions underlying the Commerce Clause also has a negative implication. Even if Congress fails to regulate transactions or shipments between states, the states are without power to regulate that sector of commerce.[50] The states are left only with the power to regulate local commerce. They have a shared power with the national Congress to regulate intrastate commerce that affects other states. Such state regulation is valid only if it does not conflict with national regulation and does not burden commerce among the several states.[51] In light of these allocations of regulatory power, the state legislatures could not regulate extraterritorial commercial transactions. That which state legislatures could not do without invading the national commerce power, the state judiciaries were also barred from doing. *Ipso facto*, the Supreme Court of the United States may not delegate to the state judiciaries the power to make binding law for interstate transactions litigated in the federal courts.

The constitutional separation of powers between the legislative and judicial branches also was no barrier, in the absence of congressional legislation on the topic, to the adoption by the Supreme Court of the law merchant as a national case law for interstate transactions. The controlling framework of analysis of the Constitution of the United States is that it is a modified and expanded version of the English Constitution extant in the 1780's.[52] Adoption of the law merchant into the English legal system in order to settle private international disputes followed the English tradition of judge-made law.[53] Since commercial law originated in customary behavior rather than from sovereign command, codification of it was not the British approach. The Courts were the governmental agency best able to adopt and modify mercantile rules from case to case as new, more efficient methods of marketing and financing were developed by the business community. Following their English tradition, the federal courts applied mercantile rules derived from English precedents or from the civil codes of France and other European nations.[54]

The phrase "in trials at common law" referred to the judicial hearing of legal actions at common law. Chief Justice John Marshall on circuit stated in 1807 that he had always conceived "the technical term 'trials at common law'" of

Section 34 to apply "to suits at common law as contradistinguished from those which come before the court sitting as a court of equity or admiralty."[55] This view is reinforced by reference to the Process Act of 1789,[56] passed five days after the Judiciary Act, that provides different procedures for actions at common law from those in equity, admiralty, and maritime jurisdiction. The latter group is according to "the course of the civil law". At the time, some states did not have equity branches in their legal systems. William Rawle explained Congress' intentional omission of "equity" in Section 34: "[a] construction that would adopt the state practice in all its extent would at once extinguish in such states the exercise of equitable jurisdiction."[57] As Justice John McLean later explained: "The rules of the High Court of Chancery of England have been adopted by the courts of the United States. . . . In exercising this jurisdiction, the courts of the Union are not limited by the chancery system adopted by any state and they exercise their functions in a state where no court of chancery has been established."[58] Thus, the negative implication of Section 34 was that conflict-of-laws rules in diversity cases should apply only to the common law in its narrower sense. By definition, this excluded the law merchant. Since common law excluded maritime law, and the general commercial law at that time was considered part of maritime law, the reasonable conclusion is that Section 34 was not applicable to commercial law.

The final clause of Section 34, "in cases where they apply," reinforces the above analysis of the status of commercial law. The primary reason to add this clause must have been to enable the Supreme Court to decide the breadth of application of the statute according to the principles of federalism. While the traditional common law was reserved to the states and would have been even without passage of Section 34, the federal judiciary was required to adopt decisional rules for those areas of the customary law that were truly national. The chief component of this national customary law was the law of nations, of which the commercial law was a major part.

This was the key distinction that Justice Story made in *Swift v. Tyson*.[59] It was between state statute law and settled state case law of a strictly local character on the one hand and customary or case law of an extraterritorial character on the other hand.[60] The latter body of law was to be governed by the law of nations, so *Swift* held that the Judiciary Act was held not to apply in this area. Since there could be only one law of nations to govern interstate and international transactions, no state statutory or case law purporting to govern controversies in the law of nations could control decisions in extraterritorial disputes decided in the federal courts.

Section 34 was a conflict-of-laws directive to the federal courts. The Supreme Court and leading commentators asserted that Section 34 merely codified for trials at common law the standing conflict-of-laws rules.[61] Although there were few American law reports at the enactment of Section 34, and even fewer decisions on conflicts of law, there was a body of law in European nations that dealt with conflicts.[62] It was argued that for the common law Section 34 was merely precautionary. It was to reaffirm that national courts were not free under their general jurisdiction in diversity-of-citizenship cases to create a federal common law. That would have meant a dual common law, so that federal decisions on matters where there was settled local state law could differ from state precedents. In fact, this is exactly what happened in the latter part of the nineteenth century and the first third of the twentieth century when the Supreme Court, misreading *Swift*, created a federal common law.[63]

Legal historians have demonstrated that before the Civil War, the federal courts adhered to the distinction outlined above.[64] They applied Section 34 to actions at common law and followed settled state rules of decision but refused to apply state law to the commercial law and other branches of the law of nations. Justice Story noted in S*wift* that Section 34 clearly applied to *in rem* and other strictly local common-law actions. He described these as "rights and titles to things having a permanent locality, such as the rights and titles to real estate and other matters immovable and intraterritorial in their nature and character."[65] The classic Supreme Court precedent holding federal courts bound by state decisions on title to property is *Jackson ex dem. St. John v. Chew*[66] and Justice Story had earlier asserted that general principle in *United States v. Crosby*.[67]

Section 34 also required federal courts to follow settled state common law generally. In *Wheaton v. Peters*,[68] an action concerning state common-law rules of copyright, Justice McLean for the Supreme Court made general observations:

> It is clear, there can be no common law of the United States. The federal government is composed of twenty-four sovereign and independent states; each of which may have its local usages, customs and common law. There is no principle which pervades the Union and has the authority of law that is not embodied in the Constitution or laws of the Union. The common law could be made a part of our federal system, only by legislative adoption. When, therefore, a common-law right is asserted, we must look to the state in which the controversy originated.[69]

It is significant that Justice Story joined in this opinion. Eight years later, he wrote the unanimous opinion in *Swift v. Tyson*,[70] affirming federal judicial adoption of the international customary commercial law for interstate transactions. Unfortunately, in writing the Swift opinion, Story failed to mention *Wheaton, Chew, or Crosby* when he distinguished local common law from the general commercial law.

A classic case applying Section 34 to statutes is *Green v. Neal's Lessee*.[71] The Supreme Court of the United States had construed a Tennessee statute of limitations relating to land claims. Some months later, the Tennessee Supreme Court gave a contrary interpretation. In *Green*, the U.S. Supreme Court explained why it would conform to the Tennessee precedents rather than its own in order not to create two rules of property on the same issue within a state.[72]

An important underlying factor was the general conflicts rule of *lex loci rei sitae* in real property cases.

This view was not followed where the Supreme Court could reverse itself only by denying the reasonable expectations of parties to contract. In *Rowan v. Runnels*,[73] the Court refused to abandon its own first interpretation of the Mississippi constitutional clause prohibiting trade in slaves that had been made in *Groves v. Slaughter*.[74] While the action was on a promissory note, the issue was not one of commercial law but of the common-law contract rule on legality of object. Since transactions totaling over $3 million had been entered in reliance on the decision in *Groves*, a subsequent contrary state precedent was rejected by the Supreme Court. In *Rowan*, the Court followed *Groves*. Writing for the Court, Chief Justice Taney refused to impair the obligations of contracts in litigation outside the field of bankruptcy. Taney admitted, however, that future contracts would be governed by the state court decisions.[75]

A special problem arose when there was no settled state law on a common-law issue. If there were no unequivocal state precedents from its highest appeals court or if precedents were in conflict in the state whose law was to be applied, Section 34 could not operate. The Supreme Court then had to apply general principles of common law found in the English law reports and those of other states. Chief Justice Marshall explained that even in a property case, it was impossible to apply *lex loci rei sitae* when the case was of first impression and there were no precedents.[76]

The Commercial Law and *Swift v. Tyson*

The federal courts early took the view that interstate and international commercial transactions were not bound by state common-law precedents. Unfortunately, the judges and justices did not seem to realize that the Commerce Clause of the Constitution mandated this view. The largest group of law-merchant cases in the United States before 1840 was in the area of marine insurance.[77] The federal courts and the state courts knowingly exercised independent judgment as they shared in adopting and clarifying a body of national customary law. In 1800, Judge Peters in a case of double insurance, stated that the United States "should have a national, uniform and generally received law-merchant."[78] In 1806, Justice Paterson reviewed the status of a settled marine insurance rule and noted: "It has grown up into a clear, known and certain rule for the regulation of commercial negotiations, and is incorporated into the law merchant of the land."[79] In all the marine insurance cases in the period to 1820, the federal courts agreed that they were applying the general commercial law.[80] In no case, even in the few instances where state courts had decided the issue differently, was it even argued that federal courts were bound by Section 34 of the Judiciary Act to follow local law.

Justice Story was thoroughly familiar with the body of decisions on marine insurance in the lower federal courts that relied on general principles of the law merchant for decision.[81] In 1836 to 1838, he wrote three opinions on circuit that treated the issue. It was not local law but law-merchant rules that would govern marine insurance.[82] Story's clearest statement of the standing law was in *Williams v. Suffolk Ins. Co.*:

> This doctrine being founded, not upon local law, but upon the general principles of commercial law, would be obligatory upon this court, even if the decisions of the state court of Massachusetts were to the contrary; for upon commercial questions of a general nature, the courts of the United States possess the same general authority, which belongs to the state tribunals, and are not bound by the local decisions. They are at liberty to consult their own opinions, guided, indeed, by the greatest deference for the acknowledged learning and ability of the state tribunals, but still exercising their own judgment, as to the reasons, on which those decisions are founded.[83]

This was the generally accepted understanding of the commercial law found in the then available treatises on the common-law system.[84]

In *Findlay's Executors v. Bank of the United States*,[85] Justice McLean on circuit resolved a conflict between Ohio and federal precedents in a case of suretyship, another branch of the law merchant. He noted that, "This great head of equity is derived from the civil law, and is founded upon immutable principles of justice and benevolence."[86] Since the Ohio precedent and the conflicting federal precedent both purported to stand on principles of general commercial law, McLean had to use independent judgment on the issue of which was correct. He adopted a principle from an opinion in the Supreme Court of the United States and noted that Chancellor Kent had adopted that view in a New York case.[87]

Many of the most notable opinions on the application of the general commercial law concerned bills of exchange. In *Buckner v. Finley*,[88] the Supreme Court made an unqualified holding that bills of exchange drawn in one state on persons living in another state were foreign bills for the purpose of applying the rules of protest. Justice Washington pointed out that almost all reported state cases took the same view.[89] He did not note the constitutional foundation. Interstate and international bills of exchange, being extraterritorial to any single state, were part of the national commerce whose regulation was delegated exclusively to the national government by the commerce power of Article 1. One of the functions of the "dormant" Commerce Clause was to prevent attempted enforcement of the conflicting statutes of two different states on any single interstate transaction.

One of the earliest expositions of the law applicable to international transactions was that of Justice Story on circuit in 1812 in *Van Reimsdyk v. Kane*.[90] The case was in equity and presented issues under the international conflict of laws. At that time, however, conflicts rules and commercial law were still considered one integrated branch of the law of nations,[91] so that principles applied here would also apply to the law merchant. Defendants, citizens of Rhode Island, through an agent in Java, had drawn a bill of exchange on a mercantile house in Amsterdam payable to plaintiff, a Dutch resident of Java. The bill of exchange had been presented to the drawee and protested for non-payment. Defendant drawers pleaded in defense that all their debts had been discharged in a proceeding under the Rhode Island insolvency statute of 1756. Without deciding whether this statute, having the effect of a general bankruptcy law, violated the constitutional prohibition on state law impairing the obligation of contracts, Story admitted its existence and exercise. The question was whether the Rhode Island insolvency statute was a bar to this legal action on an international bill of exchange, "whether the courts of the United States are bound to enforce against foreigners or citizens of other states, rightfully suing therein, the full effect of a bar of this nature."[92] In rejecting this defense, Story held that, under international conflict-of-laws rules, a valid contract made in another country could not be nullified by the insolvency law of the place where the suit was brought. Even though this action was brought in equity, Story also explained why a suit of this nature would not be subject to enforcement under Section 34 of the Judiciary Act:

> There must then be some limitation to the operation of this clause, and I apprehend such a limitation must arise whenever the subject matter of the suit is extraterritorial. In controversies between citizens of a state, as to rights derived under that state, and in controversies respecting territorial interests, in which, by the law of nations, the lex rei sitae governs, there can be little doubt, that the regulations of the statute must apply. But in controversies affecting citizens of other states, and in no degree arising from local regulations, as for instance, foreign contracts of a commercial nature, I think that it can hardly be maintained, that the laws of a state, to which they have no reference, however narrow, injudicious and inconvenient they may be, are to be the exclusive guides for judicial decision. Such a construction would defeat nearly all the objects for which the constitution has provided a national court.[93]

A leading precedent on the interpretation of interstate bills of exchange is *Coolidge v. Payson*.[94] Chief Justice Marshall affirmed a circuit court opinion of Justice Story.[95] He held that a written promise of a drawee to a drawer to accept a bill of exchange that is about to be drawn, which is communicated to a third party and induces him to take the bill, is equivalent to an actual acceptance. One fact of the case, though not in contest, was to regard a preexisting debt as valuable consideration for transfer of a bill of exchange. This was to be the primary issue in *Swift v. Tyson*. The method of interpretation was to adopt English law-merchant cases as evidence of the law and make no reference to local state law on the topic. In the circuit court, counsel for the losing defendant had cited a Massachusetts precedent.[96] The possible application of Section 34 of the Judiciary was not raised in the case.

In *Townsley v. Sumrall*,[97] Justice Story decided a case on interstate bills of exchange on the basis of law-merchant principles and without citation of authority on the key issues. One of the holdings was that a preexisting debt was a valuable consideration for a bill of exchange, the issue later contested in *Swift*. Here again, the possible application of Section 34 of the Judiciary Act was not raised.

In 1841, *in Riley v. Anderson*,[98] Justice McLean on circuit decided the same issue that was to be litigated a year later in *Swift*. An antecedent debt was held sufficient consideration upon the endorsement of a promissory note to cut off defenses that would have been good between the original parties to the instrument. Although the notes for the interstate transaction were made in Ohio, McLean refused to adopt the contrary Ohio rule. He cited *Coolidge* and *Townsley* and the English mercantile cases.

Swift v. Tyson,[99] concerning an interstate bill of exchange, required Justice Story again to construe Section 34 of the Judiciary Act of 1789. As has been noted, a significant group of circuit court opinions had held that statute did not apply to the law merchant. The specific circuit court ruling of *Riley v. Anderson*[100] one year before had decided the same issue on negotiable paper as *Swift* but did not refer to the statute. Hence, *Swift* was significant as the first Supreme Court opinion expressly ruling that the commercial law was general in nature and not subject to Section 34, so that federal courts were to use independent judgment in applying it to interstate and international transactions.

The bill of exchange was drawn in New York on the defendant Tyson in Maine who accepted it; the payee was one Norton, who indorsed it to plaintiff Swift. The bill was dishonored at maturity. It was a case of acceptance procured by fraud, the bill subsequently being taken by plaintiff in "payment" of a prior debt due from his endorser. Justice Story held that, assuming the unsettled New York law to the contrary, a pre-existing indebtedness by the endorser of a bill of exchange was consideration that would cut off defenses that were good between the original parties to the instrument.[101] The Supreme Court had twice before reached this decision on the issue following the general rule of the law merchant.[102] Thus *Swift*, certified to the Supreme Court on a narrow issue of negotiable instruments law, is an easily understandable case in its context, the commercial law. After 1860, some judges and justices found the decision puzzling because they mistakenly thought it referred to the common law.

In the key paragraph of the opinion, Story begins with an *obiter dictum* that is an excursion into abstract jurisprudence. Referring to decisions of "local tribunals," he wrote "In the *ordinary* use of language it will hardly be contended that the decisions of courts constitute laws. They are, at most, only evidence of what the laws are, and are not of themselves laws. The laws of a State are *more usually* understood to mean the rules and enactments promulgated by legislative authority thereof, or long established local customs having the force of law."[103] The words "ordinary" and "more usually" in the dictum are important qualifying terms. Local customs do have the force of law when there is a settled opinion by the highest appeals court in the jurisdiction. But in 1842, there were still relatively few settled common-law rules in the reports of the highest court of any single state. State trial courts often had to apply common-law, equity, and mercantile principles and rules by using English law reports and those of other states as evidence of the law. In any case, this excursion into jurisprudence was unnecessary. *Swift* did not rest on the definition of "laws" because, as Justice Story noted, the Supreme Court would not be bound by state statutes or decisional law when deciding issues that were extraterritorial to a state.

Story then explained why Section 34 of the Judiciary Act did not apply to the federal courts as they heard diversity cases under the general commercial law. He wrote:

> It never has been supposed by us, that the section did apply, or was designed to apply, to questions of a more general nature, not at all dependent upon local statutes or local usages of a fixed and permanent operation, as, for example, to the construction of ordinary contracts or other written instruments, and especially to questions of general commercial law, where the State tribunals are called upon to perform the like functions as ourselves, that is, to ascertain upon general reasoning and legal analogies, what is the true exposition of the contract or instrument, or what is the just rule furnished by the principles of commercial law to govern the case. And we have not now the slightest difficulty in holding, that this section, upon its true intendment and construction, is strictly limited to local statutes and local usages of the character before stated, and does not extend to contracts and other instruments of a commercial nature, the true interpretation and effect whereof are to be sought, not in the decisions of the local tribunals, but in the general principles and doctrines of commercial jurisprudence. Undoubtedly, the decisions of the local tribunal upon such subjects are entitled to, and will receive, the most deliberate attention and respect of this court; but they cannot furnish positive rules, or conclusive authority, by which our own judgments are to be bound up and governed. The law respecting negotiable instruments may be truly declared in the language of Cicero, adopted by Lord Mansfield in Luke v. Lyde, 2 Burr. R. 883, 887, to be in a great measure, not the law of a single country only, but of the commercial world. Non erit alia lex Romae, alia Athenis, alia nunc, alia posthac, sed et apud omnes gentes, et omni tempore, una eademque lex obtinebit.[104]

Justice Story itemized only two of the questions of a "more general nature" not subject to Section 34. These were the canons of documentary construction and the general commercial law.[105] Only the latter was at issue in *Swift*. Section 34 did not apply to the law merchant because all mercantile principles were totally independent of state statutes and state common law. Story cited the opinion of Lord Mansfield in the shipping case of *Luke v. Lyde*[106] to illustrate that the law of negotiable instruments, like all of the law merchant, was "not the law of a single country only, but of the commercial world."[107]

There is nothing puzzling about the *Swift* decision even though the *obiter dictum* on the meaning of the word "laws" in the opinion is ambiguous. Chief Justice Taney and other Jacksonian justices must have joined in the opinion of Justice Story because it was a reasonable declaration of standing law.[108] It was clear to competent lawyers of the time that the commercial law meant the law merchant. The Taney Court was not using law as an instrument of change to promote expansion of the national judicial function. They were deciding a narrow commercial issue, not approving the foundation of a federal common law. That illegitimate extension of *Swift* was to come later in the century when the true meaning of "commercial" law was forgotten.

Swift v. Tyson was the culmination of a series of cases on negotiable instruments that had established the distinct position of the law merchant in the common-law system. It should be noted, however, that there were some aspects of the commercial law which, under conflict-of-law rules, were decided according to the place of contract. In the law of bills of exchange, three of these items were days of grace, rates of interest, and rights to damages—all of which were determined on the basis of *lex loci.*[109]

In the same year as *Swift*, Justice Story wrote an opinion that combined both elements of the law of nations that he had mentioned in *Swift,* the canons of documentary construction and the commercial law. *Carpenter v. Providence Washington Insurance Co.*[110] concerned the construction of an interstate contract for fire insurance. Story adopted the same rationale as in *Swift* to reject state law precedents and to apply general principles of commercial law.[111]

Thirteen years after *Swift*, the Taney Court again confirmed the *Swift* rule on national mercantile law. In *Watson v. Tarpley,*[112] the Court denied the application of a Mississippi statute on bills of exchange to an interstate transaction. The statute denied legal action on a bill of exchange until after the date of its maturity. Under the law merchant, action could be brought at any time after protest and notice founded upon the refusal to pay. Justice Daniel for the Court stated that the state statute was "a violation of the general commercial law, which a state [had] no power to impose, and which the courts of the United States [were] bound to disregard."[113] In effect the Court gave the same interpretation to Section 34 of the Judiciary Act in 1855 as Justice Story had given on circuit in *Van Reimsdyk v. Kane*[114] in 1812. State rules of decision, whether statutes or decisional, did not apply to extraterritorial commercial transactions.

The Supremacy Clause

The Supremacy Clause of Article VI, Clause 2 reads as follows:

This Constitution, and the Laws of the United States which shall be made in Pursuance thereof; and all Treaties made, or which shall be made, under the Authority of the United States, shall be the supreme Law of the Land; and the Judges in every State shall be bound thereby, any Thing in the Constitution or Laws of any State to the Contrary notwithstanding.[115]

The first issue in determining the expected impact of this language in the establishment of uniform commercial law for the United States is the meaning of *Laws* in the phrases "Laws of the United States" and "Laws of any State."

As was noted in the discussion of "laws" in the Judiciary Act of 1789, the usual meaning of "laws" then included both statutory and decisional law.[116] Only if additional language or the context so demonstrated was the term limited to statutes.[117] As to "laws of the United States" in the broad context of a constitutional article mandating national supremacy there is no textual or contextual basis for less than the broadest interpretation. It is clear that the framers were concerned with national supremacy for international issues since they included in the Supremacy Clause "all Treaties made, or which shall be made under the Authority of the United States."[118]

The law of nations would be the key substantive customary law that the national judiciary would adopt and make a part of the laws of the United States. There is substantial evidence that in Article III, "laws of the United States" included the law of nations.[119] The context of Article VI seems comparable. Both the jurisdiction of federal courts and the supremacy of national law are necessary elements of a uniform legal system on which all parties to international transactions can rely. In contrast, if state courts were allowed to impose their various statutes and case law on issues of private international law that arise in state litigation, uniformity of the law of nations would be lost and forum shopping would be encouraged.

The phrase "law of any state" in the Supremacy Clause must be compared with the language "laws of the several states" in Section 34 of the Judiciary Act. As was noted, the latter included both state statute law and state common law. The context of the Supremacy Clause indicates the same broad definition of "laws." Judges in every state are bound to recognize that national law preempts conflicting state law, both statutory and decisional. Recent cases illustrate the national preemption of conflicting state common law.[120]

The future tense of the verbs in the Supremacy Clause circumscribed the scope of the clause. "Laws of the United States" applies only to laws of Congress to be enacted in consequence of its powers under this second Constitution and to those rules of the law of nations to be adopted by the national courts. As to the latter, the Supreme Court was, of course, not bound to the precedents or statutes of any nation.[121] On the other hand, to the great extent that English precedents and continental statutes coincided on issues of the law of nations, counsel could advise American ship owners and shippers of goods in interstate and international trade on the high probability of rules that would be adopted in the national courts. This prediction is supported by the pre-constitutional efforts of state supreme courts to conform to the law merchant in litigation of international transactions in hope that courts of other nations would give recognition to their judgments.[122]

The future tense of the Supremacy Clause was additional evidence of the existence of federalism. The common law of England and British amendatory statutes existing at the time of ratification were not within the class of national laws described in the Supremacy Clause. While many state constitutions and statutes expressly adopted the common law of England and even British amendatory statutes to the extent that they fit in the American setting,[123] the national constitution did not do so. The negative implication of the language of the Supremacy Clause is that "laws of the United States" in Article VI did not include the standing English or state common law. On the other hand, the exclusive power in the national government to regulate foreign relations and foreign commerce meant that only the national government could act to make the law merchant a part of American law.

Since the law merchant and admiralty are both branches of the law of nations, the operation of national preemption in admiralty cases is informative of the way the law merchant should have been treated. Under Article III, Section 2 of the Constitution, the judicial power of the United States extends to "all cases of admiralty and maritime jurisdiction."[124] The Supreme Court interpreted this clause, together with Section 9 of the Judiciary Act of 1789,[125] to give the national courts a much broader jurisdiction than the British courts of admiralty had in 1789.[126] The language of the clause is merely jurisdictional. By itself, it provides no key to the substantive law to be applied in admiralty and maritime cases.[127]

It is clear that Section 34 of the Judiciary Act could not apply to maritime cases based on events occurring on the high seas. If substantive maritime law was to have any uniformity, Section 34 also could not apply to events occurring in the territorial waters of a state.[128] In fact, it is clear that the substantive law to be applied in maritime cases was and is the maritime branch of the law of nations.[129] This has been consistently applied in maritime cases. In the recent *Moragne*[130] case, the Court utilized the traditional civil law methodology of admiralty in recognizing a customary remedy for wrongful death due to unseaworthiness.[131] Public policy was derived from a set of statutes treating the same problem but not directly applicable in the case. The Court also reemphasized the need for uniformity in private international law, the theme of *Southern Pacific v. Jensen*.[132]

The preemption of conflicting state law by national maritime law is clearly established.[133] The supremacy of national maritime law as the only means to uniformity is illustrated by recent decisions. "While states may sometimes supplement federal maritime policies, a state may not deprive a person of any substantial admiralty rights as defined in controlling acts of Congress or by interpretative decisions of this Court."[134] "A state law, even though it does not contravene an established principle of admiralty law will, nevertheless, not be applied where its adoption would impair the uniformity and simplicity which is a basic principle of the federal admiralty law."[135] The Supreme Court in the *Wilburn Boat*[136] case, concerning a marine insurance contract, stated:

> Congress has not taken over the regulation of marine insurance contracts and has not dealt with the effect of marine insurance warranties at all; hence there is no possible question here of conflict between state law and any federal statute. But this does not answer the questions presented, since in the absence of controlling Acts of Congress

this Court has fashioned a large part of the existing rules that govern admiralty. And States can no more override such judicial rules validly fashioned than they can override Acts of Congress.[137]

Maritime legal actions may begin in state courts,[138] or in the national courts. In either case, the national customary maritime law preempts state substantive statutes and common-law rules in all aspects of the litigation.[139] It makes no difference whether the maritime case is originated under admiralty jurisdiction or under diversity of citizenship.[140] The substantive maritime law is preemptive.

The preemption of Supreme Court commercial decisions could have the breadth of maritime cases only if commercial law were considered a part of maritime law for plenary federal jurisdiction. While this was the meaning of "maritime" in 1789, it has not since then been so construed by the courts. The national commercial law before 1938 was a mandate only in transactions litigated in the federal courts. Unlike maritime cases, commercial cases are subject to federal jurisdiction only when there is diversity of citizenship. All others are entirely local and are governed by state statutes and state court decisions.

In spite of their autonomy under the principle of federalism, early state courts usually recognized the Supreme Court of the United States as the final authority on the customary commercial law. Absent local statutes to the contrary, state courts recognized that the law merchant was the law of the commercial world and that a uniform national law would promote trade and economic growth. Justice Wilson referred to Mansfield and noted this in his 1790-91 lectures:

> One branch of that law, which, since the extension of commerce, and the frequent and liberal intercourse between different nations, has become of peculiar importance, is called the law of merchants. This system of law has been admitted to decide controversies concerning bills of exchange, policies of insurance, and other mercantile transactions, both where citizens of different states, and where citizens of the same state only, have been interested in the event. This system has, of late years, been greatly elucidated, and reduced to rational and solid principles, by a series of adjudications, for which the commercial world is much indebted to a celebrated judge, long famed for his comprehensive talents and luminous learning in general jurisprudence.[141]

The view of the bar on the stature of Supreme Court commercial decisions can be seen from the comments of the Justices and the official reporters. In *Coolidge v. Payson*,[142] Chief Justice Marshall decided an issue concerning bills of exchange and stated: "It is of much importance to merchants that this question should be at rest."[143] The implication was that this decision would determine the issue for all courts. Reporter Wheaton noted that Marshall's opinion would be "considered as settling the law of the country on this subject."[144]

As to *Buckner v. Finley*,[145] holding interstate bills of exchange to be foreign bills, reporter Peters noted the question was now *settled*.[146] The truth of his comment is verified by the fact that the New York courts, the only ones previously stating a contrary view, thereafter followed *Buckner*.[147] In *Riley and Amrings v. Anderson*,[148] Justice McLean made the point that he was not bound to follow Ohio decisions on the negotiability of promissory notes, but also asserted that "on all questions of a general and commercial character, the rule established by the federal courts should be followed by the local tribunal."[149]

The effect of *Swift* on state court decisions is illustrative of the attitude of judicial deference in that era. In *Carlisle v. Wishart*,[150] the Ohio Supreme Court adopted the rule of *Swift* and overruled its own prior contrary precedent. Justice Wood stated:

> It is believed that the law, as thus settled by the highest judicial tribunal in the country, will become the uniform rule of *all*, as it now is of *most* of the states. And, in a country like ours, where so much communication and interchange exists between the different members of the confederacy, to preserve uniformity in the great principles of commercial law, is of much interest to the mercantile world.[151]

The appeals courts of many states recognized *Swift* as the correct authority and applied its rule to intrastate transactions.[152] The New York Court of Appeals, however, refused to adopt the *Swift* rule on the issue.[153]

Over time, however, uniformity in state law did not prevail. In local commercial transactions, the statute and case law of the various states developed many differences.[154] Even though settled rules for federal courts did come from appeals to the Supreme Court, such rules were rejected by many state supreme courts. With state court rejection of uniform commercial law, the federal courts in this century also deviated from the *Swift* doctrine. In determining the negotiability of bills of exchange, for example, federal courts stopped applying the national law and instead applied conflict of law rules to adopt the law of one state.[155] The failure of Congress to enact national private commercial law left parties to interstate transactions in great uncertainty about which state's law would apply if controversies arose.

With the decision in *Erie v. Tompkins*,[156] the last vestiges of national commercial law disappeared. The federal courts could no longer apply national rules to interpret the Negotiable Instruments Law and other uniform codes. All commercial cases in diversity actions were thereafter treated like common law contracts. But the Supreme Court went even further. It wiped out the international conflict of law rules. In *Klaxon Co. v. Stentor Electric Mfg. Co.*,[157] it followed *Erie* and interpreted the Judiciary Act to require federal courts to follow state court decisions on the conflicts of law. *Erie* not only corrected the previous erroneous creation of a federal common law. It also led to elimination of the customary law of nations in commercial cases and in the conflicts of laws.

The application of *Erie* to the commercial law has in most cases not raised extreme problems of diverse rules because the Uniform Commercial Code is considered the federal law of commerce.[158] But in international bills of exchange controversies, the issues are more complex. In determining whether a party is a holder in due course, a federal court may choose not to apply the U.C.C. but follow alternate choice of law rules.[159] In marine insurance cases, in the absence of federal statute or settled federal decisional law, the courts will apply state law.[160] In any case there is no longer any reference to a general commercial law of the international community.

Conclusion

Much of the misunderstanding of *Swift* and confusion in its later interpretation seems to have arisen from ambiguity in language. The fact that before 1850 commercial law was a synonym of and limited to the law merchant was forgotten. The fact that common law in 1789 was almost always used in its narrow sense that excluded equity, admiralty, and law merchant was also forgotten. The national decisional law in the various branches of the law of nations was never labeled federal common law until long after *Swift*. Ambiguity could be avoided if it again was labeled national customary law.

Great justices and leading scholars have misunderstood *Swift*. Justice Holmes correctly dissented to the existence and application of federal common law,[161] but he did not understand that *Swift* was not a common-law case.[162] Since *Erie v. Tompkins*[163] was a common law tort case, textually governed by Section 34 of the Judiciary Act of 1789, Brandeis had originally written his opinion without reference to any constitutional issue.[164] It was Chief Justice Hughes who laid that issue before the Court in conference with his comment, "If we wish to overrule *Swift v. Tyson,* here is our opportunity."[165] Following this suggestion, Brandeis, for the majority, mistakenly overruled *Swift* because he too did not realize that this law-merchant opinion was not a precedent for common-law decisions.[166]

Section 34 of the Judiciary Act of 1789, as amended to substitute "civil actions" for "trials at common law," is still the national law.[167] It is not applied to admiralty,[168] but is applied to the interstate commercial law.[169] The conclusion of this study is that the latter application is wrong. The Supreme Court holds that state decisional law should regulate interstate and international commercial transactions even though the Constitution delegates this area of law exclusively to the national government. This is clearly wrong. For interstate transactions, the federal courts should apply the Uniform Commercial Code as the national law merchant, not peculiar state statutes which deviate from that code, even if they are the law of the place of contract. The federal courts should make their own interpretations of the Uniform Commercial Code using the principles of the Civil Law.[170] Under the Commerce Clause, they are not bound to follow state decisions when adopting a national law merchant to apply to transactions in commerce among the several states.

A more difficult issue arises when, in the absence of Congressional legislation, interstate transactions are litigated in the state courts. Once the national decisional law is recognized as the only constitutionally valid law for such transactions, it is clear that state courts should be bound to follow federal court precedents in such cases. The Supreme Court should acknowledge that the national customary commercial law is part of the "laws of the United States" under Article III[171] and under the Judiciary Act.[172] Then decisions of state supreme courts applying this law to interstate transactions would be subject to review in the Supreme Court upon petition for certiorari.

It is notable that recognition of a national customary commercial law will not encourage for mercantile cases the forum shopping that was characteristic of the federal common law before *Erie*. If the commercial case is interstate, national and state courts would apply the national decisional law. On the other hand, if a commercial case concerned transactions that were entirely intrastate, the courts would apply local state statutory and decisional law. The choice of law is not based on the procedural issue of whether there is diversity of citizenship. Rather, it is based on the character of the transactions.

Appendix to Chapter 6:
Law Merchant in 1789

While the existence of the law merchant as a subset of maritime law was not part of the practice of most lawyers in 1789, it was part of the available legal literature.[173] A key volume was that of Charles Molloy, *De Jure Maritimo et Navali: or a Treatise of Affairs Maritime and of Commerce*.[174] The revised ninth edition had been published in two volumes in 1769. The significance to *Swift v. Tyson*[175] was Chapter 10 on bills of exchange. In the 39 subtopics found in this chapter, there are references to key centers of trade such as London and Amsterdam that demonstrates that the customary rules are part of the law of nations. None of the topics treat the specific narrow issue that was contested in Swift. Any reader of Molloy's volumes would realize that general commercial law was not part of English common law even if heard by a common-law judge.

Justice Story's *Commentaries on the Law of Bills of Exchange*[176] was published in 1843, and this massive volume of 576 pages integrated the works of the English treatises. It must have been completed just before his *Swift* opinion, and he was able to add two citations to *Swift* before publication. The subtitle indicates that the study covers foreign and inland bills plus illustrations from the commercial law of the nations of continental Europe. Story's first chapter, on the origins of bills of exchange, has extensive citation of their origins in civil law countries.

Story's volume must not have been read by most common-law lawyers and judges in the United States. The so-called *Swift* doctrine in later cases mislabeled that case the foundation for federal common law. A series of federal common law opinions in the Court followed this erroneous doctrine.[177] An outstanding case of this misinterpretation was *Baltimore & Ohio R. Co. v. Baugh*,[178] which is treated in this chapter. Justice Brewer, for the Court, held this common-law tort case to be governed by federal common law in spite of the contrary mandate of Section 34 of the Judiciary Act of 1789. This error was pointed out by Justice Field in dissent. In *Erie R.R. v. Tompkins*,[179] another common-law tort case, Justice Brandeis correctly returned to the mandate of the Judiciary Act and applied state common law. Brandeis failed to overrule the leading erroneous opinion of Brewer in *Baugh*. Instead he mistakenly overruled the law-merchant opinion of Justice Story in *Swift*.

Even in England, where Lord Mansfield, as Chief Justice of Kings Bench, integrated the merchant customs into law, the commercial law was treated as distinct from local common law.[180] Law applied to international commerce had to be a branch of the law of nations. Before England had codified commercial law, the French Code of Commerce had been reprinted in English to facilitate trade.[181] This status of the law merchant was emphasized by Denis C. Heron, Q. C. in his 1877 volume entitled *Jurisprudence and the Relation to the Social Sciences*.[182] He even concludes with the same quotation from Cicero that Justice Story had earlier used in *Swift*:

> Commerce demands an international code for civilized nations of the earth; so that the laws of partnership, insurance, bills of exchange, shipping, and bankruptcy may be uniform. Commerce demands that there should be throughout the civilized world a uniform standard of the precious metals, and a uniform system of coinage. Commerce demands a uniform international system of weights and measures. Commerce demands a uniform system of taxation. Commerce demands that debts should be recovered with equal facility in every country, irrespective of the place of contract. Justice demands that over the entire world there should be no asylum for the criminal. Literature demands that the property in its inventions should be secured by an international law of patents. If ever there shall exist a common coinage and uniform taxation for the civilized world, with international Courts of Justice whose jurisdiction shall extend over continents, civilization will owe these advantages to the origin and progress of International Law. Then, to use the words of Cicero: There shall not be one law at Rome, another at Athens; one now, another hereafter; but one and the same law shall obtain at all places and times. Non erit alia lex Romæ, alia Athenis; alia nunc, alia posthae; sed et apud omnes gentes, et omnia tempora una eademque lex obtinebit.[183]

Notes

1. U.S. Const., Art III, § 2.
2. U.S. Const., Art. I, § 8, Cl. 3.
3. U.S. Const., Art VI, Cl. 2.
4. 41 U.S. (16 Pet.) 1 (1842).
5. See William Crosskey, *Politics and the Constitution in the History of the United States*, II, 856-60 (Univ. of Chicago, 1953); Randall Bridwell and Ralph Whitten, *The Constitution and the Common Law*, 1-4, 61-70, 90-91 (Lexington, MA: D. C. Heath, 1977); Charles Heckman, *The Relationship of Swift v. Tyson to the Status of Commercial Law in the Nineteenth Century and the Federal System*, 17 Am. J. of Legal History 246 (1973); Edwin Dickinson, *The Law of Nations as Part of the National Law of the United States*, 101 U. of Penn. L. Rev. 3, 792, 797-99 (1953).
6. Act of Sept. 24, 1789, ch. 20, § 34, 1 Stat. 92. (1789).
7. An elementary principle of *stare decisis* is that the language used in an opinion must always be read in light of the issues presented, and the ratio *decidendi* is

limited to the facts under discussion. *Cohens v. Virginia*, 19 U.S. (6 Wheat.) 264, 399 (1821); *Humphrey's Ex'r. v. United States*, 295 U.S. 602, 626-27 (1935). See, generally, Arthur Goodhart, *Determining the Ratio Decidendi of a Case*, 40 Yale L. J. 161 (1930); Julius Stone, *Legal System and Lawyers' Reasonings*, 267-74 (Stanford Univ. Press, 1964).

8.   304 U.S. 64 (1938).

9.   See Crosskey, *supra* note 5, at I, 567-70; Bridwell and Whitten, *supra* note 5, 52-53. See generally, Friedrich Savigny, *Private International Law and the Retrospective Operation of Statutes*, 194-272 (2nd. English ed., Clark, 1880).

10. *Gloucester Insurance Co. v. Younger*, 10 Fed. Cas. 495, 500 (no. 5487) (C.C.D. Mass. 1855); Joseph Story, *Commentaries on the Law of Bills of Exchange* 146-52 (2nd. ed., Little-Brown, 1847).

11. Chancellor Kent's commentaries, part V, entitled "Of the Law Concerning Personal Property" begins with a chapter on the history of maritime law followed by a survey of the law merchant. James Kent, *Commentaries on American Law*, 1019 (10th ed. Little-Brown, 1860). This historical relationship is illustrated by the English precedents in commercial law. See, e.g., *Luke v. Lyde*, 2. Burr. 882, 97 Eng. Rep. 614 (K.B. 1759); *Pelly v. Company of the Royal Exchange Assurance*, I Burr. 341, 97 Eng. Rep. 342. (K.B. 1757).

12. Joseph Story, "Progress of Jurisprudence," in *Miscellaneous Writings* 198, 214-15 (W. Story ed., Little-Brown, 1852).

13. See Bridwell and Whitten, *supra* note 5, at 61-68. See generally William Mitchell, *Essay on the Early History of Law Merchant*, ch. 2 (1904); Frederick Sanborn, *Origins of the Early English Maritime and Commercial Law* (Century, 1930); Leon Trakman, *The Law Merchant* (Rothman, 1983); Harold Berman and Colin Kaufman, *The Law of International Commercial Transactions*, 19 Harv. Int'l L. J. 221 (1978).

14. See William Holdsworth, 1 *History of English Law*, 535-44 (7th ed., Univ. of London, 1956); John MacDonnell, *Introduction to John Smith, Compendium of Mercantile Law* (10th ed., Stevens, 1890).

15. *Vanheath v. Turner*, Winch 24, 124 Eng. Rep. 20 (C.P. 1621); *Pierson v. Pounteys*, Yelverton 135, 80 Eng. Rep. 91 (K.B. 1609).

16. *Oaste v. Taylor*, Cro. Jac. 306, 79 Eng. Rep. 262. (K.B. 1613).

17. *Brandoa v. Barnett*, 12 Clark & Finnelly 787, 8 Eng. Rep. 1622 (H.L. 1846); *Ereskine v. Murray*, 2. Ld. Raym. 1542, 92 Eng. Rep. 500 (K.B. 1728); *Mogadara v. Holt*, I Show K.B. 317, 89 Eng. Rep. 597 (K.B. 1691). If evidence showed a clearly established and settled usage among merchants on the issue in contest, no evidence of particular usages of the litigants would be admitted. *Edie v. East India Co.*, 2 Burr. 1216, 97 Eng. Rep. 797 (K.B. 1761).

18. *Goodwin v. Robarts*, L.R. 10 Exch. 337, 346 (1875), affirmed, H.L., 1 App. Cas. 476 (1876).

19. See Charles Fried, *Contract as Promise* 9-21 (Harvard, 1981); Malcolm Sharp, *Promissory Liability*, 7 U. Chi. L. Rev. 1, 250 (1939-40).

20. 20 Fed. Cas. 458 (No. 11, 657) (C.C.D. Mass. 1837).

21. The true and appropriate office of a usage or custom is, to interpret the otherwise indeterminable intentions of parties, and to ascertain the nature and extent of their contracts, arising not from express stipulations, but from mere implications and presumptions, and acts of a doubtful or equivocal character. It may also be admitted to ascertain the true meaning of a particular word, or of particular words in a given instrument, when the word or words have various senses, some common, some qualified, and some technical, according to the subject matter to which they

are applied. But I apprehend that it can never be proper to resort to any usage or custom to control or vary the positive stipulations in a written contract, and a fortiori, not in order to contradict them. An express contract of the parties is always admissible to supersede, or vary, or control a usage or custom; for the latter may always be waived at the will of the parties. But a written and express contract cannot be controlled, or varied, or contradicted by a usage or custom; for that would not only be to admit parol evidence to control, vary, or contradict written contracts; but it would be to allow mere presumptions and implications, properly arising in the absence of any positive expressions of intention, to control, vary, or contradict the most formal and deliberate written declarations of the parties. *Id.* at 459.

22. *Brandoa v. Barnett,* 12 Clark & Finnelly 787, 8 Eng. Rep. I622, 1629 (H.L. 1846) (Lord Campbell).

23. It is no doubt true that negotiability can only be attached to a contract by the law merchant or by a statute; and it is also true that, in determining whether a usage has become so well established as to be binding on the Courts of law, the length of time during which-the usage has existed is an important circumstance to take into consideration; but it is to be remembered that in these days usage is established much more quickly than it was in days gone by; more depends on the number of the transactions which help to create it than on the time over which the transactions are spread; and it is probably no exaggeration to say that nowadays there are more business transactions in an hour than there were in a week a century ago. Therefore, the comparatively recent origin of this class of securities in my view creates no difficulty in the way of holding that they are negotiable by virtue of the law merchant; they are dealt in as negotiable instruments in every minute of a working day and to the extent of many thousands of pounds. It is also to be remembered that the law merchant is not fixed and stereotyped; it has not yet been arrested in its growth by being molded into a code; it is capable of being expanded and enlarged so as to meet the wants and requirements of trade in the varying circumstances of commerce, the effect of which is that it approves and adopts from time to time those usages of merchants which are found necessary for the convenience of trade; our common law, of which the law merchant is but a branch, has in the hands of the judges the same facility for adapting itself to the changing needs of the general public; principles do not alter, but old rules of applying them change, and new rules spring into existence. *Edelstein v. Schuler & Co.,* [1902] 2 K.B. 144, 154-155.

24. Thomas Scrutton, *The Influence of the Roman Law on the Law of England,* ch. 15 (1885). Justice Story commented on the origins of modern contract law: "The truth is, that the common law, however reluctant it may be to make the acknowledgment, and however boastful it may be of its own perfection, owes to the civil law, and its elegant and indefatigable commentators . . . almost all its valuable doctrines and expositions of the law of contract. The very action of assumpsit, in its modern refinements, breathes the spirit of its origin. It is altogether Roman and Praetorian." (Joseph Story, *Growth of the Commercial Law,* in *Miscellaneous Writings* 262, 280 [W. Story, ed., 1852]). See William Buckland, *A Manual of Roman Private Law,* ch. 12 (1953).

25. 43 Eliza. C. 12 (1601), *reenacted and amended* 13-14 Car. II, c. 23 (1661). See William Holdsworth, *The Development of the Law Merchant and its Courts,* in *Select Essays in Anglo-American Legal History,* 289, 329 (1907). In spite of efficient, summary procedure, the court had a short life because it was held in 1658 that the proceedings were not a bar to an action at common law. *Came v. Moye,* 2 Sid. 121, 82 Eng. Rep. 1290 (K.B. 1658).

26. See Holdsworth, *English Law, supra* note 14, at 535-44.

27. The first reported case on a negotiable instrument in the common-law courts was *Martin v. Boure,* Cro. Jac. 6, 79 Eng. Rep. 6 (Ex. Ch. 1603).

28. See Thomas Scrutton, *Elements of Mercantile Law,* 13 (London: Clowes, 1891); Francis Burdick, *What is the Law Merchant?* 2 Colum. L. Rev. 470, 479 (1902).

29. See review of this phenomenon in Cecil Fifoot, *Lord Mansfield,* ch. 4 (Oxford: Clarendon Press, 1936). William Holdsworth, 12 *History of English Law,* 524-42. (1938).

30. *Carter v. Downish,* I Show K.B. 127, 89 Eng. Rep. 492, 493 (K.B. 1689); *Williams v. Williams,* Carthew 269, 90 Eng. Rep. 759, 760 (Ex. Ch. 1693).

31. Melville Bigelow, *The Law of Bills, Notes, and Cheques,* 6 (2d ed. 1900).

32. *Lickbarrow v. Mason,* 2 T.R. 63, 100 Eng. Rep. 35, 40 (K.B. 1787).

33. 2 Burr. 882, 97 Eng. Rep. 614 (K.B. 1759).

34. James Wilson, *Works of James Wilson,* 279 (R. McCloskey ed. 1967).

35. W. Blackstone, *Commentaries on the Laws of England,* 273 (Reprint, 1979). For additional citations, see 1 Crosskey, *supra* note 5, at 33-35, 78¬79, 569.

36. Story, *supra* note 12.

37. *Walden v. LeRoy,* 2 Caines R. 263, 265 (N.Y. Sup. Ct. 1805).

38. *Petrie v. Clark,* 11 S. & R. 377, 389 (Pa. 1824).

39. *Atkinson v. Brooks,* 26 Vt. 569 (1854). He summarized the process as follows:

    The more important question growing out of the case is, perhaps, what is the true commercial rule established upon this subject? And it is of vital importance in regard to commercial usages, that they should, as far as practicable, be uniform throughout the world. And such is necessarily the ultimate desideratum, and will inevitably be the final result. It is therefore, always a question of time as to uniformity in such usages. The basis of such uniformity is convenience and justice combined. And until such rules become measurably settled by practice, they have to be treated as matters of fact, to be passed upon by juries; and when the rule acquires the quality of uniformity, and the character of general acceptance, it is then regarded as matter of law. It is thus that most of the commercial law has from time to time grown up. *Id.* at 578.

40. Act of Sept. 24, 1789, ch. 20 § 34; I Stat. 73, 92 (1789).

41. An Act to Regulate Processes in the Courts of the United States, Act of Sept. 29, 1789, ch. 21, § 2, 1 Stat. 93 (1789). For modern practice, see *Hanna v. Plumer,* 380 U.S. 460 (1965); Charles Wright, *Law of Federal Courts* 358 (4th ed. St. Paul, MI: West Publishing, 1983).

42. Crosskey, *supra* note 5, II, at 868. See also the titles of treatises on both statute and case law such as William Blackstone, *Commentaries on the Laws of England* (1765-1769); Richard Wooddeson, *A Systematical View of the Laws of England* (1792.); Zephaniah Swift, *System of the Laws of the State of Connecticut* (1795). The prior drafts of the Judiciary Act are reviewed in Charles Warren, *New Light on the History of the Federal Judiciary Act of 1789,* 37 Harv. L. Rev. 49 (1923). See critique in Wilfred Ritz, *Rewriting the History of the Judiciary Act of 1789,* 165-79 (1990).

43. See, e.g., *Jackson ex dem. St. John v. Chew,* 25 U.S. (12 Wheat.) 153 (1827); *Wheaton v. Peters,* 33 U.S. (8 Pet.) 591 (1834).

44. 149 U.S. 368, 391 (1893). In his extensive discussion of the meaning of Section 34 of the Judiciary Act of 1789 in trials at common law, Field did not mention *Swift.* One possible inference is that Field correctly understood that Section 34 did not apply to the law merchant.

45. For an example of a context where "laws" had to be a synonym for legislation, see the "necessary and proper" clause of Article I, Section 8. There, the entire article is

concerned with legislation. Similarly, the word "Laws" on the title page of a code, such as the Laws of New York, has the restricted context of legislation only.

46. 149 U.S. 398.

47. See Chapter 4.

48. See Bridwell and Whitten, *supra* note 5, at 61-62, 95.

49. U.S. Const., Amend. 10.

50. See the concurring opinion of Justice William Johnson in *Gibbons v. Ogden*, 22 U.S. (9 Wheat.) 1, 222, 224-26 (1824); *Edgar v. Mite Corp.*, 457 U.S. 624, 640 (1982).

51. *Southern Pacific Co. v. Arizona*, 315 U.S. 761 (1945); *Lewis v. BT Inv. Managers, Inc.*, 447 U.S. 27, 35-37 (1980).

52. Henry Maine, *Popular Government* 253 (London: Murray, 1886). The Constitution must be interpreted as a unified whole within the English constitutional and common-law legal environment of its adoption. *Ex parte Grossman*, 267 U.S. 87, 108-9 (1925); *United States v. Wong Kim Ark*, 169 U.S. 649, 668-72. (1898). See the comments of Justice Henry Baldwin, *Origin and Nature of the Constitution and Government of the United States*, 9 L. Ed. 869, 893-94 (1837).

53. International commerce was a significant part of the life of the nation even before the revolution. As a part of British commerce, its disputes were governed by the law merchant. After ratification of the Constitution, and absent congressional regulation, interstate commerce was of the same legal character as international. *Buckner v. Finley*, 27 U.S. (2 Pet.) 586, 590-91 (1829).

54. *Donnell v. Columbian Insurance Co.*, 7 Fed. Cas. 889, 895 (no. 3, 978) (C.C.D. Mass. 1836); *The Seneca*, 21 Fed. Cas. 1081, 1082-84 (no. 12, 670) (C.C.E.D. Pa. 1829). See J. Story, "Growth of the Commercial Law," in *Miscellaneous Writings*, 262, 268, 281 (1852).

55. *United States v. Burr*, 25 F. Cas. 187, 188 (no. 14, 694) (C.C.D. Va. 1807). This view was reiterated by Chief Justice Taney in *United States v. Reid*, 53 U.S. (12 How.) 361, 363 (1851): "The language of this section cannot, upon any fair construction, be extended beyond civil cases at common law as contra-distinguished from suits in equity."

56. 1 Stat. 93 (1789).

57. William Rawle, *A View of the Constitution of the United States of America*, 257 (Philadelphia: Carey and Lea, 1825). See *Robinson v. Campbell*, 16 U.S. (3 Wheat.) 212, 223 (1818).

58. *Pennsylvania v. Wheeling & Belmont Bridge Co.*, 54 U.S. (13 How.) 518, 563 (1852). See *United States v. Coolidge*, 25 Fed. Cas. 619, 620 (no. 14, 857) (C.C.D. Mass. 1813). Justice Story on circuit in Maine stated, "The equity jurisdiction of this court is wholly independent of the local laws of any state; and is the same in its nature and extent, as the equity jurisdiction of England, from which ours is derived, and is governed by the same principles." *Gordon v. Hobart*, in Fed. Cas. 795, 797 (no. 5, 609) (C.C.D. Me. 1836). See Gerald Dunne, *Joseph Story and the Rise of the Supreme Court* 415-20 (1970); Carl Swisher, *The Taney Period: 1836-64, 5 History of the Supreme Court of the United States*, ch. 13 (New York: Macmillan, 1974).

59. 41 U.S. (16 Pet.) 1, 19.

60. Heckman, *supra* note 5, at 247-48.

61. *Hawkins v. Barney's Lessee*, 30 U.S. (5 Pet.) 457, 464 (1831). See Peter S. Du Ponceau, *A Dissertation on the Nature and Extent of the Jurisdiction of the Courts of the United States* 36-37 (1824; reprint, Arno Press, 1972); Rawle, *View of the Constitution*, *supra* note 57, at 246-47 (1815); Walter Rose, *A Code of Federal Procedure*, 67-69 (San Francisco: Bancroft-Whitney, 1907).

62. The conflict-of-laws principles were of international origin and were thus part of the law of nations. See, e.g., *Ogden v. Saunders,* 2.5 U.S. (12. Wheat.) 213, 359 (1827) (Johnson, J.). Justice Story's treatise on the conflict of laws contains an early chapter entitled "General Maxims of. International Jurisprudence." J. Story, *Commentaries on the Conflict of Laws,* ch. 2, (1834). Story relied greatly on the writings of the European civilians and especially on Ulricus Huber, *De Conflictu Legum in Diversis Imperiis.* See Note, 3 U.S. (3 Dallas) 370-77 (1797); Earnest Lorenzen, *Huber's De Conflictu Legum,* 13 Ill. L. Rev. 375 (1919); Lorenzen, *Story's Commentaries on the Conflict of Laws,* 48 Harv. L. Rev. 18 (1934).

63. See *Erie v. Tompkins,* 304 U.S. 64, 74-76 (1938); Bridwell and Whitten, *supra* note 5, at 1-3.

64. *Id.* at 3-4, 61-97.

65. *Swift v. Tyson,* 41 U.S. (16 Pet.) 1, 18 (1842).

66. 25 U.S. (12. Wheat.) 153 (1827). See Rose, *A Code of Federal Procedure, supra,* note 61 at 71.

67. 11 U.S. (7 Cranch) 115 (1812) (Story, J.).

68. 33 U.S. (8 Pet.) 591 (1834). See G. Edward White, *The Marshall Court and Cultural Change,* 1815-35; *History of the Supreme Court of the United States,* III-IV, 384-426 (New York: Macmillan, 1988); R. Kent Newmyer, *Supreme Court Justice Story,* 140-43 (1985).

69. 33 U.S. at 658.

70. 41 U.S. (16 Pet.) 1 (1842).

71. 31 U.S. (6 Pet.) 291 (1832).

72. *Id.* at 299-300.

73. 46 U.S. (5 How.) 134 (1847).

74. 40 U.S. (15 Pet.) 449 (1841).

75. 46 U.S. (5 How.) at 139. The basic principle of *Rowan,* protecting the obligation of contract, was followed in *Gelpcke v. Dubuque,* 68 U.S. (I Wall.) 175 (184).

76. *Wilson v. Mason,* 5 U.S. (1 Cranch) 45, 94-95 (180i).

77. William Fletcher, *The General Common Law and Section 34 of the Judiciary Act of 1789,* 97 Harv. L. Rev. 1513, 1539 (1984).

78. *Thurston v. Koch,* I L. Ed. (4 Dall.) 862, 929 (C.C.D. Pa. 1800). Peters further stated, "I deem myself bound to follow what was the established law and custom of merchants of England, at the time of becoming an independent nation: not because it was the law merely of that country; but because it was, and is, our law" (*Id.* at 930).

79. *Marine Insurance Co. v. Tucker,* 7 U.S. (3 Cranch) 357, 393 (1806).

80. Fletcher, *supra* note 77, at 1576.

81. See Story, "Growth of the Commercial Law," in *Miscellaneous Writings,* 262-94 (W. Story ed., 1852).

82. *Donnell v. Columbian Insurance Co.,* 7 Fed. Cas. 889, 893-94 (no. 3,987) (C.C.D. Mass. 1836); *Robinson v. Commonwealth Ins. Co.,* 20 Fed. Cas. 1002, 1004 (no. 11,949) (C.C.D. Mass. 1838); *Williams v. Suffolk Ins. Co.,* 29 Fed. Cas. 1402, 2405 (no. 17,738) (C.C.D. Mass. 1838).

83. *Williams,* 29 Fed. Cas. at 1405.

84. Blackstone, *Commentaries on the Laws of England, supra* note 35; Richard Wooddeson, *The Elements of Jurisprudence,* 92 (1783); Samuel Marshall, *A Treatise on the Law of Insurance,* 18-20 (1st American ed., 1805); James Sullivan, *History of Land Titles in Massachusetts,* 337-38 (1801); St. George Tucker, ed., *Blackstone's Commentaries,* 429-30 (1803); Zephaniah Swift, *A Digest of the Law of Evidence in Criminal Cases and a Treatise on Bills of Exchange and Promissory Notes,* 245

(Cooke, 1810); Wilson, *Works of James Wilson,* infra note 141 and accompanying text; Peter Du Ponceau, *Dissertation on the Nature and Extent of the Jurisdiction of the Courts of the United States,* 39-41 (1824); Rawle, *supra* note 57, 225; Thomas Sergeant, *Constitutional Law,* 148-50 (2d ed., 1830). One could also cite the extrajudicial writings of Story, such as his 1821 article (see *supra* note 12).

85. 9 Fed. Cas. 62 (no. 4,791) (C.C.D. Ohio 1839).

86. *Id.* at 64.

87. *Id.* at 65.

88. 27 U.S. (2 Pet.) 586 (1829).

89. *Id.* at 592.

90. 28 Fed. Cas. 1062 (no. 16,871) (C.C.D. R.I. 1812), affirmed in part but reversed on other grounds sub nom. *Clark v. Van Reimsdyk,* 13 U.S. (9 Cranch) 153 (1815).

91. See Story, *Commentaries on the Law of Bills of Exchange, supra* note 10. The first American conflict-of-laws treatise was published in 1828. Samuel Livermore, *Dissertation on the Questions which Arise from the Contrariety of the Positive Laws of Different States and Nation,* (New Orleans: B. Levy, 1828). The first edition of Joseph Story's *Commentaries on the Conflict of Laws* was 1834.

92. 28 Fed. Cas. at 1065.

93. *Id.*

94. 15 U.S. (2. Wheat.) 66 (1817). See White, *supra* note 68, at 795-99, 810-13.

95. *Payson v. Coolidge,* 19 Fed. Cas. 19 (no. 10,860) (C.C.D. Mass. 1814).

96. 19 Fed. Cas. at 21.

97. 27 U.S. (2 Pet.) 170 (1829).

98. 20 Fed. Cas. 801 (no. 11,835) (C.C.D. Ohio 1841).

99. 41 U.S. (16 Pet.) 1 (1842). The history of this case and citations to the many commentaries thereon is in Tony Freyer, *Harmony and Dissonance* (N.Y. Univ. Press, 1981).

100. 20 Fed. Cas. 801 (no. 11,835) (C.C.D. Ohio 1841).

101. Story has been criticized for stating the entire test in terms of valuable consideration when the precedents required proof that the bill of exchange was taken in the ordinary course of business or trade. See Karl Llewellyn, *The Common Law Tradition,* 410-16 (Little-Brown, 1960).

102. *Coolidge v. Payson,* 15 U.S. (2 Wheat.) 66 (1817); *Townsley v. Sumrall,* 2.7 U.S. (2 Pet.) 170 (1829).

103. 41 U.S. (16 Pet.) at 18 (emphasis added). See 2 Crosskey, *supra* note 5, at 857-58. This jurisprudential approach was borrowed from the then-common British practice, where most recorded opinions were not settled law because they were not decided in the highest appeals court, the House of Lords. Lord Mansfield stated: "[T]he law of England would be a strange science indeed if it were decided upon precedents only. Precedents serve to illustrate principles and give them a fixed certainty. But the law of England, which is exclusive of positive law enacted by statute, depends upon principles and these principles run through all the cases according as the particular circumstances of each have been found to fall within the one or the other of them" (Jones v. Randall, I Cowper 37, 39, 98 Eng. Rep. 754, 755 [K.B. 1774]). See John Salmond, *The Theory of Judicial Precedents,* 16 L. Quart. Rev. 376, 379-80 (1900). As to the adoption by early American courts of this method of writing opinions on the basis of general principles with little citation of precedents, see Julius Goebel, "The Common Law and the Constitution," in *Chief Justice John Marshall* 101, 108-15 (W. Jones ed., Cornell Univ. Press, 1956).

104. 41 U.S. (16 Pet.) at 18-19. See. Chief Justice Taney's reaffirmation of his support for Story's opinion in Swift by his later express adoption of the Swift rationale. *Meade v. Beale,* 16 Fed. Cas. 1283, 1291 (no. 9371) (C.C.D. Md. 1850).

105. The canons of documentary interpretation and construction, though not usually classified as a part of the law of nations, can be traced to the civil law. Herbert Jolowicz, *The Roman Foundations of Modern Law,* ch. 2. (Clarendon Press, 1957). Thomas Rutherforth, *Institutes of Natural Law* 404-35 (2d. Amer. ed., 1832) relies primarily on Grotius as authority. The rules are thus international in character and not dependent on the law of any single state.

    In *Lane v. Vick,* 44 U.S. (3 How.) 464 (1845), the Court applied general canons of documentary construction to a will and refused to follow the contrary precedent of the Mississippi Supreme Court. Justice McKinley, in dissent, argued that the Court should have followed *lex loci rei sitae* because the effect of the decision was to determine title to real property. *Id.* at 482.

106. 2 Burr. 882, 97 Eng. Rep. 614 (K.B. 1759).

107. *Id.* at 617.

108. Justice Story was a nationalist on a court of states' righters. He was not the leader or even dominant on the Taney Court. For example, he felt it necessary to dissent in three leading cases during the first term that Taney was chief justice. *Charles River Bridge v. Warren Bridge,* 36 U.S. (II Pet.) 420, 583ff (1837); *New York v. Miln* 36 U.S. (11 Pet.) 102, 1530 (1837); *Briscoe v. Bank of Kentucky,* 36 U.S. (111 Pet.) 257, 328s (1837). See letter of Joseph Story to James Kent, June 26, 1837, in *Life and Letters of Joseph Story,* II, 270 (W. Story ed., 1851).

109. See, e.g., *Brown v. Van Braam,* 3 U.S. (3 Dallas) 334 (1797) (conflict-of-laws rules required that the right to damages be determined under a Rhode Island statute of 1743). See Bridwell and Whitten, *supra* note 5, at 78-79.

110. 41 U.S. (16 Pet.) 495 (1842).

111. We have not thought it necessary upon this occasion to go into an examination of the cases cited from the New York and Massachusetts Reports, either upon this last point, or upon the former point. The decisions in those cases are certainly open to some of the grave doubts and difficulties suggested at the bar as to their true bearing and results. The circumstances, however attending them, are distinguishable from those of the case now before us, and they certainly cannot be admitted to govern it. The questions under our considerations are questions of general commercial law and depend upon the construction of a contract of insurance, which is by no means local in its character or regulated by any local policy or customs. Whatever respect, therefore, the decisions of State tribunals may have on such a subject, and they certainly are entitled to great respect, they cannot conclude the judgment of this court. On the contrary, we are bound to interpret this instrument according to our own opinion of its true intent and objects, aided by all the lights which can obtained from all external sources whatsoever; and if the result to which we have arrived differs from that of these learned State courts, we may regret it, but it cannot be permitted to alter our judgment. 41 U.S. 511-512.

112. 59 U.S. (18 How.) 517 (1855). See *Oates v. National Bank,* 100 U.S. 239, 246 (1879).

113. 59 U.S. at 521. Justice Daniel was considered the most extreme states' rights proponent of the Taney Court. He would never have written this nationalist opinion if it were not a clear expression of standing law. See John Frank, *Justice Daniel Dissenting,* (Harvard U. Press, 1964).

114. 28 Fed. Cas. 1062 (no. 16,871) (C.C.D. R.I. 1812.). See *supra* notes 85 to 88 and accompanying text.

115. U.S. Const., Art. VI, cl. 2.

116. See *supra* note 42 and accompanying text.

117. The fact that an earlier draft of this clause was in terms of "the legislative acts of the United States" is not a contextual fact to limit its scope. The shift to "laws of

the United States" was most likely a deliberate choice to broaden the language to include national decisional law to be adopted by the new judiciary. See Crosskey, *supra* note 5, II, at 994. Crosskey's contrary conclusion fails to consider the law of nations as separate from the common law for application of the supremacy clause.
118. U.S. Const., Art. VI, Cl. 2.
119. See sources cited in note, *Federal Common Law and Article III: A Jurisdictional Approach to Erie,* 74 Yale L. J. 325, 335 (1964).
120. *Village of Bensenville v. City of Chicago,* 16 Ill. App. 3d 733, 306 N.E. 2.d 512. (1973) (state common law of nuisance for noise pollution preempted by the Federal Aviation Act and the Federal Noise Control Act of 1972); *In re Hendricksen's Estate,* 15 Neb. 463, 56 N.W. 2d 711, 719 (1953) (U.S. Treasury regulations relating to U.S. bonds preempt state law of decedent estates).
121. *Standard Oil Co. of New Jersey v. United States,* 340 U.S. 54, 59-60 (1950). See Story, Commentaries on the Conflict of Laws 24 (1834). The suggestion that federal courts were bound to adopt English maritime law rather than the civil codes of continental Europe on the few issues where they differed is erroneous. In *De Lovio v. Boit,* 7 Fed. Cas. 418 (No. 3, 776) (C.C.D. Mass. 1815), Justice Story held a policy of marine insurance was a maritime contract cognizable in admiralty. To reach this decision, he had to reject the restricted view that had come to prevail in England at the time the Constitution was adopted. Instead, he applied the broader rule of the civil codes. When the precisely same question finally reached the Supreme Court in 1870, Justice Story's opinion was praised as "a monument of his great erudition" and his conclusion on marine insurance was approved as correct. *Insurance Company v. Dunham,* 78 U.S. (II Wall.) I, 35 (1870). See White, *supra* note 68, at 428-44.
122. Justice M'Kean of the Pennsylvania Supreme Court, in an action on an international bill of exchange, observed:
> This is an action of very considerable importance, not only as it affects the present parties but as it affects every holder, drawer, or indorser of a bill of exchange. The honor and justice of the state are, indeed, likewise interested, that the decision should be conformably to the generally mercantile law of nations, lest a deviation should be imputed to our ignorance or disrespect, of what is right and proper. It should be remembered too, that the defendant is a stranger, and that the event of this suit can be no further obligatory, elsewhere, than as it corresponds with the universal and established usage of all countries; for, upon the present question, that, and not the local regulations of Pennsylvania, must furnish the rule of determination.

Steinmetz v. Currie, 1 U.S. (1 Dallas) 270 (Pa. 1788).
123. Richard Perry and John Cooper, eds., *Sources of Our Liberties,* 303, 309, 346, 381 (American Bar Foundation, 1959); James McClellan, *Joseph Story and the American Constitution* 189-93 (Univ. Oklahoma Press, 1971).
124. U.S. Const., Art. III, § 2.
125. 1 Stat. 76-77 (1789), as modified still in effect in 28 U.S.C. 1333 (1993).
126. *New Jersey Steam Nav. Co. v. Merchants' Bank,* 47 U.S. (6 How.) 344, 386 (1848) (contract for the carriage of goods by sea was maritime). This decision, in which Chief Justice Taney concurred, construed the breadth of the national maritime jurisdiction in an opinion comparable to that of Justice Story in *DeLovio v. Boit,* 7 Fed. Cas. 418 (no. 3, 776) (C.C.D. Mass. 1815). See *supra* note 121.
127. See Alfred Hill, *The Law-Making Power of the Federal Courts,* 67 Colum. L. Rev. 1024, 1032-33 (1967).

128. *Pope & Talbot, Inc. v. Hawn,* 346 U.S. 406, 409 (ir953); *Levinson v. Deupree,* 345 U.S. 648, 651 (1953). See Theodore Stevens, *Erie R.R. v. Tompkins and the Uniform General Maritime Law,* 64 Harv. L. Rev. 246, (1950).

129. *Sears v. The Scotia,* 81 U.S. (14 Wall.) 170, 187-88 (1872); *The Maggie Hammond v. Morland,* 75 U.S. (9 Wall.) 435, 453-53 (1870). For an earlier explanation by Justice Washington of the importance of civil codes as one source of the law of nations see *The Seneca,* 21 Fed. Cas. 1081, 1083 (no. 12,670) (C.C.E.D. Pa. 1829). See Grant Gilmore and Charles Black, *The Law of Admiralty,* 45 (Foundation Press, 2d ed. 1975); David Robertson, A*dmiralty and Federalism,* 136 (Foundation Press, 1970).

130. *Moragne v. States Marine Lines, Inc.,* 398 U.S. 375 (1970), overruling *The Harrisburg,* 119 U.S. 199 (1886).

131. See note: *The Legitimacy of Civil Law Reasoning in the Common Law: Justice Harlan's Contribution,* 82 Yale L.J. 2.58 (1972).

132. 244 U.S. 205, 215 (1917) (New York Workmen's Compensation Act held unconstitutional as applied to employees engaged in maritime work). Justice Holmes's dissent in favor of liability, as had been ruled below by the New York Court of Appeals, seems sounder. Jensen was not a maritime seaman but was a longshoreman on a gangway helping unload a ship in port. The Court's refusal to apply the saving clause of Section 9 of the Judiciary Act of 1789 (1 Stat. 76, 77, 89) governing common-law remedies seems wrong. Even though the remedy provided by the Compensation Act was unknown to the common law, it was supplementary thereto, insuring injured workmen; it was not in derogation of common law. Under the Seventh Amendment, for example, the right to trial by jury in suits at common law includes statutory civil actions for damages unknown to the common law. *Curtis v. Loether,* 415 U.S. 189 (1974).

133. See a review of the history in Dickinson, *Law of Nations, supra* note 5, at 804-16.

134. *Pope & Talbot, Inc. v. Hawn,* 346 U.S. 406, 409-10 (1953).

135. *Byrd v. Byrd,* 657 F. 2d 615, 617 (4th Cir. 1981) (admiralty rules preempt state doctrines of interspousal immunity in negligence action by wife against husband for maintaining unsafe boat).

136. *Wilburn Boat Co. v. Fireman's Fund Insurance Co.,* 348 U.S. 310 (1955).

137. *Id.* at 314. See Gilmore and Black, *Admiralty, supra* note 129, at 68-71.

138. *Garrett v. Moore-McCormick Co.,* 317 U.S. 2.39 (1942) (national customary admiralty rules on the burden of proof required to invalidate a release preempt state law).

139. *Roberson v. N.V. Stoomvaart Maatschappij,* 504 F.2d 994 (5th Cir. 1975) (state statute requiring substitution of plaintiff for the deceased within one year was preempted by national customary admiralty law). For earlier authority, see *The Moses Taylor,* 71 U.S., (4 Wall.) 411 (1866); The *Hine v. Trevor,* 71 U.S. (4 Wall.) 555 (1866).

140. *Pope & Talbot Inc. v. Hawn,* 346, U.S. 406, 410 (1953).

141. Wilson, *The Works of James Wilson,* 279 (R. McCloskey ed., 1967). In the footnote to this paragraph, Wilson quotes Justice Wilmot's statement in *Pillans v. Van Mierop.,* 3 Burr. 1663, 1670, 97 Eng. Rep. 1035, 1040 (K.B. 1765): In commercial cases, "all nations ought to have their laws conformable to each other. *Fides sevanda est; simplicitas juris gentium praevaleat."* (Faith must be kept; the simplicity of the law of nations must prevail.)

142. 15 U.S. (2. Wheat.) 66 (1817).

143. *Id.* at 75.

144. *Id.* at 76.
145. 27 U.S. (2 Pet.) 586 (1829).
146. *Townsley v. Sumrall,* 27 U.S. (2 Pet.) 170, 179, n.a. (1829).
147. See Crosskey, *supra* note 5, II, at 843.
148. 20 Fed. Cas. 801 (no. 11,835) (D. Ohio 1841).
149. *Id.* at 802.
150. 11 Ohio 172 (1842).
151. *Id.* at 191-92.
152. See, e.g., *Bank of Mobile v. Hall,* 6 Ala. 639, 644 (1844); *Bostwick v. Dodge,* I Douglas 413 (Mich. 1844) Reddic K. V. Jones, 28 N.C. 107, 110 (1847); *Allaire v. Hartshorne,* 2.1 N.J. 665, 667-68 (1847); *Blanchard v. Stevens,* 57 Mass. 162, 166 (1849).
153. *Stalker v. McDonald,* 6 Hill 93 (N.Y. 1843). The rejection of *Swift* was unnecessary in this case because the facts showed the transaction was clearly outside the ordinary course of business. See Llewellyn, *supra* note 101, 416-17.
154. For an analysis of state-court deviation from the *Swift* rule, see Charles Heckman, *Uniform Commercial Law in the Nineteenth Century Federal Courts,* 27 Emory L. J. 45, 50-51 (1978).
155. *Id.* See, e.g., *Burns Mortgage Co. v. Fried,* 2.92. U.S. 487 (1934); Frederick Beutel, *Common Law Judicial Technique and the Law of Negotiable Instruments-Two Unfortunate Decisions,* 9 Tulane L. Rev. 60, 65-67 (1934).
156. 304 U.S. 64 (1938). See analyses of Crosskey, *supra* note 5, II, at 912- 37; Wright, *supra* note 41, at 352-64. The Congress could have preempted the common law in the fact situation of Erie with a statute pursuant to the commerce clause regulating tort liabilities of carriers in commerce among the several states. *Id.* at 363 n. 17. Absent congressional preemption, Section 34 of the Judiciary Act of 1789, by incorporating established conflict-of-laws rules, mandated application of the law of the state where the tort occurred.
157. 313 U.S. 487 (1941). See critique in Henry Hart, *The Relations between State and Federal Law,* 54 Colum. L. Rev. 5, 419, 513-15 (1954) Alfred Hill, *The Erie Doctrine and the Constitution,* 53 NW. U. L. Rev. 417, 541 (1958).
158. *In re King Porter Co.,* 446 F. 2d 722, 732. (5th Cir. 1971).
159. *United Overseas Bank v. Veneers, Inc.,* 375 F. Supp. 596, 601 (D.C. Md. 1974).
160. *Walter v. Marine Office of America,* 537 F.2d 89, 94 (5th Cir. 1976).
161. *Kuhn v. Fairmont Coal Co.,* 215 U.S. 349, 370 (1910) (Holmes, J., dissenting); *Black & White Taxicab & Transfer Co. v. Brown & Yellow Taxicab & Transfer Co.,* 276 U.S. 518, 532. (1928) (Holmes, J. dissenting).
162. While Holmes's summary of *Swift* centered on the jurisprudential obiter dictum on the meaning of laws and indicates that he did not understand *Swift* as an interstate law-merchant case, his instinct was correct when he wrote: "I should leave *Swift v. Tyson* undisturbed, as I indicated in *Kuhn v. Fairmont Coal Co.,* but I would not allow it to spread the assumed dominion into new fields" (*Id.* at 535). Writing to Sir Frederick Pollock, Holmes stated that *Swift v. Tyson* "was unjustifiable in theory but did no great harm when confined to what Story dealt with 2 *Holmes-Pollack Letters,* 215 (Mark Howe ed., Harvard Univ. Press, 1941).
163. 304 U.S. 64 (1938).
164. Merlo J. Pusey, *Charles Evans Hughes,* 711 (New York: Macmillan Co., 1951). Justice Brandeis correctly asserted that judicial creation of a federal common law had a legal significance that extended beyond misconstruction of Section 34 of the Judiciary Act. The issue was constitutional because Section 34 merely reiterated for trials at common law the principle of federalism that is the truism of the Tenth

Amendment. See Henry Friendly, *In Praise of Erie*, 39 N.Y.U. L. Rev. 383, 385-91 (1964).

165. Pusey, *Hughes, supra* note 164 at 710. See Llewellyn, *Common Law Tradition, supra,* note 101, at 417.

166. Brandeis should have overruled *City of Chicago v. Robbins,* 67 U.S. (2 Blk.) 418 (1862); *Baltimore & Ohio R. Co. v. Baugh,* 249 U.S. 368 (1893); and the other cases creating a federal common law of torts.

167. Act of June 15, 1948, c. 646, 62 Stat. 944, 28 U.S.C.A. § 1652 (1966).

168. *Pope & Talbot, Inc. v. Hawn,* 346 U.S. 406, 409 (1953).

169. *United States v. Guaranty Trust Co.,* 293 U.S. 340 (1934); *Oken Frankman Livestock, etc. v. Citizens Nat.,* 605 F.2d 1082, 1085 (8th Cir. 1979).

170. Noting the civil-law origins of the law merchant, Professor Beutel asserted in writing of a predecessor code, "There is overwhelming evidence that the N.I.L. is a codification of law in the truly civilian sense, that it was so intended by the framers and the bar, and that such is the understanding of Anglo-American jurists" (Beutel, *supra* note 155, at 67, n. 20). See also Beutel, "The Necessity of a New Technique of Interpreting the N.I.L.," 6 *Tulane L. Rev.,* (19 31). As to the Uniform Commercial Code as a source for the federal law of sales, see *United States v. Wegematic Corporation,* 360 F.2d 674, 676 (2d Cir. 1966).

171. 72 Stat. 415, 28 U.S.C. § 1331 (1958).

172. U.S. Const., Art. III, § 2.

173. See Sanborn, *Origins of Early English Maritime and Commercial Law, supra,* note 13; James S. Rogers, *Early History of the Law of Bills and Notes,* (Cambridge University Press, 1995).

174. (London: T. Waller, 1769).

175. 41 U.S. (16 Pet.) 1 (1842).

176. (Boston: Little & Brown, 1843).

177. See Tony Freyer, *Harmony and Dissonance: The Swift & Erie Cases in American Federalism,* Ch. 2 (New York: New York University Press, 1981).

178. 249 U.S. 368 (1893).

179. 304 U.S. 64 (1938).

180. See note 29, *supra.* Compare David Lieberman, *The Province of Legislation Determined,* 99-121 (Cambridge University Press, 1989); James Oldham, *English Common Law in the Age of Mansfield,* 152-164 (Chapel Hill: University of North Carolina Press, 2004).

181. The French Code of Commerce was reprinted in English in Leopold Goirand, *A Treatise upon French Commercial Law,* 2d ed., (London: Stevens, 1898). The code chapter on bills of exchange begins on p. 578.

182. (Cambridge: Riverside Press, 1877).

183. *Id.* at 147.

7

Constitutional Privileges and Immunities: The Ninth Amendment and the Antimonopoly Tradition

The Fourteenth Amendment provides in part: "No state shall make or enforce any law which shall abridge the privileges or immunities of citizens of the United States."[1] This clause has been interpreted by the Supreme Court to have almost no effect.[2] The view here, based on a historical review of the English and American origins of the phrase, is that "privileges or immunities" was a synonym for constitutional limitations. The conclusion is that the states shall not make laws that abridge the constitutional limitations of citizens of the United States. The language must mean that all types and classes of civil rights of citizens protected by the Constitution against invasion by the national government are also protected from invasion by the state governments.

There is necessarily a partial redundancy here. As explained in Chapter 8, the textual meaning of the due process clause of this amendment incorporated, *inter alia*, the procedural protections of persons in the Bill of Rights as constraints against the states. The general textual language of the Privileges or Immunities Clause, while designed primarily to incorporate the substantive protections of persons in the Bill of Rights, needed generality which in effect overlapped the due process clause by protecting all civil liberties.

The language of the two clauses was probably deemed an efficient way to secure against state infringement a minimum set of civil rights to all citizens. If some state constitutions had fewer civil rights clauses than the national constitution, the national standard was to be the minimum. The objective of protecting civil rights of former slaves would not be satisfied by the Equal Protection Clause alone if any state had few express constitutional limitations and also rejected those derived from the British Constitution, the Rights of Englishmen. Furthermore, extant state constitutional limitations could be repealed in the future by amendment of state constitutions. A clear example is eminent domain, the right to just compensation for property taken by government.[3] This is effective against the national government in the Fifth Amendment. If this right was not in a state constitution in 1868 or was there but was subsequently repealed by amendment, the Privileges or Immunities Clause would still assure every citizen the right to just compensation as a remedy.

This chapter treats a neglected issue, the American significance of the British common law and constitutional tradition barring governmental grants of monopoly in the ordinary trades. The thesis is that this constitutional limitation was retained for the American people by the Ninth Amendment. The effect of the amendment is to make the limitation an original immunity of citizens of the United States. It became operative against state action by virtue of the Privileges or Immunities Clause of the Fourteenth Amendment. The conclusion is that the 5 to 4 majority decision in the *Slaughter-House Cases,*[4] upholding a state grant of monopoly in butchering, was erroneous. Of the four dissenters, the opinion of Justice Field, emphasizing the Privileges or Immunities Clause, at least pointed to the correct law based on the Anglo-American antimonopoly tradition. It will be shown that the failure to raise and argue the Ninth Amendment in that case was fatal to the decision because this was the only way to make the antimonopoly tradition an immunity of citizens of the United States.

Privileges and Immunities: Historical Meanings

The word "privileges," when used in the context of the relationship of a citizen to government, as found in the interstate Privileges and Immunities Clause of Article IV, Section 2 of the Constitution, was a synonym for the words liberties or franchises.[5] It represented a class of activities in which citizens were free to engage: affirmative or active liberties that government had no legal right to restrain. The word "immunity," when used in the context of the relationship of citizens to government, meant exemption.[6] It designated negative or passive liberties, the citizens' freedom from the legal power of government to act on some topic. It was an exemption from possible future legal liability, such as the immunity from unreasonable searches and seizures.

Privileges and immunities, or synonymous terms, had their origins in American law in the Charter of Virginia of 1606 which read as follows:

> Alsoe wee doe, for us, our heires and successors, declare by theise presentes that all and everie the parsons being our subjects which shall dwell and inhabit within everie or anie of the said severall Colonies and plantacions and everie of theire children which shall happen to be borne within the limitts and precincts of the said severall Colonies and plantacions shall have and enjoy all liberties, franchises and immunities within anie of our other dominions to all intents and purposes as if they had been abiding and borne within this our realme of Englande or anie other of our saide dominions.[7]

The phrase "liberties, franchises and immunities of free denizens or natural borne subjects" appears also in the Charter of New England of 1620,[8] in the

Charter of Maine of 1639,[9] and in the Charter of Georgia of 1732.[10] The phrase "liberties and immunities of free and natural born subjects" is in the Charter of Massachusetts Bay of 1629,[11] in the Charter of Connecticut of 1662,[12] and in the Charter of Rhode Island and Providence Plantations of 1663.[13] The Charter of Maryland of 1632 used "privileges, franchises and immunities,"[14] while the Charter of Carolina of 1663 used "liberties, franchises and privileges."[15]

The significance of the language of privileges and immunities is that it referred to the civil rights of Englishmen against their government-constitutional limitations. The colonial charters did not use the word "rights" because a colonist was not entitled to every interpersonal right created by English law for citizens of England. Since much of the detailed municipal law in England might be unsuitable in the colonies, the colonists were granted power in their charters to make their own laws, so long as these were consistent with the charters and with the part of English law which in its language was expressly made applicable to the colonies.[16]

In the declarations of civil rights made by the colonists pursuant to their limited law-making power, the privileges and immunities of Englishmen were reaffirmed. For example, the Massachusetts Body of Liberties of 1641 had a preamble which began: "The free fruition of such liberties Immunities and priviledges as humanitie, Civilitie and Christianitie call for. . . ."[17] In 1664, Richard Nicolls, Governor of New York, wrote to assure the people of Long Island that they would have "equal (if not greater freedomes & Immunityes) than any of his Majesties Colonyes in New England."[18] In 1682, William Penn proclaimed a Frame of Government of Pennsylvania in which he confirmed "these liberties, franchises and properties, to be held, enjoyed and kept by the freemen, planters, and inhabitants of the said province of *Pennsilvania* for ever."[19] Penn's Pennsylvania Charter of Privileges of 1701 confirmed the enjoyment of certain stated "Liberties, Franchises and Privileges," such as liberty of conscience and rights to witnesses and counsel in criminal cases.[20]

In the eighteenth century, as the conflicts with England increased, new resolutions were made, again using the language of privileges and immunities. In 1765, the Massachusetts legislature resolved that "no Man can justly take the Property of another without his Consent" and that "this inherent Right, together with all other, essential Rights, Liberties, Privileges and Immunities of the People of Great Britain, have been fully confirmed to them by Magna Carta. . . ."[21] Similar language was in the Resolutions of the House of Burgesses of Virginia Against the Stamp Act[22] and the Resolutions of the Stamp Act Congress,[23] both in 1765. In 1774, the colonists were still asserting loyalty to the crown, but demands for their civil rights as English subjects became more insistent. In Virginia, the Fairfax County Resolutions asserted this claim in terms of privileges, immunities, and advantages.[24] The series of intolerable acts by the English government led to the calling of the First Continental Congress. On October 14, 1774, the Congress issued its Declaration and Resolves and asserted Americans' entitlement to the civil rights of Englishmen, this time in terms of rights, liberties, and immunities.[25]

The 170 years of legal-linguistic history establishes that the words "privileges" and "immunities" had established meanings when they were included in Article IV of the Articles of Confederation.[26] They were a summary phrase to connote all constitutional rights of citizens against government, the constitutional limitations on the legitimate power of government to invade those rights.[27]

The evidence indicates that the privileges and immunities of citizens in Article IV of the Articles of Confederation were primarily those of the English Constitution. This is clearly seen from the first committee draft of July 12, 1775, in which the language in Article VI was:

> The inhabitants of each Colony shall henceforth always have the same Rights, Liberties, Privileges, Immunities and Advantages in the other Colonies, which the said Inhabitants now have, in all Cases whatever, except in those provided for by the next following Article.[28]

This was before most states had adopted constitutions, so that the phrase "which the said Inhabitants now have" had to refer to the English constitutional limitations. In other words, the Declaration of Independence discarded those parts of the English Constitution that imposed a framework of government while retaining the constitutional rights of Englishmen that the colonists had argued so long were theirs.

The final version of November 11, 1777, dropped the words "Rights," "Liberties," and "Advantages" so that the language became "privileges and immunities."[29] Each of the states, as a sovereign nation, thus agreed to give visitors from other states the benefit of its constitutional limitations. Each did not, however, want to give visitors the benefit of rights and advantages created by ordinary statutes. Citizens of a state taxed themselves to provide many benefits, such as fishing and hunting grounds, which were meant not for visitors but for the local citizens who paid for them.

The Articles of Confederation were superseded by the Constitution in 1789. The interstate Privileges and Immunities Clause of Article IV, Section 2 of the Constitution is clearly a modified form of the clause in the articles. The constitutional clause states: "The Citizens of each State shall be entitled to all Privileges and Immunities of Citizens in the Several States."[30] In the articles, the beneficiaries of comity had been the "free inhabitants" of each state, which included all free residents regardless of race.[31] In the Constitution, this was changed to "citizens." Both Chief Justice Roger Taney and Justice Benjamin Curtis later presented the view that in the late eighteenth century the words "free inhabitants," "citizens," and "the people" were synonymous.[32] They were the men and women who, as the Preamble indicates, ordained and established the Constitution.[33]

Hence, it is unlikely that this change in wording made a difference.[34] The free residents of one state, whether they had met the technical requirements of state citizenship or not, were, under English constitutional tradition, entitled to the benefit of the constitutional limitations where domiciled.[35] No common law lawyer would expect resident aliens to lose them when visiting another state. A resident alien, living in one state, would reasonably have expected, for example, the privilege of trial by jury in criminal cases and immunity from attainder in any other state he entered.

Given its derivation from Article IV of the Articles of Confederation, the interstate Privileges and Immunities Clause of the Constitution must also refer to the English constitutional limitations plus the additions to them and expansions of them found in the state constitutions. In 1789 and for some time thereafter, some states did not have bills of rights and others had only partial enumeration of the established constitutional rights inherited from England. Given this essential similarity of the state constitutional limitations in the early days of the Union and the view that the national Bill of Rights was also mostly an enumeration of previous English civil rights, it is not surprising that some persons spoke of all of them collectively. Thus, the Republicans at the time of the Civil War argued that Article IV, Section 2 was more than interstate.[36] It could connote all constitutional rights of Americans, including those found in state and federal constitutions. They argued that "in the several states" meant in the United States and was not equivalent to "of the several states." The majority interpretation, generally accepted today, restricts the clause to its interstate character. Citizens of one state, visiting a second or migrating thereto, are entitled to all the privileges and immunities found in the constitutional law of the second.[37]

The courts and commentators have largely failed to realize that privileges and immunities meant constitutional limitations. Instead of referring to the pre-Revolutionary origins of the constitutional language, they relied on the *obiter dictum* of Justice Bushrod Washington, on circuit, in *Corfield v. Coryell*,[38] and misinterpreted him. The statutory privilege in this case which was denied to out-of-state citizens was the permission to dredge for oysters in New Jersey waters. The issue clearly was statutory and not a constitutional privilege. Justice Washington commented generally:

> We feel no hesitation in confining these expressions to those privileges and immunities which are, in their nature, fundamental; which belong, of right, to the citizens of all free governments; and which have, at all times, been enjoyed by the citizens of the several states which compose this Union, from the time of their becoming free, independent, and sovereign.[39]

Some courts and commentators have labeled this *dictum* a natural law approach because of the phrase "which belong of right, to the citizens of all free governments."[40] This is probably wrong. The free governments to which Justice Washington referred were England and the nations and states with English constitutional heritage. Analysis of the whole paragraph shows that Justice Washington was not using the word fundamental in its natural law sense but in its positive law sense as a synonym for constitutional. The latter was by far the most common use of fundamental at the time.[41] He says these are the privileges and immunities which Americans have had since declaring independence and recites a list of some of the specific ones. All of these examples are positive constitutional limitations derived from our English legal heritage.[42]

Because he used the label "fundamental," Justice Washington's insight in *Corfield*, that privileges and immunities meant constitutional limitations, was misunderstood by later courts. This history has been reviewed by others and does not deserve further treatment here.[43] Two recent Supreme Court opinions illustrate the state of the law on interstate privileges and immunities. In *Baldwin v. Montana Fish & Game Commission*,[44] a state statute with substantially higher hunting licensing fees for nonresidents to hunt elk was held not to deny privileges immunities under Article IV, Section 2. Justice Harry Blackmun summarized the view of Justice Stephen Field in *Paul v. Virginia*[45] that the objective of the clause was to relieve nonresidents from "disabilities of alienage in other states." He also noted that the clause has been interpreted not to enforce natural law but to prevent states from discriminating against citizens of other states in favor of their own. The test of violation of the clause is whether the discrimination was of such significance that it would frustrate the purposes of the formation of the Union. Elk hunting "is not basic to the maintenance or well-being of the Union."[46] The Court failed to realize that the true distinction is between privileges and immunities, which are constitutional, as opposed to those rights that are created by ordinary statutes.

In *Baldwin* Justice Blackmun raised one issue pertinent to this study. He noted that earlier cases have held that the interstate Privileges and Immunities Clause prevents a state from "imposing unreasonable burdens on citizens of other States in their pursuit of common callings within the State."[47] One would expect the issue to be argued under the Commerce Clause rather than the Privileges and Immunities Clause.[48] Nonetheless, the earlier cases he cited give at least collateral support for the view that grants of monopoly in the ordinary callings and trades are unconstitutional.

In *Supreme Court of New Hampshire v. Piper*,[49] the practice of law was held to be a "privilege" under Article IV, Section 2. A rule of the New Hampshire Supreme Court limited admission to the bar to state residents. Piper lived in Vermont about four hundred yards from the New Hampshire border and passed the New Hampshire bar examination. Upon denial of admission, she brought this action. The practice of law was held a privilege "bearing on the vitality of the nation as a single entity."[50] The justifications offered by the state court were held not to be substantial reasons for difference in treatment.[51] Furthermore, the discrimination did not bear a close and substantial relationship to the State's objectives.

The treatment of Kathryn Piper here is radically different from that of Myra Bradwell in 1873, when the practice of law was held not to be a "privilege" under the Fourteenth Amendment.[52] The problem is that both cases concern equaled protection of the laws and not privileges and immunities. The practice of law is not a civil right of all persons and therefore should not be ruled a "privilege" under the Constitution. Both Piper and Bradwell were denied equal protection of the laws because they met all the requirements for admission to the bar and were still denied admission. Neither residence nor gender has a rational relationship to being a qualified attorney.

Privileges or Immunities Clause

The Privileges or Immunities Clause of the Fourteenth Amendment adopts the phrase "privileges [or] immunities of citizens" from Article IV, Section 2.[53] That part of the language of the two sections are *in pari materia* and must have the same meaning. It has been shown that 260 years of American legal-linguistic history between the Charter of Virginia and the drafting of the Fourteenth Amendment gave a clear meaning to "privileges" and "immunities" in a constitutional context. Thus, Article IV, Section 2 referred to state constitutional limitations and the Fourteenth Amendment referred to the national constitutional limitations. The national privileges and immunities of citizens of the United States are found in the original Constitution, in the Bill of Rights, and in English constitutional protections of 1791 preserved by the Ninth Amendment. Under this theory, the states are prohibited by the Fourteenth Amendment from making or enforcing any laws that would abridge the classes of civil rights against government delineated in those three sources of constitutional limitations.

The meaning of the Privileges or Immunities Clause is further confirmed by the fact that Section 1 of the Fourteenth Amendment was designed to overrule the doctrine of *Scott v. Sandford*.[54] It had been standing constitutional law under that case that a person of African descent, even if a citizen of one of the states, could not be a citizen of the United States and therefore had no protections under the national Constitution. The primary decision of this case was that persons of African descent were not entitled to the privilege of suing in courts of the United States under the interstate diverse-citizenship jurisdiction.[55] Taney further stated that such persons, even if citizens of a state, would not be entitled to state constitutional limitations guaranteed to "the citizens of each state" in Article IV, Section 2.[56]

In overruling *Dred Scott,* the Fourteenth Amendment enjoined the states from abridging all "the privileges or immunities of citizens of the United States." These were not just those of citizens of a state, such as suing in national courts on the basis of diversity of citizenship. They also included items in the original constitution such as the privilege of the writ of habeas corpus and all of the privileges and immunities guaranteed in Amendments I to VIII.[57] The most efficient way to assure minimum civil rights to former slaves and even to poor whites, who were without political power, was to make the Bill of Rights effective against states.[58] Otherwise, such fundamental privileges and immunities as those guaranteed by the First Amendment could be massively abridged by white elites controlling governments in some of the states.

This textual interpretation vindicates the dissenting views of the first Justice John M. Harlan in some early cases.[59] It also confirms the view of Justice Hugo L. Black, stated in his dissenting opinion in the 5 to 4 decision in *Adamson v. California*,[60] that the Fourteenth Amendment incorporated, *inter alia*, Amendments I to VIII of the Bill of Rights as effective against the state governments. The Court in *Adamson*, and for many years thereafter, rejected Black's view on general incorporation of most clauses of the Bill of Rights. As reviewed in Chapter 8, the later Court majorities subsequently engaged via the Due Process Clause in selective incorporation on a case by case basis, to accomplish much the same result.[61] The Court later expressly overruled the generalizations against incorporation of the immunity clauses of the Bill of Rights that had been expounded in the early case of *Maxwell v. Dow*[62] and in effect repudiated another early case denying incorporation, *O'Neil v. Vermont*.[63] In *Malloy v. Hogan*,[64] the court also overruled the specific holdings and rationales of *Adamson* and of the leading early case, *Twining v. New Jersey*,[65] which had relied on *Maxwell* to deny incorporation of the Bill of Rights. But the Court steadfastly has refused to adopt the rule of total incorporation.

The refusal of the Court to adopt the Privileges or Immunities Clause of the Fourteenth Amendment as one vehicle to incorporate those sections of the Bill of Rights against the states has created an irrationality in the law. Amendments I to IV are substantive. During the 1920's and 1930's the Court had used the doctrine of substantive due process to incorporate the First Amendment into the Fourteenth as effective against state governments.[66] In the economic regulation cases, the Court subsequently repudiated the doctrine of substantive due process as an unwarranted judicial fabrication, a usurpation of the amending power by the judiciary.[67] Since the Due Process Clause correctly refers only to procedural protections, the use of due process to incorporate the First Amendment remains an illogical anomaly in our law.

The leading case on other meaning of the Privileges or Immunities Clause is the *Slaughter-House Cases*,[68] but the issue of incorporation of the Bill of Rights by the Privileges or Immunities Clause was mentioned by the majority in the case only in dictum. As Professor John H. Ely suggests, however, a close reading of the various opinions in that case points to the possibility that all nine justices took the position that the language of the clause directed incorporation.[69] The majority opinion held that state grants of monopoly in the ordinary trades were solely an issue of state constitutional law. As to the Fourteenth Amendment, the majority stated:

[L]est it should be said that no such privileges and immunities are to be found if those we have been considering are excluded, we venture to suggest some which owe their existence to the Federal government, its National character, its Constitution, or its laws. . . . The right to peaceably assemble and petition for redress of grievances, the privilege of the writ of habeas corpus, are rights of the citizen guaranteed by the Federal Constitution.[70]

This was a clear recognition by the majority that the Privileges or Immunities Clause incorporated the First Amendment. Only one of the dissenting justices found it necessary to treat incorporation expressly. Justice Joseph P. Bradley summarized a number of the specific privileges and immunities in the Bill of Rights and then stated, "These, and still others, are specified in the original Constitution or in the early Amendments of it, as among the privileges and immunities of citizens of the United States, or, what is still stronger for the force of the argument, the rights of all persons whether citizens or not."[71]

Additional support for the incorporation theory as the reasonable meaning of the language of the Privileges or Immunities Clause at the time of adoption is found in the circuit court opinion in the first case decided under the clause. *United States v. Hall*[72] was a criminal prosecution of Ku Klux Klan members for violation of the Voting Rights Enforcement Act of 1870. The indictment that was held valid charged defendants with unlawfully preventing one Hays from exercise of freedom of speech and peaceable assembly in violation of the Constitution. Judge William Woods, who later served on the Supreme Court, quoted some of the language of *Corfield v. Coryell*[73] and then observed that the Fourteenth Amendment made the first eight amendments enforceable against the states:

We think, therefore, that the right of freedom of speech, and the other rights enumerated in the first eight articles of amendment to the constitution of the United States, are the privileges and immunities of citizens of the United States, that they are secured by the constitution, that congress has the power to protect them by appropriate legislation. We are further of opinion that the act on which this indictment is founded applies to cases of this kind, and that it is legislation appropriate to the end in view, namely, the protection of the fundamental rights of citizens of the United States.[74]

The Ninth Amendment

A thesis of this study is that one of the unenumerated rights preserved for the people by the Ninth Amendment was the prohibition of grants of domestic monopolies in the ordinary trades. The historical background of this amendment will only be summarized here, since others have treated the history in detail.[75] When the issue of a proposed declaration of civil rights was raised near the end of the Constitutional Convention, it was voted down. The debates indicate that the delegates felt that the civil rights of Englishmen against government, which they argued were theirs, did not need enumeration.[76] When the subsequent demand for an express bill of rights became so great that it was a condition of ratification, James Madison promised to introduce the proposals for amendment in the first Congress.[77]

Once the adoption of a bill of rights was agreed upon, a clause relating to unenumerated civil rights was urged for two reasons. The first was to indicate that the express restraints did not imply that Congress had been delegated power to act on the listed topics. The second was to indicate that there was no implication that unenumerated civil rights were forfeited to the national government. Madison's original proposal read as follows:

> The exceptions here or elsewhere in the Constitution, made in favor of particular rights, shall not be so construed as to diminish the just importance of other rights retained by the people, or as to enlarge the powers delegated by the Constitution; but either as actual limitations of such powers, or as inserted merely for greater caution.[78]

The language used here and Madison's proposal that it be inserted in Article I, Section 9 of the Constitution, indicate that the constraints were on the national government only and not on the states.[79]

After revision by the select committee, of which Madison was a member, the portion indicating that no additional powers in Congress were implied by the enumeration was dropped. The final version that was enacted read: "The enumeration in the Constitution, of certain rights, shall not be construed to deny or disparage others retained by the people."[80] The language states a rule of construction for those government agencies that will interpret the Constitution. It notes that certain of the civil rights of citizens against government have been enumerated in the Constitution and Bill of Rights and implies that other rights existent at the time were not. The objective is to preserve the latter. "This clause was manifestly introduced to prevent any perverse or ingenious misapplication of the well-known maxim, that an affirmation in particular implies a negation of all others."[81]

The first premise in a search for unenumerated rights is to recall that constitutional language must be interpreted as of date of adoption.[82] This is reinforced here by the key verb in the Ninth Amendment, "retained," which meant to keep hold or possession of that which one already had. Consequently, one will find the unenumerated civil rights in the substantive standing constitutional law of England and the American states in 1791.[83] None of the meager literature on the Ninth Amendment has approached its content in these terms. Irvin Kent has attempted the most comprehensive survey of unenumerated rights under four categories: (1) personal freedoms; (2) family relationships; (3) economics; and (4) participation in organized society.[84] The majority of rights he lists are really enumerated rights or derived from them, such as the right to engage in political activity or to vote or to seek office.[85] Others are those created by courts more recently and fail to meet the criterion of existence in 1791. Kent lists one right that relates to immunity from monopoly, the right to earn a livelihood.

John H. Ely argues that the literal meaning of the Ninth Amendment, as a reference to standing, unenumerated constitutional rights, is conclusively shown by its subsequent adoption in twenty-six state bills of rights.[86] The clause was not in the few partial bills of rights adopted by states before the national convention because Americans in those times must have thought it unnecessary. They automatically considered all the privileges and immunities of Englishmen as their birthright, part of their heritage.[87] After the Congress thought it wise to preserve these same unenumerated rights expressly in the Ninth Amendment, most of the later state conventions in the nineteenth century, in drafting their more comprehensive bills of rights, considered it wise also to adopt a similar clause.

One key example of an unenumerated substantive civil right is the right to possess, use, and dispose of property according to the common law rules, subject to such statutory regulation as the legislature enacts for the public welfare. This right can be traced, in part, to Chapters 28, 30, and 31 of Magna Carta and the Bill of Rights of 1689.[88] Protection of some aspects of the property right is found in two sections of the Fifth Amendment.[89] The Due Process Clause assures full and fair procedure when one is deprived of property by a rule of law. The Takings Clause assures just compensation when property is taken for public use by the national government. For 150 years, American courts have continued to cite as authority the statement of Justice Bushrod Washington that one of the fundamental or constitutional privileges and immunities of our heritage, comprehended under Article IV, Section 2 of the Constitution, is the right "to take, hold and dispose of property, either real or personal.[90] One can conclude that there was not a general protection for property in the Bill of Rights because it was such an agreed principle of Anglo-American constitutional law that restating it was unnecessary.

The antimonopoly tradition of the English Constitution, as restated in the original constitutions of two states and in the recommendations of five states to the first congress for inclusion in the Bill of Rights, was a significant element of American constitutional heritage. This was augmented in 1776 by publication of Adam Smith's *An Inquiry into the Nature and Causes of the Wealth of Nations*. His was a powerful statement for the supreme value of individual liberty and free trade as an element of that liberty. William Holdsworth recounts the substantial influence of the *Wealth of Nations* on political and legal institutions.[91] Thus, the arguments against mercantilism, which had promoted monopoly in international trade, reinforced the policy against domestic monopolies that had been confirmed in the law a century before. Like the right to property, the rule against governmental grants of monopolies in the ordinary trades was taken for granted. It was so completely accepted as part of the constitutional foundation of England and America, that enumeration was unnecessary.

The Ninth Amendment has had little hearing in the courts and has never been more than a partial basis for a Supreme Court decision.[92] The most prominent

Supreme Court case in which the Ninth Amendment was introduced as a partial basis of decision was *Griswold* v. *Connecticut*.[93] Though he did not elaborate on the Ninth Amendment, Justice William Douglas, writing for the majority in *Griswold*, listed the Ninth Amendment as one of six constitutional clauses that had penumbras combining to create a civil right of privacy. And Justice Arthur Goldberg, in his concurring opinion, relied heavily upon the Ninth Amendment.[94] From the viewpoint presented here, *Griswold* was a poor fact setting in which to raise the Ninth Amendment. In effect, both Justices Douglas and Goldberg sought to create a new constitutional right of privacy out of personal value judgments against the state statute limiting birth control. There was, however, no class of English constitutional immunities against government in 1791 relating to privacy in the general sense under which a statute preventing birth control could be subsumed.[95] The Justices, therefore, had no textual support for a Ninth Amendment argument, and it is unfortunate that *Griswold* stands as the foremost reference to the meaning of the amendment.[96]

Antimonopoly Tradition in England

The tradition against governmental grants of domestic monopolies in England seems to have begun with Chapter 41 of Magna Carta.[97] This chapter was designed to protect one small sector of competition, that of foreign merchants. Since these merchants had not been protected by the common law of the land, King John had extracted large tolls from them, impeding the introduction to England of types of goods not previously known there or not amenable to efficient production there. Chapter 41 guaranteed them safe conduct, liberty to buy and sell, and confirmation of the ancient rates of "customs."[98]

The right of the English sovereign to grant monopolies to inventors and to persons introducing new goods from abroad as a reward for benefit given to the community was always recognized as part of the common law prerogative.[99] In theory, a monopoly could not be granted by the crown without some consideration moving to the public, since monopolies were considered to be in derogation of the common right to freedom of trade. In practice, however, the sovereigns of England from the fourteenth to the sixteenth centuries granted all types of monopolies, some as royal favors, and some to finance the crown treasury. Royal grants of monopolies to merchants were common. Consequently, Parliament enacted statutes in the fourteenth century designed to curtail these grants.[100]

During this era, the superiority of parliament was not established. Kings granted monopolies in spite of statutory prohibitions. The response of Parliament was to reenact statutes asserting the liberty of English merchants to buy and sell goods without governmental restraint.[101] William Cunningham quotes Sandys' paper on "Instructions towchinge the Bill for Free Trade" on the broad scope of the 1497 statute.[102] In the sixteenth century, patents of monopoly were issued to promote the introduction into England of the advanced knowledge on industrial arts on the continent. In the latter part of the century, however, Queen Elizabeth granted many patents of monopoly on commodities in general use such as alum, salt, soap, and playing cards. Universal discontent led to an address from the Commons to the Queen in 1597 and a declaratory bill in Parliament to restore common law freedom of trade.[103] The Queen responded with a concession that the courts could determine the legality of patents of monopoly. This was followed by a proclamation revoking some of the patents, and the bill in Commons was withdrawn.

The common law rule that monopolies were void unless they were for the common good is cited in two leading cases. In *Davenant v. Hurdis*,[104] the Company of Merchant Tailors had been empowered in its charter from the crown, which had been confirmed by Parliament, to make ordinances to govern the corporation. One ordinance required each member to send at least one-half of the cloth sent out to be dressed to another member of the corporation. The penalty for violation was ten shillings for each cloth. The ordinance was held void as a monopoly in violation of the common law.

The second leading case was *Darcy v. Allin*,[105] best known as the *Case of Monopolies*. In 1598, the Queen had granted Darcy a patent for the manufacture and transport of playing cards for twenty-one years. Darcy brought this action against Allin, who began manufacture of cards in competition. The grant was held void as a monopoly against the common law and in violation of earlier statutes protecting free trade. The case is famous as the most comprehensive statement of the common law of monopolies at the beginning of the seventeenth century. The exaggerations of Lord Coke that crown grants of monopolies had been forbidden by law since Magna Charta became part of the accepted law.[106] The significance of this case in Anglo-American constitutional law has not been overlooked. Professor James B. Thayer of Harvard Law School included a full report in his *Cases on Constitutional Law*.[107]

The *Case of Monopolies* was reinforced in 1614 by the Kings Bench decision in *Cloth Workers of Ipswich*.[108] This was an action for a penalty by the Corporation of Tailors of Ipswich charging that defendant had practiced the trade of tailor without serving an apprenticeship of seven years. The royal charter granting the monopoly was held unenforceable since it took away the common law right of any man to work at a lawful trade. The rule was reiterated in the *Dublin Corporation Case*,[109] an action in *quo warranto* holding a crown grant of monopoly to a guild of merchants within one city to be void. These cases are evidence that control of trades by the guilds, dating back at least to the thirteenth century, was in decline.

In spite of the decision in the *Case of Monopolies*, King James continued to exercise his royal prerogative to issue patents of monopoly. The number became so great that the House of Commons filed petitions of protest with King James in 1606 and 1610. The second provoked a declaration of the King, or *Book of Bounty*, that monopolies were against the laws of the realm.[110] Finally, on July

10, 1621, King James issued a proclamation revoking certain monopolies.[111] The culmination of these protests was the proceeding in the House of Commons against Sir Giles Mompesson for abuse of monopolies.[112] He was expelled from the House.

Another petition of grievance of the Commons against monopolies in 1623 led to a second legal milestone of constitutional status in England, the Statute of Monopolies.[113] The first section declared all royal grants of domestic monopolies to be void. The second section provided that the validity of letters patent should be determined by the courts according to the common law. The third section disabled all persons and corporations from exercising monopolies. The fourth section gave any party aggrieved by action of a monopoly a right to recover treble damages and double costs. Other sections provided exemptions of fourteen years for new manufactures.

Section 9 of the Statute of Monopolies exempted municipalities and existing corporations or companies of craftsmen or merchants. This is easily understandable in the mercantilist setting of the times. It was 150 years before the free market philosophy of Adam Smith. Nevertheless, the decisions in the *Davenant, Ipswich*, and *Dublin Corporation* cases indicate that monopoly power in corporations was limited. In the seventeenth century, persons outside the corporations could enter the same trade in competition if they could find customers not concerned by the lack of a guild stamp of quality.

Despite the rule of *Darcy v. Allin* and the Statute of Monopolies, King Charles continued to assert his prerogative to grant monopolies to corporations for the sale of many manufactures.[114] The Company of Playing-Card makers, for example, and received a patent in 1615 and was awarded another in 1637.[115] In 1631, as a technique of taxation, an office was erected for the sealing of playing cards, which further entrenched the monopoly.[116] This resurgence of monopolies again provoked many protests from the Commons. In response, the King issued proclamations in 1639 and 1640 canceling most patents of monopoly.[117] This marked the decline of the monopoly system. In 1641 the Parliament abolished the Court of Star Chamber, where many patents of monopoly had been enforced.[118] During the commonwealth patents were not granted, and after the restoration, Charles II agreed to submit patent applications to the Royal Society for examination to determine invention. The Bill of Rights of 1689[119] abolished the royal prerogative and established parliamentary supremacy. The Commons, having fought the battle against monopolies and won, has never since issued a patent for a domestic monopoly except for invention.[120]

Under the conventions of the English Constitution, the *Case of Monopolies* and the Statute of Monopolies were established fundamental law in 1791 when the Ninth Amendment preserved unenumerated civil rights.[121] The fact that legislative supremacy in England made it possible for Parliament to reverse its long-standing view and start granting domestic monopolies has no bearing on legislative power in the United States. A key function of the United States Bill of Rights was to impose constitutional limitations on both the executive and the legislative branches. Madison, in proposing the national Bill of Rights, noted the great differences between the English and United States Constitutions. He observed that "it may not be thought necessary to provide limits for the legislative power in that country, yet a different opinion prevails in the United States.... The people of many States have thought it necessary to raise barriers against power in all forms and departments of Government. . . ."[122]

Antimonopoly Tradition in America

With the *Case of Monopolies* and the Statute of Monopolies enunciating one of the claimed liberties or immunities of Englishmen, the American colonists could also claim the same benefits by virtue of the colonial charters.[123] Pursuant to the authority granted in their charters, the colonists enacted local law consistent with the charters. The first mention of monopolies was in the Massachusetts Body of Liberties of 1641.[124] Item 9 therein states, "No monopolies shall be granted or allowed amongst us, but of such new Inventions that are profitable to the Countrie, and that for a short time."[125] The Body of Liberties was adopted at the time the greatest victories were won in England against crown grants of monopolies to domestic companies. It was adopted by the General Court of Massachusetts only after consideration by the magistrates and elders in each town and publication for the citizens. As one historian has commented, "a more careful process of legislation is perhaps nowhere recorded."[126]

William Penn, in *The Excellent Priviledge of Liberty & Property Being the Birth-Right of Born Subjects of England*,[127] also examined monopolies. In the section of this pamphlet that is a commentary on Magna Carta, largely from Lord Coke, Penn wrote of Chapter 29 (Chapter 39 in the revised version) and described some practices that were against the law of the land. After summarizing the facts of *Davenant v. Hurdis*[128] and *Darcy v. Allin*,[129] he concluded: "Generally all Monopolies are against the great charter because they are against the Liberty and Freedom of the Subject, and against the Law of the Land."[130]

No other mention of monopolies has been found in the American constitutional documents of the seventeenth century. Sir Edwin Sandys, who played a leading role in obtaining the revised royal charters of Virginia of 1609 and 1612,[131] was one of the outspoken opponents of the grants of monopolies to companies in England. Since Sandys prepared the first draft of the charter of 1609 and did not specifically mention monopolies, historians can only hypothesize that the general protection for free trade in the charter was sufficient to preclude grants of monopoly.[132]

In the eighteenth century, the issue of constitutional immunity against monopolies did not arise until the American Revolution. This can be understood only in light of the fact that the colonists claimed all the constitutional protections of Englishmen,[133] which included the benefit of the Statute of Monopolies and its antecedent common law. When the first state constitutions were enacted, starting with Virginia in 1776, the conventions were more concerned with the structure of their new governments than with civil rights. Only seven states enacted a bills of rights while four more included some civil rights within their constitutions.[134] These states codified only part of the existing English constitutional limitations. Connecticut and Rhode Island did not adopt constitutions and continued state government under their colonial charters. In this context of partial codification, it is not surprising that only two states included specific constitutional provisions against monopolies. The Maryland Constitution of November 3, 1776, contained the following clause: "XXXIX. That monopolies are odious, contrary to the spirit of free government, and the principles of commerce; and ought not to be suffered."[135] The similar clause of the Constitution of North Carolina of December 14, 1776, stated: "XXIII. That perpetuities and monopolies are contrary to the genius of a free State, and ought not to be allowed."[136] One reasonably can conclude that these two constitutional clauses merely codify one element of the standing constitutional law of all Americans, derived from their heritage as English citizens.

Upon adoption of the proposed national constitution by the convention of 1787, the dominant issue in the ratification controversies was whether an express bill of rights should be appended.[137] In his first letter to Madison commenting on the proposed constitution, Jefferson wrote:

> I will now add what I do not like. First the omission of a bill of rights providing clearly and without the aid of sophisms for freedom of religion, freedom of the press, protection against standing armies, *restriction against monopolies,* the eternal and unremitting force of the habeas corpus laws, and trials by jury. . . . Let me add that a bill of rights is what the people are entitled to against every government on earth, general or particular, and what no just government should refuse, or rest on inference.[138]

In so writing, Jefferson seemed to attach as much importance to the English constitutional immunity from grants of monopoly as he did to those privileges and immunities which eventually appeared in the First Amendment.

Five of the states that ratified the Constitution and urged adoption of an express Bill of Rights recommended a prohibition on monopolies. The proposal of the Massachusetts Convention of February 6, 1788 was "[t]hat Congress erect no Company of Merchants with exclusive advantages of commerce."[139] New Hampshire and North Carolina adopted the same language on June 21, 1788 and August 1, 1788, respectively.[140] The New York recommendation of July 26, 1788 was "[t]hat the Congress do not grant Monopolies or erect any Company with exclusive Advantages of Commerce."[141] The belated ratification of Rhode Island on May 29, 1790 contained the same recommendation as New York.[142] While the Rhode Island proposal came too late to have had an effect on Congress in its decisions on which rights should be enumerated in the Bill of Rights, the proposal indicates one more state that found this issue significant. This must be compared with the fact that only four states considered it necessary for express statement in the Bill of Rights of provisions for due process of law, speedy and public trial, and the rights to assembly and petition.[143]

The surprising facts were that neither Virginia nor Maryland recommended a prohibition of monopolies. George Mason of Virginia, major author of the Virginia Declaration of Rights of 1776, refused to sign the constitution in 1787, primarily because it failed to contain a bill of rights.[144] One of his stated objections was that "Congress may grant monopolies in trade and commerce."[145] There is no explanation why Mason did not persuade the Virginia Convention to include a ban on monopolies among its twenty recommendations for a bill of rights. Maryland had adopted a prohibition on monopoly in its state constitution.[146] Hence, it is also difficult to understand why Maryland did not propose the same constraint on the national government.

The express prohibition of monopolies was not among the amendments offered in Congress by Madison nor among those reported by the Select Committee of the House of Representatives. Proposals on the floor of the House and the Senate to add prohibitions on monopolies were defeated.[147] Since Madison had to assuage the Federalists, who controlled both Houses and thought a bill of rights was unnecessary, he eschewed controversial topics that might engender substantial opposition in ratification.

There is no expressed explanation why the Due Process Clause was expressly included in the Bill of Rights and the ban on monopolies was not. Both received the recommendation of four states before action by the Congress. It is clear, however, that those civil rights which were not expressly included in the Bill of Rights were to be preserved. This was the sole purpose of the Ninth Amendment.

Slaughter-House Cases

The *Slaughter-House Cases*[148] was provoked by the grant from the legislature of Louisiana in 1869 to one corporation of a monopoly over the slaughtering of animals for food in New Orleans. Over a thousand trained butchers were deprived of a living, and there was a general feeling of outrage in the community.[149] The result was several hundred suits for injunctions. Five of the actions, either attacking or attempting to enforce the monopoly, were heard on writ of error to the Supreme Court of the United States.[150] After the monopoly had been upheld in the Louisiana Supreme Court and before the appeal was heard in the Supreme Court of the United States, an action to enjoin enforcement of the Louisiana judgments was heard in the United States Circuit Court for Louisiana.[151] Justice Joseph Bradley, on circuit, was of the view that the state grant of monopoly violated the Civil Rights Act[152] and the Privileges or Immunities Clause of the Fourteenth Amendment. As to the latter, he declined to submit a general definition, stating: "But so far as relates to the question in hand, we may safely say it is one of the privileges of every American citizen to adopt and follow such lawful industrial pursuit—not injurious to the community—as he may see fit, without unreasonable regulation or molestation, and without being restricted by any of those unjust, oppressive, and odious monopolies or exclusive privileges which have been condemned by all free governments. . . ."[153]

He noted exceptions to the antimonopoly rule for inventions, for structural monopolies such as railroads, canals, and turnpikes, and for regulating sale of intoxicating drinks and drugs. In this case, however, he found the pretense of a health regulation false. He stated: "But this pretense is too bald for a moment's consideration. It certainly does confer on the defendant corporation a monopoly of a very odious character. If it be not fairly and fully within the definition of a monopoly given in the great case of monopolies (11 Coke, 85), it is difficult to conceive of a case which would be within it."[154] Justice Bradley denied the injunction, however, reasoning that section 3 of the Judiciary Act of 1793[155] prohibited federal courts from enjoining proceedings in state courts.

When the cases from the Louisiana Supreme Court reached the Supreme Court of the United States, they were affirmed by a vote of 5 to 4.[156] Writing for the majority, Justice Samuel Miller asserted that the appellant's argument rested wholly on the assumption that the privileges and immunities guaranteed by Article IV, Section 2, and the Fourteenth Amendment were the same,[157] and consequently rejected that assumption. Justice Miller's assertion, however, was erroneous. Retired Justice John A. Campbell, for the appellants, had merely used ambiguous language. He should have argued more precisely that both classes of privileges and immunities had the same foundation in English constitutional law. Every lawyer and most educated citizens knew that while the state and national bills of rights had many clauses in common, they also had some constitutional limitations that differed. However, Justice Miller went further and, in effect, asserted, also erroneously, that the two sets of privileges and immunities did not overlap—that only state constitutions and interstate Privileges and Immunities Clause protected the many civil rights derived from our English heritage that Justice Washington had labeled *fundamental*.[158] The national privileges and immunities, he reasoned, were only those enumerated in the national Constitution or implied by it, such as the right to travel to the seat of government.

Justice Miller viewed the appellant's argument to be that the Fourteenth Amendment made the Supreme Court of the United States the final arbiter on all civil rights, state and national. Part of the effect would have been to make the Court the final reviewer of state legislation under state constitutions. Having given this extreme, and arguably wrong, interpretation to appellants' arguments, Justice Miller of course rejected them as inconsistent with the structure and spirit of the constitutional division of powers between national and state governments. He concluded that the right to pursue a common calling free from grants of monopoly to others was solely an issue of state privileges and immunities under state constitutional law. Not being enumerated in the Constitution or Bill of Rights, Miller argued it posed no federal issue under the Fourteenth Amendment. He concluded that the Louisiana courts, with their French legal tradition, had the final say when they held the grant of monopoly constitutional.[159]

Professor Louis Lusky, in a penetrating critique of Justice Miller's opinion, calls it an anomaly and considers it based on shabby reasoning.[160] He argues that it also is intellectually dishonest;[161] in that Justice Miller deliberately misquoted Article IV, Section 2 to end with "of the several states,"[162] and trimmed a quotation from *Corfield v. Coryell* to hide the fact that it harmed rather than helped his argument.[163] Furthermore, Professor Lusky argues that Justice Miller denied that Congress had ever undertaken to define any of the privileges or immunities of citizens of the United States, even though the Civil Rights Act of 1866 had an extensive, though incomplete, enumeration.[164] Given Lusky's critique and many prior ones,[165] it is surprising that Justice Miller's opinion is still part of our standing constitutional law. Yet the Supreme Court has held to the opinion that the Privileges or Immunities Clause is without significant effect.[166]

Justice Stephen Field, for the four dissenters in the *Slaughter-House Cases*, viewed the privileges and immunities of citizens of the United States to be much broader. Although he incorrectly held the privileges and immunities protected by the Fourteenth Amendment to be the same as those protected by the Comity Clause of Article IV, he correctly viewed the civil rights derived from our English heritage and labeled by Justice Washington as "fundamental" as not only the foundation of state privileges and immunities but also the foundation of national privileges and immunities.[167] In effect, he held both privileges and immunities clauses to be types of equal protection clauses. Unfortunately, however, and unlike the majority opinion, Field found it unnecessary even to mention the issue whether the Privileges or Immunities Clause incorporated the Bill of Rights. If he *had* adopted the incorporation principle, his opinion would have more closely paralleled the viewpoint of this study and would have been a stronger argument against the Louisiana statute.

Justice Field showed that the substantive privilege or immunity in question in the *Slaughter-House Cases*, immunity from government grants of domestic monopolies in the ordinary trades, was part of our English constitutional heritage. He stated: "All such grants relating to any known trade have been held by all the judges of England, whenever they have come up for consideration, to be void at common law as destroying the freedom of trade, discouraging labor and industry, restraining persons from getting an honest livelihood, and putting it in the power of grantees to enhance the price of commodities."[168]

Field cited the *Case of Monopolies*,[169] *Davenant v. Hurdis*,[170] and the Statute of Monopolies[171] as authorities. He then cited the Declaration and Resolves of the First Continental Congress as preserving these "indubitable rights and liberties" for Americans.[172] He further noted state cases applying the rule against monopolies and concluded by tying the immunity to "the right of free labor, one of the most sacred and imprescriptible rights of man."[173]

The one major legal argument that appellants failed to raise and that could and should have enabled them to win was the applicability of the Ninth Amendment to the states. The political and legal context of the adoption of the Ninth Amendment demonstrates that the national government was, like the state governments, based on the English constitutional tradition, and Justice Field was therefore right to assert that the antimonopoly tradition of English constitutional law was part of our national law. If only the Ninth Amendment had been pleaded in the *Slaughter-House Cases* and the history of its origins argued, Justice Field possibly could have persuaded at least one more justice that the rule against monopolies was part of the Bill of Rights. The incorporation of the Bill of Rights by the Privileges or Immunities Clause as effective against state governments already had been at least noted by the majority, and, consequently, grants of domestic monopolies for ordinary goods or services, whether by the national or the state governments, could have been held unconstitutional.[174]

Ignored until recently, the unenforced Ninth Amendment has left citizens of the United States without the full benefit of their unenumerated substantive civil rights. One result is that Congress has been free to pass regulatory statutes whose effect is equivalent to outright grants of domestic monopolies for ordinary goods and services.[175] In addition, the misconstrued Fourteenth Amendment has left citizens of the United States without remedies against infringement by state governments of unenumerated national civil rights. State statutes granting monopolies in the ordinary trades flourish in many jurisdictions.[176] Overruling the *Slaughter-House Cases* would revive the privileges or immunities clause and enable challenge of modern state regulatory statutes granting monopoly power.

Appendix to Chapter 7: English Constitutional Foundation to The U.S. Bill of Rights

The legal background to and foundation upon which the Bill of Rights was created has not received adequate recognition by the Constitutional historians. The view that Americans inherited the civil rights of Englishmen and could surely enforce them against the state and national governments that they created explains why some men at the Constitution Convention thought a U.S. Bill of Rights was unnecessary.[177] The civil rights of citizens that were declared by the Continental Congress essentially restate the rights of Americans to the English constitutional limitations.

These foundations strongly support the view that the generalization of Chief Justice John Marshall limiting all of the Bill of Rights to the national government in *Barron v. Baltimore*[178] was in error. The litigation concerned what is today classified as inverse condemnation. The city has diverted streams that lowered water levels greatly, making wharves owned by Barron unusable. He claimed that the city took his property without just compensation in violation of the Fifth Amendment. A unanimous Supreme Court held that Baltimore had a governmental right to control water levels and thus there was no condemnation. This is still the law. In 1956, Congress exercised its power to preempt the entire flow of water in a navigable river, depriving the riparian owners of their former use of water.[179] The Supreme Court held that the owners had no vested claim in the waters that could be recognized by the judiciary as constituting "private property."

The problem with *Barron* was that Chief Justice Marshall's rationale was an unnecessary generalization that none of the Bill of Rights applied to the states. He held that the Fifth Amendment's requirement of just compensation was a constraint only on the national government and not on the state governments. In fact, the civil right to just compensation for condemnation of property can be traced to Chapter 28 of Magna Carta.[180] Its restatement in the Fifth Amendment merely proclaimed an inherent right that all English settlers in America considered enforceable against all governments that they created.

One can hypothesize a test whether the Court would follow Marshall's generalization. If the Maryland legislature had decided in 1835 (two years after *Barron*) that a larger parade ground was needed in front of the capital building, it could have ordered direct condemnation of an adjacent city block of land occupied by small shops. Absent an eminent domain clause in 1835 in the state constitution, the state could have refused to pay compensation to the owners of the condemned land. When the landowners brought an action in federal court for just compensation under the Fifth Amendment, their counsel would have argued firstly the distinction between alleged inverse condemnation and clear facts of direct condemnation with clearly measurable losses. They would then have argued the above noted precedents of English constitutional limitations that the founders brought to America and that these could be asserted against all our governments. The later Supreme Court could have found that Chief Justice Marshall, though correct on riparian inverse condemnation, was in error in his generalization in *Barron*.

This viewpoint is shared in the chapter by Professor William W. Crosskey, a renowned textualist. It was entitled "The Supreme Court's Destruction of the Constitutional Limitations on State Authority, Contained in the Original Constitution and Initial Amendments."[181] Crosskey pointed out that only the First Amendment and the appeals clause of the Seventh Amendment were confined to Congress. Thus, a textualist would argue that the other clauses of the Bill of Rights, some of which were longstanding English constitutional law, would apply to the nation and to the states. In the Constitution of 1789, before passage of the Bill of Rights, the framers may have been unsure whether the novel national government that they were creating, outside the common law tradition,[182] would be bound by the established civil liberties in English constitutional law. In Article 1, Section 9, they prohibited suspension of the writ of habeas corpus by the Congress. The framers did not deem it necessary to add habeas corpus to the prohibitions on the states in Article 1, Section 10. They must have presumed that the people in the states had a continuing right against state governments that prevailed since enactment of the English Habeas Corpus Act of 1679. In fact, by 1791 only three states had protected the privilege of habeas corpus in their state constitutions.[183] The failure of the other ten states to do likewise would not limit the protection of all Americans by the English Act. The Ninth Amendment reconfirmed application of the English Act in all the states.

There are many implications from the conclusion that the civil rights in the English "unwritten" constitution were considered by Americans to prevent oppression and to be binding on all governments that they created. First it must be noted that the fine study of this topic by A. E. Dick Howard, *The Road from Runnymede: Magna Carta and Constitutionalism in America,*[184] has been overlooked by most historians.[185] These data establish the legal and social contexts in which the Bill of Rights and state constitutional limitations were drafted. They also explain the main function of the Ninth Amendment to insure that all English constitutional limitations that were not detailed in the U.S. Bill of Rights would still prevail here. A prime example was the English prohibition on government grants of monopolies in the ordinary trades, as explained in this chapter.

Two documents enacted by the Continental Congress demonstrate that most of the Bill of Rights derives from the English charters, statutes, and key judicial opinions that, by convention, are known as the English Constitution. Their existence is strong evidence that the unlimited language in Amendments II through VIII of the Bill of Rights (except for the appeals clause in Amendment VII) was applicable to both the nation and the states. The first of these was the *Declaration and Resolves of the First Continental Congress* in 1774. The key civil rights sections declare:

That the inhabitants of the English colonies in North America, by the immutable laws of nature, the principles of the English constitution, and the several charters or compacts, have the following RIGHTS:

> *Resolved,* N. C. D. 1. That they are entitled to life, liberty and property: and they have never ceded to any foreign power whatever, a right to dispose of either without their consent.

> *Resolved,* N. C. D. 2. That our ancestors, who first settled these colonies, were at the time of their emigration from the mother country, entitled to all the rights, liberties, and immunities of free and natural-born subjects, within the realm of England.

> *Resolved,* N. C. D. 3. That by such emigration they by no means forfeited, surrendered, or lost any of those rights, but that they were, and their descendants now are, entitled to the exercise and enjoyment of all such of them, as their local and other circumstances enable them to exercise and enjoy.

* * *

> *Resolved,* N. C. D. 5. That the respective colonies are entitled to the common law of England, and more especially to the great and inestimable privilege of being tried by their peers of the vicinage, according to the course of that law.

Resolved, 6. That they are entitled to the benefit of such of the English statutes, as existed at the time of their colonization; and which they have, by experience, respectively found to be applicable to their several local and other circumstances.
Resolved, N. C. D. 7. That these, his majesty's colonies, are likewise entitled to all the immunities and privileges granted and confirmed to them by royal charters, or secured by their several codes of provincial laws.
Resolved, N. C. D. 8. That they have a right peaceably to assemble, consider of their grievances, and petition the king; and that all prosecutions, prohibitory proclamations, and commitments for the same, are illegal.[186]

The second applicable document of the Continental Congress was the Northwest Ordinance of 1787 which was subsequently adopted by the first U.S. Congress in 1789. Only the first two articles declare civil rights of persons:

ARTICLE I. No person, demeaning himself in a peaceable and orderly manner, shall ever be molested on account of his mode of worship, or religious sentiments, in the said territory.
ARTICLE II. The inhabitants of the said territory shall always be entitled to the benefits of the writs of *habeas corpus,* and of the trial by jury; of a proportionate representation of the people in the legislature, and of judicial proceedings according to the course of the common law. All persons shall be bailable, unless for capital offences, where the proof shall be evident, or the presumption great. All fines shall be moderate; and no cruel or unusual punishment shall be inflicted. No man shall be deprived of his liberty or property, but by the judgment of his peers, or the law of the land, and should the public exigencies make it necessary, for the common preservation, to take any person's property, or to demand his particular services, full compensation shall be made for the same. And, in the just preservation of rights and property, it is understood and declared, that no law ought ever to be made or have force in the said territory, that shall, in any manner whatever, interfere with or affect private contracts, or engagements, *bona fide,* and without fraud previously formed.[187]

The introduction to the resolves declares the rights of the settlers in the colonies to the benefit of the principles of the English Constitution. Resolve number 7 asserts the rights of colonists to the privileges and immunities of royal charters. When incorporated in the Fourteenth Amendment, the language of "privileges and immunities" is adopted for enforcement of the national constitutional limitations against the states. Resolve number 8, asserting the English constitutional right peaceably to assemble and to petition the chief executive would be effective against the state governments after the American Revolution. These two English constitutional privileges were restated in the First Amendment as constraints on the national Congress.

In the Northwest Ordinance, Article 1 adopts the English constitutional protection of freedom of religion, a protection for minorities where there exists an established national church. In 1787, it was unknown whether any of the future northwest states would adopt a particular Christian religion as established by law. Article 2 restates many English constitutional limitations to be effective in the Northwest. They are restated in the Bill of Rights, Amendments II through

VIII, and, in light of their English history, should have been held effective against state governments.

Saenz v. Roe[188] is the leading recent action in which the Supreme Court has attempted partially to revitalize the Privileges or Immunities Clause of the Fourteenth Amendment. The case concerned a California statute limiting temporary assistance to needy families' benefits. Those moving to California from another state with lower welfare benefits than California would receive the lower amount for the first year. In holding this differential treatment unconstitutional, the Court majority first noted that the constitutional right to move to another state was guaranteed by Article 4, Section 2.[189] The Court correctly cited *Shapiro v. Thompson*,[190] that it was constitutionally impermissible for a state to enact durational residency requirements for the purpose of inhibiting the migration by needy persons into the state. This penalty on a person moving to another state violated the Equal Protection Clause. The Court in *Saenz* asserted that state statutes imposing inequality on newly arrived citizens violated the Citizenship Clause and the Privileges or Immunities Clause of the Fourteenth Amendment.[191] This is noted as supported by *obiter dicta* in the *Slaughter-House Cases*.[192] It is inconsistent with the textualist meaning of constitutional privileges or immunities, which by definition means the U.S. Constitution plus any others in the English constitution that are protected by the Ninth Amendment. Welfare benefits are statutory, not constitutional. Their equality is a substantive issue, enforceable by the Equal Protection Clause.

Notes

1. U.S. Const., Amend. 14, § I. See Richard Cortner, *The Supreme Court and the Second Bill of Rights* (Madison: Univ. of Wisconsin Press, 1981); Michael K. Curtis, *No State Shall Abridge: The Fourteenth Amendment and the Bill of Rights* (Durham, NC: Duke Univ. Press, 1986); Akhil Reed Amar, *The Bill of Rights: Creation and Reconstruction*, Ch. 8 (New Haven: Yale Univ. Press, 1998); Leonard W. Levy, *Origins of the Bill of Rights* (New Haven: Yale Univ. Press, 1999).
2. *Colgate v. Harvey*, 96 U.S. 404 (1935), overruled in *Madden v. Kentucky*, 309 U.S. 83 (1940).
3. U.S. Const., Amend. 5.
4. 83 U.S. (16 Wall.) 36 (1873).
5. William Blackstone, 2 *Commentaries on the Laws of England*, 37 (1765) Reprint (Chicago: Univ. of Chicago Press, 1979); Charles Viner, 8 *A General Abridgement of Law and Equity 508* (2d ed., London: Robinson 1791). The usage is traced to Magna Carta in *Commonwealth v. Alger*, 61 Mass. (7 Cush.) 53, 71 (1851).
6. See Giles Jacob, *Law Dictionary*, 389 (1811). In the *Slaughter-House Cases*, 83 U.S. (16 Wall.) 36 (1873), retired Justice Campbell, for appellants, cited similar definitions. See Nathaniel Lindley, *An Introduction to the Study of Jurisprudence*, Secs. 30-32, app. note § 31 (1855). Reprint (Littleton, CO: F. B. Rothman, 1985).
7. Francis Thorpe, ed., 7 *The Federal and State Constitutions, Colonial Charters and Other Organic Laws*, 3788 (1909) [hereinafter cited as Colonial Charters]. The same language was repeated in Virginia's revised charters of 1609 and 1612. *Id.*, Vol. 7 at 3800, 3805. The earlier letters patent to Sir Humfrey Gylberte and Sir

Walter Raleigh granted colonialists the "privileges of free denizens," *Id.,* Vol. 1 at 51, 55.

8. *Id.,* Vol. 3 at 1839.

9. *Id.* at 1635.

10. *Id.,* Vol. 2 at 773.

11. *Id.,* Vol. 3 at 1857. The Charter of Massachusetts Bay of 1691 used the terms "liberties and immunities." *Id.,* at 1881.

12. *Id.,* Vol. 2 at 533.

13. *Id.,* Vol. 6 at 32.30.

14. *Id.,* Vol. 3 at 1681.

15. *Id.,* Vol. 5 at 2747, 2765.

16. See A. E. Dick Howard, *The Road from Runnymede,* 103-4 (Charlottesville: Univ. of Virginia Press, 1968).

17. Richard Perry and John Cooper, *Sources of Our Liberties* 148 (Chicago: American Bar Foundation, 1959).

18. Letter from Richard Nicolls to the residents of Long Island (1664), quoted in Howard, *supra* note 16, at 71.

19. Perry and Cooper, *supra* note 17, at 212.

20. *Id.* at 256.

21. The Massachusetts Resolves, October 29, 1765, reprinted in Edmund Morgan, *Prologue to Revolution,* 56 (Chapel Hill: Univ. of North Carolina Press, 1959).

22. The resolutions provided in part as follows:

> *Resolved,* That the first Adventurers and Settlers of this his Majesty's Colony and Dominion of Virginia brought with them, and transmitted to their Posterity, and all other his Majesty's Subjects since inhabiting in this his Majesty's said Colony, all the Liberties, Privileges, Franchises and Immunities, that have at any Time been held, enjoyed, and possessed, by the people of Great Britain.

> *Resolved,* that by two royal Charters, granted by King James the First, the Colonists aforesaid are declared entitled to all Liberties, Privileges, and Immunities of Denizens and natural Subjects, to all Intents and Purposes, as if they had been abiding and born within the Realm of England.

> *Resolutions of the House of Burgesses of Virginia against the Stamp Act,* reprinted in Howard, *Runnymede, supra* note 16, at 430.

23. Resolution II of the Stamp Act Congress provided: "That his Majesty's liege subjects in these colonies, are entitled to all the inherent rights and liberties of his natural born subjects, within the Kingdom of Great Britain" (Resolution II of the Stamp Act Congress, reprinted in Arthur E. Sutherland, *Constitutionalism in America,* 135 (New York: Blaisdell Pub. Co., 1965). On the constitutional importance of the Stamp Act crisis, see Edmund Morgan and Helen Morgan, *The Stamp Act Crisis,* 295 (Chapel Hill: Univ. of North Carolina Press, 1953).

24. The resolutions provided in part as follows:

> *Resolved,* That this Colony and Dominion of Virginia cannot be considered as a conquered country, and, if it was, that the present inhabitants are the descendants, not of the conquered, but of the conquerors. That the same was not settled at the national expense of England, but at the private expense of the adventurers, our ancestors, by solemn compact with, and under the auspices and protection of, the British Crown, upon which we are, in every respect, as dependent as the people of Great Britain, and in the same manner subject to all his Majesty's just, legal, and constitutional prerogatives; that our ancestors, when they left their native land, and settled in America, brought with them, even if the same had not been confirmed by Charters, the civil Constitution and form of Government of the country they came from, and

were by the laws of nature and Nations entitled to all its privileges, immunities, and advantages, which have descended to us, their posterity, and ought of right to be as fully enjoyed as if we had still continued within the Realm of England.

Fairfax County Resolutions, reprinted in Howard, *Road from Runnymede, supra* note 16, at 423-33.

25. *Journals of the Continental Congress,* 68 (1904). See Appendix, *infra,* for reprint of the resolves.

26. *Articles of Confederation,* Art. IV, reprinted in 9 *Journals of the Continental Congress,* 908 (1907).

27. For a detailed, comprehensive review of this development, see Howard, *supra* note 16, at 1-202.

28. 5 *Journals of the Continental Congress,* 547 (1906). Article VII of the first draft read as follows: "The Inhabitants of each Colony shall enjoy all the Rights, Liberties, Privileges, Immunities, and Advantages, in Trade, Navigation, and Commerce, in any other Colony, and in going to and from the same from and to any Part of the World, which the Natives of such Colony . . . enjoy."

29. The final version of Article IV read: "The better to secure and perpetuate mutual friendship and intercourse among the people of the different states in this union, the free inhabitants of each of these states, paupers, vagabonds, and fugitives from justice excepted, shall be entitled to all privileges and immunities of free citizens in the several states; and the people of each State shall have free ingress and regress to and from any other State, and shall enjoy therein all the privileges of trade and commerce, subject to the same duties, impositions, and restrictions, as the inhabitants thereof respectively" (9 *Journals of the Continental Congress,* 1908 [1907]).

30. U.S. Const., Art. IV, § 2. See Edward Dumbauld, *The Constitution of the United States,* 406-414 (Norman: Univ. of Oklahoma Press, 1964).

31. On June 25, 1778, South Carolina delegates moved to amend Article IV by inserting the word "white" between the words "free" and "inhabitants," so that constitutional protections would be available only to white visitors from other states. This was defeated, eight states against two, and one state had a divided delegation. 11 *Journals of the Continental Congress,* 652 (1908).

32. *Scott v. Sandford,* 60 U.S. (19 How.) 393, 403-4, 585 (1857). Justice Curtis, following the canons of documentary construction, reported that he had examined the forms of expression commonly used in the *State Papers* of 1789. *Id.* at 584.

33. U.S. Const., Preamble.

34. Madison seems in error in suggesting that free inhabitants who were not technically citizens of their state of domicile would have greater privileges under this clause in a state they visited than at home. He seems to confuse civil rights and rights of citizenship, e.g., voting. *Federalist* No. 42, at 291-92. (J. Madison) (E. Bourne ed., 1947).

35. See generally, Albert V. Dicey, *Introduction to the Study of the Law of the Constitution,* ch. 5 (London: Macmillan, 7th ed. 1908); Joseph Story, *2 Commentaries on the Constitution of the United States,* 499 (Boston: Hilliard, Gray, 1833).

36. Lysander Spooner, *The Unconstitutionality of Slavery* (1845; reprint New York: B. Franklin, 1965), and Joel Tiffany, *A Treatise on the Unconstitutionality of American Slavery* (Cleveland, OH: J. Calyer, 1849), are cited on the issue in Jacobus ten Broek, *The Antislavery Origins of the Fourteenth Amendment,* 49-50, 86-93 (Berkeley: Univ. of California Press, 1951). As part of antislavery constitutional theory, Tiffany and others felt that the opinion in *Barron v. Baltimore,* 32. U.S. (7

Pet.) 243 (1833) was wrong, and that the Bill of Rights, except Amendments I and VII, which expressly referred to Congress and the federal courts, was a constraint on the states. See Howard J. Graham, *Everyman's Constitution,* 174-84 (Madison, WI: State Historical Society, 1968).

37. See *supra* notes 34-35 and accompanying text.

38. 6 F. Cas. 546 (C.C.E.D. Pa. 1823) (no. 3,230) (New Jersey statute forbidding non-residents from gathering oysters in state's waters did not violate Article IV, § 2.).

39. *Id.* at 551. The opinion continues as follows:
What these fundamental principles are, it would perhaps be more tedious than difficult to enumerate. They may, however, be all comprehended under the following general heads: Protection by the government; the enjoyment of life and liberty, with the right to acquire and possess property of every kind, and to pursue and obtain happiness and safety; subject nevertheless to such restraints as the government may justly prescribe for the general good of the whole. The right of a citizen of one state to pass through, or to reside in any other state, for purposes of trade, agriculture, professional pursuits, or otherwise; to claim the benefit of the writ of habeas corpus; to institute and maintain actions of any kind in the courts of the state; to take, hold and dispose of property, either real or personal; and an exemption from higher taxes or impositions than are paid by the other citizens of the state; may be mentioned as some of the particular privileges and immunities of citizens, which are clearly embraced by the general description of privileges deemed to be fundamental: to which may be added, the elective franchise, as regulated and established by the laws or constitution of the state in which it is to be exercised. These, and many others which might be mentioned, are, strictly speaking, privileges and immunities, and the enjoyment of them by the citizens of each state, in every other state, was manifestly calculated (to use the expressions of the preamble of the corresponding provision in the old articles of confederation) "the better to secure and perpetuate mutual friend-ship and intercourse among the people of the different states of the Union."
Id. at 551-52.

40. See *Hague v. CIO,* 307 U.S. 496, 511 (1939); Laurence Tribe, *American Constitutional Law,* 1251-1255 (New York: Foundation Press, 3rd ed., 2000).

41. The expression "fundamental" law as a synonym for constitutional became current during the controversy over the tax known as ship money around 1635. Dicey, *supra* note 35, at 141. This usage continued on through the eighteenth century. John W. Gough, *Fundamental Law in English Constitutional History,* 207 (Oxford: Clarendon Press, rev. ed. 1971). Some colonies used "fundamental" to label their basic laws adopted pursuant to their charters, such as the *Fundamental Orders of Connecticut* (1639), the *Fundamentals of Massachusetts* (1646), and *Fundamental Laws of West New Jersey* (1676). Dean Pound noted that early American lawyers equated the idea of fundamental law with the "law of the land," to which all official and governmental action was bound to conform. Roscoe Pound, *The Development of Constitutional Guarantees of Liberty,* 61 (New Haven, CT: Yale Univ. Press, 1957). He further stated: "American lawyers were taught to believe in a fundamental law which, after the Revolution, they found declared in written constitution" (*Id.* at 78). See *Bayard v. Singleton,* 1 N.C. (Mart.) 48 (1787).
The other use of "fundamental law," as a reference to natural law, was used in America in the 1770s primarily in political writings to rationalize the Revolution. See Charles F. Mullett, *Fundamental Law and the American Revolution,* 1760-1776 (1933).

42. See Chapter 4 on the English origins of property rights.

43. See Roger Howell, *The Privileges and Immunities of State Citizenship* (Baltimore: Johns Hopkins Univ. Press, 1918); Tribe, *American Constitutional Law, supra* note 40, at 1255-1270; S. Doc. no. 82, 92nd Cong., 2d Sess., 830-38 (1973).

44. 436 U.S. 371 (1978).

45. 75 U.S. (8 Wall.) 168, 180 (1869).

46. 436 U.S. at 388.

47. *Id.* at 383, 386 (citing *Ward v. Maryland,* 79 U.S. (12 Wall.) 418 (1871), which concerned a discriminatory tax on nonresidents for the privilege of selling goods produced in other states). See also *Toomer v. Witsell,* 334 U.S. 385 (1948) (discriminatory license fees for nonresident commercial shrimpers).

48. Article IV of the Articles of Confederation provided nonresidents with protection of "privileges and immunities of free citizens" and of "privileges of trade and commerce." In the Constitution the protection for privileges of trade and commerce was moved to Article I, Section 8, Clause 3, and Article I, Section 10, Clause 2.

49. 470 U.S. 2.74 (1985).

50. *Id.* at 279.

51. The New Hampshire Court asserted that nonresidents would be less likely: (1) to become and remain familiar with local rules and procedures; (2) to behave ethically; (3) to be available for court proceedings; and (4) to do pro bono and other volunteer work in the State. *Id.* at 285.

52. *Bradwell v. Illinois,* 83 U.S. (16 Wall.) 130 (1873). As to Bradwell's admission to the bar by the Illinois legislature, see Jane M. Friedman, *America's First Woman Lawyer,* 28 (Buffalo, NY: Prometheus Books, 1993); H.B. Hurd, ed., *Revised Statutes of the State of Illinois,* 169 (1874).

53. The words "citizens of the United States" in the Fourteenth Amendment are not words of limitation. They were necessary to help define which class of civil rights were to be protected and were not inserted to limit the persons protected. John R. Green, *The Bill of Rights, the Fourteenth Amendment and the Supreme Court,* 46 Mich. L. Rev. 869, 904 (1948). See Simeon E. Baldwin, *The Citizen of the United States,* 2 Yale L. J. 85 (1893). On the meaning of "citizens" in Article IV, see *supra* notes 32 and 33 and accompanying text.

54. 60 U.S. (19 How.) 393 (1857). The Supreme Court's express view that a purpose of Section 1 of the Fourteenth Amendment was to overrule *Dred Scott* is stated in the *Slaughter-House Cases,* 83 U.S. (16 Wall.) 36, 73 (1873). See Curtis, *No State Shall Abridge, supra* note 1, at 26-56.

55. Chief Justice Roger B. Taney wrote "the question is simply this: can a negro, whose ancestors were imported into this country, and sold as slaves, become a member of the political community formed and brought into existence by the Constitution of the United States, and as such become entitled to all the Rights, and privileges, and immunities, guaranteed by that instrument to the citizen?" *Scott, 60* U.S. (19 How.) at 403. His answer was negative.

56. 60 U.S. at 406, 422-23.

57. For the evidence that the Fourteenth Amendment made the Bill of Rights effective against the states, see William W. Crosskey, 2 *Politics and the Constitution in the History of the United States,* 1089-95 (Chicago: Univ. of Chicago Press, 1953); Harry Flack, *The Adoption of the Fourteenth Amendment,* 233 (Baltimore, MD: Johns Hopkins Univ. Press, 1908); Howard J. Graham, *Our "Declaratory" Fourteenth Amendment,* reprinted in *Everyman's Constitution* 295, 316-17 (1968).

58. See the critique of *Barron v. Baltimore,* 32 U.S. (7 Pet.) 243 (1833) in the appendix to this chapter, note no. 178.

59. On application of the Bill of Rights to criminal procedures in the states, see Loren P. Beth, *John Marshall Harlan,* 216-222 (Lexington: Univ. Press of Kentucky, 1992). See generally, Akhil Reed Amar, *The Constitution and Criminal Procedures* (New Haven, CT: Yale Univ. Press, 1997).

60. 332 U.S. 46, 68-12.3 (1947) (Black, J., dissenting). The pursuit of the differing and conflicting subjective intents of the framers of the Fourteenth Amendment by Justice Black and Professor Fairman is a prime example of the futile search for intent when the correct methodology requires search for textual meaning of language. See Charles Fairman, *Does the Fourteenth Amendment Incorporate the Bill of Rights?* 2 Stan. L. Rev. 5 (1949). Compare Amar, *The Bill of Rights, supra,* note 1, at 181-206; Curtis, *No State Shall Abridge, supra* note 1, at 92-130.

61. See *Duncan v. Louisiana,* 391 U.S. 145, 148, (1968). In the *Palko* case, which is cited as the standard for selective incorporation, immunity from double jeopardy had been held not implicit in the 1791 concept of ordered liberty. *Palko v. Connecticut,* 302. U.S. 319, 32.4 (1937). *Palko* was overruled in *Benton v. Maryland,* 395 U.S. 784 (1969). The *Palko* Court's view was not consistent with Blackstone: "It is contrary to the genius and spirit of the law of England to suffer any man to be tried twice for the same offense in a criminal way, especially if acquitted upon the first trial" (4 Blackstone, *Commentaries, supra* note 5, at 259). In fact, all of the first eight amendments are explicit requirements of ordered liberty.

62. 176 U.S. 581 (1900), overruled in *Duncan v. Louisiana,* 391 U.S. 146, 149 n. 14 (1968). In *Maxwell* the majority opinion had upheld a felony jury of eight persons and denied that the Fourteenth Amendment incorporated the Sixth Amendment. *Duncan* validated the textual analysis of the dissent of Justice Harlan in *Maxwell:*
"I am of opinion that under the original Constitution and the Sixth Amendment, it is one of the privileges and immunities of citizens of the United States that when charged with crime they shall be tried only by a jury composed of 12 persons; consequently, a state statute authorizing the trial by a jury of eight persons of a citizen of the United States, charged with crime, is void under the Fourteenth Amendment declaring that no State shall make or enforce any law that 'shall abridge the privileges or immunities of citizens of the United States."
"I am also of opinion that the trial of the accused for the crime charged against him by a jury of eight person was not consistent with the 'due process of law' prescribed by the Fourteenth Amendment."
176 U.S. at 612-13. Compare *Williams v. Florida* 399 U.S. 78 (1970) (trial by a jury of a six in a non-capital felony in a state prosecution does not violate the Sixth Amendment by incorporation); *Apodaca v. Oregon,* 406 U.S. 404 (1972) (While unanimous verdict is required in federal criminal trials, a 10 to 2 verdict in a state criminal trial did not violate the due process clause.)

63. 144 U.S. 323 (1892), *questioned in* Furman v. Georgia, 408 U.S. 238, 325 (1972). The dissent of Justice Field in *O'Neill,* explaining the true meaning of privileges and immunities of citizens of the United States, is reviewed in Curtis, *No State Shall Abridge, supra* note I, at 189-91.

64. 378 U.S. 1, 6 (1964). The epistemology of overruling is explained above in the appendix to Chapter 2. As to the constitutional issue in *Adamson,* see Richard H. Helmholz et al, *The Privilege Against Self-Incrimination* (Chicago: Univ. of Chicago Press, 1997); Leonard W. Levy, *Origins of the Fifth Amendment: The Right Against Self-Incrimination* (Chicago: Ivan R. Dee, 1999).

65. 211 U.S. 78 (1908), overruled in *Malloy v. Hogan,* 378 U.S. 1, 6 (1964); *Griffin v. California,* 380 U.S. 609 (1965). In *Twining,* Justice Harlan had written a forceful

dissent. The later overruling proved that Harlan's textual analysis was the correct privileges or immunities and due process meaning of the clauses. He concluded that compelling a person to incriminate himself violated the legal maxim *Nemo Tenetur Seipsum Accusare* and "shocks or ought to shock the sense of right and justice of every one who loves liberty." 211 U.S. at 114.

66. See, e.g., *Cantwell v. Connecticut,* 310 U.S. 296 (1940); *De Jonge v. Oregon,* 2.99 U.S. 353 (1937); *Near v. Minnesota,* 2.83 U.S. 697 (1931); *Gitlow v. New York,* 268 U.S. 652 (1925).

67. See, e.g., *Ferguson v. Skrupa,* 372 U.S. 726, 730 (1963), *overruling Adams v. Tanner,* 244 U.S 590 (1917); *Day-Brite Lighting v. Missouri,* 342 U.S. 421, 423 (1952). See Chapter 8, notes 153-174 and accompanying text.

68. 83 U.S. (16 Wall.) 36 (1973). See infra notes 148-176 and accompanying text for a further discussion of the *Slaughter-House Cases.*

69. John H. Ely, *Democracy and Distrust,* 196 n. 59 (Cambridge: Harvard Univ. Press, 1980).

70. 83 U.S. (16 Wall.) at 79. In commenting on the meaning of Amendments XIII through XV in the context of the history of the times at their adoption, Justice Miller asserted: "Fortunately that history is fresh within the memory of us all, and the leading features, as they bear upon the matter before us, free from doubt" (*Id.* at 68).

71. 83 U.S. (16 Wall.) at 118-19 (Bradley, J., dissenting).

72. *United States v. Hall,* 26 F. Cas. 79 (C.C.S.D. Ala. 1871) (No. 15, 282). See Curtis, *No State Shall Abridge, supra* note 1, at 171-72; R. Kaczorowski, *The Politics of Judicial Interpretation,* 14-17 (Dobbs Ferry, NY: L Oceana Publications, 1985); Lou Falkner Williams, *The Great South Carolina Ku Klux Klan Trials, 1871-1872,* 131-135 (Athens: Univ. of Georgia Press, 1996).

73. 6 F. Cas. 546 (C.C.E.D. Pa. 1823) (No. 3230).

74. *United States v. Hall,* 26 F. Cas. at 82.

75. See Randy E. Barnett, ed., *The Rights Retained by the People: The History and Meaning of the Ninth Amendment* (Fairfax, VA: George Mason Univ. Press, 1989); Mark N. Goodman, *The Ninth Amendment* (Smithtown, NY: Exposition Press, 1981); Bennett Patterson, *The Forgotten Ninth Amendment* (Indianapolis, IN: Bobbo-Merrill, 1955); James Kelley, *The Uncertain Renaissance of the Ninth Amendment,* 33 U. Chi. L. Rev. 814 & nn.2 & 5 (1966); Russell Caplan, *History and Meaning of the Ninth Amendment,* 69 Va. L. Rev. 223 (1983).

76. Max Farrand, 2 *The Records of the Federal Convention of 1787,* at 582, 587-88 (New Haven, CT: Yale Univ. Press, rev. ed. 1937); *Id.* III, at 143-44, 161-62. See *Federalist* No. 84, book II, 152-58 (Hamilton) (E. Bourne ed., 1947).

77. See Julius Goebel, *Antecedents and Beginnings to 801,* vol. 1, *History of the Supreme Court of the United States,* 430-39 (1971); Edward Dumbauld, *The Bill of Rights and What It Means Today,* 33-38 (Norman: Univ. of Oklahoma Press, 1957); Leslie Dunbar, *James Madison and the Ninth Amendment,* 42 Va. L. Rev. 617, 630 (1956).

78. *Debates and Proceedings in the Congress of the United States,* 452 (J. Gales and W. Seaton eds., 1834). Madison's explanation of reasons for the clause was made on June 8, 1789, as follows:

It has been objected also against a bill of rights, that, by enumerating particular exceptions to the grant of power, it would disparage those rights which were not placed in that enumeration; and it might follow, by implication, that those rights which were not signaled out, were intended to be assigned into the hands of the General Government, and were consequently insecure. This is one of the most plausible arguments I

have ever heard urged against the admission of a bill of rights into this system; but, I conceive, that it may be guarded against, I have attempted it, as gentlemen may see by turning to the last clause of the fourth resolution.
Id. at 456.

79. *Livingston v. Moore*, 32. U.S. (7 Pet.) 551 (1833). See Dumbauld, *The Bill of Rights, supra* note 77, at 207-8.

80. U.S. Const., Amend. IX.

81. Story, 2 *Commentaries on the Constitution, supra* note 35, § 1905.

82. See Chapter 2, notes 43 and 44 and accompanying text.

83. The Ninth Amendment refers only to substantive constitutional law because the due process clause of the Fifth Amendment was designed to incorporate, *inter alia,* all procedural protections of standing English constitutional law. *Murray's Lessee v. Hoboken Land & Improvement Co.,* 59 U.S. (18 How.) 272 (1855). See Van Loan, *Natural Rights and the Ninth Amendment,* 48 B.U.L. Rev. 1, 13-14 (1968).

84. Irvin Kent, *Under the Ninth Amendment What Rights Are the "Others Retained by the People?"* 28 Fed. B. J. 219 (1970).

85. *Id.* at 234-35.

86. Ely, *Democracy and Distrust, supra* note 69, at 203.

87. See John P. Reid, *In an Inherited Way,* 49 S. Calif. L. Rev. 1109, 1120-23 (1976).

88. Gottfried Dietze, *In Defense of Property,* 52-59 (1963).

89. U.S. Const., Amend. V.

90. *Corfield v. Coryell,* 6 F. Cas. 546 (C.C.E.D. Pa. 1823) (No. 3,230). See *Shelley v. Kraemer,* 334 U.S. I, 10 (1948).

91. William Holdsworth, 11 *History of English Law,* 392-94, 507-12 (Boston: Little Brown, 7th ed. 1938).

92. Cases in which the Ninth Amendment has been pleaded are reviewed in Patterson, *supra* note 75, at 19-26; and Kelley, *supra* note 75, at 825-32; Lyman Rhoades and Rodney Patula, *The Ninth Amendment,* 50 Den. L. J. 153 (1973).

93. 381 U.S. 479 (1965).

94. *Id.* at 492.

95. A search through Blackstone, *Commentaries, supra* note 5, and William Holdsworth, *History of English Law* (1903-1938) reveals no such category. The dynamics of the common law that had led to the development of the private tort remedy for invasion of privacy should have no bearing on public law. See Erwin N. Griswold, *The Right to Be Let Alone,* 55 Nw.U. L. Rev. 2. 17 (1960); Charles Warren and Louis Brandeis, *The Right to Privacy,* 4 Harv. L. Rev. 193 (1890). The historical dynamics of the common law are explained in Edward H. Levi, *An Introduction to Legal Reasoning,* 8-27 (Chicago: Univ. of Chicago Press, 1948).

96. *Griswold,* 381 U.S. at 522.

97. "All merchants shall have safe and secure exit from England, and entry to England, with the right to tarry there and to move about as well by land as by water, for buying and selling by the ancient and right customs, quit from all evil tolls, except (in time of war) such merchants as are of the land at war with us. And if such are found in our land at the beginning of the war, they shall be detained, without injury to their bodies or goods, until information be received by us, or by our chief justiciar, how the merchants of our land found in the land at war with us are treated; and if our men are safe there, the others shall be safe in our land" *Magna Charta,* ch. 41, translated and reprinted in William McKechnie, *Magna Carta,* 399 (Glasgow: J. Maclehose, 2d ed. 1914).

98. McKechnie, *supra* note 97, at 399-400.

99. See Harold G. Fox, *Monopolies and Patents,* 57 (Univ. of Toronto Legal Series, 1947).
100. 9 Edw. 3, Stat. 1, ch. 1 (1335); 25 Edw. 3, Stat. 4, ch. 2. (1350); 2 Rich. 2., Stat. 1, ch. 1 (1378).
101. See, e.g., 12, Hen. 7, ch. 6 (1497).
102. Sandys argued: "All free Subjects are borne inheritable as to ther Lands, soe alsoe to the free exercise of ther industrie in those trads wherto they applie themselves and wherby they are to live. Merchandise being the chiefe and richest of all other, and of greater extent and importance than all the rest, it is against the naturall right and liberty of the Subjects of England to restrain it into the hands of some fewe" (Sandys, *Instructions towchinge the Bill for Free Trade,* quoted in William Cunningham, 2 *The Growth of English Industry and Commerce,* 287 (Cambridge, England: Univ. Press, 5th ed., 1912).
103. Fox, *supra* note 99, at 74-75.
104. *Moore* K.B. 576, 72 Eng. Rep. 769 (K.B. 1599) See Fox, *Monopolies supra* note 99, at 311.
105. 11 Coke 84, 77 Eng. Rep. 1260 (K.B. 1602). See John W. Gordon, *Monopolies by Patents and the Statutable Remedies Available to the Public* 193-231 (London: Stevens and Sons, 1897); D. S. Davies, *Further Light on the Case of Monopolies,* 48 L.Q. Rev. 394 (1932).
106. See Donald O. Wagner, *Coke and the Rise of Economic Liberalism,* 6 Econ. Hist. Rev. 30 (1935). See generally Holdsworth, 4 *History of English Law, supra* note 91, at 63-62 (1924).
107. James B. Thayer, *Cases on Constitutional Law* (1895), reprinted in Pound, *Development, supra* note 41, at 145-48.
108. 11 Coke 53a, 77 Eng. Rep. 12, 18 (K.B. 1614).
109. Palmer 1, 81 Eng. Rep. 949 (K.B. 1619).
110. See Fox, *Monopolies and Patents, supra* note 99, at 330.
111. *Id.* at 336.
112. *State Trials,* II, 1119, 1130-32. (T. Howell ed., 1816).
113. 21 Jac. 1, ch. 3 (1624). See Joseph R. Tanner, *Constitutional Documents of the Reign of James I,* at 268-272 (Cambridge Univ. Press, 1930).
114. See Fox, *Monopolies and Patents, supra* note 99, at 130.
115. *Id.* at 180.
116. John Rushworth, 2 *Historical Collections of Private Passages of State,* 103 (London: D. Browne, 1721).
117. See Fox, *supra* note 99, at 129.
118. 16 Car. 1, ch. 10 (1640).
119. Perry and Cooper, *Sources of Our Liberties, supra* note 17, at 222.
120. Hermann Levy, *Monopolies, Cartels and Trusts in British Industry,* 62-72 (1927). (New York: A.M. Kelley Reprint, 1968).
121. On the constitutional conventions in England, see Dicey, *The Law of the Constitution, supra* note 35, at ch. 14.
122. *Debates and Proceedings in the Congress of the United States,* 436 (J. Gales and W. Seaton eds., 1834). See Zachariah Chafee, *How Human Rights Got into the Constitution* 19-21 (Boston: Boston Univ. Press, 1952). See also Chapter 3, notes 53-56 and accompanying text.
123. See *supra* notes 7-15 and accompanying text.
124. *The Colonial Laws of Massachusetts* 1672, at 33-61 (W. Whitmore ed., 1890).
125. *Id.* at 35.

126. Paul S. Reinsch, *The English Common Law in the Early American Colonies,* in 1 Select Essays in Anglo-American Legal History, 367, 373 (Boston: Little Brown, 1907).

127. William Penn, *The Excellent Privilege of Liberty & Property Being the Birth-Right of the Free-Born Subjects of England* (1687), excerpts reprinted in: Howard, *Road from Runnymede, supra* note 16, at 413-25.

128. Moore 576, 72 Eng. Rep. 679 (K.B. 1599).

129. 11 Coke 84, 77 Eng. Rep. 1260 (K.B. 1602).

130. Howard, *Road from Runnymede, supra* note 16, at 421.

131. See 7, *Colonial Charters, supra* note 7, 3790, 3802.

132. See 1, *The Genesis of the United States,* 207, Alexander Brown ed., (Boston: Houghton Mifflin, 1891); Edward Channing, *History of the United States,* I, 193 (New York: Macmillan, 1928).

133. See supra notes 7-15.

134. Perry and Cooper, *Sources of Our Liberties, supra* note 17, at 309-10. See Robert Rutland, *The Birth of the Bill of Rights* 41-77 (Chapel Hill: Univ. of North Carolina Press, 1955).

135. See 3 *Colonial Charters, supra* note 7, 1686-1691.

136. See 5 *Colonial Charters, supra* note 7, 2788. After Tennessee was established as a separate state, it adopted the same prohibition. 6, *Colonial Charters, supra* note 7, 3423.

137. See Story, 1 *Commentaries on the Constitution, supra* note 35, §§ 301, 304; Vol. 2, §§ 1858-68.

138. Letter from Jefferson to Madison (Dec. 2.0, 1787), reprinted in T. Jefferson, 12 *The Papers of Thomas Jefferson,* 438, 440 (J. Boyd ed. 1955) (emphasis added). The need for a clause in the Bill of Rights prohibiting monopolies was repeated in letters to Madison in 1788 and in 1789. *Id.,* Vol. 13 at 440, 442.; *Id.,* Vol. 14 at 364, 368.

139. *Debates in the Several State Conventions on the Adoption of the Federal Constitution,* I, 323 (J. Elliot ed., 1836) [hereinafter cited as *Debates*].

140. *Id.* at 326; *Id.,* Vol. 3, 210-215.

141. *Id.,* I at 330.

142. *Id.* at 337. Congress completed action on the Bill of Rights on September 25, 1789, and sent the proposal to the states for ratification.

143. See Dumbauld, *Bill of Rights, supra* note 77, at 160-65 for tables showing the sources of the Bill of Rights.

144. See James Madison, 5 *Writings,* 34, G. Hunt ed., (New York: Putnam, 1906).

145. *Debates, supra* note 139, I at 496. See Kate Rowland, 2 *The Life of George Mason,* 387, 389, 1725-92, (New York: G. P. Putnam, 1892).

146. See generally, 3 *Colonial Charters, supra* note 7, 1690.

147. J. Senate 122 (1st Cong., 1789); J. H. Rep. 111 (1st Cong., 1789). See Dumbauld, *Bill of Rights, supra* note 77, at 24, 34.

148. 83 U.S. (16 Wall.) 36 (1873). See Ronald M. Labbé and Jonathan Lurie, *The Slaughterhouse Cases* (Lawrence, KA: Univ. Press of Kansas, 2003); Earl M. Maltz, *The Fourteenth Amendment and the Law of the Constitution,* 85-112 (Durham: Carolina Academic Press, 2003); Charles Fairman. *Reconstruction and Re-union, 1864-88, Vol. 6, History of the Supreme Court of the United States,* 1864-88, 1320-63 (New York: Macmillin, 1971); Mitchell Franklin, *The Foundation and Meaning of the Slaughterhouse Cases,* 18 Tulane L. Rev. 1, 218 (1943); Richard L. Aynes, *Constricting the Law of Freedom: Justice Miller, the Fourteenth Amendment and the Slaughter-House Cases,* 70 Chicago-Kent L. Rev. 627 (1994).

149. Charles Warren, 2 *The Supreme Court in United States History,* 533-61 (Boston: Little Brown, 1926).

150. See Arnold J. Lien, *Concurring Opinion,* 111 n. 8 (St. Louis: Washington Univ. Studies, 1957).

151. *Live-Stock Assoc. v. Crescent City Co.,* 15 F. Cas. 649 (C.C.D. La. 1870) (no. 8,408).

152. An Act to Protect All Person's in the United States in their Civil Rights and Furnish the Means of their Vindication, 14 Stat. 27 (1866).

153. 15 F. Cas. at 652.

154. *Id.* at 653.

155. An Act to Establish the Judicial Courts of the United States, 1 Stat. 333, 335 (1845).

156. *Slaughter-House Cases,* 83 U.S. (16 Wall.) at 82.

157. *Id.* at 74. See Crosskey, *Politics and the Constitution, supra* note 58 at 1127-1130; Richard L. Aynes, *Constricting the Law of Freedom: Justice Miller, the Fourteenth Amendment and the Slaughter-House Cases,* 70 Chi-Kent L. Rev. 627, 653-655 (1994).

158. See *supra* notes 38-42 and accompanying text. Cf. Louis Lusky, *By What Right?* 191 (Charlottesville, Va.: Michie, 1975).

159. *State v. Fagan,* 22 La. Ann. 545 (La. 1870).

160. Lusky, *supra* note 158 at 197, 198.

161. *Id.* at 194.

162. *Slaughter-House Cases,* 83 U.S. (16 Wall.) at 75. Justice Bradley in dissent, stated: "It is pertinent to observe that both the clause of the Constitution referred to, and Justice Washington in his comment on it, speak of the privileges and immunities of citizens in a state; not of citizens of a state" (*Id.* at 117 [Bradley, J., dissenting] [emphasis added]).

163. 83 U.S. (16 Wall.) at 76. See Lusky, *By What Right? supra* note 158, at 195-196.

164. Lusky, *supra* note 158 at 196.

165. See, e.g., Tribe, *American Constitutional Law, supra* note 40; Crosskey, 2 *Politics and the Constitution, supra* note 58, at 1119-30 (1953); Edwin Borchard, *The Supreme Court and Private Rights,* 47 Yale L. J. 1051, 1063 (1938); William L. Royal, *The Fourteenth Amendment: The Slaughter-House Cases,* 4 S.L. Rev. (n.s.) 558 (1878); M. F. Taylor, *The Slaughter-House Cases,* 3 S.L. Rev. 476 (1874).

166. See *supra* note 2.

167. Referring to the Privileges and Immunities Clause of Article IV, Field stated:
    What the clause in question did for the protection of the citizens of one State, against hostile and discriminating legislation of other states, the fourteenth amendment does for the protection of every citizen of the United States against hostile and discriminating legislation against him in favor of others, whether they reside in the same or in different States. If under the fourth article of the Constitution equality of privileges and immunities is secured between citizens of different States, under the fourteenth amendment the same equality is secured between citizens of the United States. . . . Now, what the clause in question does for the protection of citizens of one State against the creation of monopolies in favor of citizens of other States, the fourteenth amendment does for the protection of every citizen of the United States against the creation of any monopoly whatever. The privileges and immunities of citizens of the United States, of every one of them, is secured against abridgement in any form by any State. The fourteenth amendment places them under the guardianship of the National authority.
    Slaughter-House Cases, 83 U.S. (16 Wall.) at 100-101 (Field, J., dissenting).

168. 83 U.S. (16 Wall.) at 102 (Field, J., dissenting).
169. 77 Eng. Rep. 1260 (K.B. 1602).
170. 72 Eng. Rep. 769 (K.B. 1599).
171. 21 Jac. 1, ch. 3 (1623).
172. See *supra* note 25.
173. *Slaughter-House Cases*, 83 U.S. (16 Wall.) at 110 (Field, J., dissenting).
174. Two other legal arguments in the *Slaughter-House Cases* received summary disposition by the majority. The Court rejected substantive due process in one sentence. *Id.* at 81. For the recent law on substantive due process, see Chapter 8. In light of the later overwhelming rejection of this concept by the Supreme Court with respect to economic regulation, Justice Miller clearly was correct, and dissenting Justice Bradley clearly was wrong. The dissent of Justice Bradley is considered one of the historical foundations of substantive due process. 83 U.S. at 114-15, 122-23 (Bradley, J., dissenting). The Court also rejected an argument based on equal protection, stating that the equal protection clause was primarily for protection of freed slaves and that the plaintiffs had made no case for creating an exception. *Id.* at 81. See Chapter 9.
175. See, e.g., Richard Ippolito and Robert Masson, *The Social Cost of Government Regulation of Milk*, 21 J. L. & Econ. 33 (1978); Neal Smith, *The Monopoly Component of Inflation in Food Prices*, 14 U. Mich. J. L. Reform 149 (1981); Thomas Moore, *The Beneficiaries of Trucking Regulation*, 21 J. L. of Econ. 327, 342. (1978).
176. See, e.g., *New Motor Vehicle Board v. Orrin W. Fox Co.*, 439 U.S. 96 (1978); *City of New Orleans v. Dukes*, 42.7 U.S. 2.97 (1976); Thomas Moore, *The Purpose of Licensing*, 4 J. L. & Econ. 93 (1961); Edmund Kitch, Mare Issacson and Daniel Kasper, *The Regulation of Taxicabs in Chicago*, 14 J. L. & Econ. 285 (1971).
177. Edward Dumbauld, *The Bill of Rights and What It Means Today*, 4-6 (Norman: Univ. of Oklahoma Press, 1957).
178. 32 U.S. (7 Pet.) 243 (1833).
179. *United States v. Twin City Power Co.*, 350 U.S. 222 (1956). See Richard A. Epstein, *Takings: Private Property and the Power of Eminent Domain*, 67-73 (Cambridge, MA: Harvard Univ. Press, 1985).
180. See Howard, *The Road from Runnymede, supra,* note 16 at 38, 210; J.A.C. Grant, *The Higher Law Background of the Law of Eminent Domain*, 6 Wis. L. Rev. 67 (1931). While this chapter was stated in terms of the taking of chattels, the later English statutes secured the principle for real property. *Attorney General v. DeKeyser's Royal Hotel* [1920] A.C. 508 (House of Lords). See Philip Nichols, 1 *Law of Eminent Domain,* § 1.21 (Albany, NY: Mathew Bender, 3d ed., 1985).
181. Crosskey, 2 *Politics and the Constitution, supra* note 58 at ch. 30.
182. Section 34 of the Judiciary Act of 1789, by requiring federal courts to apply state common law, reinforced the view that the national government was not a common law jurisdiction. See *supra*, Chapter 4.
183. See Edward Dumbauld, *The Bill of Rights* 164 (Norman: Univ. of Oklahoma Press, 1957). As to the origins of habeas corpus, see Robert J. Sharpe, *The Law of Habeas Corpus* (Oxford: Clarendon Press, 1989); William F. Duker, *A Constitutional History of Habeas Corpus* (Westport: Greenwood Press, 1980).
184. *Supra* note 16.
185. Raoul Berger, *Government by Judiciary,* (Indianapolis: Liberty Fund, 2d ed. 1997), does not list Howard in his bibliography.
186. *Documents Illustrative of the Formation of the Union of the American States,* H. Doc. 398, 69th Cong., 1st Sess., 1927, at 1-5.

187. *Id.* at 47-54. Enacted at 1 Stat. 50-53 (1789). See Peter S. Onuf, *Statehood and Union: A History of the Northwest Ordinance,* 60-64 (Bloomington: Indiana Univ. Press, 1987).
188. 526. U.S. 489 (1999).
189. *Id.* at 501-02, citing U.S. Const., Art. IV, Sec. 2.
190. 394 U.S. 618, 634 (1969).
191. 526 U.S. at 502-05.
192. 83 U.S. (16 Wall.) 36, 80 (1873). See Kevin C. Newsom, *Setting Incorporationism Straight: A Reinterpretation of the Slaughter-House Cases,* 109 Yale L. J. 643, 658-87 (2000).

8

Procedural Essence of Due Process: Judicial Error of Substantive Scope

The most elementary and persistent classification in law is that between procedure and substance. While the law of procedure has been codified, the ultimate standards for required procedure are constitutional. Thus, national and state constitutions stipulate specific procedural protections for persons accused of crimes plus the general protection of due process of law for fairness in both criminal and civil proceedings.

The due process clauses in the Fifth and Fourteenth Amendments are technical terms of the law.[1] Under the basic common-law canons of documentary construction, the latter clause must make good against the states every procedural constraint the former imposed on the national government.[2] This study presents the evidence that due process meant "required or appropriate procedure." Under the basic epistemological requirement of consistency of truths, substantive due process was an oxymoron.[3] The clauses had no substantive content, and the judicial creation of liberty of contract was an invasion of the legislative power. The possible usurpation of legislative power by the appointed elite of the judiciary, the Supreme Court majority, is one key aspect of the countermajoritarian difficulty.[4] This study demonstrates that most briefs filed in the major Supreme Court cases to oppose the imposition of liberty of contract failed to argue the original textual meanings of the due process clauses as solely procedural constraints.

The creation of substantive due process in the late nineteenth century was confirmed for regulation of business in *Lochner v. New York*[5] in 1905 and continued until overruled in *West Coast Hotel Co. v. Parrish*[6] in 1937. During that period a significant set of Supreme Court opinions invalidated statutes regulating labor relations, utility rates, and other business practices. The common criticism of scholars is that the argued reasonableness or unreasonableness of regulations had no measurable standard, and therefore judicial decisions turned on the socio-economic biases of the justices. But some scholars, like most justices, failed to recognize or to admit that substantive due process was usurpation of legislative power. Thus, they did not realize that the later total rejection of liberty of contract by a set of Supreme Court overrulings that began in 1937, was not a "constitutional revolution," but was a set of totally justified corrections.[7]

Constitutional language, ratified by the people of a democracy, was not designed to be redefined to fit the social biases of five or six members of the Supreme Court. A textual interpretation of constitutional language, as understood by educated readers of the time, was the only language ratified by the people. The first element of interpretation was the then existing common-law canons of documentary construction. The framers were known to be aware of such canons collected in Coke's *Institutes*. The most prominent was *Contemporanea expositio est optima et fortissima in lege*,[8] that is, contemporaneous exposition in the best and strongest in the law. The need to brief this principle fully cannot be emphasized enough.

Valid interpretation of the due process clauses begins with the canon of documentary construction that technical words are to be given the technical meaning unless this is repelled by the context.[9] This must be taken in light of another canon of construction that words are not construed in isolation; they have meaning only as part of a clause and a section of a document. In order to resolve any ambiguity, we must resort "to the context, and shape the particular meaning so as to make it fit that of the connecting words and agree with the subject matter."[10] These canons dictate that the due process clauses be interpreted as integrated wholes in light of their technical sense in the law of the time.

The clauses do not protect "liberty" or "property" in isolation. In a proper judicial proceeding, one's liberty or one's property may be taken as a punishment or remedy so long as there is compliance with all the required procedures of law. The judicial creation of constitutional liberty of contract was inefficient because justices' unpredictable personal views of reasonable regulation, based on laissez-faire economic biases, were imposed on the law. Such rulings precluded definition and consequently fostered litigation. The hundreds of cases in federal courts between 1890 and 1937, seeking judicial remedies under that theory, represent a great economic waste by courts, lawyers, and the litigants.

Textual Meaning: Required Procedure

It is uncontested legal history that in 1791, process was a synonym for procedure.[11] A typical example of process as the usual way of referring to judicial procedure was the first federal statute regulating procedures in lower federal court. It was the "Act to Regulate Processes in the Courts of the United States."[12] The bill that led to the enactment was the "Senate Process Bill."[13] The leading law dictionary defined process as proceedings in legal actions from the beginning to the end.[14] The usual way of comparing procedures was to speak of different "modes of process."[15]

Legal historians have established that in 1791 due process of law meant required or appropriate procedure in the broadest sense.[16] The constitutional context indicates that the constraint is imposed on all three departments of government. In a criminal prosecution, a convicted defendant may be deprived of his life, liberty, or property. In a civil lawsuit, a losing defendant may be deprived of his property. In either case, there is a required judicial procedure. Daniel Webster explained it as "a law which hears before it condemns; which proceeds upon inquiry and renders judgment only after trial."[17] Legislative due process would require the Congress and state assemblies to follow all their respective constitutional and statutory procedures for enacting laws. The Supreme Court will void any statute that denies required procedures.[18] And, under due process, executive officers must administer laws in ways which give citizens such full and fair hearings as are appropriate to the particular administrative functions.

An explicatory definition of due process or required procedure of law has three elements. The first two were explained by Justice Benjamin Curtis in the leading case of *Murray's Lessee v. Hoboken Land and Improvement Company* in 1855:

> The Constitution contains no description of those processes which it was intended to allow or forbid. It does not even declare what principles are to be applied to ascertain whether it be due process. It is manifest that it was not left to the legislative power to enact any process which might be devised. The article is a restraint on the legislative as well as on the executive and judicial powers of the government, and cannot be so construed as to leave Congress free to make any process "due process of law," by its mere will. To what principles, then, are we to resort to ascertain whether this process enacted by Congress, is due process? To this the answer must be twofold. We must examine the Constitution itself, to see whether this process be in conflict with any of its provisions. If not found to be so, we must look to those settled usages and modes of proceeding existing in the common and statute law of England, before the emigration of our ancestors, and which are shown not to have been unsuited to their civil and political condition by having been acted on by them after the settlement of this country.[19]

The first category enumerated by Justice Curtis includes the various specific "process" or procedural guarantees of the Fourth, Fifth, Sixth, and Eighth amendments and those in the original constitution. His second category notes the constitutional incorporation of the then existing procedural guarantees under the common and statute law of England. This second group of limitations is directly supported by the language of the Ninth Amendment: "The enumeration in the Constitution of certain rights shall not be construed to deny or disparage others retained by the people." In 1884, Justice John Marshall Harlan confirmed that due process included this second category of guarantees "which had long been deemed fundamental in Anglo-Saxon institutions." He went on to quote Justice Joseph Story: "It was under the consciousness of the full possession of the rights, liberties and immunities of British subjects that the colonists in almost all the early legislation of their respective assemblies insisted upon a declaratory Act, acknowledging and confirming them."[20]

Justice Curtis had no need to supply further explanation because the "process" in the *Hoboken* case conformed to the Constitution and had been followed as Common Law in England. But there must be a third category of due process. The framers of the Fifth Amendment clearly contemplated that the Congress would pass new procedure statutes. And the Congress, in framing the Fourteenth Amendment, contemplated that the state legislatures would pass new procedure statutes. Furthermore, executive officers of both the nation and the states could be expected to invent novel procedures for the new administrative agencies created by Congress and the state legislatures. While conforming to the specific process guarantees of Amendments Five to Eight, any of the innovative procedures of later legislatures or administrators might have an essential unfairness or inequity to the persons governed. Hence, in addition to the two elements of due process explained by Justice Curtis, there must have been a third, general limitation on all procedures of all departments of government. They must also be *fair* and *equitable* under the general value standards of American society.

This final aspect of due process of law is not subject to more precise definition than "total fairness" in procedure, including notice, hearing, and decision making.[21] It is summarized by Justice Benjamin Cardozo as those procedures that embody "some principle of justice so rooted in the traditions and conscience of our people as to be ranked as fundamental."[22] While reflecting traditional notions of fair play and substantial justice, the concept is not static. As Justice Felix Frankfurter has written, "It is thus not a stagnant formulation of what has been achieved in the past but a standard for judgment in the progressive evolution of the institutions of a free society."[23]

One basic implication of *Murray's Lessee* has received little recognition by the Supreme Court. Since due process is a phrase of comprehensive connotation that firstly includes the particular procedural guarantees of the original constitution and the Bill of Rights, the Due Process Clause of the Fourteenth Amendment must incorporate Amendments Five through Eight. This creates a partial redundancy, since the Privileges or Immunities Clause also incorporated the entire Bill of Rights for citizens of the United States. It was the failure to understand and answer the incorporation implications of *Murray's Lessee* that led the Court majority in the indictment case of *Hurtado v. California*[24] and other procedural cases to deny incorporation.[25] It was only in the 1960s that most of the erroneous denials of incorporation were overruled.[26]

In *Davidson v. New Orleans*,[27] Justice Samuel Miller emphasized the total procedural character of the due process clauses. An assessment on real estate in New Orleans for draining the swamps of the city was upheld against a charge that it violated the Due Process Clause of the Fourteenth Amendment. If "those laws provide for a mode of confirming or contesting the charge thus imposed, in ordinary courts of justice, with such notice to the person, or such proceeding in regard to the property as is appropriate to the nature of the case, the judgment in such proceedings cannot be said to deprive the owner of his property without due process of law, however obnoxious it may be to other objections."[28] The statute contested here clearly provided the required procedures of law. In contrast, Miller pointed out that a statute confiscating property without hearing on the issue of compensation would violate due process. "It seems to us that a statute which declared in terms, and without more, that the full and exclusive title of a described piece of land, which is now in A, shall be and is hereby vested in B, would, if effectual, deprive A of his property without due process of law, within the meaning of the constitutional provision."[29] In this sense, the taking of property by the state cannot be solely statutory. Owners are entitled to a judicial due process to which the substantive constitutional right to just compensation is inextricably entwined.

Justice Miller noted that while there had been little litigation under the Due Process Clause of the Fifth Amendment, the docket in his day was crowded with cases under the Due Process Clause of the Fourteenth. "There is here abundant evidence that there exists some strange misconception of the scope of this provision as found in the XIVth Amendment."[30] Petitioners were requesting review of the merits of legislation, a reversal on the basis of the Court's view of the substance of the law. The pressure on the Court to adopt substantive due process was growing.

Textual Meaning of Liberty

From the history of the due process clauses, it is clear that the word "liberty" meant freedom from imprisonment or detention by agents of government. Thus "liberty" in the context of fair procedures was not a synonym for "civil liberties," a term which includes all of the constitutional limitations against government.[31] The historical evidence that the word "liberty" in the due process clauses was concerned only with freedom of movement of the individual, immunity from imprisonment, was assembled and published by Charles Shattuck in 1891.[32]

The thirty-ninth article of Magna Carta reads "No freeman shall be taken, or imprisoned, or disseized, or outlawed, or banished, or any ways destroyed; nor will we pass upon him, nor send upon him, unless by the legal judgment of his peers, or by the law of the land."[33] The same declaration of rights is confirmed in more precise language in 28 Ed. III, c.3 as follows: "No man, of whatever estate or condition that he be, shall be put out of land or tenement, nor taken nor imprisoned, nor put to death, without being brought in answer by due process of law."[34] It's clear that the original language "No freeman shall be taken or imprisoned" was equivalent to the modern term "liberty of the person" and that these earliest procedural protections applied to the criminal law. Language similar to that in Magna Carta is found in the Massachusetts Body of Liberties in 1641,[35] and the early constitutions of Pennsylvania, Maryland, North Carolina, and Vermont.[36]

William Blackstone's *Commentaries* define personal liberty of individuals as used in the context of the thirty-ninth chapter of Magna Carta. "This personal liberty consists in the power of the loco-motion, of changing situation, or removing one's person to whatsoever place one's own inclination may direct; without imprisonment or restraint, unless by due course of law."[37] Blackstone then records the statutes that expressly demonstrate the criminal law origins of the due process protection in that no freeman shall be imprisoned or detained without cause shown, to which he may make answer according to law.[38] He then explains the relationship between due process of the criminal law and the right to personal liberty protected by the Habeas Corpus Act of 1679.[39] Shattuck points out that Blackstone considered only life, liberty, and property of chapter thirty-nine to be absolute rights of individuals.[40] In contrast, substantive civil liberties such as religious, press, speech, and political liberties were unknown and unclaimed in England into the seventeenth century. Even thereafter, they were subject to parliamentary regulation.

The Supreme Court's isolation and misinterpretation of the word "liberty" in the due process clauses had its major negative effects on the working class as statutes regulating maximum hours of work and minimum wages were held unconstitutional.[41] It was unfortunate that state and national legislators who had responded to public demand and passed those laws did not eventually propose a constitutional amendment to replace the word "liberty" in the clauses.[42] A careful revision also would have replaced "process" with it's synonym, "procedure." Such a revised clause would have read as follows: "No person shall be executed, imprisoned, or divested of property rights without full judicial hearing that utilizes fair and impartial procedure." Essentially, this substitution would have returned U.S. law to equal the English statute protecting due process of law in 28 Ed. III, c. 3. This was the original meaning of the Due Process Clause when the Fifth Amendment was ratified in 1791.

Creation of Substantive Limitations

Substantive due process is the label for holding unconstitutional those regulatory statutes which the court finds to be unreasonable interferences with liberty or property. The approach was created by lawyers, especially Thomas M. Cooley, who convinced courts to ignore and eliminate from consideration the phrase "due process of law" from the end of the two constitutional clauses.[43] In this group of cases, the clause came to be understood as "No person shall be deprived of life, liberty or property" whenever a court could be convinced that a statute was unreasonable. The Supreme Court majority adopted a constitutional ideology for individualism that was based on a premise of inherent antagonism between the people and the government.[44] While rejecting a theory of natural rights, Cooley viewed human rights against government as incorporated in an organically growing Constitution. He asserted that preexisting common-law rights of freedom of contract and unfettered property were preserved in the

Constitution by virtue of implied limitations. The sanctity of these vested rights, while not present in specific clauses, was found from reading the constitutional limitations as a unified whole. Judicial review was a necessary instrument to enforce the implied limitations on the substance of relations between the individual and the state. The judicial expansion of constitutional meanings was viewed by Cooley as a direct response to the expression of popular will which was superior to that of elected legislators.

Freedom of contract was elevated to a constitutional principle. Business lawyers created the idea as part of the laissez-faire philosophy of the business community. They convinced the majority of the justices to use it in holding unconstitutional federal and state statutes which attempted to regulate prices, wages, and other business practices. Thus, the will of the people for regulated economic development in order to remedy asserted market failures was many times frustrated by the courts. Arrogating unto themselves the status of a superlegislature, they held the regulatory statutes unreasonable and therefore unconstitutional. The negative public reaction to this usurpation of the legislative power by the Court was noted by Professor Frankfurter in 1937.[45]

The legal arguments to convert liberty and property into distinct constitutional standards began in state courts before the Civil War.[46] Howard J. Graham records the extrajudicial rise of substantive due process in the antislavery movement and litigation of the rights of free Negroes.[47] The leading case in which a court clearly adopted the doctrine was the 1856 decision of *Wynehamer v. The People*[48] in the New York Court of Appeals. That Court held unconstitutional a state prohibition act which barred the sale of liquor except for medicinal purposes and forbade storing all other existing liquor in any place other than a dwelling house. This criminal statute declared that liquors kept in any other place were a nuisance and provided for summary destruction. Such change of property rights was found unreasonable and therefore held to violate the state due process guaranty, although such uncompensated forfeiture was not unusual in prohibition statutes. Analogous modern laws provide for summary destruction of other dangerous drugs.

The *Dred Scott* case[49] was the first opinion under the Fifth Amendment to distort "due process of law" into "due substance of law." As a second aspect of that case, the Supreme Court held the Missouri Compromise of 1820 unconstitutional. The statute prohibited slavery in certain territories west of the Mississippi.[50] Dred Scott had been taken into Illinois and into the western territory by his master.[51] Unfortunately, the lawsuit to enforce the prohibition of slavery was filed after he was removed to the slave state, Missouri. In holding the federal law invalid, Chief Justice Roger Taney indicated that, under the due process clause, the owners of slaves had a vested right in their slave property that was absolute.[52] His implication was that the total prohibitions of slavery in the Illinois Constitution and in the federal statute for the western territory were not effective for a slave brought temporarily into those territories. Taney's opinion was error when issued, as demonstrated in the eloquent dissenting opinion of Justice Curtis.[53] As candidate Abraham Lincoln said: "We think the Dred Scott decision is erroneous. We know the court that made it has often over-ruled its own decisions, and we shall do what we can to have it to over-rule this."[54] *Dred Scott* was overruled by the Thirteenth and Fourteenth amendments.[55]

Substantive due process under the Fourteenth Amendment was initiated by Justice Joseph Bradley in his dissenting opinion in the *Slaughter-House Cases*[56] of 1873. Under the pretense of enacting sanitary regulations, the legislature of Louisiana granted a corporation of seventeen citizens a monopoly on the slaughter of meat in New Orleans. The five-person majority of the Supreme Court upheld this grant. Justice Bradley emphasized that the Due Process Clause afforded substantive protection to liberty and property. He asserted: "This right to choose one's calling is an essential part of that liberty which it is the object of government to protect; and a calling, when chosen, is a man's property and right."[57]

The main development of substantive due process took place after 1885. In *Mugler v. Kansas*,[58] the Supreme Court in 1887 upheld a state statute prohibiting the manufacture and sale of intoxicating liquors. The statute was a measure to protect public health, safety, and morals. Justice Harlan, for the Court, acknowledged that the police power is constitutionally vested in the legislative branch of the government, but he did not limit due process to procedure. He mistakenly asserted that the courts "are at liberty—indeed, are under a solemn duty—to look at the substance of things, whenever they enter upon the inquiry whether the Legislature has transcended the limits of its authority."[59] The brief of the State Attorney General had not treated the original meaning of due process of law.

In *Powell v. Pennsylvania*,[60] the Court in 1888 approved a state statute prohibiting the manufacture and sale of oleomargarine against challenges under the Due Process and Equal Protection clauses. Justice Harlan, for the Court, correctly stated that the issue was legislative. But he mistakenly cautioned that the courts would have to hold a statute unconstitutional if it invaded the right to liberty.[61] Harlan thus ignored the brief of counsel for Pennsylvania that defined due process of law as a procedural constraint and therefore not applicable to this case. In fact, the sole purpose of the legislation in this case was to promote monopoly power in one of the ordinary trades, the dairy industry. This clearly violates the Anglo-American constitutional tradition against governmental grants of monopoly in the ordinary trades.[62]

Allgeyer v. Louisiana[63] stands as the founding case in which the Supreme Court expressly confirmed substantive due process as constitutional law. A Louisiana statute created a deliberate barrier to interstate commerce by making it a misdemeanor for its citizens to contract for insurance with companies outside the state that had not complied with state law requiring them to have an agent within the state. In *Hooper v. California*,[64] two years earlier, the Supreme Court had upheld a state statute requiring out-of-state insurance companies to file a bond as a condition of doing business within the state. But in *Hooper*, the insurance contract was entered in California by local agents of the New York insurer. In *Allgeyer* there was no local agent. The contract was a New York contract because the offer sent from Louisiana to purchase marine insurance was accepted in New York. Justice Rufus Peckham, for a unanimous Court, held the Louisiana statute unconstitutional. He recognized the authority of a state to regulate the local agents of foreign insurance companies, as in *Hooper*. But here he held that a New York contract could not be regulated by Louisiana. He ignored the fact that there was a violation of the Commerce Clause, probably because the Court had earlier erroneously held that interstate contracts of insurance were not "articles of commerce."[65] Instead, he followed the obiter dicta of Justice Harlan in *Powell v. Pennsylvania*[66] and misconstrued the word "liberty" in the Due Process Clause of the Fourteenth Amendment to include key elements of liberty of contract.

The brief of Allgeyer and Co., as appellants, centers on the Due Process Clause of the Fourteenth Amendment. While the Commerce Clause is listed in the assignment of errors, none of the argument treats the scope and breadth of that clause.[67] The situs of the contract had been fixed as New York in the earlier related case of *State v. Williams*.[68] A state act enforcing a state constitutional clause fixing conditions upon which foreign corporations may engage in business in a state may not be applied to regulate foreign corporations who have no agent in the state.[69] All these propositions are argued as part of freedom of contract protected by the Fourteenth Amendment.

The brief of the State of Louisiana, of only seven pages, failed to penetrate the constitutional issue. A factual argument was made that notices to the New York insurer of specific shipments to be covered by the contractual policy demonstrate that the contract is executed in Louisiana.[70] This argument is questionable since the insurance contract covered all marine risks for shipments from Louisiana to ports in Europe and all payments for losses would be processed and mailed form New York. There is total failure to make any argument or the basis of the original meanings of "due process" and of "liberty" in the context of the due process clause. It is not surprising that Justice Peckham's opinion adopts Allgeyer's arguments based on liberty of contract.

Regulation of Hours of Work

The laissez-faire bias of the court majority offered employers a good likelihood of successful attack on statutes limiting hours of work or setting minimum wages.[71] In many states, organized labor interests had convinced the legislatures to pass laws remedying asserted market failures in this field. Limiting hours of work was urged as a health and safety measure that would reduce the short-run supply of labor (total hours worked) but materially protect the health of workers and in the long run increase the total supply of healthy laborers. This analysis may have overlooked the facts of the real world. At the turn of the century, immigrant workers, unschooled in the English language, worked at a market wage that was very low. They may have needed seventy hours of work in order to purchase what they considered the necessities of life. In any case, the legislative policy issues of whether limiting hours of factory work was wise or unwise were not delegated to the judiciary.

In *Holden v. Hardy*,[72] in 1898, the Court upheld a Utah health and safety statute setting a maximum eight-hour day for workers in dangerous occupations at smelters and underground mines. Justice Henry Brown, for the majority noted: "These employments when too long pursued the legislature has judged to be detrimental to the health of the employees, and, so long as there are reasonable grounds for believing that this is so, its decision upon the subject cannot be reviewed by the Federal courts."[73] This followed the findings of facts, as reviewed by the Supreme Court of Utah.[74] But Brown noted that this rule might not apply to ordinary employments. Justices David Brewer and Rufus Peckham dissented without opinions.

The briefs for appellee, State of Utah, failed to argue that the Due Process Clause was only a procedural protection or even to make any distinction between procedure and substance. The main argument was for the high presumption of the constitutionality of statutes which originates in the separation of governmental powers.[75] The only argument that came close to attacking substantive due process was that the Federal Constitution has no application to statutes of the several states unless such statutes encroach upon one of the powers expressly surrendered to Congress or are in direct violation of some constitutional restriction upon the state.[76] But this was insufficient to prevent Justice Brown from confusing procedural and substantive cases in his opinion.

Lochner v. New York,[77] a 5 to 4 decision that should have been looked upon as highly questionable, unsettled law, became the leading early labor case. Ignoring the judicial notice of facts in the lower courts,[78] Justice Peckham, for the Supreme Court majority, held a New York law limiting hours of work in bakeries to ten per day and sixty per week to be unconstitutional. Justices Brown, Fuller, and McKenna abandoned the rational majority of *Holden* to join Justices Brewer and Peckham to form the new majority in *Lochner*. The high presumption of the constitutionality of statutes was not mentioned. Peckham departed from the principle enunciated in *Holden* that legislative determination of a detriment to health was not reviewable in a federal court if there were reasonable grounds for belief in the detriment. He cited *Allgeyer* for the constitutional principle of liberty of contract and reversed the lower courts. He asserted "that there can be no fair doubt that the trade of baker, in and of itself, is not an unhealthy one to that degree which would authorize the legislature to interfere with the right to labor, and with the right of free contract on the part of the individual, either as employer or employee."[79] Professor Roscoe Pound criticized the assumption of equal bargaining power of employers and employees as a fallacy "to everyone acquainted at first hand with actual industrial conditions."[80] Pound correctly concluded that constitutional liberty of contract was a judicial usurpation of legislative power.

Justice Peckham described the methodology of a superlegislature: "In every case that comes before this court, therefore, where legislation of this character is concerned, and where the protection of the Federal Constitution is sought, the question necessarily arises: Is this a fair, reasonable, and appropriate exercise of the police power of the state, or is it an unreasonable, unnecessary, and arbitrary interference with the right of the individual to his personal liberty, or to enter into those contracts in relation to labor which may seem to him appropriate or necessary for the support of himself and his family?"[81] The majority found that the limit of the police power had been reached and reversed the New York Court of Appeals.

Justice Harlan, for three of the dissenters, noted *Allgeyer* and concurred in the view that the state may not unduly interfere with freedom of contract.[82] But he cited authority that the Court may not reverse state regulations unless they are "so utterly unreasonable and extravagant in their nature and purpose that the property and personal rights of the citizen are unnecessarily, and in a manner wholly arbitrary, interfered with or destroyed without due process of law."[83] He noted authorities on diseases of workers that reported on the physical hardship of bakers. The regulations here were not plainly and palpably beyond all question arbitrary.

The *Lochner* case is most famous for the separate dissent of Justice Oliver Wendell Holmes and his fundamental attack on substantive due process:

> This case is decided upon an economic theory which a large part of the country does not entertain. If it were a question whether I agreed with that theory, I should desire to study it further and long before making up my mind. But I do not conceive that to be my duty, because I strongly believe that my agreement or disagreement has nothing to do with the right of a majority to embody their opinions in law. . . . The Fourteenth Amendment does not enact Mr. Herbert Spencer's Social Statics. . . . [A] Constitution is not intended to embody a particular economic theory, whether of paternalism and the organic relation of the citizen to the state or of *laissez faire*. It is made for people of fundamentally differing views, and the accident of our finding certain opinions natural and familiar, or novel, and even shocking, ought not to conclude our judgment upon the question whether statutes embodying them conflict with the Constitution of the United States.[84]

Unfortunately, Justice Holmes failed to add an explanation that his opinion was based on the original meaning of due process that "process" was a synonym for "procedure." The definition precluded substantive review.[85] If Holmes had emphasized the conservative nature of his textualist original interpretation, he might have been able to persuade one or more of the majority justices to join him in judicial restraint and formed a different majority. Substantive due process would have been less influential and its effective time would not have been labeled the *Lochner* era.

Justice Holmes may have failed to discuss the meanings of "process" and "liberty" in the Due Process Clause of the Fourteenth Amendment because the briefs for appellant Lochner and for appellee New York failed to discuss them. The brief for Lochner of forty-six pages devotes ten pages to the Equal Protection Clause, which was not treated by the Supreme Court.[86] The rest of the argument is devoted to the assertion that the bakery statute was not a reasonable exercise of the police power under the Due Process Clause. The main theme was that this was not a statute for the protection of health. New York precedents and major treatises are quoted to argue that the judiciary must be allowed to rule whether a statute really has the objective of protection of health or safety or the prevention of fraud.[87]

The brief for New York by Attorney-General Julius M. Mayer contained only nineteen pages plus statutory appendices. Mayer first argued that the Supreme Court lacked jurisdiction to hear a constitutional issue when this was not pleaded or argued in the trial court.[88] The issue was not set forth in the demurrer to the indictment. When the demurrer was overruled, there was no trial and Lochner was fined $50. The judges in the New York Court of Appeals had mentioned the Fourteenth Amendment and had affirmed Lochner's conviction.

Most of the New York brief is devoted to arguing that the bakery statute was a proper exercise of the police power.[89] While the statutory chapter is labeled "Labor Law," it is clear that it regulated the health of workers. Even though there were no trial court findings of fact, the brief made reference to the judicial notice of the New York Court of Appeals on the unhealthful character of the baker's occupation. Hence, regulation is a matter of legislative discretion with which courts are not authorized to interfere. All this argument is made without mentioning the language of the Fourteenth Amendment.

In *Muller v. Oregon*,[90] in 1908, the *Lochner* majority view on reasonableness was not followed. The Court unanimously affirmed the Oregon judicial validation of a law limiting hours of work for women to ten per day and sixty per week. Louis D. Brandeis, counsel for Oregon, realized the Court had assumed the role of a superlegislature. Consequently, he filed a brief of over 100 pages that was essentially like a presentation of facts to a legislative committee.[91] Brandeis's brief reviewed scientific opinion to the effect that long hours of work were especially dangerous to women because of their physical structure and their maternal functions. Justice David Brewer upheld this state regulation as an exception to the *Lochner* doctrine of liberty of contract.[92] The Oregon statute not only protected the health of women, but, "as healthy mothers are essential to vigorous offspring, the physical well-being of woman becomes an object of public interest and care in order to preserve the strength and vigor of the race."[93]

The legal part of the Oregon brief, as distinct from the social-economic data, was only twenty-four pages.[94] The argument begins by noting that the term "police power" had never had a fixed definition. Counsel asserts that the Oregon statute does not prohibit women from entering employment contracts but only regulates hours.[95] Numerous state court cases are cited that upheld regulation of hours of work for women on health grounds.

Neither the Fourteenth Amendment nor any of its parts is mentioned in the brief. The meanings of "process" and "liberty" are not treated. Rather than attack the fundamental interpretive errors of the *Lochner* majority, the brief distinguishes *Lochner* as a case concerned with men and not the health issues of women.[96] One must conclude the Brandeis missed the primary legal issue of the meaning of constitutional language.

By 1917, in *Bunting* v. *Oregon*,[97] the Court voted 5 to 3 to sustain a state law limiting hours of work in manufacturing for both men and women to ten per day. The statute required time-and-a-half pay for overtime, which the majority held to be a penalty and not a wage regulation. Since the law expressly stated that it was the interest of the state in the physical well-being of its citizens and that work in excess of ten hours was injurious to health, it was presumptively valid.[98] The lower courts had found that ten hours was a usual work day in Oregon. Therefore, the statute was not unreasonable or arbitrary.[99] Since this was a general statute, not limited to dangerous occupations like *Holden,* it was presumed by most commentators, including conservative Chief Justice William Howard Taft, to have overruled *Lochner, sub silentio.*[100]

Neither the brief of the Attorney General of Oregon nor that of Felix Frankfurter for the National Consumers' League treated the meaning of the language in the Due Process Clause of the Fourteenth Amendment.[101] Brandeis had originally been employed by the league to defend the law, but before the case came up for argument he was appointed to the Court. Frankfurter took over for Brandeis and filed a long brief of economic data to demonstrate that long hours of work were detrimental to health.

Minimum Wage Legislation

Two cases concerning the constitutionality of state minimum wage legislation reached the Supreme Court of the United States. In *Stettler v. O'Hara*[102] in 1917, the Court affirmed without opinion by a *per curiam* vote of 4 to 4, a unanimous Oregon Supreme Court judgment upholding the validity of the state minimum wage law for women. In *Adkins v. Children's Hospital,*[103] in 1923, the Court affirmed by a vote of 5 to 3 a decision of the U.S. Court of Appeals of the District of Columbia holding a federal minimum wage law for women as unconstitutional violation of liberty of contract. By the times of these cases, the deficient briefs of the earlier cases concerning liberty of contract and the consequent court opinions adopting liberty of contract meant that substantive due process was an established part of constitutional law. So that Louis D. Brandeis, the lead attorney in the nation arguing in support of labor legislation, could write in partial error in 1915: "These things are perfectly clear: First, that the constitution does protect 'liberty'; and second that the right to contract is a part of 'liberty.'"[104]

Before *Adkins*, four state courts, including Oregon, had ruled on the validity of minimum wage legislation for women. The Minnesota Supreme Court in cases in 1917 and 1920 upheld the law with six justices in favor and none opposed.[105] In Arkansas, the court sustained the legislation by a vote of four to one, though one of the majority refrained from dissent only because he thought that the legislation was entitled to the benefit of the Supreme Court tie until it was broken.[106] The Supreme Court of Washington, in two opinions in 1918, upheld the wage legislation by a total of eleven justices with none opposed.[107] Adding the votes in the four state Supreme Courts, minimum wage legislating for women was viewed constitutional by twenty-seven justices and viewed invalid by only two justices. Three of the four courts were unanimous in favoring the statutes.

Adkins v. Children's Hospital[108] concerned an attack on the federal Minimum Wage Law of the District of Columbia of 1918. Children's Hospital sued Adkins and other members of the Minimum Wage Board who had set a minimum wage for women of $16.50 per week or $71.50 per month on the grounds that the statute was an unconstitutional invasion of liberty of contract protected by the Fifth Amendment. The Supreme Court of the District of Columbia dismissed the action. In a highly irregular double hearing, the court of appeals first approved and then reversed the lower court.[109] The brief for the Wage Board in the court of appeals by Felix Frankfurter contained sixty pages of legal argument and 430 pages of economic data on costs of living and wage scales.[110] While the legal argument of Frankfurter attacked liberty of contract as applied to wage agreements, he failed to argue the original meaning of "liberty" in the due process context as freedom from imprisonment. He also failed to argue the original meaning of "process" as a synonym for procedure.

Upon appeal to the Supreme Court, Justice George Sutherland, for the five-justice majority, affirmed the court of appeal.[111] He reiterated the oft-repeated judicial error that liberty of contract is guaranteed by the due process clauses of the Fifth and Fourteenth Amendments. "That the right to contract about one's affairs is a part of the liberty of the individual protected by this clause is settled by the decisions of this court, and is no longer open to question."[112] In spite of the long list of cases cited by Sutherland, going back to *Allgeyer*, he made the common lawyer's error of asserting a constitutional interpretation was settled, not just for lower courts but also for the Supreme Court. The later overruling of *Adkins* demonstrated that Sutherland was wrong.[113]

Sutherland emphasized that, in light of the Nineteenth Amendment, the majority would not treat wages of women differently from that of men. Here again he erred. The Nineteenth Amendment concerned equal voting rights while the minimum wage statute here primarily concerned women's physical health. He mistakenly asserted that the statute was invalid because it exacted from employers an arbitrary payment even though the statute did not require employers to hire any person whose productivity would be less than her wages.[114]

Chief Justice William H. Taft dissented and Justice Edward Sanford joined his opinion. Taft accepted the view that liberty under the Fifth and Fourteenth amendments may extend to economic matters. After reviewing the earlier cases he concluded: "I do not feel, therefore, that either on the basis of reason, experience, or authority, the boundary of the police power should be drawn to include maximum hours and exclude a minimum wage."[115] Taft then submitted that the reasoning of Justice David Brewer in *Muller v. Oregon*, "that woman's physical structure and the performance of maternal functions place her at a disadvantage in the struggle for subsistence,"[116] was persuasive. The reasoning of *Muller* on hours of work should be applied to minimum wage regulation in this case.

Justice Holmes dissented and, while failing to discuss original meaning of "due process of law," he did explain why the term "liberty" did not include liberty of contract. He noted a number of earlier Supreme Court opinions that had upheld statutes regulating business against due process challenges. The Court's later overruling of *Adkins* verifies Holmes' dissent here as the correct law of the case:

> The earlier decisions upon the same words in the Fourteenth Amendment began within our memory and went no farther than an unpretentious assertion of the liberty to follow the ordinary callings. Later that innocuous generality was expanded into the dogma, Liberty of Contract. Contract is not specially mentioned in the text that we have to construe it. It is merely an example of doing what you want to do, embodied in the word liberty. But pretty much all law consists in forbidding men to do some things they want to do, and contract is no more exempt from law than other acts. . . .
>
> *Muller v. Oregon*, I take it, is as good law today as it was in 1908. It will need more than the Nineteenth Amendment to convince me that there are no differences between men and women, or that legislation cannot take those [physical] differences into account. I should not hesitate to take them into account if I thought it necessary to sustain this Act. But after *Bunting v. Oregon* I had supposed that it was not necessary, and that Lochner v. New York would be allowed a deserved repose.[117]

In *Adkins*, as was true in *Lochner*, Justice Holmes's failure in dissent to make a complete analysis of the original meaning of the Fifth Amendment Due Process Clause can in part be blamed on the deficient brief of appellant. Felix Frankfurter filed a legal brief of 66 pages followed by an economic-data brief of 1138 pages.[118] Unlike *Muller*, the "Brandeis" brief here failed to impress the Court. Justice Brandeis recused himself in *Adkins* even though he had no part in preparing this case. It was true that much of arguments and supporting data in *Adkins* had been offered to the Court in *Stettler*, the earlier case in which Brandeis was counsel.

Frankfurter's legal brief begins with the presumption of constitutionality of acts of Congress so that invalidity must be demonstrated beyond a reasonable doubt. The ends of the legislation, to protect the health and morals of women and minors in the district, were surely legitimate. Frankfurter's conclusion was that the so-called "liberties" of which the Children's Hospital claimed to be deprived were merely "fanciful and theoretical and not substantial."[119] As to the Constitution, Frankfurter never mentioned the original meanings of "process" and "liberty" in the context of the Fifth Amendment.

The majority view in *Adkins* was applied by the Court to invalidate minimum wage statutes for women in Arizona and Arkansas in 1925 and 1927.[120] In these two cases, the justices who had dissented in *Adkins* bowed to what they had considered an erroneous constitutional decision. Justice Brandeis, who had not participated in *Adkins*, dissented. The last case to invalidate a state minimum wage statute was in 1936 in *Morehead v. New York ex rel. Tipaldo*,[121] a 5 to 4 decision. The restricted appeal in this case concerned only whether the facts were distinguishable from *Adkins* because no review of the constitutional issue was requested in the petition for writ of certiorari to the Supreme Court. Justice Stone, in dissent, argued in vain but correctly that it was error to avoid an underlying constitutional issue.

Regulation of Business Practices

There were some overruled cases in which the Supreme Court had voided state regulation of business practices. *Adams v. Tanner*[122] was issued in 1917 and overruled in 1963. The people of the state of Washington, by an initiative measure in 1914, had enacted the Employment Agency Law that prohibited the collection of fees from workers by employment agencies. The purpose in time of great unemployment was to stop impositions and extortions by employment agencies on the poorest job seekers. Plaintiffs, agency owners, sued the state Attorney General, to enjoin enforcement of the initiative statute on the grounds of violation of the Due Process Clause of the Fourteenth Amendment. Plaintiffs argued that the statute in effect decreed the end of private employment agencies. The district court dismissed the action. Upon appeal, Justice James C. McReynolds, writing for the Court, reversed the dismissal, citing *Allgeyer v. Louisiana*[123] as authority for broad liberty of contract under due process.

Justice Brandeis wrote a dissent in which Justices Holmes and Clarke concurred.[124] While he failed to argue the meaning of "due process," he explained the rational basis for the statute. He cited a 1912 report of the U.S. Bureau of Labor that collected evidence on how the employment agencies had swindled and defrauded those who sought employment.

In *Burns Baking Co. v. Bryan*,[125] the Court invalidated a Nebraska statute designed to prevent deception by requiring loaves of bread must weigh one-half pound, one pound, or multiples thereof. The aspect that the Court declared an unreasonable violation of due process was the statutory prescribed tolerance of only two ounces in excess of the minimum weight per loaf. Rejecting the lower courts finding of facts, the Court found that it was impossible to manufacture bread without frequently exceeding this tolerance. Justices Brandeis and Holmes dissented. Brandeis disagreed with the factual finding but failed to treat the original meaning of due process. He concluded:

It is not our province to weigh evidence. . . . To decide, as a fact, that the prohibition of excess weights "is not necessary for the protection of the purchasers against imposition and fraud by short weights," that it "is not calculated to effectuate that, purpose;" and that it "subjects bakers and sellers of bread" to heavy burdens is, in my opinion, an exercise of the powers of a super-legislature—not the performance of the constitutional function of judicial review.[126]

In 1934, the *Burns Baking Co.* opinion was distinguished on the basis of a slight difference in facts. In effect, this was an overruling. In *P. F. Peterson Baking Co. v. Bryan,*[127] the Court upheld a newer Nebraska statute regulating bread sizes against a due process challenge. In the new statute, the allowed tolerance for shrinkage was three ounces per pound as compared to a tolerance of only two ounces in the earlier statute invalidated in the *Burns* case.

Liggett Co. v. Baldrige[128] was decided in 1928 and overruled in 1973. The case concerned state legislation impairing market competition by barring chain drug stores. The Pennsylvania statute required that no new drug stores be opened or acquired unless every stockholder or partner is a licensed pharmacist. Two new drug stores acquired by the Liggett chain were refused permits. Justice George Sutherland, for the Court, correctly held that this statute was not one that protected public health since other statutes of the state totally protected the quality of work by pharmacists. Then Sutherland incorrectly held that Liggett's business was a property right protected by the due process of the Fourteenth Amendment. He concluded that since the statute had no relation to public health, it rested on conjecture and was arbitrary. Hence, it was unconstitutional. Justice Holmes wrote a dissent, in which Justice Brandeis concurred, correctly maintaining that the substance of this law could not be tested by the Due Process Clause.[129]

In this case and others treated in Chapter 10, there was a failure of counsel to brief the Equal Protection Clause.[130] That clause was the appropriate substantive constraint. The question here was whether drugstores owned by individual pharmacists and those owned by corporate chains would be in like positions in free markets. If the Equal Protection Clause had been presented at trial and in the Supreme Court, the decision of Justice Sutherland of like circumstances of firms would have been correct. The opinion could have been unanimous and never overruled.

Price Regulation and the Public Interest Concept

State regulation of carrier rates and other prices was adopted largely at the political demand of agricultural interests as a remedy for the market failure of monopoly. History shows, however, that in the railroad industry the carriers supported rate regulation as a technique to reinforce price fixing cartels.[131] State regulation of rates or prices was first upheld by the Supreme Court in *Munn v. Illinois*[132] in 1876, with two justices dissenting. The fourteen grain elevators in Chicago were controlled by nine business firms whose storage rates were set by agreement between the firms. The state statute setting maximum rates that the

Chicago warehousemen could charge was a police regulation to limit monopoly pricing. Chief Justice Morrison Waite, for the majority, held this regulation was not an unconstitutional deprivation of property without due process of law. He held it a legislative question whether a business was "affected with a public interest" and likewise a legislative question of what rates were reasonable. "For protection against abuses by legislatures, the people must resort to the polls, not to the courts."[133] Justice Stephen Field, in dissent, urged adoption of substantive due process. He viewed governmental regulation to control and limit monopoly pricing by unincorporated firms as subversive to the rights of property and liberty. This was clearly inconsistent with Field's strong views against governmental grants of monopoly in his dissent in the *Slaughter-House Cases*.[134]

The effectiveness of *Munn v. Illinois* was short-lived. As more states passed statutes regulating intrastate rates, the reasonableness of the rates was repeatedly challenged under the Due Process Clause. In the *Railroad Commission Cases,* Chief Justice Waite admitted that railroad rates can not be set so low that it "mounts to a taking of private property for public use without just compensation, or without due process of law.[135] By 1890 in *Chicago, Milwaukee & St. Paul Ry. v. Minnesota,*[136] essentially the entire court was won over to substantive due process. "The question of the reasonableness of a rate of charge for transportation by a railroad company, involving as it does the element of reasonableness both as regards the company and as regards the public, is eminently a question for judicial investigation, requiring due process of law for its determination."[137] This view was confirmed in 1898 in *Smyth v. Ames,*[138] in which the Court invalidated a Nebraska regulation of railroad rates. The distinction between confiscatory and unreasonable rates disappeared. "What the company is entitled to ask is a fair return upon the value of that which it employs for public convenience."[139] The Supreme Court became a superlegislature to review the reasonableness of rates in all regulated industries.

The regulation of prices in various industries by state legislatures, which attempted to follow the method in *Munn v. Illinois,* were many times held by the Supreme Court to be an unreasonable invasion of "property" under the Due Process Clause.[140] The Court took the dictum from the *Munn* case that warehouses were "affected with a public interest," and used this concept to reverse its ruling that it was a legislative question to determine which industries needed regulation. From 1923 to 1932, the Court majority voided price regulation in five major decisions by interposing its view that these industries were not "affected with a public interest."

Tyson & Bros. v. Banton,[141] was decided in 1927 and overruled in 1965. The Court held unconstitutional a New York statute that declared the theater business to be affected with a public interest and limited the resale price of theater tickets to fifty cents over the box office price. The statute was aimed at ticket brokers, who were labeled mere appendages of the theaters companies. Justice Sutherland, for the Court, asserted that "the right of the owner to fix a price at which his property shall be sold or used is an inherent attribute of the property itself, and, as such within the protection of the due process of law clauses of the 5th and 14th Amendments."[142] The Court found that the theater business had not been devoted to a public use. It was not comparable to grain elevators as in *Munn v. Illinois*. Rather, the interest of the public in theaters fell below that for food, clothing, and shelter markets, that, absent an emergency, were viewed as not subject to price regulation. The statutory declaration of public interest was held not to bind the Court.

Justices Holmes, Brandeis, and Stone dissented. Justice Holmes concluded:

> I think the proper course is to recognize that a State legislature can do whatever it sees fit to do unless it is restrained by some express prohibition in the Constitution of the United States or of the State, and that courts should be careful not to extend such prohibitions beyond their obvious meaning by reading into them conceptions of public policy that the particular court may happen to entertain.
>
> Coming down to the case before us I think, as I intimated in Adkins v. Children's Hospital, that the notion that a business is clothed with a public interest and has been devoted to the public use is little more than a fiction intended to beautify what is disagreeable to the sufferers. The truth seems to me to be that, subject to compensation when compensation is due, the legislature may forbid or restrict any business when it has a sufficient force of public opinion behind it.[143]

Ribnik v. McBride[144] was decided in 1928 and overruled in 1941. The case concerned a New Jersey law requiring licensing of private employment agencies and submission by such agencies of a schedule of fees to be charged to prospective employers and employees for approval by the Commissioners of Labor. Citing *Tyson & Bros. v. Banton* and *Adkins v. Children's Hospital* as authority, the Court held that regulation of fees charged by agencies violated the Due Process Clause of the 14th Amendment. The agencies were held analogous to brokers and not firms with a "public interest" that the law contemplated as a basis for legislative price control. Justice Harlan Stone dissented with the concurrence of Justices Holmes and Brandeis. Stone concluded: "I cannot accept as valid the distinction on which the opinion of the majority seems to me necessarily to depend, that granted constitutional power to regulate there is any controlling difference between reasonable regulation of price, if appropriate to the evil to be remedied, and other forms of appropriate regulation which curtail liberty of contract or the use and enjoyment of property."[145]

In *New State Ice Co. v. Liebmann*,[146] an Oklahoma statute had declared that the manufacture of ice for sale and distribution to users was a public business and required a certificate of public convenience and necessity for entry. The Corporation Commission was delegated power to license ice producers. Manufacture of ice without a license was a misdemeanor. New State Ice Co. was a licensed manufacturer. Liebmann, without a license, built an ice plant, planning to sell ice, and New State filed an action to enjoin his entering the ice business. The Supreme Court, in a 6 to 2 decision, affirmed dismissal of the action on the basis that ice manufacture was not a business affected with a public interest, so that regulation violated due process. Justice Brandeis, without treating the meaning of due process, wrote a long dissent in which Justice Stone concurred. As to due process, Justice Brandeis was correct in his dissent when he concluded, "The notion of a distinct category of business 'affected with a public interest' employing property 'devoted to a public use,' rests upon historical error."[147] But the facts of the case show an objective to create local monopolies in ice manufacture by barring entry of new firms.[148] The facts are most closely analogous to the *Slaughter-House Cases*[149] in that the statute was designed to bar entry into an ordinary trade. As Justice Sutherland wrote, "We are not able to see anything peculiar in the business here in question which distinguishes it from ordinary manufacture and production."[150] If tested under the Privileges or Immunities Clause, as noted in Chapter 7, or the Equal Protection Clause, the statute should have been invalidated. *New State Ice Co.* presented an ideal opportunity to overrule the *Slaughter-House* decision.

This survey of the rise of substantive due process reviewed only the leading cases. From 1890 to 1937, there were over 150 cases before the Supreme Court on the validity of economic regulations under the due process clause.[151] The majority of the cases upheld state regulatory statutes, but the others were significant enough to impede substantially the economic controls which were justified by market failures. If the majority of the Court had adhered to the rejection of substantive due process that was clearly enunciated in *Davidson v. New Orleans*,[152] most of the later cases would never have reached the Supreme Court.

Repudiation of Constitutional Liberty of Contract: Holmes and Brandeis Vindicated

The vindication of Justice Holmes' constitutional method began in 1934. *Nebbia v. New York*[153] initiated the decline that led to the ultimate demise of substantive due process as a standard to judge economic regulation. The Court finally discarded the concept of "business affected with a public interest." The 5 to 4 decision upheld the constitutionality of a New York law delegating to the Milk Control Board the authority to set minimum retail prices for milk. The opinion was written by Justice Roberts, who, with Chief Justice Hughes, switched from the majority in the *New State Ice*[154] case, which had interposed the economic due process barrier, to the majority in this case, which rejected economic due process. He noted that "neither property rights nor contract rights are absolute; for government cannot exist if the citizen may at will use his property to the detriment of his fellows, or exercise his freedom of contract to work them harm. Equally fundamental with the private right is that of the public to regulate it in the common interest"[155] He interpreted *Munn v. Illinois* as holding that "affected with a public interest" is the equivalent of "subject to the exercise of the police power."[156] Consequently he concluded: "It is clear that there is no closed class or category of businesses affected with a public interest. . . . The phrase 'affected with a public interest' can, in the nature of things, mean no more than an industry, for adequate reason, is subject to control for the public good."[157]

From an economics viewpoint, the statute in *Nebbia* was predestined to fail its objective of raising farm incomes.[158] It was a microeconomic policy reaction to the macroeconomic problem of a large drop in aggregate demand. Legislated minimum retail prices could only result in less total sales, the amount of decrease depending on the elasticity of demand. By eliminating price competition in milk retailing, the statute guaranteed the mark-up of distributors at the expense of consumers.

The great reversal on the constitutionality of minimum wage legislation came in 1937 coinciding with President Roosevelt's proposed court-packing plan.[159] In *West Coast Hotel Co. v. Parrish*,[160] the Court upheld the constitutionality of the Washington state minimum wage law for women and minors. In doing so, it expressly overruled the *Adkins* opinion of 1923 and in effect overruled the *Morehead* decision of 1936.[161] In fact, the 5 to 4 decision in *West Coast Hotel Co. v. Parrish* came about without a change in Court personnel from the Morehead case. Like his behavior in *Nebbia v. New York*,[162] which had upheld regulation of minimum retail prices for milk, Justice Roberts again made a quick switch from supporting due process as a barrier to economic regulation to its denial. This was the same Roberts who was later to complain that too many overrulings tend "to bring adjudications of this tribunal into the same class as a restricted railroad ticket good for this day and train only."[163]

Chief Justice Hughes, for the majority, affirmed the Washington Court but held that *Adkins* had to be reexamined because the language in the due process clauses in the Fifth and Fourteenth amendments were *in pari materia*.[164] While he failed to review the original meaning of "liberty," and cited the erroneous generalization in *Allgeyer* and *Lochner* that liberty of contract is protected by the Fourteenth Amendment, Hughes did attack the breadth of such claims. He quoted from the dissents of Chief Justice Taft and Justice Holmes in *Adkins* as authoritative interpretations of due process clauses. Hughes concluded with the correct textual analysis.

> The Constitution does not speak of freedom of contract. It speaks of liberty and prohibits the deprivation of liberty without due process of law. In prohibiting that deprivation the Constitution does not recognize an absolute and uncontrollable liberty. Liberty in each of its phases has its history and connotation. But the liberty safeguarded is liberty in a social organization which requires the protection of law against the evils which menace the health, safety, morals and welfare of the people . . . The guarantee of liberty does not withdraw from legislative supervision that wide department of activity which consists of the making of contracts, or deny to government the power to provide restrictive safeguards. Liberty implies the absence of arbitrary restraint, not immunity from reasonable regulation and prohibitions imposed in the interests of the community.[165]

The brief for appellee Parrish was only four pages long and mostly distinguished *Adkins* from this case.[166] The *amicus curiae* brief of the Attorney General of Washington and his two assistants was twenty-six pages.[167] This brief centered on the reasonable and nondiscriminatory nature of the wage regulation for women, citing analogous regulation of hours of work in *Muller* and *Bunting* and price regulation in *Nebbia*. In fact, *Nebbia* had ended the idea that the public interest was limited to monopoly industries. The final part of the brief argued the wide scope of state police power and the consequent discretion in the legislature to determine the necessity for laws protecting public health, safety, and morals. Neither of these two briefs discussed the Fourteenth Amendment or the meaning of the language in the due process clauses.

Seven years after *Nebbia, Ribnik v. McBride*[168] was overruled in 1941 in *Olsen v. Nebraska*.[169] The Nebraska Supreme Court had invalidated a state statute fixing the maximum compensation which private employment agencies might collect from an applicant for employment. Following the *Ribnik* precedent, the Nebraska court had held the statute unconstitutional under the Due Process Clause of the Fourteenth Amendment. Justice Douglas, for the U.S. Supreme Court, reversed the Nebraska ruling. His overruling of *Ribnik* concluded: "We are not concerned, however, with the wisdom, need, or appropriateness of the legislation. Differences of opinion on that score suggest a choice which should be left where . . . it was left by the Constitution—to the States and to Congress."[170]

Adams v. Tanner was overruled in 1963 in *Ferguson v. Skrupa*.[171] A Kansas statute made it a misdemeanor for any person to engage in the business of debt adjusting except lawyers. Skrupa, a non-lawyer debt adjuster, brought this action to enjoin enforcement of the statute on the ground that it violated the Due Process Clause of the Fourteenth Amendment. The district court granted relief and the Supreme Court reversed. Justice Hugo L. Black, for the court wrote:

> The doctrine that prevailed in Lochner, Coppage, Adkins, Burns, and like cases—that due process authorizes courts to hold laws unconstitutional when they believe the legislature has acted unwisely—has long since been discarded. We have returned to the original constitutional proposition that courts do not substitute their social and economic beliefs for the judgment of legislative bodies, who are elected to pass laws. As this Court stated in a unanimous opinion in 1941, "We are not concerned with the wisdom, need, or appropriateness of the legislation." Legislative bodies have broad scope to experiment with economic problems, and this Court does not sit to "subject the State to an intolerable supervision hostile to the basic principles of our Government and wholly beyond the protection which the general clause of the Fourteenth Amendment was intended to secure."[172]

Tyson & Bros. v. Banton was finally overruled per curiam in 1965 in *Gold v. DiCarlo*.[173] The quotations here are from the district court opinion that was affirmed. A licensed ticket broker in New York sued to enjoin enforcement of a New York law making it unlawful to resell a ticket for a public amusement event at a price more than $1.50 over the price printed on the ticket. The district court held it was not bound by res judicata to follow *Tyson* and denied the injunction. Judge Kaufman, for the court, wrote:

> Nebbia's approach was reaffirmed in Olsen v. Nebraska, which upheld a statute regulating the fees charged by employment agencies. The Court there stated, in effect, that Tyson's standard had been discarded. And, most recently, in Ferguson v. Skrupa, Justice Black not only declared that Tyson's philosophy had been abandoned, but quoted the rationale of Justice Holme's dissent in that case with approval. We would be abdicating our judicial responsibility if we waited for the Supreme Court to use the express words "We hereby overrule Tyson," as the plaintiffs contend we should, before recognizing that the case is no longer binding precedent but simply a relic for the constitutional historians.[174]

Conclusion

Commentators today rightly ask how five or more members of the Supreme Court, an appointed elite, could have undertaken to reverse policies of elected legislatures regulating hours of work and minimum wages. Most important, these justices were members of the same socio-economic class as employers, not manual laborers.[175] They refused to recognize the views of minority justices that the majority in most such cases were ignoring the findings of fact in trial courts and ignoring the high presumption for the constitutionality of statutes; consequently the majority were usurping legislative power.

As to the composition of socially biased Court majorities, one factor that was totally unpredictable was presidential decisions to appoint justices to the Court that the president may not have known had extreme socio-economic biases. A prime example was President Wilson's appointment of James C. McReynolds in 1914.[176] The leading cases of *Lochner* and *Adkins* were each decided by five men. If one or two men of the *Lochner* and *Adkins* majorities had been other persons with the humility like Holmes to set aside their personal socio-economic biases and recognize the conservative correctness of Holmes' original reasoning in dissent, substantive due process might have been curtailed.

Perhaps the most important judicial failure that led to the creation of substantive due process can be traced to the primary position of precedent in common-law reasoning and its application to statutory reasoning, an emphasis on precedent in the education of lawyers in the common-law system.[177] Most lawyers, judges, and scholars failed to recognize that there is one fundamental exception to the rule of precedent, and that is for constitutional cases in the highest appeals court.[178] In the federal system, this is the Supreme Court of the United States. As Justice Frankfurter proclaimed, "The ultimate touchstone of constitutionality is the Constitution itself and not what we have said about it."[179] Justice Scalia, in his recent book, restates this fundamental principle as he characterizes the law of the national government as a Civil Law System.[180] The correct methodology in Supreme Court constitutional interpretation is to search in each case for the original meaning of the ratified language. As a consequence, while lower courts are bound to follow general interpretations of a constitutional clause made in the Supreme Court, the Court itself is not bound by its earlier constitutional decisions. Given the great difficulties of securing amendments to the Constitution, the Court must have the power to correct its earlier errors of interpretation by overruling past decisions.

In light of this special methodology in Supreme Court constitutional interpretations, such early majority decisions and opinions as *Allgeyer* and *Lochner* that misconstrued the Due Process Clause were mistakenly viewed by some conservative justices as binding on the Court in later cases. As Justice Frankfurter indicated, however, there is no such thing as settled constitutional law for the Supreme Court. It was the failure of leading justices, including the great senior Harlan, to recognize that earlier court's creation or adoption of liberty of contract as part of the due process clauses was not binding on them. As was noted, even Justice Brandeis committed the fallacy of treating a limited liberty of contract as a binding part of due process.[181] It was only Justice Holmes who, from his great *Lochner* dissent onward, denounced the creation of substantive due process.

The thesis of this study is that the briefs of lawyers opposing substantive due process have suffered the same mistaken application of precedent in constitutional cases in the Supreme Court as had the Court itself. The lawyers have failed to brief and argue the textual meanings of constitutional language as the sole constraint binding on the Court. They have also failed to brief the key structural barrier in the Constitution, the separation of governmental powers.[182] A brief can state a conclusion that the earlier Supreme Court usurped legislative power by creating substantive due process. But fully briefing the functions of separated powers reminds a court that the mandated checks and balances are achieved by strict adherence to its province by each of the three departments of government.

The briefing remedies necessary to combat and to overrule substantive due process are still a live and current issue. While economic due process is finished, substantive due process was totally resurrected by the Supreme Court creation of a constitutional right to privacy. *Griswold v. Connecticut*[183] was a contrived case to test a disused state statute that made it a crime to use artificial birth control.[184] Defendants were a director of Planned Parenthood and a Yale professor of medicine who were convicted of abetting violation of the statute. In reversing the conviction and finding an invasion of a constitutional right of privacy, Justice Douglas, for the majority, had great trouble in finding a basis for the decision in constitutional language. He finally asserted that there are "penumbras formed by emanations" from the First, Third, Fourth, Fifth, and Ninth amendments that result in a general guarantee of privacy.[185] Justices Harlan and White wrote concurring opinions, specifically relying on the concept of liberty in the Fourteenth Amendment. Justice Black, joined by Justice

Stewart, dissented and criticized substantive due process as usurpation of the amending clause, as he had done in the majority opinion of the *Ferguson* case two years earlier.[186]

In *Roe v. Wade*,[187] the Court invalidated a Texas law making it a crime to secure an abortion. Justice Blackmun, for the majority, concluded that a right of privacy could be found in the word "liberty" in the Fourteenth Amendment and that this privacy included a right to abortion. Justice White, joined by Justice Rehnquist, dissented. He stated: "I find nothing in the language or history of the Constitution to support the Court's judgment. The Court simply fashions and announces a new constitutional right for pregnant mothers and, with scarcely any reason or authority for its action, invests that right with sufficient substance to override most existing state abortion statutes."[188] Taken out of context, this conclusion overstates the objection to substantive due process. If a constitutional right to choice of abortion were re-litigated, the Supreme Court might uphold the right to choose on the basis of the Equal Protection Clause.[189]

Notes

1. The Fifth Amendment states in part: "No Person shall be . . . deprived of life, liberty, or property, without due process of law." In spite of its unqualified language and its origin in the fundamental rights of Englishmen, the Fifth Amendment was interpreted by the Supreme Court in an eminent domain case as a limit only on the national government. *Barron v. Baltimore*, 32 U.S. (7 Pet.) 243 (1833). The Fourteenth Amendment, Section 1 put the same limitation on the states: "nor shall any state deprive any person of life, liberty, or property without due process of law."

2. *Adamson v. California*, 332 U.S. 46, 68-123 (1947) (Black, J., dissenting).

3. Charles L. Black, *A New Birth of Freedom*, 87-106 (New York: Grosset/Putnam, 1997); John H. Ely, *Democracy and Distrust: A Theory of Judicial Review*, 18 (Cambridge: Harvard Univ. Press, 1980); Henry P. Monaghan, *Our Perfect Constitution*, 56 NYU L. Rev. 351-361 (1981). See generally, Leslie F. Goldstein, *In Defense of the Text* (Savage, MD: Rowman & Littlefield, 1991).

4. See Alexander M. Bickel, *The Least Dangerous Branch*, 16-23 (New York: Bobbs-Merrill, 1962); Martin S. Flaherty, *The Most Dangerous Branch*, 105 Yale L. J. 1725 (1996); Barry Friedman, *The Road to Judicial Supremacy: The History of the Countermajoritarian Difficulty*, Part 1, 73 NYU L. Rev. 333 (1998).

5. 198 U.S. 45 (1905). See generally, Barry Cushman, *Rethinking The New Deal Court* 47-105 (New York: Oxford Univ. Press, 1998); Sidney Fine, *Laissez-Faire and the General-Welfare State: A Study of Conflict in American Thought, 1865-1901* (Ann Arbor: Univ. of Michigan Press, 1956); Stephen, Siegel, *Understanding the Lochner Era*, 70 Va. L. Rev. 187 (1984).

6. 300 U.S. 379 (1937), overruling *Adkins v. Children's Hospital*, 261 U.S. 525 (1923).

7. See Robert G. McClosky, *Economic Due Process and the Supreme Court: An Exhumation and Reburial*, Sup. Ct. Rev. 34 (1962).

8. Edward Coke, 2 *Institutes of the Laws of England*, 11 (London: Flesher and Young, 1642). See Jack N. Rakove, *Original Meanings: Politics and Ideas in the Making of the Constitution*, 339-365 (New York: Alfred A. Knopf, 1996); Henry P. Monaghan, *Stare Decisis and Constitutional Adjudication*, 88 Colum. L. Rev. 723, 725-27 (1988); Antonin Scalia, *Originalism: the Lesser Evil*, 57 U. Cin. L. Rev. 849, 853 (1989).

9.   Joseph Story, 1 *Commentaries on the Constitution of the United States*, § 453 (Boston: Hilliard, Gray, 1833).

10. *Id.* at § 452.

11. For the historical origins of the due process clauses, see William S. McKechnie, *Magna Carta*, ch. 39 (Glasgow: J. Maclehose, 2d ed. 1914); Melville Bigelow, *History of Procedure in England from the Norman Conquest*, 155 (London: Macmillan, 1880). The earliest meaning of process was as a synonym for writ and hence the phrase "service of process." By the 14th century and the use of the phrase "due process of law," process became a synonym for procedure. See Keith Jurow, *Untimely Thoughts: A Reconsideration of the Origins of Due Process of Law*, 19 Am. J. Legal Hist. 265 (1975).

12. 1 Stat. 93 (1789).

13. See Julius Goebel, *History of the Supreme court of the United States, vol. 1, Antecedents and Beginnings to 1801*, 509 (New York, Macmillan, 1971).

14. Giles Jacob, *Law-Dictionary* (London: R. Ware, 7th ed. 1756), s.v. Process.

15. Goebel, *supra* note 13, at 514.

16. On the textual meaning of the Fourteenth Amendment, see William W. Crosskey, 2 *Politics and the Constitution in the History of the United States*, 1103-1116 (Chicago: Univ. of Chicago Press, 1953); Michael Kent Curtis, *No State Shall Abridge* (Durham: Duke Univ. Press, 1986); Louis B. Boudin, 2 *Government By Judiciary*, 355-373 (New York: William Godwin, Inc., 1932). Ely, *Democracy and Distrust, supra* note 3; Monaghan, *Our Perfect Constitution, supra* note 3.

17. *Dartmouth College v. Woodward*, 17 U.S. (4 Wheat.) 518, 581 (1819) (argument of Daniel Webster).

18. See A.E. Dick Howard, *The Road from Runnymede: Magna Carta and Constitutionalism in America*, 303-305 (Charlottesville: Univ. of Virginia Press, 1968).

19. 59 U.S. (18 How.) 272, 276-277 (1855).

20. *Hurtado v. California*, 110 U.S. 516, 539 (1884) (Harlan, dissenting).

21. See *International Shoe Co.* v. *Washington*, 326 U.S. 310, 316 (1945).

22. *Snyder v. Massachusetts*, 291 U.S. 97, 105 (1934).

23. *Malinski v. New York*, 324 U.S. 401, 414 (1945).

24. 110 U.S. 516 (1884) (grand jury clause of Fifth Amendment not applicable to the states.) The dissent of Justice Harlan clearly demonstrated that under the rule of *Murray's Lessee*, due process incorporated Amendments Five through Eight. *Id.* at 542-543. See Crosskey, 2 *Politics and the Constitution, supra* note 16, at 1136-1141.

25. See, e.g., *Maxwell v. Dow*, 176 U.S. 581 (1900) (Sixth Amendment right to jury trial not applicable to states), overruled in *Duncan v. Louisiana*, 391 U.S. 145 (1968); *Twining v. New Jersey*, 211 U.S. 78 (1908) (Fifth Amendment privilege against self incrimination not applicable to the states), overruled in *Malloy v. Hogan*, 378 U.S. 1 (1964); *Palko v. Connecticut*, 302 U.S. 319 (1937) (Fifth Amendment immunity from double jeopardy not applicable to states), overruled in *Benton v. Maryland*, 395 U.S. 784 (1969).

26. See *Duncan v. Louisiana*, 319 U.S. 145 (1968).

27. 96 U.S. 97 (1878).

28. *Id.* at 105.

29. *Id.* at 102. Later in the opinion, Miller emphasizes in this case that the issue of just compensation was not before the Court. *Id.* at 105.

30. *Id.* at 104.

31. For the more general definition of liberty as the absence of arbitrary power of officials under British constitutionalism, see John P. Reid, *The Concept of Liberty*

in the Age of the American Revolution, 74-83 (Chicago: Univ. of Chicago Press, 1988).

32. Charles Shattuck, *The True Meaning of the Term "Liberty" in Those Clauses in the Federal and State Constitutions Which Protect "Life, Liberty, and Property,"* 4 Harv. L. Rev. 365 (1891).

33. Richard L. Perry, ed., *Sources of Our Liberties,* 17 (Chicago: American Bar Foundation, 1952). On the American adoption of chapter 39 of *Magna Carta,* see Howard, *Road From Runnymede, supra,* note 18 at 488-89; Story, 2 *Commentaries, supra,* note 9 at § 1789.

34. Perry, *Sources of Our Liberties, supra,* note 33 at 74.

35. *Id.* at 148.

36. *Id.* at 330, 348, 355, 366.

37. William Blackstone, 1 *Commentaries on the Laws of England,* 130 (1765) (Reprint, Chicago: Univ. of Chicago Press, 1979).

38. *Id.* at 131.

39. 31 Car. 2, c.2 (1679).

40. Shattuck, *True Meaning, supra,* note 32 at 377-78.

41. See *Lochner v. New York* at note 84, *infra,* and *Adkins v. Children's Hospital* at note 108, *infra.*

42. A search of records showed only one proposed amendment relating to redefining the Due Process Clause. It was introduced by Congressman Emanuel Celler on June 5, 1939 and referred to the Committee on the Judiciary. See John R. Vile, ed; 2 *Proposed Amendments to the U. S. Constitution 1787-2001,* at item 754 (Clark, NJ: Lawbook Exchange Ltd., 2003).

43. Benjamin R. Twiss, *Lawyers and The Constitution: How Laissez Faire Came to the Supreme Court,* ch. 2 (Princeton, NJ: Princeton Univ. Press, 1942); Arnold M. Paul, *Conservative Crisis and the Rule of Law,* 221-237 (Ithaca, NY: Cornell Univ. Press, 1960); Bernard Siegan, *Economic Liberties and the Constitution,* (Chicago: Univ. of Chicago Press, 1980).

44. See Clyde E. Jacobs, *Law Writers and the Courts,* 3-63 (Berkeley: Univ. of California Press, 1954); Edward S. Corwin, *Liberty Against Government,* 116-168 (Baton Rouge: Louisiana State Univ. Press, 1948).

45. Max Freedman, ed., *Roosevelt and Frankfurter, Their Correspondence, 1928-1945,* 384 (Boston: Little Brown, 1967). See comment, supra, at page 56.

46. Corwin, *Liberty Against Government, supra,* note 44 at ch. 3; Edward Corwin, *Due Process of Law Before the Civil War,* 24 Harv. L. Rev. 366, 460 (1911).

47. Howard J. Graham, *Procedure to Substance: Extra-Judicial Rise of Due Process,* 1830-1860, 40 Calif. L. Rev. 483 (1952), reprinted in *Everyman's Constitution,* ch. 5 (Madison, WI: State Historical Society, 1968).

48. 13 N.Y. 378 (1850) (State act barring sale of liquor held unconstitutional). See Corwin, *Liberty Against Government, supra* note 44, at 100-103.

49. *Scott v. Sandford,* 60 U.S. (19 How.) 393 (1857). See Don E. Fehrenbacher, *The Dred Scott Case* (New York: Oxford Univ. Press, 1978); E. S. Corwin, *The Doctrine of Judicial Review,* ch. 4 (Princeton, NJ: Princeton Univ. Press, 1914); Charles Warren, 2 *The Supreme Court in United States History,* ch. 26 (Boston: Little Brown, 1926).

50. Limitation on Slavery, 16th Cong., Sess. 1, Ch. 22, Sec. 8, 3 Stat. 548 (1820).

51. The Illinois constitution of 1848, Art. 13, § 16, contained an absolute prohibition on slavery in the state. This was notice to all owners in slave states not to bring slaves into Illinois because no person could be held in slavery there. This notice met the procedural requirements of due process. *Rodney v. Illinois Central Railroad Co.,* 19 Ill. 42 (1857).

52. 60 U.S. (19 How.) at 450.
53. *Id.* at 564.
54. Speech at Springfield, Illinois, June 26, 1857, Reprinted in 2 *Collected Works of Abraham Lincoln* 398, 401 (New Brunswick, NJ: Rutgers Univ. Press, 1953).
55. U.S. Constitution, Amend. 14.
56. 83 U.S. (16 Wall.) 36 (1873). See 2 Warren, *Supreme Court, supra* note 49, at ch. 32.
57. 83 U.S. (16 Wall.) at 122.
58. 123 U.S. 623 (1887). See brief for State of Kansas, 31 L. Ed. 207.
59. 123 U.S. at 661.
60. 127 U.S. 678 (1888). See brief for Pennsylvania, 32 L. Ed. 254 (1888).
61. 127 U.S. at 686-687.
62. See Chapter 7.
63. 165 U.S. 578 (1897).
64. 155 U.S. 648 (1895).
65. *Paul v. Virginia,* 75 U.S. (8 Wall.) 168, 183 (1869), overruled, *United States v. South-Eastern Underwriters Ass'n,* 322 U.S. 533 (1944).
66. 127 U.S. 678 (1888).
67. *Allgeyer,* Appellant's Brief 15. See 13 *Landmark Briefs and Arguments of the Supreme Court of the United States: Constitutional Law,* 154-188, Philip B. Kurland and Gerhard Casper, eds., (Arlington, VA: Univ. Publications of America, 1975)(hereafter cited as *Landmark Briefs*).
68. 46 La. Ann. 922, 15 So. 290 (1894).
69. *Allgeyer,* Appellant's Brief 24.
70. *Allgeyer,* Appellant's Brief 4.
71. See Siegan, *Economic Liberties and the Constitution, supra,* note 43 at ch. 5; Roscoe Pound, *Liberty of Contract,* 18 Yale L. J. 454 (1919).
72. 169 U.S. 366 (1898).
73. 169 U.S. at 395. See Robert J. Glennon, *Justice Henry Billings Brown: Values in Tension,* 44 Colorado L. Rev. 553 (1973).
74. *Holden v. Hardy,* 14 Utah 98, 46 P. 756 (1896). See *State v. Holden,* 46 P. 1105 (1896).
75. *Holden,* Appellee's Brief, 42 L. Ed. 786.
76. *Id.*
77. 198 U.S. 45 (1905). See Owen M. Fiss, *Beginnings of the Modern State, 1888-1910,* vol. 8, *History of the Supreme Court of the United States,* ch. 6 (New York: Macmillan, 1993); Herbert Hovenkamp, *The Political Economy of Substantive Due Process,* 40 Stan. L. Rev. 379 (1988); Charles W. McCurdy, *The "Liberty of Contract" Regime in American Law,* in Harry N. Scheiber, ed., *The State and Freedom of Contract* 161, 163 (Stanford Univ. Press, 1998).
78. "The regulations instituted by this statute were for the purpose of protecting the health of the employees . . . When we consider the intense heat of the rooms where baking is done, and the flour that floats in the air and is breathed by those who work in bakeries, there can be but little doubt that prolonged labor, day and night, subject to these conditions, might produce a diseased condition of the human system." *People v. Lochner,* 73 App. Div. 120, 76 N.Y.S. 396, 402 (1902), affirmed, 177 N.Y. 145, 69 N.E. 373 (1904). See comments of Paul Kens, *Judicial Power and Reform Politics: The Anatomy of Lochner v. New York,* 115-29 (Lawrence: Univ. of Kansas Press, 1990); Archibald Cox, *The Court and the Constitution,* 130-137 (Boston: Houghton Mifflin, 1987).

79. 198 U.S. at 59.
80. Pound, *Liberty of Contract, supra,* note 71 at 454. See Morton J. Horwitz, *The Transformation of American Law,* 1870-1960, 34 (New York: Oxford Univ. Press, 1992); William F. Duker, *Mr. Justice Rufus W. Peckham: The Police Power and the Individual in a Changing World,* 1980 B.Y.U.L. Rev. 47 (1980).
81. 198 U.S. at 56. See the earlier extreme laissez-faire views of Peckham when he was on the New York Court of Appeals. *People v. Budd,* 117 N.Y. 1, 45-47 (1889) (Peckham, dissenting).
82. 198 U.S. at 65-66. Justice Harlan was joined in dissent by Justices White and Day.
83. *Id.* at 67, citing *Gundling v. Chicago,* 177 U.S. 183, 188 (1900).
84. 198 U.S. at 75-76. For critiques supporting the dissent of Justice Holmes, see Ernst Freund, *Limitations of Hours of Labor and the Federal Supreme Court,* 17 Green Bag 411 (1905); Learned Hand, *Due Process of Law and the Eight-Hour Day,* 21 Harv. L. Rev. 495 (1908); Roscoe Pound, *Liberty of Contract, supra* note 71.
85. Justice Holmes was essentially a philosopher who turned to law and was immune from the laissez-faire business ideology of the times. See Felix Frankfurter, *Mr. Justice Holmes and the Supreme Court,* 55 (Cambridge, MA: Harvard Univ. Press, 1938).
86. *Lochner,* Brief for Plaintiff in Error 7-18. See 14 *Landmark Briefs* 653.
87. *Id.,* 18-40.
88. *Lochner,* Brief for Defendants in Error 2-3. See 14 *Landmark Briefs* 715.
89. *Id.,* 10-19.
90. 208 U.S. 412 (1908).
91. See Louis D. Brandeis, *Living Law,* 10 Ill. L. Rev. 461 (1916); Alpheus T. Mason, *Brandeis: A Free Man's Life,* 248-52 (New York: Viking Press, 1946).
92. On the issue of women's health, see *State v. Muller,* 48 Ore. 252, 85 P. 855 (1906).
93. *Muller,* 208 U.S. at 421.
94. *Muller v. Oregon,* Brief for the State of Oregon. See 16 *Landmark Briefs* 37.
95. *Id.* at 10.
96. *Id.* at 18-19.
97. 243 U.S. 426 (1917). Justice McKenna, who had joined the majority in *Lochner,* wrote the opinion sustaining the Oregon law. Justice White, who had dissented in *Lochner,* changed sides and dissented in *Bunting.*
98. 243 U.S. at 435.
99. *Id.* at 438. See *State v. Bunting,* 71 Ore. 259, 139 P. 731 (1914).
100. See statement to this effect by Chief Justice Taft. *Adkins v. Children's Hospital,* 261 U.S. 525, 528 (1923) (dissenting opinion); Thomas Powell, *The Logic and Rhetoric of Constitutional Law,* 15 J. Phil., Psych & Scientific Method 654 (1918), reprinted in *Essays in Constitutional Law,* 85, 98 (R. McCloskey ed. 1962).
101. 243 U.S. at 430.
102. 243 U.S. 629 (1917). See Thomas R. Powell, *The Constitutional Issue in Minimum-Wage Legislation,* 2 Minn. L. Rev. 1 (1971).
103. 261 U.S. 525 (1923). See David Card and Alan B. Krueger, *Myth and Measurement: The New Economics of the Minimum Wage* (Princeton: Princeton Univ. Press, 1995).
104. Louis D. Brandeis, *The Constitution and the Minimum Wage,* The Survey 490, 494 (Feb. 6, 1915).
105. *Williams v. Evans,* 139 Minn 32, 165 N.W. 495 (1917); *Miller Telephone Co. v. Minimum Wage Commission,* 145 Minn. 262, 177 N.W. 341 (1920).

106. *State v. Crowe*, 130 Ark. 273, 197 S.W. 4 (1917).
107. *Larsen v. Rice*, 100 Wash. 642, 171 P. 1037 (1918); *Spokane Hotel Co. v. Younger*, 113 Wash. 359, 194 P. 595 (1920).
108. 261 U.S. 525 (1923), *overruled, West Coast Hotel Co. v. Parrish*, 300 U.S. 379 (1937). See Cushman, *Rethinking the New Deal Court, supra* note 5, at 66-83; Robert L. Hale, *Freedom through Law: Public Control of Private Governing Power*, 430-460 (New York: Columbia Univ. Press, 1952; Charles Grove Haines, *Minimum Wage Act for District of Columbia Held Unconstitutional*, 59 Amer. L. Rev. 581, 592 (1924);
109. *Children Hospital v. Adkins*, 284 F. 613 (C.A.D.C., 1922). See dissent to double hearing by Chief Justice Smyth at *Id.*, 623. See commentary of Thomas R. Powell, *The Judiciality of Minimum Wage Legislation*, 37 Harv. L. Rev. 545, 547 (1924).
110. *Children Hospital*, Brief for Appellees. See 21 *Landmark Briefs* 435.
111. *Adkins v. Children's Hospital*, 261 U.S. 525 (1923). See Joel F. Paschal, *Mr. Justice Sutherland: A Man Against the State*, 119-26 (New York: Greenwood Press, 1951).
112. 261 U.S. at 545.
113. *West Coast Hotel Co. v. Parrish*, 300 U.S. 379, 400 (1937).
114. 261 U.S. at 558-59. For a refutation of Justice Sutherland's economic fallacy, see Powell, *The Constitutional Issue in Minimum-Wage Legislation, supra* note 102, at 3, 6.
115. 261 U.S. at 566. Taft's conclusion was publicly confirmed in the anonymous editorial comment in 1923 by the eminent U.S. District Court Judge, Learned Hand, that Sutherland's majority opinion in *Adkins* enforced "The Legal Right to Starve." See Gerald Gunther, *Learned Hand: The Man and the Judge*, 251 (New York: Alfred A. Knopf, 1994).
116. 208 U.S. 412 (1908).
117. 261 U.S. at 569-70.
118. *Adkins*, Brief for Appellants, 2 vols. See 21 *Landmark Briefs* 359.
119. *Id.* at lii.
120. *Murphy v. Sardell*, 269 U.S. 530 (1925), *Donham v. West-Nelson Co.*, 273 U.S. 657 (1927).
121. 298 U.S. 587 (1936), holding overruled in *West Coast Hotel Co. v. Parrish*, 300 U.S. 379 (1937).
122. 244 U.S. 590 (1917), overruled in *Ferguson v. Skrupa*, 372 U.S. 726 (1963).
123. 165 U.S. 578 (1897).
124. *Adams*, 244 U.S. at 597.
125. 264 U.S. 504 (1924). See *Jay Burns Baking Co. v. McKelvie*, 108 Neb. 674, 189 N.W. 383, (1922), for state Supreme Court affirming trial court finding of facts supporting the regulation. See the earlier opinion upholding a city ordinance setting standard bread sizes. *Schmidinger v. Chicago*, 226 U.S. 578 (1913).
126. 264 U.S. at 534.
127. 290 U.S. 570 (1934).
128. 278 U.S. 105 (1928), *overruled, North Dakota Pharmacy Bd. v. Snyder's Stores*, 414 U.S. 156 (1973).
129. 278 U.S. at 115.
130. See Chapter 10 notes 201 and 208 and accompanying texts.
131. See Gabriel Kolko, *Railroads and Regulation* (Princeton, NJ: Princeton Univ. Press, 1965); Paul W. MacAvoy, *The Economic Effects of Regulation: The Trunk-Line Railroad Cartels and the Interstate Commerce Commission Before 1900* (Cambridge: M.I.T. Press, 1965).

132. 94 U.S. 113 (1877). On the Granger cases, see Warren, 2 *Supreme Court in United States History, supra* note 49, at 574-589; Carl B. Swisher, *Stephen J. Field: Craftsman of the Law,* 362-95 (Chicago: Univ. of Chicago Press, 1969); Edmund Kitch and Clara Bowler, *The Facts of Munn v. Illinois,* 1978 Sup. Ct. Rev. 313 (1978).

133. 94 U.S. at 134. The brief for the State of Illinois prevailed against a charge that the statute violated the due process clause even though it contained no analysis of the meaning of "liberty" or "process." 7 *Landmark Briefs,* 631-657. See dissent of Justice Field, opposing regulation. 94 U.S. at 136.

134. 83 U.S. (16 Wall.) 36, 102 (1873). See Conant, *Antimonopoly Tradition Under the Ninth and Fourteenth Amendments, supra* note 62, at 823-28.

135. 116 U.S. 307, 331 (1886).

136. 134 U.S. 418 (1890). See Fiss, *Beginnings of the Modern State, supra* note 77, at 185-221.

137. 134 U.S. at 458. See Edward S. Corwin, *The Supreme Court and the Fourteenth Amendment,* 7. Mich. L. Rev. 643 (1909), Reprinted in Corwin, *American Constitutional History,* 67, 83-87 (New York: Harper & Row, 1964).

138. 169 U.S. 466 (1898). On the "fair value" fallacy in rate-making, see Robert L. Hale, *Freedom through Law, supra,* note 108, at 461-500.

139. 169 U.S. at 547. The fair value fallacy was finally rejected in *Federal Power Commission v. Hope Natural Gas Co.,* 320 U.S. 591 (1944). Justice Douglas wrote, "The heart of the matter is that rates cannot be made to depend on 'fair value' when the value of the going enterprise depends on earnings under whatever rates may be anticipated." *Id.,* at 601.

140. *Wolff Packing Co. v. Court of Industrial Relations,* 262 U.S. 522 (1923) (Kansas compulsory arbitration act as applied to the meat-packing industry); *Tyson & Bro. United Theatre Ticket Offices v. Banton,* 273 U.S. 418 (1927), overruled in *Gold v. DiCarlo,* 380 U.S. 520 (1965) (per curiam), *affirming* 235 F. Supp. 817, 819 (S.D.N.Y. 1964) (New York statute limiting prices in the resale of theater tickets to fifty cents in excess of box-office price); *Ribnik v. McBride,* 277 U.S. 350 (1928) overruled in *Olsen v. Nebraska,* 313 U.S. 236 (1941) (New Jersey law requiring licensing and price regulation of employment agencies; *Williams v. Standard Oil Co.,* 278 U.S. 235 (1929) (Tennessee statute regulating gasoline prices); *New State Ice Co. v. Liebmann,* 285 U.S. 262 (1932) (Oklahoma statute requiring license to enter ice business). See Robert L. Hale, *Freedom Through Law: Public Control of Private Governing Power,* 400-429 (New York: Columbia Univ. Press, 1952).

141. 273 U.S. 418 (1927), *overruled,* Gold v. DiCarlo, 380 U.S. 520 (1965).

142. *Id.* at 429.

143. *Id.,* at 446-447.

144. 277 U.S. 350 (1928), overruled, *Olsen v. Nebraska,* 313 U.S. 236 (1941).

145. *Id,* at 373.

146. 285 U.S. 262 (1932). See Alpheus T. Mason, *Brandeis: A. Free Man's Life,* 607-608 (New York: Viking Press, 1946).

147. 285 U.S. at 302-303.

148. *Id.* at 279.

149. 83 U.S. (16 Wall.) 36 (1873). See Chapter 7.

150. 285 U.S. at 279.

151. See Benjamin F. Wright, *The Growth of American Constitutional Law,* 154 (Chicago: Univ. of Chicago Press, 1967).

152. 96 U.S. 97 (1878).

153. 291 U.S. 502 (1934). See Cushman, *Rethinking the New Deal Court, supra* note 5, at 78-83; Hale, *Freedom through Law, supra* note 108, at 425-429.

154. 285 U.S. 263 (1932). See notes 146-150 and accompanying text.
155. *Nebbia,* 291 U.S. at 523.
156. *Id.* at 533.
157 *Id.* at 536.
158. See Siegan, *Economic Liberties, supra* note 43, at 138-143.
159. See House Doc. 142, 75th Cong., 1st sess. (1937); Robert Jackson, *The Struggle for Judicial Supremacy,* 187-196, 328-353 (New York: Alfred A. Knopf, 1941); William Leuchtenburg, *The Supreme Court Reborn,* 82-162 (New York: Oxford Univ. Press, 1995); Daniel A. Farber, *Who Killed Lochner?,* 90 Georgetown L. J. 985 (2002), Reviewing G. Edward White, *The Constitution and the New Deal* (Cambridge: Harvard Univ. Press, 2000).
160. 300 U.S. 379 (1937). The Supreme Court of Washington had upheld Parrish's claim for minimum wages pursuant to the 1913 state statute, as it had done in two earlier cases, on the basis of the reserved police powers of the states. *Parrish v. West Coast Hotel Co.,* 185 Wash. 581, 55 P. 2d. 1083 (1936). See Charles A. Leonard, *A Search for a Judicial Philosophy: Mr. Justice Roberts and the Constitutional Revolution of 1937* (Port Washington, N.Y.: Kennikat Press, 1971).
161. 300 U.S. at 400.
162. 291 U.S. 502 (1934).
163. *Smith* v. *Allright,* 321 U.S. 649, 699 (1944).
164. *West Coast Hotel,* 300 U.S. at 389-90.
165. *Id.* at 391-92. Justice Sutherland dissented, erroneously implying that his majority opinion in *Adkins* upholding liberty of contract conformed to the original meaning of the due process clause. *Id.* at 402-404.
166. *West Coast Hotel,* Brief of Appellees.
167. *Id.,* Brief of Amici Curiae.
168. 277 U.S. 350 (1928).
169. 313 U.S. 236 (1941).
170. *Id.* at 246.
171. 372 U.S. 726 (1963).
172. *Id.* at 730.
173. 380 U.S. 520 (1965), *affirming, Gold v. DiCarlo,* 235 F. Supp. 817 (S.D.N.Y. 1964).
174. 235 F. Supp. at 819
175. Justice Holmes observed in a speech in 1897, "When socialism first began to be talked about, the comfortable classes of the community were a good deal frightened. I suspect this fear has influenced judicial action both here and in England, yet it is certain that it is not a conscious factor in the decisions to which I refer. I think that something similar has led people who no longer hope to control the legislatures to look to the courts as expounders of the Constitutions, and that in some courts new principles have been discovered outside the bodies of those instruments, which may be generalized into acceptance of the economic doctrines which prevailed about fifty years ago." Oliver W. Holmes, *The Path of the Law,* 10 Harv. L. Rev. 457 (1897), reprinted in Holmes, *Collected Legal Papers* 167, 184 (1920).
176. See, e.g., *Nebbia v. New York,* 291 U.S. 502, 558 (1934) (McReynolds, dissenting): "The adoption of any 'concept of jurisprudence' which permits facile disregard of the Constitution as long interpreted and respected will inevitably lead to its destruction." This statement was a plea favoring the series of erroneous Supreme Court opinions applying constitutional liberty of contract. See Laurence Tribe, *God Save This Honorable Court,* 31-40 (New York: Random House, 1985).

177. The historical primacy of precedent was based on Coke's writings and decisions of the common-law courts. "So steeped were the eighteenth-century lawyers in Coke's teachings, for Coke's *Institutes* were the most authoritative law books available to them and they were dealing with a tradition, not a code, that the controversial literature of the era of the Revolution, if it is to be understood, must be read or interpreted by a common-law lawyer." Roscoe Pound, *The Development of Constitutional Guarantees of Liberty,* 57 (New Haven: Yale Univ. Press, 1957).

178. See Edward H. Levi, *Introduction to Legal Reasoning,* 57-102 (Chicago: Univ. of Chicago Press, 1961).

179. *Graves v. New York,* 306 U.S. 466, 491-92 (1939), overruling *Dobbins v. Commissioners of Erie County,* 41 U.S. (16 Pet.) 435 (1842); *Collector v. Day,* 78 U.S. (11 Wall.) 113 (1871); *New York ex rel. Rogers v. Graves,* 299 U.S. 401 (1937); *Brush v. Commissioner,* 300 U.S. 352 (1937).

180. Antonin Scalia, *A Matter of Interpretation: Federal Courts and the Law,* 3-47 (Princeton, NJ: Princeton Univ. Press, 1997). See supporting comment of Professor Lawrence Tribe. *Id.* 65-94.

181. "Despite arguments to the contrary which had seemed to me persuasive, it is settled that the due process clause of the 14th Amendment applies to matters of substantive law as well as to matters of procedure." *Whitney v. California,* 274 U.S. 357, 373 (1927) (Brandeis, concurring).

182. See M. Elizabeth Magill, *The Real Separation in Separation of Powers Law,* 86 Va. L. Rev. 1127 (2000).

183. 381 U.S. 479 (1965). For background to this case, see Alexander Bickel, *The Least Dangerous Branch,* 143-56 (1962). For a critique of this case and of the subsequent development by the Supreme Court of a constitutional right of privacy, see James Stoneking, *Penumbras and Privacy,* 87 W. Va. L. Rev. 859 (1985).

184. See *Poe v. Ullman,* 367 U.S. 497 (1961), on the disused nature of the statute.

185. *Griswold,* 381 U.S. at 484. See continued use of substantive due process in *Lawrence v. Texas,* 539 U. S. 558 (2003).

186. "The Due Process Clause with an 'arbitrary and capricious' or 'shocking to the conscience' formula was liberally used by this Court to strike down economic legislation in the early decades of this century, threatening, many people thought, the tranquility and stability of the Nation. See, e.g., *Lochner v. New York.* That formula, based on subjective considerations of "natural justice," is no less dangerous when used to enforce this Court's views about personal rights than those about economic rights. I had thought that we had laid that formula, as a means for striking down state legislation, to rest once and for all in cases like *West Coast Hotel Co. v. Parrish; Olsen v. Nebraska ex rel. Western Reference & Bond Assn.,* and many other opinions."
Griswold at 522-23.

187. 410 U.S. 113 (1973). See Archibald Cox, *The Role of the Supreme Court in American Government* 113 (New York: Oxford Univ. Press, 1976); John H. Ely, *The Wages of Crying Wolf: A Comment on Roe v. Wade,* 83 Yale L. J. 1205 (1970); Richard A. Epstein, *Substantive Due Process by Any Other Name: The Abortion Cases,* 1973 Supreme Court Rev. 159; *Symposium on the Law and Politics of Abortion,* 77 Mich. L. Rev. 1579-1827 (1979).

188. 410 U.S. at 221.

189. Ruth Colker, *Equality Theory and Reproductive Freedom,* 3 Texas J. Women and the Law 99 (1994); Ruth Bader Ginsburg, *Some Thoughts on Autonomy and Equality in Relation to Roe v. Wade,* 63 N.C.L. Rev. 375 (1985).

9
Injunctions against Labor Unions:
Antitrust and Due Process

Judicial bias by Supreme Court majorities against labor unions was another element of the American economy in the twentieth century until the great over-rulings of 1937 onward.[1] Unions were held to have violated the Sherman Anti-trust Act and the employers' liberty of contract under the due process clauses. In *A.F. of L. v. American Sash Co.*[2] (1949), Justice Felix Frankfurter commented on the earlier Supreme Court majority's bias against the working class:

[U]nionization encountered the shibboleths of a pre-machine age and these were reflected in juridical assumptions that survived the facts on which they were based. Adam Smith was treated as though his generalizations had been imparted to him on Sinai and not as a thinker who addressed himself to the elimination of restrictions which had become fetters upon initiative and enterprise in his day. Basic human rights expressed by the constitutional conception of "liberty" were equated with theories of *laissez faire*. The result was that economic views of confined validity were treated by lawyers and judges as though the Framers had enshrined them in the Constitution. This misapplication of the notions of the classic economists and resulting disregard of the perduring reach of the Constitution led to Mr. Justice Holmes' famous protest in the *Lochner* case against measuring the Fourteenth Amendment by Mr. Herbert Spencer's Social Statics. Had not Mr. Justice Holmes' awareness of the impermanence of legislation as against the permanence of the Constitution gradually prevailed, there might indeed have been "hardly any limit but the sky" to the embodiment of "our economic or moral beliefs" in that Amendment's "prohibitions."[3]

From the viewpoint of workers, trying to bargain for wages and working conditions, the fundamental issues were freedom of association and freedom of speech. Freedom of association had been established as a common law principle in *Commonwealth v. Hunt*[4] in 1842. A workman had been discharged from his employment because he had refused to follow the Rules of the Boston Journeyman Bootmakers' Society. Hunt and six other leaders of the society were charged with criminal conspiracy and convicted. Upon appeal, Chief Justice Lemuel Shaw reversed the convictions and held that the purpose of the union was not unlawful. Refusal to work with a non-member of the Society was not a criminal purpose.

The issue of freedom of speech was concerned with strikers informing workers in related industries and others not to buy the products of their employers so long as the strike continued. This is labeled a secondary boycott because it includes those other than the strikers. After a passage of the Sherman Antitrust Act[5] of 1890, there was one major treble—damage action under the statute against a union and one major action for common-law conspiracy resulting in injunction against a union. In *Loewe v. Lawlor,*[6] the United Hatters of North America attempted to unionize Loewe's hat factory. As part of the this campaign, the Hatters sent organizers to Loewe's customers, urging them not to purchase and retail Loewe's hats and warning them of a boycott if they continued dealing with Loewe. At the request of the union, the American Federation of Labor placed Loewe on its "we don't patronize" list. The Supreme Court held the union liable for treble damages, noting that the Sherman Act forbade all combinations that obstructed the free flow of commerce among the several states.

In *Gompers v. Bucks Stove and Range Co.,*[7] in a dispute over increasing the work day from nine hours to ten hours, the workers went on strike and were replaced by non-union employees. The local union announced a boycott and made a public appeal against Bucks Stove. The American Federation of Labor put Buck Stove on the "we don't patronize" published list. After one year, Buck Stove filed an action for injunction against union officials and the unions for conspiracy. An injunction was issued and upheld by the Supreme Court. The secondary boycott was held a conspiracy. Justice Joseph Lamar referred to *Loewe v. Lawlor* by analogy, but this case was not actually brought under the Sherman Act.

The Clayton Act and Antitrust

Beginning early in the twentieth century, there were pressures from organized labor for exemption from the Sherman Act.[8] Proposals for amendment to exempt labor unions from liability passed one house of Congress but failed to be enacted.[9] The long-run determined campaign of the labor movement was finally rewarded in 1914 by the passage of Sections 6 and 20 of the Clayton Act. Labor unions were to be exempted from both the Sherman Act and other injunctions that would impede unionization. Unfortunately, conservative majorities of the Supreme Court gave these sections the narrowest effect.

Section 6 of the Clayton Act was an addition to the antitrust laws:

> The labor of a human being is not a commodity or article of commerce. Nothing contained in the antitrust laws shall be construed to forbid the existence and operation of labor, agricultural, or horticultural organizations, instituted for the purposes of mutual help, and not having capital stock or conducted for profit, or to forbid or restrain individual members of such organizations from lawfully carrying out the legitimate objects thereof; nor shall such organizations, or the members thereof, be held or construed to be illegal combinations or conspiracies or conspiracies in restraint of trade, under the antitrust laws.[10]

Section 20 of the Clayton Act was designed to limit the power of federal courts to issue injunctions against certain types of labor actions in industrial disputes. The first paragraph stated:

> No restraining order or injunction shall be granted by any court of the United States, or a judge or the judges thereof, in any case between an employer and employees, or between employers and employees, or between employees, or between persons employed and persons seeking employment, involving, or growing out of, a dispute concerning terms or conditions of employment, unless necessary to prevent irreparable injury to property, or to a property right, of the party making the application, for which injury there is no adequate remedy at law. . . .[11]

The second paragraph of Section 20 recited acts which "any person or persons, whether singly or in concert" could do and still be immune from injunction. As to this set of cases, federal courts were barred from enjoining persons "from ceasing to patronize or to employ any party to such dispute, or from recommending, advising, or persuading others by peaceful and lawful means so to do."[12] This language must have been chosen to protect those who engaged in secondary boycotts.

In reviewing the cases under the Clayton Act, it is of prime importance to note the key opinions that were overruled. Since the basic epistemological effect of overruling is to declare the earlier opinion was invalid when decided, these cases are persuasive evidence of the class bias of the Supreme Court majority. A related issue in some of those earlier opinions is their refusal to accept findings of facts by trial judges in favor of unions. This is done *sub silentio* by the Supreme Court by merely stating a set of facts contrary to that of the trial court. Such action violates the canon of the law of evidence that appeals courts will not reverse findings of fact of trial courts unless they are against the manifest weight of the evidence.[13]

Duplex Printing Press Co. v. Deering[14] was the first case concerning the labor exemption from antitrust in the Clayton Act to reach the Supreme Court. Duplex was a manufacturer of newspaper printing presses in Michigan. The local union had a strike pending against Duplex, hoping to secure a closed shop, an eight-hour day, and a union scale of wages. The defendants were not Duplex employees but officers of the International Association of Machinists in New York. Duplex sought an injunction to stop defendants from inducing haulers and installers of presses at newspapers from cooperating with the strike and refusing to handle Duplex machines. This was clearly a secondary boycott case.

In the district court, Judge Martin F. Manton found that the strike was totally peaceful. He concluded that there was nothing in the record which warranted granting an injunction.[15] In light of the language of the Clayton Act, the findings of fact in the district court were not against the manifest weight of the evidence and should have determined appeals.

The court of appeals affirmed the dismissal by a vote of 2 to 1. Judge Charles Hough concluded that the widely known purpose of Section 20 (perhaps in conjunction with Section 6) was to legalize the secondary boycott.[16] Judge Learned Hand concurred.[17]

The Supreme Court majority opinion, by Justice Mahlon Pitney, reversed the court of appeals and gave Section 20 of the Clayton Act the narrowest possible construction. In order to exclude statutory protection for the New York officers of the national union, the defendants were held not to be "employees" as that term was used in Section 20.[18] This ignored the fact that these officers were the elected agents of all union workers in that industry and were surely agents of union employees of Duplex. So that even though no working employees of Duplex were directly involved in the boycott activity, the lower courts had correctly construed the entire union as an integrated entity for collective bargaining.

Contrary to the findings of fact in the trial court, Pitney described a fear of violence resulting from defendants implementation of their secondary boycott. He asserted that defendants warned customers not to purchase or install Duplex presses and threatening them with loss if they do so.[19] This included threats that customers and truckers might face sympathetic strikes in their trades. Pitney's conclusion was that the secondary boycott was not exempt from injunction under Section 6 or Section 20 of the Clayton Act. Consequently injunction was appropriate to stop a conspiracy in violation of Section 1 of the Sherman Act.

When Pitney's majority interpretation was later overruled, it became clear that the only correct textual analysis on *Duplex* in the Supreme Court was the dissent of Justice Louis D. Brandeis, in which Justice Oliver W. Holmes and Justice John H. Clarke concurred.[20] Brandeis noted the underlying idea presented to the committees in Congress which reported the Clayton Act and concluded:

> The resulting law set out certain acts which had previously been held unlawful, whenever courts had disapproved of the ends for which they were performed; it then declared that, when these acts were committed in the course of an industrial dispute, they should not be held to violate any law of the United States. In other words the Clayton Act substituted the opinion of Congress as to the propriety of the purpose for that of differing judges; and thereby it declared that the relations between employers of labor and workingmen were competitive relations, that organized competition was not harmful and that it justified injuries necessarily inflicted in its course. . . . But Congress did not restrict the provision to employers and workingmen *in their employ*. By including "employers and employees" and "persons employed and persons seeking employment" it showed that it was not aiming merely at a legal relationship between a specific employer and his employees.[21]

Justice Brandeis concluded with a comment on the jurisprudence of separated powers.[22]

Bedford Cut Stone Co. v. Journeymen S.C. Assoc.[23] was a second opinion concerning secondary boycotts to be overruled. Plaintiffs were twenty-four quarriers and fabricators of Indiana limestone. Prior to 1921, defendant union had a closed shop with these employers for cutting the stone. In 1921, plaintiffs and the union failed to reach a new working agreement. Plaintiffs then employed non-union stone cutters. In response, the union ordered its members to stop cutting stone which had already been partly cut by non-union labor. Then came a strike and lockout by plaintiffs. The union urged its members in other states not to work on stone cut by non-union workers. Plaintiff charges this was restraint of trade in commerce among the states in violation of the Sherman Act.

The trial court dismissed the action. The court of appeals affirmed the dismissal with the following conclusion: "We are of opinion that under the facts appearing appellees were within their rights in thus undertaking to induce members of their craft to refrain from further cutting upon stone which had before been partly cut by nonunion labor, notwithstanding such refusal might have tended in some degree to discourage builders from specifying appellants' stone, and thus to reduce the quantity of their product which would enter interstate commerce."[24]

In the Supreme Court, Chief Justice William H. Taft, writing the majority opinion, reversed the court of appeals.[25] Following the *Duplex* holding, the acts here were also held a secondary boycott, not exempt from injunction under Section 20 of the Clayton Act. In spite of the findings of fact by the lower courts, this powerful combine of the plaintiffs was found injured by the unreasonable restraint of trade in commerce by the union urging all members not to work on stone cut by non-union workers.

Justice Brandeis, with the concurrence of Justice Holmes, dissented. He emphasized the reasonableness of the restraints as follows:

> The manner in which the journeymen's unions acted was also clearly legal. The combination complained of is the cooperation of persons wholly of the same craft, united in a national union, solely for self-protection. No outsider—be he quarrier, dealer, builder or laborer—was a party to the combination. No purpose was to be subserved except to promote the trade interests of members of the journeymen's association. There was no attempt by the unions to boycott the plaintiffs.[26]

State statutes limiting injunctions against striking employees, similar to Section 20 of the Clayton Act, were also attacked in the courts. In *Truax v. Corrigan*,[27] an Arizona statute barred such injunctions issued in labor disputes unless necessary to protect property against violence. Truax owned a restaurant where striking employees patrolled the streets carrying banners and passing handbills to inform the public of their cause. Truax sought an injunction, charging that his loss of business invaded his property right in the business. The trial court found for defendants. The Arizona Supreme Court affirmed the denial of injunction since the strikers had only engaged in peaceful dissemination of information.[28] "If any person conducting a business elects to disregard the demands of his employees, and such employees strike for that reason, no right of the employer is violated if the striking employees advertise the cause of the strike."[29]

The U.S. Supreme Court reversed the judgment by a vote of 5 to 4. Chief Justice Taft, for the Court, held that there was an invasion of property rights in violation of the Due Process Clause and the Equal Protection Clause of the Fourteenth Amendment. The claim of a property right to conduct a lawful business was a novel technique to subsume the claim as property under the due process clause. The plaintiffs could then assert a substantive constitutional right under than clause, a mere extension of the fallacy of *Lochner v. New York.*[30] The clause in this penal statute excepting ex-employers was also held a violation of the Equal Protection Clause.

Chief justice Taft found facts directly contrary to the lower court's. He held that the strikers did not engage in lawful persuasion. He asserted that the strikers were "compelling every customer or would-be customer to run the gauntlet of most uncomfortable publicity, aggressive and annoying importunity, libelous attacks, and fear of injurious consequences, illegally inflicted to [Truax's] reputation and standing in the community."[31] He concluded, "Violence could not have been more effective. It was moral coercion by illegal annoyance and obstruction, and it thus was plainly a conspiracy."[32]

Justices Holmes, Brandeis, Clarke, and Pitney dissented. Justice Holmes rejected the labeling a going business as "property" under the Fourteenth Amendment:

> The dangers of a delusive exactness in the application of the Fourteenth Amendment have been adverted to before now. Delusive exactness is a source of fallacy throughout the law. By calling a business "property" you make it seem like land, and lead up to the conclusion that a statute cannot substantially cut down the advantages of owner-ship existing before the statute was passed. An established business no doubt may have pecuniary value and commonly is protected by law against various unjustified injuries. But you cannot give it definiteness of contour by calling it a thing. It is a course of conduct and like other conduct is subject to substantial modification according to time and circumstances both in itself and in regard to what shall justify doing it a harm.[33]

By 1937, Chief Justice Charles E. Hughes and Justice Owen Roberts voted with the liberals who favored labor legislation. The four remaining conservatives became a dissenting minority. In *Senn v. Tile Layers Protective Union,*[34] the Wisconsin Supreme Court had affirmed the dismissal of an action to enjoin picketing of plaintiff's business and the publishing of plaintiff as unfair to organized labor. The Wisconsin Labor Code protected the unions in giving publicity to labor disputes and peaceful picketing by barring injunctions by employers.[35] The 5 to 4 decision here in the U.S. Supreme Court held that this statute did not violate the Due Process Clause of the Fourteenth Amendment.

Plaintiff Senn had never served an apprenticeship as a tile layer. The union demand that only union tile layers work on jobs would bar Senn from laying tiles; he could not work tiles with employees. Justice Brandeis, for the majority, held that the denial of injunction by the state supreme court was conclusive construction of a state statute, binding on the U.S. Supreme Court.[36] In contrast, no such finding had been made in the *Truax* case where the Supreme Court found facts contrary to the lower courts. But Brandeis chose to distinguish *Senn* from *Truax,* quoting that the Supreme Court opinion in the latter case found non-peaceful libelous attacks and abusive epithets.

The Norris-LaGuardia Act[37] of 1932 was firstly designed to remedy the narrow interpretation the Supreme Court had given to Section 20 of the Clayton Act. The first section of the 1932 act mandated a broad immunity from injunctions growing out of labor disputes. The second section recognized the necessity for workers to have full freedom of association, self-organization, and designation of representatives of their own choosing to negotiate terms and conditions of their employment. The third section outlawed yellow dog contracts. The fourth section barred injunctions in labor disputes and listed nine types of specific situations in which injunctions could not be issued.

One year after *Senn,* the Supreme Court confirmed its broad view of the Norris-LaGuardia Act. Lower courts, relying on extremist precedents, such as *Duplex,* had held the Act inapplicable. Their injunctions against unions were reversed. In *Lauf v. E.G. Skinner & Co.,*[38] the Court held that, under Section 13 of the act, there was a labor dispute between union organizers and Skinner even though the thirty-five employees of Skinner had refused to join the union. In *New Negro Alliance v. Sanitary Grocery Co.,*[39] an organization of African-Americans had picketed Sanitary Grocery to cause them to include hiring African-American sales clerks as a part of their employment policies. This too was held a labor dispute and a lower court injunction was reversed. In *International L.G.W. Union v. Donnelly G. Co.,*[40] an unanimous Supreme Court issued a *per curiam* opinion reversing a lower court injunction against the union. The union picketing and boycott had been held by two judges of a special three-judge federal trial court not to be a labor dispute but a conspiracy in violation of the antitrust laws.[41]

The ultimate explanation of the remedial function of the Norris-La Guardia Act of 1932 in reinforcing the labor sections of the Clayton Act was in *United States v. Hutcheson.*[42] Anheuser-Busch contracted for the erection of additional plant for its brewery in St. Louis. The firm had employees in two unions, the carpenters and the machinists, which were in long-term conflict over the erection and dismantling of machinery. Anheuser-Busch had an agreement with the unions whereby disputed jobs were given to the machinists and the carpenters agreed to submit all disputed jobs to arbitration. In 1939, the carpenters refused to submit to arbitration and called a strike against Anheuser-Busch and the construction companies. They not only picketed the brewery but sent circulars to all union carpenters to refrain from buying Anheuser-Busch beer. Four officials of the carpenter's union were indicted under the Sherman Act for criminal combination and conspiracy.

Justice Frankfurter, for the Court, affirmed the district court's order sustaining a demurrer to the indictment. It was not necessary to determine whether the secondary boycott here would have been legal under the rule of the *Duplex* case. The Norris-La Guardia Act defined "labor dispute" to include secondary boycotts within its exemptions from injunction. Justice Frankfurter concluded:

> The underlying aim of the Norris-LaGuardia Act was to restore the broad purpose which Congress thought it had formulated in the Clayton Act but which was frustrated, so Congress believed, by unduly restrictive judicial construction. This was authoritatively stated by the House Committee on the Judiciary. "The purpose of the bill is to protect the rights of labor in the same manner the Congress intended when it enacted the Clayton Act, which act, by reason of its construction and application by the Federal courts, is ineffectual to accomplish the congressional intent." The Norris-LaGuardia Act was a disapproval of *Duplex Printing Press Co. v. Deering,* and *Bedford Cut Stone Co. v. Journeymen Stone Cutters' Assn.,* as the authoritative interpretation of §20 of the Clayton Act, for Congress now placed its own meaning upon that section. The Norris-LaGuardia Act reasserted the original purpose of the Clayton Act by infusing into it the immunized trade union activities as redefined by the later Act. In this light §20 removes all such allowable conduct from the taint of being a "violation of any law of the United States," including the Sherman Law.[43]

Employee Contracts Not to Join Unions

Employment contracts in which employers' bargaining power enabled them to compel employees to promise not to join or to remain in labor unions were labeled "yellow dog" contracts.[44] Both federal and state statutes prohibiting such contracts were held by the Supreme Court to violate liberty of contract under the due process clauses of the Fifth and Fourteenth Amendments. The leading early opinions were the *Adair* and *Coppage* cases.[45] Both of these were expressly overruled by the Supreme Court after its repudiation of constitutional liberty of contract in 1937.

Adair v. United States[46] concerned Section 10 of the Erdman Act of 1898[47] in which Congress prohibited rail carriers in interstate commerce from conditioning employment of workers that they not become or remain members of a labor union. Adair, agent of the Louisville & Nashville Railroad Co., discharged an employee because of his membership in a labor union. Trial Judge Andrew M. Cochran held that while the precedents indicated that liberty of contract could protect ordinary private businesses from some types of regulation, common carriers could be subject to a greater level of regulation.[48] The purpose of Section 10 was to prevent interruption of interstate commerce on railroads by strikes, lockouts, and boycotts. "The only possible ground for holding said section is in violation of the fifth amendment is that it has no real and substantial relation to the free course of interstate commerce. I believe that it has such relation thereto. . . . I am constrained, therefore, to hold that said section is not unconstitutional for this reason."[49]

In the Supreme Court, Justice John M. Harlan wrote the majority opinion reversing the trial court. He cited *Allgeyer v. Louisiana*[50] and *Lochner v. New York*,[51] the two cases founding constitutional liberty of contract. Harlan held that union membership did not relate to health, safety, or morals of workers. He concluded that Section 10 invaded rights of liberty and property under the due process clause of the Fifth Amendment.[52] Thus Harlan ignored the view of the trial court that regulated railroads were an industry affected with a public interest. Harlan gave no weight to grants of monopoly from government that justified rate regulation, the prime example.

Justice Harlan did hold the criminal sanction litigated here was severable from the rest of the Erdman Act. "This decision is therefore restricted to the question of the validity of the particular provision in the act of Congress making it a crime against the United States for an agent or officer of an interstate carrier to discharge an employee from its service because of his being a member of a labor organization."[53] One can hypothesize that a money remedy against the railroad might have prevailed.

Harlan also found Section 10 to be invalid under the Commerce Clause.[54] In spite of the fact that a successful union might negotiate higher wages that raised railroad cost structures and in time affected interstate rail rates, Harlan found that there was no connection between union membership and interstate commerce.

Justices Joseph McKenna and Holmes dissented. McKenna emphasized that railroads as a regulated industry were a business affected with a public interest.[55] Thus, the carriers had less freedom of contract than other industries. He suggested that Congress had the power to decide which classes of employment contracts would reduce strikes that interfered with commerce.

Justice Holmes made a more direct attack on substantive due process even though he failed to note the essence of its original meaning, that it was an oxymoron:

> The section simply prohibits the more powerful party to exact certain undertakings, or to threaten dismissal or unjustly discriminate on certain grounds against those already employed. I hardly can suppose that the grounds on which a contract lawfully may be made to end are less open to regulation than other terms. So I turn to the general question whether the employment can be regulated at all. I confess that I think that the right to make contracts at will that has been derived from the word liberty in the amendments has been stretched to its extreme by the decisions; but they agree that sometimes the right may be restrained. Where there is, or generally is believed to be, an important ground of public policy for restraint the Constitution does not forbid it, whether this court agrees or disagrees with the policy pursued.[56]

Holmes disposed of the commerce clause issue in two sentences. "I suppose that it hardly be denied that some of the relations of the railroads with unions of railroad employees are closely enough connected with commerce to justify legislation by Congress. If so, legislation to prevent the exclusion of such unions from employment is sufficiently near."[57]

Coppage v. Kansas,[58] in 1915, followed the federal rule in *Adair* by holding a state statute that barred yellow dog contracts to violate the due process clause of the Fourteenth Amendment. Since the majority opinion in *Adair* had ruled out effects of labor contracts on interstate commerce, the Kansas court could rule on the validity of its state statute as applied to an interstate railroad. Hedges was employed as a switchman by the St. Louis & San Francisco Railway Co. He refused to sign a yellow dog contract and was discharged. The railroad superintendent was charged with a misdemeanor under the Kansas statute that made it illegal for an employer to coerce or demand a contact from an employee not to join a union.

The superintendent was convicted at trial and this ruling was affirmed by the Supreme Court of Kansas.[59] On appeal, Justice Mahlon Pitney, for the majority, reversed the Kansas Court, finding the attempt of that court to distinguish the facts of *Adair* to be ineffective. He held that unless *Adair* was to be overruled, that decision was controlling upon the controversy in *Coppage.* The due process clauses of the Fifth and Fourteenth amendments had the same effect when an employer was deprived of liberty or property for threatening an employee of discharge because of his membership in a labor union.[60]

Justices William R. Day, Hughes, and Holmes dissented. Day wrote, "The law should be as zealous to protect the Constitutional liberty of the employee as it is to guard that of the employer. A principal object of this statute is to protect the liberty of the citizen to make such lawful affiliations as he may desire with organizations of his choice. It should not be necessary to the protection of the liberty of one citizen that the same right in another citizen be abridged or destroyed."[61] Day distinguished this case from *Adair* because that case rested on a criminal penalty.

Justice Holmes dissented, treating freedom of contract as a common-law principle subject to legislative limitation, not a constitutional immunity of employers:

> I think the judgment should be affirmed. In present conditions a workman not un-naturally may believe that only be belonging to a union can he secure a contract that shall be fair to him. If that belief, whether right or wrong, may be held by a reasonable man, it seems to me that it may be enforced by law in order to establish the equality of position between the parties in which liberty of contract begins. Whether in the long run it is wise for the workingmen to enact legislation of this sort is not my concern, but I am strongly of opinion that there is nothing in the Constitution of the United States to prevent it, and that *Adair v. United States* and *Lochner v. New York,* should be overruled. I have stated my grounds in those cases and think it unnecessary to add others that I think exist. See further *Vegelahn v. Guntner,* [and] *Plant v. Woods.* I still entertain the opinions expressed by me in Massachusetts.[62]

One of the unfortunate effects of the *Adair* and *Coppage* opinions was to encourage employers to adopt yellow dog contracts in states that had no law designed to prohibit such clauses. A key example just two years after *Coppage* was *Hitchman Coal & Coke Co. v. Mitchell*[63] in West Virginia. The Supreme Court majority, freed from national or state legislative control, could exercise its bias against labor unions.

The workers at the Hitchman mine had been represented by the United Mine Workers union. When negotiations for a wage increase failed, there was a strike, and after a time the union was no longer paying benefits to the workers. Workers who needed to return to work were required to make verbal and written promises not to be members of the union. Union workers in mines in other states were concerned that Hitchman could sell coal at a lower price than their employers, and this would put pressure on their own wage negotiations. Consequently, the union branch in West Virginia recruited members and thus urged them to violate their yellow dog contracts.

Hitchman filed suit against the union officials, who were not employees, for trying to persuade its employers to breach employment contracts and join the union. The district court granted a perpetual injunction against the union leaders on two grounds.[64] First, the union action was found to be a common-law conspiracy in unreasonable restraint of trade. Second, the union recruitment endeavored by unlawful means to induce breach of contract by the Hitchman employees. While the district court opinion was reversed by the circuit court of appeals, the latter was again reversed by the Supreme Court. The findings of the district court were accepted with some minor changes.

Justice Brandeis wrote a dissenting opinion in which Justices Holmes and Clarke concurred.[65] Brandeis found nothing in the common law or statutes of West Virginia that made the union an unlawful organization or an unlawful conspiracy. No conspiracy to shut down or otherwise injure Hitchman was proved. Defendants, in negotiating with Hitchman, were not themselves inducing employees to join the union but rather were trying to persuade Hitchman to enter a collective bargaining agreement with the union. The yellow dog contracts signed by the workers were contracts at will. These workers could join the union and leave employment while negotiations continued by the union to secure a union shop. The decree enjoined "threat, violence, or intimidation" when there was no evidence that any of these union officials engaged in such illegal behavior.

Although not specifically concerned with yellow dog contracts, the issue of freedom of association of railroad workers in their independent unions reached the Supreme Court again in 1930. Section 2 of the Railway Labor Act of 1926, designed to protect independent rail unions, provided in part: "Representation for the purpose of this Act shall be designated by the respective parties . . . without interference, influence or coercion exercised by either party over the self-organization or designation of representatives by the other."[66] In *Texas & N.O.R. Co. v. Brotherhood Ry. & S.S. Clerks,*[67] the railroad challenged the constitutionality of this statute as violative of the First and Fifth Amendments. The independent brotherhood had represented the majority of railway clerks since 1918. In 1925, when negotiations for a wage increase failed, the railroad instigated the formation of a company union and endeavored to intimidate and coerce members of the brotherhood to leave their union and join the company union. The U.S. District Court issued a temporary injunction which the railroad violated by recognizing the company union.[68] The district court held the railroad in contempt. It directed the railroad to disestablish the company union, reinstate the brotherhood as representatives of the clerks, and restoration to service of certain employees who had been discharged. On final hearing, the temporary injunction was made permanent. The circuit court of appeals affirmed the decree.[69]

The first major ruling by the Supreme Court was a principle of evidence based on the fact that only the trial courts observe the witnesses and judge their credibility. Findings of fact in which a district court and a court of appeals concur will be accepted by the Supreme Court unless clear error is shown.[70] In this case, both lower courts considered the evidence of intimidation and coercion and resolved any conflicts in favor of the brotherhood. In historical contrast, this issue of presumptions in favor of trial court findings of fact does not appear to have been pleaded and briefed in either the *Adair* or *Coppage* cases.

Chief Justice Charles E. Hughes, for a unanimous court, affirmed the decree of injunction.[71] His view of the effects on commerce among the several states by the input negotiations of workers and railroads coincided with that of the dissenters in *Adair.* "The power to regulate commerce is the power to enact all appropriate legislation for its protection and advancement . . . to adopt measures to promote its growth and insure its safety . . . to foster, protect, control and restrain. . . . Exercising this authority, Congress may facilitate the amicable settlements of disputes which threaten the service of the necessary agencies of interstate transportation."[72]

The court also held that there was no deprivation for employers of freedom of contract in alleged violation of the First and Fifth Amendments. *Adair* and *Coppage* were held inapplicable. "The Railway Labor Act of 1926 does not interfere with the normal exercise of the right of the carrier to select its employees or to discharge them. The statute is not aimed at this right of the employers but at the interference with the right of employees to have representative of their own choosing."[73]

As noted, yellow dog contracts were expressly prohibited by Section 3 of the Norris LaGuardia Act of 1932. This was reinforced by the National Labor Relations Act of 1935,[74] which mandated collective bargaining in industries in commerce among the several states. The section on declaration of policy reviews the inequality of bargaining power between the individual worker and large firms of employers. The statute concludes:

Experience has proved that protection by law of the right of employees to organize and bargain collectively safeguards commerce from injury, impairment, or interruption, and promotes the flow of commerce by removing certain recognized sources of industrial strife and unrest, by encouraging practices fundamental to the friendly adjustment of industrial disputes arising out of differences as to wages, hours, or other working conditions, and by restoring equality of bargaining power between employers and employees.[75]

Notes

1. See Dianne Avery, *Images of Violence in Labor Jurisprudence: The Regulation of Picketing and Boycotts*, 37 Buffalo L. Rev. 1 (1989).
2. 335 U.S. 538 (1949).
3. *Id.* at 543.
4. 45 Mass. (4 Met.) 111 (1842). See Elias Lieberman, *Unions Before the Bar* 16-28 (New York: Harper & Brothers, 1950); Walter Nelles, *Commonwealth v. Hunt*, 32 Colum. L. Rev. 1128 (1932).
5. 29 Stat. 209 (1890), 15 U.S.C.A. 1 (1997).
6. 208 U.S. 274 (1908). See Lieberman, *supra* note *4*, at 56-70.
7. 221 U.S. 418 (1911). See Lieberman, *supra,* note 4, at 71-83.
8. Felix Frankfurter and Nathan Greene, *The Labor Injunction,* chs. 3 and 4 (New York: Macmillan Co., 1930).
9. *Id.* at 140-141.
10. 38 Stat. 731 (1914),15 U.S.C.A. § 17 (1997).
11. 38 Stat. 738 (1914), 29 U.S.C.A. § 52 (1998).
12. *Id.*
13. See George Christie, *Judicial Review of Findings of Fact,* 87 NW U.L. Rev. 14 (1992); Henry Monaghan, *Constitutional Fact Review,* 85 Colum. L. Rev. 229 (1985). Rule 52 of the Federal Rules of Civil Procedure states: "Findings of fact, whether based on oral or documentary evidence, shall not be set aside unless clearly erroneous, and due regard shall be given to the opportunity of the trial court to judge of the credibility of the witnesses."
14. 254 U.S. 443 (1921), *overruled, United States v. Hutcheson,* 312 U.S. 219, 236 (1941). See Lieberman, *supra.* note 4, at 96-107.
15. "A peaceful and orderly strike, not to harm others, but to improve conditions, has never been held to be a violation of the law. The object here to establish an eight-hour day with a minimum scale of wages in this particular industry was a lawful purpose, and, unless something was done in violation of the law, the complainant cannot be heard to complain." *Duplex Printing Co. v. Deering,* 247 F. 192, 198 (S.D.N.Y. 1917).
16. *Duplex Printing Co. v. Deering,* 252 F. 722,748 (2d Cir. 1918).
17. "I think that section 20 of the Clayton Act has legalized secondary boycotts in cases between an employer and employees, and that this was such a case, at least after the strike was declared on August 27. I do not think that the section applies only when the employer is plaintiff and his present or former employees are the defendants." *Id.*
18. 254 U.S. at 471.
19. *Id.* at 468.
20. *Id.* at 479.
21. *Id.* at 486-488.

22. "All rights are derived from the purposes of the society in which they exist; above all rights rises duty to the community. The conditions developed in industry may be such that those engaged in it cannot continue their struggle without danger to the community. But it is not for judges to determine whether such conditions exist, nor is it their function to set the limits of permissible contest and to declare the duties which the new situation demands. This is the function of the legislature which, while limiting individual and group rights of aggression and defense, may substitute processes of justice for the more primitive method of trial by combat." *Id.* at 488.

23. 274 U.S. 37 (1927), *overruled, United States v. Hutcheson,* 312 U.S. 219, 236 (1941). See Lieberman, *supra* note 4 at 164-172.

24. *Bedford Cut Stone Co. v. Journeyman S.C. Assoc.,* 9 F. 2d 40 (1925).

25. 274 U.S. at 55.

26. 274 U.S. at 60.

27. 257 U.S. 312 (1921). See Lieberman, *supra* note 4, at 118-126.

28. 20 Ariz. 7, 176 P. 570 (1918).

29. *Id.* at 571.

30. 198 U.S. 45 (1905).

31. 257 U.S. at 328.

32. *Id.*

33. *Id.* at 342.

34. 301 U.S. 468 (1937). See Lieberman, *supra* note 4, 15 173-180.

35. 301 U.S. at 475.

36. *Id.* at 477.

37. 47 Stat. 70 (1932), 29 U.S.C.A. §101-§115 (1998).

38. 302 U.S. 323 (1938).

39. 302 U.S. 552 (1938).

40. 304 U.S. 243 (1938).

41. *Donnelly Garment Co. v. International L.G.W. Union,* 21 F. Supp. 807 (W.D. Mo. 1937).

42. 312 U.S. 219 (1941). See Lieberman, *supra* note 4, at 241-251.

43. 312 U.S. at 236.

44. See Barry Cushman, *Doctrinal Synergies and Liberal Dilemmas: the Case of the Yellow Dog Contract,* 1992 Supreme Court Review 235. Daniel Ernst, *The Yellow Dog Contract and Liberal Reform, 1917-1932,* 30 Labor History 251 (1989).

45. *Adair v. United States,* 208 U.S. 161 (1908), overruled, *Lincoln Fed. L.U. v Northwestern I & M. Co.,* 335 U.S.525, 536 (1949); *Coppage v. Kansas,* 236 U.S. 1 (1915), overruled *Phelps Dodge Corp. v. National Labor Rel. Bd.,* 313 U.S. 177, 187 (1941). See Daniel Ernst, *The Yellow Dog Contract and Liberal Reform, 1917-1932,* 30 Labor History 251 (1989).

46. 208 U.S. 161 (1908). For timely criticism of the *Adair* case, see Richard Olney, Discrimination Against Union Labor—Legal? 42 Am. L. Rev. 161 (1908); Roscoe Pound; *Liberty of Contract,* 18 Yale L.J. 454 (1909). See Lieberman, *Unions Before the Bar, supra* note 4, at 44-55; Robert L. Hale, *Freedom Through Law,* 390-397 (New York: Columbia Univ. Press, 1952); Thomas R. Powell, *Collective Bargaining Before the Supreme Court,* 33 Pol. Sci. Q. 396, 397-403 (1918).

47. 30 Stat. 424 (1898). See Gerald Eggert, *Railroad Labor Disputes* (Ann Arbor: Univ. of Michigan Press, 1967).

48. *United States v. Adair,* 152 F. 737 (E.D. Ky. 1907).

49. *Id* at 759.

50. 165 U.S. 578 (1897).

51. 198 U.S. 45 (1905).
52. *Adair,* 208 U.S. at 174-176. See Owen M. Fiss, *Troubled Beginnings of the Modern State, 1888-1910,* Vol. 8 *History of the Supreme Court of the United States,* 166-172 (New York, Macmillan Pub. Col, 1993).
53. 208 at U.S. at 180.
54. 208 U.S. at 176-180. This restricted view of the Commerce Clause was inconsistent with its plenary original meaning. *NLRB v. Jones & Laughlin Steel Corp.,* 301 U.S. 1 (1937); *Wickard v. Filburn,* 317 U.S. 111 (1942).
55. 208 U.S. at 181. Justice McKenna's dissent essentially adopted the reasoning of the district court that was reversed by the majority opinion. *United States v. Adair,* 152 F. 737 (E. D. Ky. 1907).
56. 208 U.S. at 191.
57. *Id.* at 190.
58. 236 U.S. 1 (1915). See Powell, *Collective Bargaining, supra,* note 46, at 414-426.
59. *State v. Coppage,* 87 Kan. 752, 125 P. 8 (1912).
60. 236 U.S. at 11.
61. *Id.* at 40.
62. *Id.* at 26-27.
63. 245 U.S. 229 (1917). See Lieberman, *supra* note 4, at 84-95.
64. *Hitchman Coal & Coke Co. v. Mitchell,* 202 F. 512 (N.D.W. Va. 1912), reversed, 214 F. 685 (C.C.A. 4, 1914).
65. 245 U.S. at 263.
66. 44 Stat. 577 (1926), 45 U.S.C.A. §152 (1998).
67. 281 U.S. 548 (1930).
68. *Brotherhood of Ry. And S.S. Clerks v. Texas & N. O.R. Co.,* 25 F. 2d 873 (D.C.S.D. Texas 1928).
69. *Texas & N.O.R. Co. v. Brotherhood of Ry. And S.S. Clerks,* 33 F. 2d 13 (5th Cir. 1929).
70. 281 U.S. at 559. See *Virginian Ry. v. System Federation,* 300 U.S. 515, 542 (1937).
71. 281 U.S. at 570. Justice McReynolds took no part in this decision.
72. 281 U.S. at 570.
73. *Id.* at 571.
74. *49 Stat.* 449 (1935), 29 U.S.C.A. §151 (1998).
75. *Id.*

10

Equal Protection Clause:
Rights of Persons and Firms

The first thesis of this chapter is the fundamental conflict between the Equal Protection Clause of the Fourteenth Amendment and the racial caste system enforced by state segregation laws. The overwhelming evidence reviewed herein established that the separate-but-equal doctrine of the majority in *Plessy v. Ferguson*[1] was a legal fiction. The caste system so roundly condemned by Justice Harlan in his *Plessy* dissent continued into the twentieth century with the open denial of equal education, segregation in public places, refusal of employment in most manufacturing and retailing, and even peonage. Sociologists cited herein have demonstrated the overwhelming proof that the foremost function of caste systems is to deny equality. It has long been textbook knowledge in social psychology that racism is a subset of ethnic stratification.[2] Throughout the South, there existed a caste system as degrading to African-Americans as that in India for untouchables.[3] If one understands the worldwide character of ethnic stratification, one can begin to comprehend the severity of the problems in overcoming it. With *Plessy* as standing law, later Supreme Court majority decisions approving segregation statutes in a social context of racism must have aggravated the problem.[4] They could not have contributed to a solution. The evidence of the racial caste system in the United States for a hundred years after the Civil War demonstrates that the majority opinion in *Plessy* was error.[5]

The series of Supreme Court opinions upholding state segregation laws demonstrated that the Court majority relied on *Plessy* as a precedent. The justices ignored the canon of interpretation that the highest appeals court is not bound by *stare decisis* when making a constitutional interpretation.[6] As Justice Felix Frankfurter proclaimed, "The ultimate touchstone of constitutionality is the Constitution itself and not what we have said about it."[7] Since the whole NAACP strategy was to challenge every state segregation statute against the Constitution itself, counsel in those cases deserve only small blame for not briefing and arguing the canon of construction. It is elementary that the Court must not rely on its own past errors by mistakenly following past constitutional opinions. The hesitancy of the Court to overrule past cases because large sectors of the public have relied on such cases should not apply where the past case has led to inhumane treatment of a minority.

The second thesis of this chapter is that the Equal Protection Clause should reinforce the privileges or immunities clause as a bar to state grants of monopoly power to private persons and firms. As explained in Chapter 6, the Anglo-American antimonopoly tradition, as retained against the national government by the Ninth Amendment and enforceable against the states through the Privileges or Immunities Clause, should have barred state grants of monopoly in the ordinary trades. The Equal Protection Clause should have supplemented this by barring all unequal state regulation of persons and firms that were found to be in like circumstances.

The legal standard for violation of equal protection in the area of economic and business regulation has been the rational-basis test:[8] to define a class subject to legislation all that is required is that the distinctions drawn have some relevance to the purpose for which the classification is made.[9] But it is always possible to define the legislative purpose of a statute in such a way that the statutory classification is rationally related to it.[10] And furthermore, if the legislative record shows multiple purposes of a statute, the classification need be related to only one of them. Thus the Court need not openly recognize that some statutes are designed for the monopolistic exploitation of consumers. It can find some other aspect of public health, safety, or welfare to be the statutory objective.

In a system of representative government where most legislation is sponsored by special interest groups, attempts to purchase grants of monopoly power from legislators are pervasive.[11] While the Fourteenth Amendment was adopted primarily to protect the civil rights of former slaves, the comprehensive language of the Equal Protection Clause has clear application to the economy. Whether state statutes foreclose tobacco farming to Afro-Americans or instead to persons not raising tobacco at the time of the passage of the restrictive statute, all excluded farmers are denied equal treatment under the law. The Equal Protection Clause has been applied by the courts to some economic activities,[12] but the thesis here is that it should have had a much broader application. The possible correct utilization of the Equal Protection Clause in the field of economic regulation has been impaired by the error of substantive due process.

Equal Protection: Textual Meaning

The final clause of Section I of the Fourteenth Amendment provides "that no state shall deny to any persons with in its jurisdiction the equal protection of the laws."[13] Following generally accepted rules of documentary construction, the clause must be viewed as a complement to the earlier clauses in Section I and also as having a specific function of its own.[14]

The Privileges or Immunities Clause was designed to make all national constitutional limitations protecting citizens effective against the states.[15] The Due Process Clause mandated full and fair procedure to any person whose life, liberty, or property was to be taken by a state.[16] The Equal Protection Clause complemented the earlier ones by providing a specific substantive protection for all persons within a state in order to bar oppressive state legislation that would not have contravened the earlier prohibitions. Equal protection does not refer to fundamental civil liberties that are protected by the privileges or immunities clause. Rather, it primarily concerns statutes that classify persons in order to regulate human behavior in some substantive way.[17] The most prominent examples of application of the clause have been to the classification of children by race involved in the state regulation of public schools.

Unlike the Privileges or Immunities Clause and the Due Process Clause, both of which had hundreds of years of legal-linguistic history, the Equal Protection Clause brought new language to the Constitution.[18] The word "equal" is found in natural-law contexts in the Declaration of Independence and in the "free and equal" clauses of some state constitutions.[19] These clauses were the basis in a few states for the judicial termination of slavery where it was a dying institution opposed by the majority of citizens.[20] The clauses did not function as controlling law on other topics.

The word "protection" is derived from the Latin term meaning "to cover or to save from harm." Equal protection means equal coverage for all persons.[21] The shield of the law is to be the same for any individual or firm found by the courts to come within the definition of "person."[22] The close connection between the idea of equality and its protection by government was stated by Senator Timothy Howe, abolitionist from Wisconsin: "I have thought that it belonged to republican institutions to carry out, to execute the doctrines of the Declaration of Independence, to make men equal. That they are not equal in social estimation, that they are not equal in mental culture, that they are not equal in physical stature, I know very well; but I have thought the weaker they were the more the government was bound to foster and protect them. If government be designed for the protection or the weak, certainly the weaker men are the more they need its protection."[23]

In this context, the word "laws" must mean both the common law and statutes. The hearings in the 39th Congress demonstrate that one primary purpose of the Equal Protection Clause was to invalidate the black codes that had been adopted by many of the southern states.[24] Another primary purpose was to assure equality in the right to contract and to hold property, key elements of the common law.[25] Even the objective of overruling the doctrine of *Scott v. Sandford*[26] vindicated a common-law principle, that persons of African descent could be free and equal citizens of the nation. This was the principle that Lord Mansfield had enunciated in 1772 in *Somerset's Case,*[27] when he held that a slave brought into England could resist return to the colonies and receive a judicial ruling that he was a free person.

The phrase "equal protection of the laws" must mean that persons in like circumstances are to receive the same treatment.[28] There is no issue of inequality if persons are not in like circumstances. Barbers and lawyers do not expect to take the same state licensing examination to enter their professions. Equal protection thus requires classification in order to determine if persons are in like circumstances in relation to a constitutionally valid statutory objective. Legislative classification defines the class to which the law applies. Most statutes are not generally legislation applying to all persons in the state, but rather are special laws regulating a particular group. "Indeed, the greater part of all legislation is special, either in the extent to which it operates, or the objects sought to be attained by it."[29]

The idea of equality before the law in the Anglo-American legal system has its beginnings in chapter 40 of the Magna Charta, which states: "To no one will we sell, to no one will we refuse or delay, right or justice."[30] As one key aspect of the English concept, "Rule of Law" means "equality before the law, or the equal subjection of all classes to the ordinary law of the land administered by the ordinary law courts."[31] The protection was incorporated in the Massachusetts Body of Liberties of 1641 as follows: "Every person within this Jurisdiction, whether Inhabitant or forreiner shall enjoy the same justice and law, that is generally for the plantation, which we constitute and execute one towards another without partialitie or delay."[32] The religion clause of the Massachusetts Constitution of 1780 declared that "every denomination of Christians, demeaning themselves peaceably, and as good subjects of the common wealth, shall be equally under the protection of the law."[33]

The absence of express equal protection clauses in most state constitutions at that time can probably be attributed to the existence of slavery. After ratification of the Fourteenth Amendment, the dicta on equality became more general. As Chief Justice Morrison Waite observed: "The equality of the rights of citizens is a principle of republicanism. Every republican government is in duty bound to protect all its citizens in the enjoyment of this principle, if within its power. That duty was originally assumed by the states; and it still remains there. The only obligation resting upon the United States is to see that the States do not deny the right. This the amendment guaranties, but no more. The power of the National Government is limited to the enforcement of this guaranty."[34]

Since the Equal Protection Clause was adopted primarily to protect the legal rights of former slaves, the foremost group of cases under the clause have concerned racial segregation. These cases illustrate the difficult issues of interpretation when a constitutional clause incorporates the ideals of revolutionary change in a society. The language of the clause, drafted by the radical Republicans on the Committee of fifteen on reconstruction, was couched in the broadest possible terms in order to express the committee's ideals of a legal system where all persons were absolutely equal.[35] Although the language did not treat social or political equality,[36] its mandate for legal equality was unequivocal.

The inclusive character of the language in the Equal Protection Clause must be emphasized because a few recent scholars have erroneously suggested that the alleged intent of some of the framers controls and narrowly limits its meaning.[37] Their argument is that evidence of the intent of some members of the 39th Congress, though highly controversial and not within the knowledge of the ratifiers, can be used to cut the meaning of the language to a fraction of its facial definition to ordinary readers of those times.[38] By asserting that the comprehensive language of the Fourteenth Amendment was designed solely to constitutionalize the narrower language of the Civil Rights Act of 1866,[39] they conclude that wholly different language is equivalent. This attempt to curtail the meaning of the language of the clause by interpretation violates a basic canon of documentary construction.[40]

Section I of the Civil Rights Act of 1866 provided former slaves with the same right to contract, to sue, and to hold property as whites for "the full and equal benefit of all laws and proceedings for the security of person and property, as is enjoyed by white citizens."[41] This language is narrower in scope than "the equal protection of the laws" in the Fourteenth Amendment. As noted, the latter applies to all laws, both common law and statutes. There is no doubt that one primary function of the Fourteenth Amendment was to supply a constitutional foundation for the Civil Rights Act. Congressman John A. Bingham of Ohio, the radical Republican who was later the primary author of Section I of the Fourteenth Amendment, opposed the Civil Rights Act because he thought that Congress was without power to pass such bill.[42] He indicated that a legal foundation for this act and for the original antidiscrimination clause that had been deleted from the final act could be secured only by constitutional amendment. But the equality of civil rights that were provided in the 1866 act did not include equality under statutes dispersing public benefits. State statutes providing public education only for whites would not violate the 1866 act. The language of the Equal Protection Clause of the Fourteenth Amendment was broader and would apply to all state statutes, including those dispensing state benefits, and to all regulations of the marketplace that might be administered to the detriment of nonwhites.

For efficient judicial review of cases arising under the Equal Protection Clause, the courts should have adopted a two-step process of analysis. The first issue is whether there is a constitutionally valid objective. "The sovereign might not draw distinctions between individuals based solely on differences that are irrelevant to a legitimate governmental objective."[43] This would apply both to trial judges in common-law actions and to legislatures. If a trial judge in common-law litigation should indicate by language or rulings that he will grant motions to exclude all members of a certain race, religion, or ethnic group from serving on juries, his objective is constitutionally invalid.[44] Similarly, a state statute limiting jury service to whites is also invalid.[45] In these examples, the objective of the judge or the statute is discrimination on the basis of race or some other arbitrary characteristic. The unequal treatment makes the actions unconstitutional, whether or not prohibited by federal statute.[46] The Supreme Court has consistently held that the judiciary has the power to enforce the Fourteenth Amendment whether or not Congress has passed an enforcement statute pursuant to Section 5.[47]

The second step to test conformity to the Equal Protection Clause is necessary only if there has been a finding of a constitutionally valid objective of the common-law rulings or statute in question. If such finding has been made, the second test is whether the classification that has been adopted assigns all persons who are in like circumstances or "similarly situated" to the same class.

In applying this two-step analysis to the case of school segregation by race, for example, the first finding should be whether the objective of the statutes was arbitrary separation on the basis of race. If so, an immediate conclusion of unconstitutionality should follow. But if the court should find that the statutory objective was to subsidize elementary and secondary education and regulate quality in the operation of schools, then the second test would have to be applied: the determination if all persons similarly situated were treated equally. The persons similarly situated for purpose of education are all children. Separating any one or group of them on the basis of non-educational criteria would be arbitrary and therefore unequal. Legislative segregation on the basis of race, religion, height, weight, country of ancestor's origin, or any other non-educational criterion is a badge of differentiation that indicates inequality.

Equality of Persons: Racial Segregation

The economic theory of racial discrimination postulates that there exists a dominating ethnic group in a society and that many of the members of that group have a taste not to associate with members of the other ethnic groups.[48] The extent that members of the dominant group refuse to engage in value-increasing exchanges with other groups, incomes of both groups are reduced. Before World War I in the United States, African-Americans were largely barred from skilled trades and factory work and were relegated by a caste system to the lowest income levels.[49] In a caste society, transactions between dominant and dominated members are not discouraged so long as minority members remain in the areas and tasks assigned by the system of their group. Contractual relations between whites and African-Americans after the Civil War were necessary for the functioning of the economy in the south. Whites entered sharecropping agreements with African-Americans in rural areas and hired them as unskilled labor in urban areas.[50] Large numbers of African-American women worked as domestic laborers in white homes.

A key factor maintaining the lower caste status of the African-Americans after the Civil War was separate and unequal education.[51] Before passage of the Fourteenth Amendment, there were few public schools in the South, and most states provided public schools only for whites. Other states required African-Americans to pay separate taxes for their own schools. The percentage of African-Americans children in school rose from 1.9 in 1860 to 9.9 in 1870 and to 33.8 in 1880, but it dropped to 31.1 in 1900.[52] Even though some courts held that dual systems of taxes violated equal protection,[53] county administrators allocated general tax funds on an unequal per capita basis, largely in favor of white schools.[54] Thus, the assumption in the South that African-Americans were being educated at the expense of whites was false.

Racial segregation and economic deprivation were interrelated phenomena. In those southern states with large African-American populations, the underinvestment in public education left the economy with a large segment of semiliterate persons, ill prepared to hold jobs in an industrializing economy.[55] Part of the lag in economic development in the South must be attributed to this limited investment in African-American public education.

If the courts had followed the textual meaning of the Equal Protection Clause, statutes requiring racial separation would have been invalidated upon the enactment of the Fourteenth Amendment. Such laws are today immediately suspect because their objective is discriminatory—treating some persons as second-class citizens.[56] But the invidious character of statutory racial classification had been recognized by the Court as early as the *Strauder* case of 1870, where Justice William Strong observed: "The words of the Amendment, it is true, are prohibitory, but they contain a necessary implication of a positive immunity, or right, most valuable to the colored race—the right to exemption from unfriendly legislation against them distinctively as colored,—exemption from legal discriminations which are steps toward reducing them to the condition of a subject race."[57]

A few racial segregation laws have an antebellum origin.[58] Although the rural South had the ultimate caste system in slavery, a few major cities had large numbers of free African-Americans. Segregation laws and ordinances were enacted in these cities to define and defend the caste system for free African-Americans. The Civil War brought an end to the slavery and an end to statutory racial segregation in public places for a long period of time. It was more than ten years after the federal troops left the South in 1877 that the first state segregation statute for public places was passed.[59] The capitulation to racism allowed extremist views to take control of social relations through legislation. The essence of white supremacy was to relegate and maintain African-Americans in a lower caste, and this was the function of segregation laws.[60]

The background to the state-mandated racial segregation in *Plessy* is a set of inconsistent Supreme Court opinions that demonstrate the interactions between the Commerce Clause and the Equal Protection Clause of the Fourteenth Amendment. The national case law began during reconstruction in Louisiana in *Hall v. De Cuir*.[61] The Constitution of Louisiana provided that "All persons shall enjoy equal rights and privileges upon any conveyance of a public character."[62] The statute of 1869 concerning exclusion of passengers who refused to pay or who misbehaved had a proviso: "Said rules make no discrimination on account of race or color. . . ."[63] Mrs. De Cuir, "a person of color," was an intrastate passenger on defendant's interstate steamboat on the Mississippi River. She was denied a cabin on the upper deck, which was reserved for white persons. She sued for damages under the statute and prevailed in the state courts. The Louisiana Supreme Court held that the state constitutional clause and statute did not regulate commerce but merely reinforced a standing duty under common and civil law that common carriers treat all passengers alike.[64]

On writ of error, the U.S. Supreme Court reversed the Louisiana ruling, holding the state law to violate the Commerce Clause of Article I, Section 8. Since different states along the route could have different rules on racial mixing, the state law was held an unconstitutional burden on commerce. "If the public good requires such legislation, it must come from Congress and not from the States."[65] The vessel was duly enrolled and licensed under federal law to engage in the coasting trade. As Chief Justice Marshall had explained in *Gibbons v. Ogden*,[66] the integration of interstate and intrastate commerce on public carriers barred state regulation.

The key problem with this case is that Congress had acted, but too late for this action. The Civil Rights Act of March 1, 1875 provided:

> That all persons within the jurisdiction of the United States shall be entitled to the full and equal enjoyment of the accommodations, advantages, facilities, and privileges of inns, public conveyances on land or water, theatres, and other places of public amusement; subject only to the conditions and limitations established by law, and applicable alike to citizens of every race and color, regardless of any previous condition of servitude.[67]

While this statute was passed after the trial in *De Cuir* and two months after the Louisiana Supreme Court opinion, its existence apparently was not pleaded on appeal by counsel for De Cuir as a national policy deserving equitable consideration. Since the federal statute was remedial, providing for $500 damages, the Supreme Court could have taken notice of it as a national antidiscrimination policy and then given recognition to operation of the state statute with the same policy for intrastate trips prior to March 1, 1875. This would have recognized concurrent state and federal jurisdiction over local commerce until Congress exercised its plenary power over commerce to preempt local regulation.[68]

An alternative approach by the Supreme Court would have been a structural analysis holding that constitutional limitations such as the Fourteenth Amendment take a higher status in law than delegated powers such as the commerce power. The state law against discrimination on public conveyances had the same objective as the more general Equal Protection Clause of the Fourteenth Amendment for all state laws. The court at that time only hypothesized segregation statutes in adjacent states. It is those hypothetical segregation statutes that would have violated equal protection and burdened commerce among the several states, not the Louisiana statute enforcing equal protection in public conveyances.

In the *Civil Rights Cases*[69] of 1883 the Supreme Court invalidated the Civil Rights Act of 1875 without consideration of the Commerce Clause.[70] As quoted above, the act provided for full and equal accommodations in common carriers, inns, theaters, and places of amusement. Only one of the five cases concerned carriers; i.e., *Robinson v. Memphis & Charleston R. Co.* The railroad's main line ran from Memphis to Chattanooga in Tennessee but it was connected to three successive lines that extended to Lynchburg, Virginia, so that the four lines together operated as a major east-west route in interstate commerce.[71] Robinson sued for statutory damages of $500 because the railroad conductor refused to allow Robinson's wife to ride in the ladies car, as she appeared to be a person of African descent.[72]

Since the Civil Rights Act was adopted pursuant to Section 5 of the Fourteenth Amendment, the briefs of counsel and the opinions centered on equal protection and did not treat the Commerce Clause. Justice Joseph Bradley, for the majority, held sections 1 and 2 of the Civil Rights Act unconstitutional because the Fourteenth Amendment applied to state action and not usually to the behavior of private firms.[73] The inference is that if a federal court found a state statute mandating racial discrimination to violate the Fourteenth Amendment, then the Civil Rights Act could be a valid remedy against persons or firms. Or if a state constitution or statute provided for non-discrimination on the basis of race and state officers failed to enforce it, the Civil Rights Act would be a valid remedy against persons or firms.

Since the Court held that the Equal Protection Clause applied only to discriminatory state statutes, it ruled that it was not necessary to examine arguments based on the legal theory of Senator Sumner and his associates in proposing the civil rights bill that carriers and inns were regulated by common-law duties to serve all paying travelers decent in appearance and conduct.[74] Under Sumner's view, the Civil Rights Act was merely a supplemental national control for regulated industries to effect directly the ban on racial discrimination mandated by the Equal Protection Clause.[75] Sumner had argued that "The pending bill simply reinforces this rule, which without Congress ought to be sufficient. But since it is set at naught by an odious discrimination, Congress must interfere."[76]

The lone dissent of Justice John M. Harlan in the *Civil Rights Cases*, covering thirty-seven pages in the official reports, rejects the stilted formalism of the majority and emphasizes constitutional and statutory purposes.[77] Harlan reviewed the antislavery origins of the Thirteenth and Fourteenth amendments to show the breadth of their purposes. The express power in Section 2 of the Thirteenth Amendment for congressional enforcement was for eradication of slavery and all burdens and disabilities which constituted badges of slavery and servitude.[78] The Civil Rights Act of 1866 was the first legislative act to protect fundamental rights that were the essence of civil freedom.[79] Harlan concluded that freedom of former slaves "necessarily involved immunity from, and protection against, all discriminations against them, because of their race, in respect of such civil rights as belong to freemen of other races."[80] Harlan reviewed the precedents describing the common-law obligations of operators of common carriers, inns, and places of public amusement. He concluded that racial discrimination in these regulated industries was a badge of servitude and that the Thirteenth Amendment by itself was a constitutional foundation for the Civil Rights Act of 1875.

The failure of counsel to plead the Commerce Clause as an additional constitutional basis of the Civil Rights Act of 1875 and the failure of Justice Harlan to argue the Commerce Clause missed what could have been the strongest argument. Transactions of common carriers are in commerce among the several states, and this was later illustrated by the broad construction of the commerce power that the Supreme Court applied to railroads after passage of the Interstate Commerce Act of 1887.[81] The *Shreveport Cases*[82] and others embodied the principle that commerce among the several states extended to local activities that affected rail movements between states or railroad earnings. This was in effect the application of the broad principles enunciated by Chief Justice John Marshall in *Gibbons v. Ogden*.[83] Ninety years after passage of the Civil Rights Act of 1875, Congress exercised its restored plenary power over commerce and enacted legislation similar to the 1875 act, barring racial discrimination in places of public accommodation. This part of the Civil Rights Act of 1964[84] was held constitutional.[85]

The next major interstate carrier opinion was inconsistent with the commerce rule of *Hall v. De Cuir*[86] and hence inconsistent with the original constitutional policy explicated in *Gibbons*. In *Louisville, New Orleans, and Texas Ry. Co. v. Mississippi*,[87] the Court upheld a Mississippi statute of 1888 requiring railroads to provide separate accommodations for the "white and colored races." The statute applied only to intrastate commerce, and the litigation tested only the carrier's duty to provide facilities, not the segregation of passengers. The carrier demonstrated that adding coaches at the state line would increase operating expenses and claimed that this would burden interstate commerce. Justice David Brewer, for the court, accepted as authoritative the Mississippi Court's construction of the statute that discounted the effect of the added expenses. Justice Harlan, joined by Justice Bradley, dissented,[88] arguing correctly that the facts were within the rule of *Hall v. De Cuir*. The defendant was an interstate carrier and the clear objective of the statute was to segregate all passengers, including interstate travelers.

While the racist ideology permeating white society may have affected the majority justices, another possible explanation of these discrepant cases is that between the two trials the Supreme Court had begun its assumption of power to cut the scope of the Commerce Clause to a fraction of its original meaning.[89] After 1870, the Court issued opinions that excluded most local commerce from national regulation. An exception after 1890 was the national control of intrastate freight rates under the Interstate Commerce Act. State statutes in the South requiring racial segregation on all passenger trains were enforced as regulations of local commerce. Beginning in 1937, the Court restored the Commerce Clause to its broad original meaning, applying to all local commerce that affected other states, and in 1946 state segregation statutes for transport of persons were invalidated.[90]

Plessy was Error

The Louisiana legislature passed the rail segregation statute in 1890, requiring carriers to provide "equal but separate accommodations for the white, and colored races, by providing two or more coaches for each passenger train, or by dividing the passenger coaches by a partition."[91] An exception, demonstrating that some close racial mixing conforming to the caste system, was approved, provided that the act would not apply "to nurses attending children of the other race." The railroads had opposed the statute because of the increased costs of providing separate cars. An African-American Citizens Committee was organized to raise funds in order to challenge the constitutionality of the statute.[92] Homer A. Plessy, who was seven-eighths white, was chosen to challenge the statute. This demonstrated the arbitrary nature of the statute.[93]

In June, 1892, Plessy purchased a first-class ticket for the East Louisiana Railway, an intrastate carrier, for a trip form New Orleans to Covington, Louisiana. When he insisted on boarding the first-class coach, which was reserved for whites, Plessy was arrested for violating the segregation statute. The prosecution filed an information and Plessy was arraigned in October. Counsel for Plessy promptly filed a motion to dismiss the action, a fourteen-point plea to the jurisdiction of the criminal court. The state's demurrer to the plea was allowed but the case was not set for trial. Since the state law would not have allowed any appeal from a criminal conviction, counsel for Plessy immediately petitioned the Louisiana Supreme Court for a writ of certiorari and prohibition against trial judge Ferguson to review the denial of the motion to dismiss the information. The Supreme Court of Louisiana granted certiorari and, after hearing the appeal, decided against Plessy.[94]

A writ of error was filed in the Supreme Court of the United States in 1893, but Plessy's counsel encouraged delay because he thought the current majority of the Court had views favoring segregation. The delay was not helpful. The opinion of Justice Henry B. Brown in 1896 affirmed the Louisiana decision, with only Justice Harlan dissenting.[95] As to the Thirteenth Amendment, the Court followed the Louisiana opinion in holding it was limited to slavery and involuntary servitude. Segregation laws were held not to be of that class.[96]

This lawsuit and similar legal actions demonstrated that segregation itself was highly resented. Justice Brown, for the majority, thus made an assumption of fact that was clearly against the manifest weight of the available evidence. Justice Brown first admitted that "the object of the amendment was undoubtedly to enforce the absolute equality of the two races before the law."[97] But he erroneously concluded: "We consider the underlying fallacy of the plaintiff's argument to consist in the assumption that the enforced separation of the two races stamps the colored with a badge of inferiority. If this be so, it is not by reason of anything found in the act, but solely because the colored race chooses to put that construction upon it."[98] But from time immemorial, the primary function of caste systems has been to impose and perpetuate inequality.

Justice Brown's erroneous assumption that enforced segregation was not racial discrimination had been repudiated by a unanimous Court twenty-three years before *Plessy*. In *Railroad Co. v. Brown*,[99] the Court had recognized the congressional declaration that segregation in transportation was negative discrimination, not equality. The charter to the railroad included a clause that "no person shall be excluded from any car on account of color."[100] The carrier provided separate-but-equal cars for white and colored. Mrs. Brown, a "colored" woman, attempted to sit in the "white" car and was ejected. A judgment for Mrs. Brown against the railroad was affirmed by a unanimous Supreme Court. The inequality was explained: "Congress, in the belief that this discrimination was unjust, acted. It told this company, in substance, that it could extend its road in the District as desired, but that this discrimination must cease, and the colored and white race, in the use of the cars, be placed on an equality."[101]

Justice Harlan was the lone dissenter. His opinion centered on the Thirteenth and Fourteenth amendments as a combined protection of individual liberty which meant he failed to analyze the meaning of the language in the crucial Equal Protection Clause that applied to wrongful discrimination. He first noted the statutory exemption for "nurses attending children of the other race," an example of approving interracial contact so long as caste relationships prevailed.[102] He then cited the authorities that common carriers were public highways delegated the right to eminent domain. He concluded that the civil rights of citizens do not permit such a public authority to know the race of those entitled to patronize them.[103] Racial distinctions are inconsistent with equality of civil rights of citizens and with personal liberty. The purpose of the amendments was to secure to former slaves and their descendents the civil rights that the white race enjoyed.[104] Everyone knew that the purpose of the racial segregation statute was to interfere with personal liberty so that whites and blacks could not choose to occupy the same public conveyance on a public highway.[105]

Justice Harlan concluded that racial segregation of former slaves was a badge of second-class citizenship and therefore a denial of equal protection. "There is no caste here. Our constitution is color-blind, and neither knows nor tolerates classes among citizens. In respect of civil rights, all citizens are equal before the law."[106] He concluded: "In my opinion, the judgment this day rendered will, in time, prove to be quite as pernicious as the decision made by this tribunal in *the Dred Scott* case."[107] As many commentators predicted, Justice Harlan has been vindicated on the meaning of equal protection.[108] The modern Court has unqualifiedly asserted that: "The Equal Protection Clause was intended to work nothing less than the abolition of all caste-based and invidious class-based legislation."[109]

The *Plessy* decision fostered the ideology of racial separation and statutes enforcing racial segregation for almost sixty years. The decision was more than just a travesty of justice. It was part of the common understanding of Americans in 1890 that racial segregation was a badge of inferior status. This truth is confirmed by historians and sociologists who in this century have made scientific studies of the origins of "jim crow."[110] Charles Black has characterized the acceptance of the separate-but-equal doctrine as the point where "the curves of callousness and stupidity intersect at their respective maxima."[111] Robert Harris has labeled *Plessy* "a compound of bad logic, bad history, bad sociology, and bad constitutional law."[112]

Segregation in Public Education

The doctrine of *Plessy* confirmed the constitutionality of a caste society. Applied to education, it validated existing segregation of public schools[113] and discouraged legal attacks on segregation because all trial courts would be bound to follow the precedent of *Plessy*. An African-American community, one generation out of slavery and largely illiterate, was at the mercy of the white supremacists who had instigated the passage of segregation statutes. The result was not a society that was separate and equal. Like other caste systems, it was a society that was separate and unequal.[114] The most pronounced aspect was highly inferior schools for African-Americans and in many areas the absence of public high schools for them.[115]

The school segregation cases began in 1850, long before the Fourteenth Amendment, with a key Massachusetts decision that was overruled by legislative action. *Roberts v. City of Boston*[116] challenged regulations of the Boston School Committee assigning "colored" children to 2 of the 161 primary schools in Boston. The plaintiff, a five-year-old "colored" girl, attempted to enter the school nearest her home, a distance of 900 feet, and was denied admission.[117] The segregated school was 2,100 feet from her home. The qualification of instructors in white and "colored" schools was equal, and the physical deficiencies of the "colored" school appear not to have been put in issue. Chief Justice Lemual Shaw, for the Supreme Judicial Court, upheld the Boston School Committee. The clause of the Massachusetts Declaration of Rights, "All men are born free and equal,"[118] was a natural-law proclamation, not operative law. "The province of a declaration of rights and constitution of government, after directing its form, is to declare great principles and fundamental truths, to influence and direct the judgment and conscience of legislators in making laws, rather than to limit and control them, by directing what precise laws they shall make."[119] Charles Sumner, for the plaintiff, had argued that discrimination on the basis of race was a perpetuation of caste and necessarily a violation of equality.[120] The court upheld the discretion of the School Committee and held that separate schools did not violate any constitutional rights. But the *Roberts* decision was law for only five years. Citizens organized and convinced the legislature that separate schools were in their nature unequal. In 1855 the Massachusetts legislature enacted a statute prohibiting the separation of children in schools on the basis of race, color, or religious opinion.[121] Given the factual basis of the legislative rejection of the Roberts decision, the opinion should never have stood as a precedent for separate-but-equal schools.

After the Civil War, radical Republicans began what was to be an unsuccessful campaign to end racial segregation in the public schools. The new constitutions of 1868, drafted by the conventions controlled by the radicals in Louisiana and South Carolina, expressly prohibited racial segregation in public schools.[122] In 1870, the radicals in Congress were successful in incorporating bars against racial segregation in state schools as a condition subsequent in the acts to readmit Mississippi, Texas, and Virginia to the Union.[123] These conditions were subsequently evaded.

The controversies over school segregation in the Congress demonstrate that most members recognized that the power to order racially mixed schools was within the power of Congress under Section 5 of the Fourteenth Amendment.[124] Under the leadership of Senator Sumner, the proposal for what would become the Civil Rights Act of 1875 contained a clause for equal rights in common schools and institutions of learning authorized by law, but this was deleted from the final bill.[148]

For fifty years after *Plessy*, the African-American community, with few lawyers and few friends among skilled white lawyers who would donate time to an impoverished group, did not begin a direct attack on school segregation. Instead, most actions centered on showing the inequality of schools for African-Americans. In *Cumming v. County Board of Education*,[126] a high school for sixty African-Americans was closed in order to convert the building to a primary school for about three hundred African-Americans. The Constitution of Georgia mandated racially segregated primary schools for all children supported by taxation. In violation of this clause, four hundred or more "colored" children had been turned away from primary education for lack of buildings and teachers.[127] Absent adequate taxation, closure of the African-American High School was adopted as the only financially feasible remedy for this denial. The county provided a high school for white girls and assisted a county denominational high school for white boys.[128] The African-American plaintiffs, alleging violation of the Fourteenth Amendment to the Constitution but failing to center on the Equal Protection Clause, sued to enjoin the collection of taxes to support white high schools until a public high school was also provided for African-Americans. The school board denied that African-Americans were barred from high school since, for the same small tuition of the public high school for white girls, non-whites could attend any one of three "colored" denominational high schools in Augusta.[129]

The Supreme Court affirmed a decision for defendants. Plaintiffs had made no objection to the segregated school system. The entire case turned on plaintiff's prayer for a remedy detrimental to education. Justice Harlan, for the Court, stated that if plaintiffs had drafted a prayer that the school board, out of funds under its control, be ordered to establish and maintain a high school for "colored" children and the board refused because of their race, "different questions might have arisen in the state court."[130] This case is surely not a retreat from Justice Harlan's powerful dissent in *Plessy*. It is clear that this ruling created a very narrow precedent for lower courts.

In *Berea College v. Kentucky*,[131] the state mandate of racial segregation was extended to private colleges. The state statute made it a crime "for any person, corporation, or association of persons to maintain or operate any college, school or institution, where persons of the white and negro races are both received as pupils for instruction."[132] Berea was a private sectarian college dedicated to Christian equality that admitted African-Americans equally with whites and had thereby violated the statute. The college was fined $1000 for teaching whites and non-whites in the same place at the same time. The Supreme Court sustained the conviction by a vote of 7 to 2 on the ground that the college had failed to change its charter to exclude African-Americans. Justice Brewer, for the Court, upheld the state statute on the theory that it had been applied only to the corporate entity, the college.[133] This was a rejection of constitutional supremacy in favor of a caste system. Justices Harlan and Day dissented.[134] This case was overruled in 1954.

The *Berea College* opinion was a significant expansion of the doctrine of *Plessy* to non-regulated industries. As a result, laws were passed throughout the South requiring racial segregation in public places, including privately operated facilities such as restaurants, theaters, and pool halls.[135]

The validity of state racial segregation was assumed in *Gong Lum v. Rice*,[136] in which the Court affirmed the denial of admission of a Chinese-American girl to a white high school in Mississippi. The plaintiffs did not challenge the state segregation statute but only the refusal to admit a Chinese to the white school. The plaintiff failed to plead that there was no "colored" high school in a district overlapping that of the white high school or one nearby. Consequently, the Court assumed that such a high school existed even though Mississippi was notorious for not providing public high schools for African-Americans.[137] The Court held that denial of admission of a Chinese citizen of the United States to the white high school was not a denial of equal protection of the laws, citing *Plessy v. Ferguson*.[138] Like *Plessy*, this opinion was destined to be overruled.

The background to *Brown v. Board of Education of Topeka* was a set of Supreme Court opinions from 1938 to 1950, all of which concerned admission to law schools or graduate schools. These cases centered on unequal treatment of African-Americans, and plaintiffs did not directly challenge the *Plessy* ruling on separate but equal. In 1938, the Court in the *Gaines* case, by a vote of 6 to 2, ordered the segregated University of Missouri Law School to admit African American Lloyd Gaines, holding that the state's offer to subsidize Gaines's tuition to an out-of-state law school was not equal treatment.[139] In 1948, the Court in the *Sipuel* case ordered the Oklahoma Board of Regents to provide Ada Sipuel with a legal education in conformity with the Equal Protection Clause.[140] Rather than admit her to the University of Oklahoma Law School, the board set aside a small section of the state capitol and assigned three law teachers to teach non-white students. Upon challenge to this sham of a law school, the Court held that the issue of a separate law school had not been raised on appeal in the action and denied mandamus to compel compliance with its earlier opinion.[141] After one year, the Oklahoma officials stopped financing the one-student law school. Sipuel had filed a second lawsuit, and though she lost at the trial, state officials admitted her to the University of Oklahoma Law School. She was graduated in 1951.

In 1950, two opinions were issued on the same day concerning unequal graduate education. In *Sweatt v. Painter,*[142] Chief Justice Fred Vinson, for a unanimous court, ordered a plaintiff's admission to the University of Texas Law School. He held that the small separate law school that the state had created for African-Americans was unequal to that at the University of Texas, citing size of faculty and student body, law review, moot court, scholarship funds, national honors, and relations of students to leading alumni. He also refused "petitioner's contention that *Plessy v. Ferguson* should be reexamined in the light of contemporary knowledge respecting the purposes of the Fourteenth Amendment and the effects of racial segregation."[143] In *McLaurin v. Oklahoma S. Regents,*[144] the unanimous Court ordered the University of Oklahoma to cease the internal segregation of a doctoral student in education pursuant to a state statute. He had been ordered to sit apart in an anteroom next to the classroom and at specified separate tables in the library and cafeteria. McLaurin was handicapped in his pursuit of education by the prohibition of intellectual commingling with other students. Like Sweatt, McLaurin had been denied a personal and present right of equal protection.[145]

In *Henderson v. United States,*[146] racial segregation in dining cars of Southern Railway was tested against section 3(1) of the Interstate Commerce Act. The statute made it unlawful for a railroad in interstate commerce "to subject any particular person . . . to any undue or unreasonable prejudice or disadvantage in any respect whatsoever."[147] In this case, an African-American was denied dining car service because the one table in the car that was conditionally reserved for "Negroes" had some white passengers and the plaintiff was not allowed to occupy the one empty seat. This clearly violated the statutory standard and the district court's dismissal of plaintiff's action was reversed. The unusual procedure of this case was the intervention of the Justice Department on behalf of Henderson and in opposition to the Interstate Commerce Commission.

From a historical viewpoint, there was great significance to the intervention of the Justice Department in the last three cases. In the *Sweatt* and *McLaurin* cases, the Solicitor General filed a single combined brief in which counsel analyzed the original meaning of the Equal Protection Clause of the Fourteenth Amendment.[148] The brief then reviewed *Strauder v. West Virginia*[149] and other cases that noted the requirement for broad construction of the Fourteenth Amendment. The conclusion here and in the *Henderson* brief filed shortly before was that the "separate but equal" doctrine of *Plessy v. Ferguson* was wrong as a matter of law, history, and policy. For the first time, United States attorneys urged the Court to repudiate the doctrine and overrule *Plessy*.[150] While the Court side-stepped the fundamental issue of "separate but equal," these briefs document the views of the Justice Department in 1950.

Brown v. Board of Education[151] was the leading case that held segregation in public schools to violate the Equal Protection Clause. Since Kluger has written a comprehensive study of this case and its background, there is only a summary here.[152]

In the four cases that were on appeal together in *Brown*, attorneys for the plaintiffs seeking admission to white schools presented the testimony of many expert witnesses on the demeaning character of enforced segregation of minority children.[153] While three of the trial courts ruled that they were bound to follow *Plessy*, one of these, the Topeka Court, made a finding of fact accepting the social science evidence on the detrimental effect of segregation on the Afro-American children.[154] In the Delaware case, the district court found the inequalities of education of such magnitude that they ordered immediate admission of the Afro-American children to the white schools.[155] The chancellor also found that segregation itself results in an inferior education for Afro-American children, but he did not rest his decision on that ground.[156]

The Supreme Court in *Brown* held for the plaintiffs in all the cases. The stigma of being a member of a lower caste was thoroughly demonstrated,[157] so that Chief Justice Warren's conclusion was clearly supported by the records of the four cases. "To separate them from others of similar age and qualifications solely because of their race generates a feeling of inferiority as to their status in the community that may affect their hearts and minds in a way unlikely ever to undone . . . We conclude that in the field of public education the doctrine of 'separate but equal' has no place. Separate educational facilities are inherently unequal."[158]

Critics of Warren who label this conclusion as unprincipled failed to reflect on the fatal errors of reasoning by Justice Brown in *Plessy*. Warren's opinion was based on the rejection of a caste system as articulated by Justice Harlan in dissent in *Plessy*. In essence, the textual meaning of the Equal Protection Clause mandated a color-blind Constitution.[159] Judicial compromises made it impossible for Warren to be as articulate as Harlan had been in his *Plessy* dissent and write a full explanation of equal protection.

Many critics of Chief Justice Warren fail to note that the Court followed *Brown* with a per curiam overruling of *Plessy*. But it is an elementary application of epistemic principle that inconsistent applications of a given constitutional clause cannot both be correct law. State laws requiring racial segregation in intrastate public transportation cannot be both constitutional and also unconstitutional. So that in 1956 when *Plessy* was finally overruled in the intrastate bus case, *Gayle v. Browder*,[160] *Plessy* was demonstrated to have been an erroneous opinion. The error took place in 1896, not in 1954 when Warren refused to follow it. Consequently, all lower court decisions that had relied on the generalizations of *Plessy* to uphold state segregation laws in many areas of state activity were also erroneous.[161] It is truly unfortunate that the Court in *Browder* did not write an opinion explaining its overruling, but this also may have been a compromise decision.

The Court in *Brown* had heard argument on whether the original understanding of the Equal Protection Clause was to invalidate segregated schools. After review of the sources, the court concluded that, at best, they are inconclusive. Bickel demonstrates that history cannot answer the question of whether a particular set of acts occurring today do or do not violate broad general constitutional principles such as the Equal Protection Clause of the Fourteenth Amendment. "It is thus quite apparent that to seek in historical materials relevant to the framing of the Constitution, or in the language of the Constitution itself, specific answers to specific present problems is to ask the wrong questions. With adequate scholarship, the answer that must emerge in the vast majority of cases is no answer."[162] Most of the hundreds of representatives at the ratifying conventions did not speak on the need for special schools for illiterate, former slave children. But even if they had spoken and said that separate and equal public facilities for the races satisfied the Equal Protection Clause at that time, this would not control courts today. The findings of facts at trials in 1951 that racial separation was a badge of inferior status would require a holding of unconstitutionality regardless of the views of ratifiers in the social context of 1867 and 1868.

In the companion case to *Brown*, *Bolling v. Sharpe*,[163] the Court held that segregation of public schools in the District of Columbia violated the Due Process Clause of the Fifth Amendment. Since due process meant required procedure and there is no Equal Protection Clause in the Fifth Amendment, the reasoning of *Bolling* is much more difficult than *Brown*. The Court resorted to substantive due process. "Classifications based solely upon race must be scrutinized with particular care, since they are contrary to our traditions and hence constitutionally suspect."[164] The Court concluded: "Segregation in public education is not reasonably related to any proper governmental objective, and thus it imposes on Negro children of the District of Columbia a burden that constitutes an arbitrary deprivation of their liberty in violation if the Due Process Clause."[165] A more direct approach would have established a national civil right to equal protection from the English right to equal justice as founded in Chapter 40 of *Magna Carta* and preserved by the Ninth Amendment.[166] It is argued that in a true democracy, equal protection of the law is a self-evident truth.[167] In this framework, the proclamation of equality in the Declaration of Independence can be viewed both as a statement of natural law and of positive law.

Equality of Firms in the Market

An efficient economy requires that business firms receive equal protection of the law. The efficiencies resulting from division of labor in large-scale factory production could occur only if underlying risk capital could be secured from large numbers of small investors. These stockholders had no part in day-to-day management, so that there was separation of ownership from control.[168] They would invest only if they were guaranteed limited liability. Nicholas Murry Butler remarked in 1911 on the legal technique of limited liability: "I weigh my words, when I say that in my judgment the limited liability corporation is the greatest single discovery of modern times . . . Even steam and electricity are far less important than the limited liability corporation, and they would be reduced to comparative impotence without it."[169]

In light of the economic realities it is not surprising that Chief Justice Waite announced for the Court in *Santa Clara County v. Southern Pacific R. Co.*[170] that "The court does not wish to hear argument on the question whether the provision in the Fourteenth Amendment to the Constitution, which forbids a state to deny to any person within its jurisdiction the equal protection of the laws, applies to these corporations. We are all of opinion that it does."[171] While a corporation is not a citizen within the meaning of the Privileges or Immunities Clause,[172] it is a person within the meanings of the Due Process and Equal Protection clauses. The right of corporations to equal protection of the laws has been reaffirmed by the Court many times though its application to specific controversies has been uneven.[173]

The Supreme Court's treatment of the Equal Protection Clause in the marketplace begins with its refusal to apply the principle in the 5 to 4 decision in the *Slaughter House Cases.*[174] Justice Samuel Miller, for the majority, held that the pervading purpose of the amendments was to protect the newly emancipated Afro-Americans, and that no strong case of other state oppression had been made in this action.[175] From an economic viewpoint, the refusal to apply the Equal Protection Clause to stop this state grant of monopoly for twenty-five years in an ordinary trade, like the refusal to apply the Privileges or Immunities Clause, was patently wrong. All butchers were in like circumstances for the enactment of any health or safety statute, and the creation of a monopoly was not necessary for any police regulation of the trade. On the contrary, the grant of monopoly was not only an injury to all other butchers. It was an injury to the public as consumers, forcing them to pay monopoly prices for butchering services and for meat. The Equal Protection Clause should have been a second, additional basis for invalidating the statute granting the monopoly by enforcing the Anglo-American constitutional precedents against governmental grants of monopoly in the ordinary trades.

In 1879, the State of Louisiana adopted a new constitution, which read in part: "The monopoly features in the charter of any corporation now existing in the State, save such as may be contained in the charters of railroad companies, are hereby abolished."[176] In *Butchers Union Co. v. Crescent City Co.*[177] the Supreme Court held that the grant of monopoly which had been validated in the *Slaughter-House Cases* was legally terminated. Justice Miller, for the majority, emphasized the contract clause. After holding that the grant was a contract, he adopted the rule of *Stone v. Mississippi*[178] that the state may not contract to surrender its police power to regulate industry. Justices Joseph Bradley and Stephen Field wrote concurring opinions. Adopting their dissenting views in the *Slaughter-House Cases* that the original grant of monopoly was void, they restated their opinions that the grant violated the Privileges or Immunities Clause.[179] Justice Bradley also noted a violation of the Equal Protection Clause. "If it is not a denial of equal protection of the laws to grant to one set of men, the privilege of following an ordinary calling in a large community, and to deny it to all others, it is difficult to understand what would come within the constitutional prohibition."[180]

One of the earliest cases under the Equal Protection Clause concerned both racial and monopoly issues. In *Yick Wo v. Hopkins*,[181] a San Francisco ordinance made it unlawful to operate a laundry in a wooden building without a permit from the board of supervisors. Yick Wo proved that his wooden laundry had equipment that was not a fire hazard but was refused a permit. In fact, two hundred other Chinese laundry operators were denied permits while only one of eighty non-Chinese laundry operators with wooden buildings was denied a permit. Though the ordinance was neutral on its face, it was obviously administered to grant a monopoly to non-Chinese. Justice Stanley Matthews, for the Court, reversed the convictions for operating laundries without permits. "The fact of this discrimination is admitted. No reason for it is shown, and the conclusion cannot be resisted, that no reason for it exists except hostility to the race and nationality to which the petitioners belong, and which in the eye of the law is not justified."[182]

Statutory monopoly in the labor market was invalidated under the Equal Protection Clause in *Truax v. Raich*.[183] An Arizona statute required firms employing five or more workers to reserve 80 percent of its positions for United States citizens. In an action by a resident alien, the Supreme Court affirmed a holding that a person could not be denied opportunity for employment. Chief Justice Charles E. Hughes noted that "It requires no argument to show that the right to work for a living in the common occupations of the community is of the very essence of the personal freedom and opportunity that it was the purpose of the Amendment to secure."[184] He concluded: "If this could be refused solely on the ground of race or nationality, the prohibition of the denial to any person of the equal protection of the laws would be a barren form of words."[185]

Absent a classification based on race or alienage, the Equal Protection Clause has not been utilized significantly to protect the right to compete in markets. A key early example was *Powell v. Pennsylvania*,[186] in which a state law prohibiting the manufacture and sale of oleomargarine was upheld. The Court devoted the bulk of the opinion to a denial of relief under substantive due process. It then disposed of the equal protection claim in one unreasoned sentence by noting that the statute applied to all makers of margarine.[187] The avowed purpose of the statute was the protection of public health, but the trial court had denied admission in evidence of all offers of proof of the healthfulness of the margarine.[188] In fact, the purpose of the statute was to confer monopoly power on the dairy interests. Suppliers of butter and of margarine are in like circumstances as competitors in the market place and should have been treated equally. As the New York Court of Appeals previously had said in voiding a similar statute: "Who will have the temerity to say these constitutional principles are not violated by an enactment which absolutely prohibits an important branch of industry for the sole reason that it competes with another, and may reduce the price of an article of food for the human race? . . . Equal rights to all are what are intended to be secured by the establishment of constitutional limit to legislative power, and impartial tribunals to enforce them."[189]

Outside the field of taxation, few cases have found a violation of equal protection in state statutes regulating business. In 1902, an Illinois antitrust statute that exempted agricultural products in the hands of the producer was invalidated.[190] Since small farmers engaged in joint marketing are not in like circumstances with large manufacturers who conspire in restraint of trade, the decision seems wrong. It has been overruled.[191] In *Smith v. Cahoon*[192] the Court invalidated a Florida statute under equal protection that required certain private motor carriers to obtain Certification and insurance but did not require it of others. In *Mayflower Farms* v. *Ten Eyck*,[193] the anticompetitive New York Milk Control Act that set minimum prices for sellers without well-advertised trade names below that of established firms was held to violate equal protection because it in effect barred entry of new firms. In *Hartford Co. v. Harrison*,[194] Georgia statute was held to violate equal protection when it permitted mutual insurance companies to act through salaried resident employees but denied the same agencies to stock companies.

Morey v. Doud[195] was a leading exception to the Court's usual refusal to invalidate economic regulation on the grounds of violating equal protection. An Illinois act for licensing of currency exchanges that contained a special exemption for American Express Co. was held arbitrary. It was clear that the legislative purpose was "to afford the public *continuing* protection"[196] in its transactions with currency exchanges. While American Express Co. was a large, financially sound firm at the passage of the statute, the exemption would continue even if its financial conditions changed. The effect of barring rival firms from selling money orders in retail establishments was discriminatory because it created a closed class of one firm for preferential treatment.[197] The sound reasoning of *Morey* in holding a grant of monopoly to violate the Equal Protection Clause was overruled in *City of New Orleans v. Dukes*.[198] A city ordinance banning pushcart food vendors in the French Quarter exempted those who had previously been operating there for eight years or more. Only two vendors came under this exception and they had operated in the area for over twenty years. The plaintiff had operated in the area only two years but demonstrated that she had invested money and time in developing a trade in reasonable reliance on the right to participate in that market. The Supreme Court upheld the ordinance as rationally related to a legitimate state interest.[199] The decision illustrates the fallacy of the rationality test. The ordinance was rationally related to the objective of preserving "the appearance and custom valued by the Quarter's residents and attractive to tourists."[200] But the plaintiff was in like circumstances with other vendors who had invested in reliance on the existence of that market and should have been treated in the same way.

A similar reversal of an antimonopoly holding took place for statutes whose effect was to bar the entry into a state of chain drug stores. In *Liggett Co. v. Baldridge*,[201] the Court had invalidated a Pennsylvania statute requiring all stockholders of drug stores to be registered pharmacists. No detriment to public health could arise from ownership of drug stores by corporate chains because other state statutes prohibited the sale of impure drugs and required that prescriptions be compounded by registered pharmacists.[202] The problem with the decision was that it rested primarily on substantive due process rather than equal protection. No analysis was made of the efficiencies that would derive from competition of chain and local drug stores as equal participants in free markets. *Liggett* was overruled in 1973 in *North Dakota State Bd. v. Snyder's Drug Stores*,[203] sustaining a state statute requiring that a corporate owner of a pharmacy must have a majority of its stock owned by registered pharmacists. Here again the reasoning centered on substantive due process.[204] The Court missed the point that all owners of drug stores are in like circumstances as competitors in markets and that protection of public health was a separate issue.

The Supreme Court's great deference to state legislatures in refusing to protect equal access to the marketplace is exemplified by the 5 to 4 decision in *Kotch v. Board of River Port Pilot Com'rs*.[205] A Louisiana statute restricted piloting of ocean vessels on the Mississippi into New Orleans to persons appointed by the governor upon recommendation of a state board composed of the pilots themselves. The unlimited discretion of board members enabled them to recommend their relatives and friends exclusively for the required six months apprenticeship. Plaintiffs, with at least fifteen years experience elsewhere as pilots, sought relief under the Equal Protection Clause. Justice Black, for the majority, upheld the law and adopted the rational basis test. The object of the law was to secure "the safest and most efficiently operated pilotage system practicable. We cannot say that the method adopted in Louisiana for the selection of pilots is unrelated to this objective."[206] Here again one sees persons in like circumstances denied access to markets by state statute. Justice Rutledge, for the dissenters, stated, "The door is thereby closed to all not having blood relationship to presently licensed pilots. Whether the occupation is considered as having the status of `public officer' or of highly regulated private employment, it is beyond legislative power to make entrance to it turn upon such a criterion."[207]

Other cases centering on the rejection of substantive due process have failed to give adequate analysis to parallel claims of violation of equal protection. *Williamson v. Lee Optical Co.*[208] is a prime example. An Oklahoma statute aimed at reinforcing monopoly power in optometrists and ophthalmologists prohibited others, such as opticians, from fitting lenses to a face or duplicating or replacing lenses into frames without a prescription from the named professionals. The effect was to forbid an optician from doing these mechanical tasks at minimal cost to consumers. In upholding the statute, Justice Douglas, for the Court, failed to discuss whether opticians were similarly situated with the doctors in guaranteeing quality work in duplicating a cracked lens or in placing old lenses in new frames and fitting them to the buyer's face. Instead, he generalized: "The prohibition of the Equal Protection Clause goes no further than the invidious discrimination. We cannot say that point has been reached here."[209]

The filled milk cases represent another instance where discriminatory legislation was approved as conforming to due-process standards and valid claims of violation of equal protection were sidestepped.[210] The conclusion here is that the famous *Carolene Products*[211] decision was wrong. Strict scrutiny of economic regulation under the Equal Protection Clause to prevent monopolistic exploitation of consumers is just as important as defending the political rights of "discrete and insular minorities."[212] Filled milk is a combination of non-fat milk and vegetable oils that can be manufactured for approximately one-half the price of evaporated milk. It was bought mainly by very low-income people, a discrete social minority. The farm bloc in many states caused their legislatures to pass statutes absolutely prohibiting the sale of filled milk even though it was healthful food and could clearly be labeled as "not evaporated milk or cream." In the leading case of *Sage Stores Co. v. Kansas*,[213] the Supreme Court affirmed a 4 to 3 decision of the Kansas Supreme Court upholding such a prohibitory statute. Nutritional inferiority and possible deception of retailers in spite of well-labeled cans was emphasized. The U.S. Supreme Court summarily disposed of the equal protection issue using a rational basis test.[214]

In *Strehlow v. Kansas State Board of Agriculture*,[215] the truth finally prevailed. In *Strehlow*, the Kansas Court overruled its *Sage Stores* decision, noting that the dissent in 1943 had "hit the nail on the head."[216] The food was found wholesome, nutritious, and healthful. It was clearly labeled and not conducive to deception or fraud. As applied to this product, the statute was held to violate the Due Process and Equal Protection clauses. The opinion followed an earlier finding of a U.S. District Court that the similar Arkansas statute as applied to filled milk violated the Equal Protection Clause.[217]

On the national level, the Filled Milk Act of 1923 that had been passed by pressure of the dairy interests prohibited its shipment in interstate commerce. In *Carolene Products Co. v. United States*,[218] the federal statue was upheld against a due process challenge as a protective against fraudulent substitution for milk. This was in spite of a finding of equal nutritional value.[219] In 1972, a U.S. District Court made an opposite finding, relying on the concept of equal protection as incorporated in the due process clause of the Fifth Amendment.[220] The application of the prohibition to filled milk and not to other products combining non-fat milk and vegetable oils was discriminatory. Without mentioning the leading case of *Bolling v. Sharpe*,[221] the district court presumed that the Due Process Clause incorporated equal protection of the laws.

In a significant number of other cases, the Supreme Court has denied equal protection to persons in business firms through summary application of the rational basis test. Absent argument on whether parties were in like circumstances in relation to a valid statutory purpose, the Court in many cases failed to consider the true issue. In *Goesaert v. Cleary*,[222] it upheld a Michigan statute forbidding women to be licensed as bartenders unless they were wives or daughters of the male owner of the bar. Three dissenting justices argued that the act denied equal protection to female owners of bars since they and their daughters were not permitted to tend their bar.[223] In *Daniel v. Family Security Life Ins. Co.*,[224] the Court upheld a South Carolina statute that forbade insurance companies and their agents from engaging in the undertaking business and forbade undertakers from serving as sales agents for life insurance companies. The evidence had shown that insurance companies represented by morticians and those not so represented were in like circumstances as competitors in the market. The district court had found the statute to be "arbitrary and discriminative" since its sole objective was to restrain competition.[225]

In *Ferguson v. Skrupa*,[226] the Court upheld a Kansas statute that prohibited any person other than lawyers from engaging in the business of debt adjustment. Persons skilled in problems of family finance and budgeting were barred from competing with lawyers. Evidence showed that some states had regulated any abuses of debt adjusting without eliminating competition of those persons who might be most skilled in the field.[227] In *Martin v. Walton*,[228] the Court upheld a Kansas Supreme Court rule that required a member of the Kansas bar residing nearby in Missouri to appear with local associate counsel when appearing in Kansas courts. Since all members of the bar must be presumed to know the procedural law of the state, the only purpose of the rule must have been to reduce competition. The dissenters found the statute "invidious in its application."[229]

Recent decisions have continued the rejection of the plea for equal protection in the marketplace. In *Rice v. Norman Williams Co.*,[230] claims under the Sherman Act and the Supremacy Clause were combined with the issue of equal protection. California liquor wholesalers had induced the state legislature to enact a "designation" statute under which a licensed wholesaler was prohibited from buying any brand of distilled liquor unless he was designated as the authorized wholesaler by the distiller who owned the brand name. The objective was to create monopoly wholesalers for each brand and thus prevent intrabrand competition by preventing a California wholesaler from acquiring branded liquor from an out-of-state wholesaler. Reversing the California Court of Appeal, the Supreme Court held that there was not a *per se* violation of the Sherman Act because the distiller's designation of an exclusive wholesaler was a vertical non-price restraint.[231] As to the Equal Protection Clause, the Court held that the discrimination between designated and non-designated wholesalers was rationally related to the statute's legitimate purpose. The asserted purpose was to restrain intrabrand competition in order to foster interbrand competition.[232] There was no evidence that this interaction ever had occurred or could occur in the marketing structure of the liquor industry. In fact, interbrand competition was the weakest of the two because of the contrived product differentiation due to distillers' intensive advertising of brand names.[233] The statutory curtailment of intrabrand rivalry wiped out the most effective element of competition in liquor marketing by depriving wholesalers in like circumstances of equal opportunity in the marketplace.

In theory, the Equal Protection Clause as applied to markets should reinforce the national commerce power in protecting and maintaining a nationwide free economy. In a few instances, however, the Congress has delegated an aspect of the commerce power to the states. In *Northeast Bancorp v. Board of Governors, FRS*,[234] a federal statute required bank holding companies to obtain approval of the Federal Reserve Board before they acquired any bank and prohibited such acquisition by an out-of-state holding company unless it was authorized by the state in which the bank was located. Connecticut and Massachusetts passed statutes allowing only out-of-state bank holding companies of New England to acquire in-state banks and only on the basis of reciprocal privileges. The Supreme Court unanimously upheld the state statutes against challenges under the Commerce, Compact, and Equal Protection clauses of discrimination against bank holding companies outside New England. As to the equal protection challenge, this opinion in part faces the issue of whether New England bank holding companies are in like circumstances with those outside New England. Regional bank holding companies combined "the beneficial effect of increasing the number of banking competitors with the need to preserve a close relationship between those in the community who need credit and those who provide credit."[235]

Notes

1. 163 U.S. 537 (1896), overruled in *Gayle v. Browder*, 352 U.S. 903 (1956).
2. Tamotsu Shibutani and Kian M. Kwan, *Ethnic Stratification: A Comparative Approach,* 224-250 (New York: Macmillan Co., 1965).
3. See Susan Bayly, *Caste, Society and Politics in India from the Eighteenth Century to the Modern Age* (Cambridge: Cambridge Univ. Press, 2001).
4. See Leon F. Litwack, *Been in the Storm So Long: The Aftermath of Slavery* (New York: Vintage Books, 1979); C. Vann Woodward, *Reunion and Reaction: The Compromise of 1877 and the End of Reconstruction* (New York: Oxford Univ. Press, 1966); David A.J. Richards, *Conscience and the Constitution: History, Theory, and Law of the Reconstruction Amendments,* 150-56 (Princeton, NJ: Princeton Univ. Press, 1993).
5. Kenneth L. Karst, *Belonging To America: Equal Citizenship and the Constitution* 21-27, 64-69 (New Haven: Yale Univ. Press, 1989). "The fact is that *Plessy* may have been stillborn, for it never developed beyond a fictional excuse for discrimination. The states adhered to the 'separate' part of the doctrine but never took notice of the 'equal' proposition." Philip B. Kurland, *Politics, the Constitution, and the Warren Court,* 89 (Chicago: Univ. of Chicago Press, 1970).
6. See Edward H. Levi, *An Introduction to Legal Reasoning,* 57-61 (Chicago: Univ. of Chicago Press, 1961); Albert R. Blaustein and Andrew H. Field, *"Overruling" Opinions in the Supreme Court,* 57 Mich. L. R. 151 (1958).
7. *Graves v. New York,* 306 U.S. 466, 491-92 (1939).
8. *City of New Orleans v. Dukes,* 427 U.S. 297, 303 (1976); *Williamson v. Lee Optical Co.,* 348 U.S. 483, 489 (1955); *Smith v. Cahoon,* 283 U.S. 553, 567 (1931).
9. Laurence H. Tribe, *American Constitutional Law,* 1439-43, 2d ed., (Meineola, NY: Foundation Press, 1988).
10. *Note, Legislative Purpose, Rationality, and Equal Protection,* 82 Yale L. J. 123, 128 (1972). See Gerald Gunther, *The Supreme Court 1971 Term, Forward: A Model for a Newer Equal Protection,* 86 Harv. L. Rev. 1 (1972).
11. See George Stigler, *The Theory of Economic Regulation,* 2 Bell J. Econ.& Mgmnt. Sci. 3 (1971); Sam Peltzman, *Toward a More General Theory of Regulation,* 19 J. Law & Econ. 211 (1976).
12. See, e.g., *Morey v. Dowd,* 354 U.S. 459 (1957), overruled in *City of New Orleans v. Dukes,* 427 U.S. 297, 306 (1976).
13. U.S. Const., Amend. 14, §1. See William E. Nelson, *The Fourteenth Amendment: from Political Principle to Judicial Doctrine* (Cambridge: Harvard Univ. Press, 1988).
14. Chief Justice Marshall noted the rule of construction: "It cannot be presumed that any clause in the Constitution is intended to be without effect; and, therefore, such a construction is inadmissible, unless the words require it," *Marbury v. Madison,* 5 U.S. (1 Cranch) 137, 174 (1803).
15. Congressman John A. Bingham, who drafted section 1 of the Fourteenth Amendment, asserted that the prime purpose of the Privileges or Immunities Clause was to overrule the Supreme Court's opinion in *Barron v. Baltimore,* 32 U.S. (7 Pet.) 243 (1833) and make the immunities that are enumerated in the Bill of Rights effective against the state governments. Cong. Globe, 39th Cong., 1st Sess., 1089-90 (Feb. 28, 1866); *Id.* 1292 (Mar. 8, 1866). The senate leader on the Fourteenth Amendment, Jacob M. Howard, asserted the same point and added that enforcement of the Bill of Rights against the states together with the Equal Protection Clause were necessary to protect the black man in his fundamental rights as a citizen and

wipe out the caste system. Cong. Globe, 39th Cong., 1st Sess., 2765-66 (May 23, 1866). See Akhil Reed Amar, *The Bill of Rights: Creation and Reconstruction,* 163-87 (New Haven, CT: Yale Univ. Press, 1998); Michael Kent Curtis, *No State Shall Abridge: The Fourteenth Amendment and the Bill of Rights* 57-91 (Durham, NC: Duke Univ. Press, 1986); Richard L. Aynes, *On Misreading John Bingham and the Fourteenth Amendment,* 103 Yale L. J. 57 (1993). Compare Chapter 7.

16. See authorities cited in William W. Crosskey, 2 *Politics and the Constitution in the History of the United States* 1103-16, 1377-78 (Chicago: Univ. of Chicago Press, 1953).

17. It also bars unequal application of common-law rules. *Jersey Shores, etc. v. Estate of Baum,* 84 N.J. 137, 417 A.2d 1003, 1007 (1980).

18. On the early meanings of political equality as a self-evident truth, see Jack R. Pole, *The Pursuit of Equality in American History,* ch. 2 (Berkeley: Univ. of California Press, 1978).

19. Francis Thorpe, ed., *The Federal and State Constitutions, Colonial Charters and Other Organic Laws,* VII, 3812-13 (1909) (Virginia); id., V, 3081-82 (Pennsylvania); id., VI, 3739 (Vermont); id., IV, 2453 (New Hampshire); id., III, 1888-1889 (Massachusetts); id., I, 536-37 (Connecticut), id., V, 2599 (New Jersey).

20. Robert M. Cover, *Justice Accused: Antislavery and the Judicial Process,* ch. 3 (New Haven, CT: Yale Univ. Press, 1975).

21. See Jacobus tenBroek, *The Antislavery Origins of the Fourteenth Amendment* 175-79 (Berkeley: Univ. of California Press, 1951).

22. See Howard Jay Graham, E*veryman's Constitution* 566-70 (Madison: State Historical Society of Wisconsin, 1968).

23. Cong. Globe, 39th Cong., 1st Sess., 438 (Jan. 26, 1866).

24. See tenBroek, *supra* note 19, at 163-64.

25. Cong. Globe, 39th Cong., 1st Sess., 2764-65 (May 23, 1866).

26. 60 U.S. (19 How.) 393 (1857).

27. 1 Loft's Rep. 1, 20 Howell's State Trials 1, 98 Eng. Rep. 499 (1772). See William M. Wiecek, *Somerset: Lord Mansfield and the Legitimacy of Slavery in the Anglo-American World,* 42 U. Chi. L. Rev. 86 (1974).

28. *Plyler v. Doe,* 457 U.S. 202, 216 (1982); *Royster Guano Co. v. Virginia,* 253 U.S. 412, 415 (1920). See Joseph Tussman and Jacobus tenBroek, *The Equal Protection of the Laws,* 37 Calif. L. Rev. 341, 345 (1949). As to the questionable utility of a rational basis test in modern equal protection opinions of the Supreme Court, see Robert F. Nagel, *Constitutional Cultures: The Mentality and Consequences of Judicial Review,* 84-105 (Berkeley: Univ. of California Press, 1989).

29. *Home Insurance Co. v. New York,* 134 U.S. 594, 606 (1890).

30. William McKechnie, *Magna Carta* 395 (Glasgow: J. Maclehose, 2d ed. 1914). Note the judicial citation of *Magna Charta* for equal protection in *Malinski v. New York,* 324 U.S. 401, 413-14 (1945) (Frankfurter, J.); *Griffin v. Illinois,* 351 U.S. 12, 16-17 (1956) (Black, J.). See A.E. Dick Howard, *The Road from Runnymede,* 311-15 (Charlottesville: Univ. Press of Virginia, 1968).

31. A. Dicey, *Introduction to the Study of the Law of the Constitution* 202 (London: Macmillan, 10th ed. 1962). As to colonial Americans' claims to equality of rights with citizens in England, see John A. Reid, *Constitutional History of the American Revolution* 60-64, 82-86 (Madison: Univ. of Wisconsin Press, 1986).

32. Richard L. Perry and John C. Cooper, *Sources of Our Liberties* 148 (Chicago: American Bar Foundation, 1959).

33. *Id.* at 375.

34. *United States v. Cruikshank,* 92 U.S. 542, 555 (1876).

35. Michael W. McConnell, *Originalism and the Desegregation Decisions,* 81 VA. L. Rev. 947 (1995); John P. Frank and Robert Munro, *The Original Understanding of "Equal Protection of the Laws,"* 1972 Wash. U.L.Q. 421, 432. Compare, Bickel, *The Original Understanding of the Segregation Decision,* 69 Harv. L. Rev. 1 (1955)
36. Political rights of former slaves were protected in U.S. Const., amend. XIV, §2, and in Amend. XV.
37. Paul Dimond, *Strict Construction and Judicial Review of Racial Discrimination under the Equal Protection Clause,* 80 Mich. L. Rev. 462, 494-502 (1982).
38. See, e.g., Raoul Berger, *Government by Judiciary,* ch. 10 (Cambridge, MA: Harvard Univ. Press, 1977); Charles Fairman, *Does the Fourteenth Amendment Incorporate the Bill of Rights?* 2 Stan. L. Rev. 5, 44 (1949).
39. Act of April 9, 1866, c. 31, 14 Stat. 27.
40. *United States v. Wong Kim Ark,* 169 U.S. 649, 699 (1898).
41. See *supra* note 39.
42. Cong. Globe, 39th Cong, 1st sess., 1290-92 (Mar. 9, 1866). See Horace E. Flack, *The Adoption of the Fourteenth Amendment* 30-31 (Baltimore, MD: Johns Hopkins Press, 1908).
43. *Reed v. Reed,* 404 U.S. 71, 76 (1971); *Lehr v. Robertson,* 463 U.S. 248, 265 (1983).
44. *Ex parte Virginia,* 100 U.S. 339 (1879).
45. *Strauder v. West Virginia,* 100 U.S. 303 (1880).
46. *Ex parte Virginia,* 100 U.S. 339 (1879)
47. See *Oregon v. Mitchell,* 400 U.S. 112, 264n (1970) (Brennan, J.).
48. See Gary Becker, *The Economics of Discrimination* (Chicago: Univ. of Chicago Press, 2d ed. 1971); Richard Posner, *The Economics of Justice,* 351-63 (Cambridge: Harvard Univ. Press, 1983).
49. Richard Kluger, *Simple Justice,* 52-53 (New York: Alfred A. Knopf, 1975); Gunnar Myrdal, 1 *An American dilemma,* ch. 13(New York: Harper & Bros, 1944), Charles Johnson, *Patterns of Negro Segregation,* ch. 4 (New York, Harper & Bros, 1943).
50. C. Vann Woodward, *Origins of the New South* (Baton Rouge: Louisiana State Univ. Press, 1951); Eli Ginzberg and Alfred S. Eichner, *The Troublesome Presence*: *American Democracy and the Negro,* ch. 8 (New York: Free Press, 1964).
51. Meyer Weinberg, *A Chance to Learn: The History of Race and Education in the United States,* ch. 2 (New York: Cambridge Univ. Press, 1977).
52. *Id.* at 44. The percentage of Negro children enrolled in school rose to 44.8 in 1910; 53.5 in 1920; 60.3 in 1930; and 68.4 in 1940. *Id.*
53. *Claybrook v. Owensboro,* 16 F. 297, 302 (D.C.Ky. 1883); *Puitt v. Commissioners,* 94 N.C. 514, 519 (1886) (ruling under Art. 9, §2 of N.C. Constitution).
54. Weinberg, *A Chance to Learn, supra* note 51, at 48. In 1920-1921, in the nineteen Black counties of Mississippi where 78.1 percent of the population was Negro, per capita public school expenditure on white children was $30.22, while the per capita expenditure on Negro children was $3.59. The latter was 11.9 percent of the former. *Id.* at 60.
55. On the optimum social investment in education, see Gary Becker, *Human Capital* (New York: National Bureau of Economic Research, 2d ed. 1975).
56. Suspect classification has been explained by the Court:

Some classifications are more likely than others to reflect deep-seated prejudice rather than legislative rationality in pursuit of some legislative objective. Legislation predicated on such prejudice is easily recognized as incompatible with the constitutional understanding that each person is to be judged individually and is entitled to equal justice under the law. Classifications treated as suspect tend to be irrelevant to any proper legislative goal. . . . Legislation imposing special disabilities upon groups disfavored by virtue of circumstances beyond their control suggests the kind of "class or caste" treatment that the Fourteenth Amendment was designed to abolish.

Pyler v. Doe, 457 U.S. 202, 216 n. 14 (1982). See Judith Baer, *Equality under the Constitution*, ch. 5 (Ithaca, NY: Cornell Univ. Press, 1983); Hans Linde, *Due Process of Lawmaking*, 55 Neb. L. Rev. 197, 201-2 (1976).

57. *Strauder v. West Virginia*, 100 U.S. 303, 307-8 (1880).

58. See Roger A. Fischer, *The Segregation Struggle in Louisiana*, ch. 1 (Urbana: Univ. of Illinois Press, 1974).

59. C. Vann Woodward, *The Strange Career of Jim Crow* 16 (New York: Oxford Univ. Press, rev. ed. 1957); Howard N. Rabinowitz, *Race Relations in the Urban South*, ch. 8 (New York: Oxford Univ. Press, 1978).

60. Gion Johnson, *The Ideology of White Supremacy*, 1876-1910, in James Sprunt Studies in History and Political Science, XXXI, Essays in Southern History, 124, 136-140 (F.M. Green ed. 1949).

61. 95 U.S. 485 (1878).

62. *Id.*

63. *Id.* at 486.

64. *De Cuir v. Benson*, 27 La. Ann. 1, 5 (1875).

65. 95 U.S. at 490.

66. 22 U.S. (9 Wheat.) 1 (1824).

67. Civil Rights Act of 1875, ch. 14, 18 Stat. 335 (1875).

68. See *Wilson v. Black Bird Creek Marsh Company*, 27 U.S. (2 Pet.) 245, 252 (1829), where Chief Justice Marshall upheld Delaware control of a small, navigable creek but noted that Congress could exercise its plenary power over commerce in such cases and the national law would preempt that of a state.

69. 109 U.S. 3 (1883).

70. See Michael W. McConnell, *Originalism, supra,* note 35 at 949, 984-1086 (1995) for a complete history of the enactment of the Civil Rights Act. Compare Kurt H. Wilson, *The Reconstruction Desegregation Debate,* 17-45 (East Lansing: Michigan State Univ. Press, 2002).

71. John F. Stover, *American Railroads,* 42-3 (Chicago: Univ. of Chicago Press, 2d ed., 1997).

72. *Civil Rights Cases*, 109 U.S. at 5.

73. "It does not authorize Congress to create a code of municipal law for the regulation of private rights; but to provide modes of redress against operation of state laws, and action of state officers, executive or judicial, when these are subversive to fundamental rights specified in the amendment." 109 U.S. at 11.

74. *Id.* at 19.

75. Cong. Globe, 42d Cong., 2d Sess. 383 (Jan. 15, 1872).

76. *Id.* Sumner had quoted as authority on common carrier duties Justice *Story's Commentaries on the Law of Bailments* and Parsons *Contracts. Id.* See Wilson, *Reconstruction Desegregation Debate, supra* note 70 at 47-75.

77. *Civil Rights Cases*, 109 U.S. at 26.

78. *Id.* at 35.

79. Civil Rights Act of 1866, ch. 31, §1, 14 Stat. 27 (1866).

80. *Civil Rights Cases*, 109 U.S. at 36. This view of Justice Harlan was finally vindicated in *Jones v. Alfred H. Mayer Co.*, 392 U.S. 409 (1968) (Civil Rights Act of 1866 was a valid enforcement pursuant to Section 2 of the Thirteenth Amendment and forbids private racial discrimination in real-estate transactions).

81. 24 Stat. 379 (1887).
82. *Houston, E. & W. Texas Ry. v. United States*, 234 U.S. 342 (1914).
83. 22 U.S. (9 Wheat.) 1 (1824).
84. 78 Stat. 214 (1964), 42 U.S.C.A. 2000a-2000a-6 (1994).
85. *Heart of Atlanta Motel v. United States*, 379 U.S. 241 (1964); *Katzenbach v. Mc-Clung*, 379 U.S. 294 (1964).
86. 95 U.S. 485 (1878) See *supra*, notes 61 to 65 and accompanying text.
87. 133 U.S. 587 (1890).
88. *Id.* at 593-95.
89. See Chapter 4, *supra.*
90. 328 U.S. 373 (1946).
91. Louisiana Acts, 1890, no. 111.
92. See Otto H. Olsen, *Carpetbagger's Crusade: The Life of Albion Winegar Tourgee* 312-31 (Baltimore, MD: Johns Hopkins Univ. Press, 1965).
93. See Barbara J. Fields, *Ideology and Race in American History*, in J. Morgan Kousser, *Religion Race and Reconstruction: Essays in Honor of C. Vann Woodward* 143, 144 (New York: Oxford Univ. Press, 1982); Ashley Montagu, *Man's Most Dangerous Myth: The Fallacy of Race*, 5th ed. (New York: Oxford Univ. Press, 1974); Ashley Montagu, *The Myth of Blood*, 6 Psychiatry 15-19 (1943).
94. Ex parte Plessy, 45 La. Ann. 80, 11 So. 948 (1892). See Charles A. Lofgren, *The Plessy Case: A Legal-Historical Interpretation*, ch. 3 (New York: Oxford Univ. Press, 1987).
95. *Plessy v Ferguson* 163 U.S. 537 (1896). See Lofgren, *Plessy Case*, supra note 94 at 148-95; Benno C. Schmidt, Jr., *Principle and Prejudice: The Supreme Court and Race in the Progressive Era. Part 1: The Heyday of Jim Crow*, 82 Colum L. Rev. 463, 465-70 (1982).
96. *Plessy*, 163 U.S. at 542.
97. *Id.* at 544.
98. *Id.* at 551. On structural issues in mental fabrications, see Erving Goffman, *Frame Analysis*, ch. 6 (Boston; Northeastern Univ. Press, 1974).
99. 84 U.S. (17 Wall.) 445 (1873).
100. *Id.* at 452.
101. *Id.* at 452-53.
102. 163 U.S. at 553.
103. *Id.* at 554.
104. *Id.* at 556.
105. *Id.* at 557.
106. *Id.* at 559.
107. *Id.*
108. Richard Watt and Richard Orlikoff, *The Coming Vindication, of Mr. Justice Harlan*, 44 Ill. L. Rev. 13 (1949); Alan F. Westin, *John Marshall Harlan and the Constitutional Rights of Negroes: The Transformation of a Southerner*, 66 Yale L. J. 637 (1957).
109. *Plyler v. Doe*, 457 U.S. 202, 213 (1982). See Paul R. Dimond, *The Anti-Caste Principle—Toward A Constitutional Standard for Review of Race Cases*, 30 Wayne L. Rev. 1 (1983).
110. Eric Foner: *Reconstruction: America's Unfinished Business, 1863-1877* (New York: Harper & Row, 1988); Franklin Johnson, *Development of State Legislation Concerning the Free Negro*, 1919 (Reprint, Westport: Greenwood Press, 1979); Myrdal, 1 *An American Dilemma*, *supra* note 49, chs. 28-31; Howard N. Rabinowitz, *Race Relations in the Urban South* 329-39 (New York: Oxford Univ. Press, 1978).

111. Charles L. Black, *The Lawfulness of the Segregation Decision*, 69 Yale L.J. 421, 422 n. 8 (1960).

112. Robert J. Harris, *The Quest for Equality* 101 (Baton Rouge: Louisiana State Univ. Press, 1960).

113. *United States v. Buntin*, 10 F. 730 (C.C.S.D. Ohio, 1882). See note on public school segregation following this case. *Id*. at 737.

114. Leon F. Litwack, *The Trouble in Mind: Black Southerners in the Age of Jim Crow* (New York: Alfred A. Knopf, 1998); Myrdal, *American Dilemma*, *supra* note 49; John Dollard, *Caste and Class in a Southern Town* (New Haven, CT: Yale Univ. Press, 1937); E. Franklin Frazier, *The Negro Family in the United States* (Chicago: Univ. of Chicago Press, 1939).

115. Weinberg, *A Chance to Learn*, *supra* note 51; Henry Bullock, *A History of Negro Education in the South* (Cambridge: Harvard Univ. Press, 1967); Louis Harlan, *Separate and Unequal* (Chapel Hill: Univ. of North Carolina Press, 1958); Horace Bond, *The Education of the Negro in the American Social Order* (Englewood Cliffs: Prentice Hall, 1934).

116. 59 Mass. (5 Cush.) 198 (1850). See Levy and Jones, "Jim Crow Education; Origins of the 'Separate But Equal' Doctrine," in Leonard Levy, *Judgments: Essays on American Constitutional History*, 316-41 (Chicago: Quadrangle Books, 1972); Roderick T. Baltimore and Robert F. Williams, *The State Constitutional Roots of the "Separate But Equal" Doctrine: Roberts v. City of Boston*, 17 Rutgers L. J. 537 (1986).

117. 59 Mass. (5 Cush.) at 200.

118. Mass. Declaration of Rights, Art. 1. (1780). See Perry and Cooper, *Sources of Our Liberties*, *supra* note 32 at 374.

119. 59 Mass. (5 Cush.) at 206-7. The later assertion of Chief Justice Taft that the Massachusetts constitutional injunction was the same as the Equal Protection Clause of the Fourteenth Amendment was in error. *Gong Lum v. Rice*, 275 U.S. 78, 86 (1927).

120. 59 Mass. (5 Cush.) at 201. See Charles Sumner, 3 *Works*, 51-100 (Boston: Lee and Shepard, 1909).

121. Mass. St. 1855, ch. 256 sec. 1; Mass. Gen. Stat., ch. 41, sec. 9 (1860).

122. Alfred Kelly, *The Congressional Controversy Over School Segregation*, 64 Am. Hist. Rev. 537, 540 (1959).

123. *Id*.

124. *Id*. at 542-44.

125. McConnell, *Originalism and the Desegregation Decisions*, *supra* note 35, at 987-1086.

126. 175 U.S. 528 (1899), overruled, *Brown v. Board of Education,* 347 U.S. 483, 491, 494-95 (1954).

127. *Id*. at 532.

128. *Id*. at 542.

129. *Id*. at 534.

130. *Id*. at 545.

131. 211 U.S. 45 (1908).

132. 1904 Ky. Acts 181.

133. *Id.*

134. *Id*. at 67. See Andrew Kull, *The Color-Blind Constitution,* 126-130 (Cambridge, MA: Harvard Univ. Press. 1992).

135. Kluger, *Simple Justice, supra*, note 49 at 88.

136. 275 U.S. 78 (1927), overruled, *Brown v. Board of Education,* 347 U.S. 483, 491, 494-95 (1954).

137. 275 U.S. at 84. See *Rice v. Gong Lum,* 139 Miss. 760, 104 So. 105 (1925).

138. 275 U.S. at 86.

139. *Missouri ex rel. Gaines v. Canada,* 305 U.S. 337 (1938).

140. *Sipuel v. Board of Regents,* 332 U.S. 631 (1948). See Ada Fisher, *A Matter of Black and White: Autobiography of Ada Lois Sipuel Fisher* (Norman: Univ. of Oklahoma Press, 1996).

141. *Fisher v. Hurst,* 333 U.S. 147, 150 (1948). Justices Murphy and Rutledge dissented.

142. 339 U.S. 629 (1950).

143. *Id.* at 636.

144. 339 U.S. 637 (1950).

145. *Id.* at 642. See Note, *The Fall of An Unconstitutional Fiction—The "Separate but Equal" Doctrine,* 30 Nebraska L. Rev. 69, 76-78 (1950).

146. 339 U.S. 816 (1950).

147. 54 Stat. 898, 902, 49 U.S.C.A. § 3(1) (1940).

148. *Sweatt v. Painter* and *McLaurin v. Oklahoma S. Regents, Memorandum for the United States as Amicus Curiae.*

149. 100 U.S. 303 (1880).

150. *Sweatt* and *McLaurin Memorandum* 9-10; *Henderson v. United States, Brief For The United States* 38-40. See Philip Elman, *The Solicitor General's Office, Justice Frankfurter, and Civil Rights Litigation 1946-1960,* 100 Harvard L. Rev. 817, 820-22 (1987).

151. 349 U.S. 254 (1954).

152. Kluger, *Simple Justice, supra,* note 49. See Michael J. Klarman, *From Jim Crow to Civil Rights* (New York: Oxford Univ. Press, 2004).

153. 347 U.S. 483 (1954). The four cases were from Kansas, South Carolina, Virginia, and Delaware.

154. *Brown v. Board of Education,* 98 F. Supp. 797 (D. Kan. 1951). See Kluger, *supra* note 49, at 424.

155. *Belton v. Gebhart,* 32 Del. Ch. 343, 87 A. 2d 862 (1952).

156. *Id.* at 865.

157. See Erving Goffman, *Stigma: Notes on the Management of Spoiled Identity* (Englewood Cliffs, NJ: Prentice Hall, 1963); Karst, *Belonging to America, supra,* note 5 at 21-27.

158. *Brown,* 347 U.S. at 494-495.

159. See Michael W. McConnell, *The Originalist Case for Brown v. Board of Education,* 19 Harvard J. Law & Public Policy 457 (1996).

160. 352 U.S. 903 (1956) (*per curiam*), *aff'g, Browder v. Gayle,* 142 F. Supp. 707 (M.D.Ala. 1956). "We think that Plessy v. Ferguson has been impliedly, though not explicitly, overruled, and that, under the later decisions, there is now no rational basis upon which the separate but equal doctrine can be validly applied to public carrier transportation. . . ." *Id.* at 717. See Philip B. Kurland, *Politics, the Constitution, supra* note 5, at 71.

161. *Baltimore v. Dawson,* 350 U.S. 877 (1955) (segregated beaches); *Holmes v. Atlanta,* 350 U.S. 879 (1955) (golf courses); *New Orleans Parks Ass'n v. Detiege,* 358 U.S. 54 (1958) (parks).

162. Alexander Bickel, *The Least Dangerous Branch,* 102 (Indianapolis, IN: Bobbs-Merrill, 1962). For similar views, see Terrance Sandalow, *Constitutional Interpretation,* 79 Mich. L. Rev. 1033, 1036 (1981); Dimond, *Strict Construction supra,* note 37.

163. 347 U.S. 497 (1954).

164. Id. at 499, citing *Korematsu v. United States*, 32.3 U.S. 214 (1944); *Hirabashi v. United States*, 320 U.S. 81 (1943).
165. 347 U.S. 500.
166. See *supra* notes 30-33 and accompanying text.
167. See Pole, *The Pursuit of Equality, supra*, note 18.
168. See Adolph Berle and Gardiner Means, *The Modem Corporation and Private Property* (rev. ed., New York: Harcoourt-Brace, 1968).
169. Nicholas M. Butler, *Politics and Business,* in *Why Should We Change Our Form of Government?* 77, 82 (New York: Scribners, 1912).
170. 118 U.S. 394 (1886). See Peter C. Magrath, *Morrison R. Waite,* 221-24 (New York: Macmillan, 1963); Graham, *Everyman's Constitution, supra* note 22 at 566-70.
171. 118 U.S. at 396.
172. *Orient Insurance Co. v. Daggs,* 172 U.S. 557, 561 (1899). This follows the rule that corporations are not citizens under the Privileges and Immunities Clause of U.S. Const., Art. IV, 82. *Pembina Mining Co. v. Pennsylvania,* 125 U.S. 181, 187 (1888).
173. *Metropolitan Life Ins. Co. v. Ward,* 470 U.S. 869, 881 (1985); *Western & Southern L. I. Co. v. Bd. of Equalization,* 451 U.S. 648, 66o (1981*); Grosjean v. American Press Co.,* 297 U.S. 233, 244 (1936).
174. 83 U.S. (16 Wall.) 36 (1873).
175. *Id.* at 81.
176. *Butchers Union Co. v. Crescent City Co.,*111 U.S. 746, 748 (1884).
177. 111 U.S. 746 (1884).
178. 101 U.S. 814 (1880).
179. 111 U.S. at 754, 760.
180. 111 U.S. 766. Justice Field quoted Adam Smith, *Wealth of Nations*, bk. 1, ch. 10: "The property which every man has in his own labor, as it is the original foundation of all other property, so it is the most sacred and inviolable. The patrimony of the poor man lies in the strength and dexterity of his own hands, and to hinder his employing this strength and dexterity in what manner he thinks proper, without injury to his neighbor, is a plain violation of this most sacred property. It is a manifest encroachment upon the just liberty both of the workman and of those who might be disposed to employ him. As it hinders the one from working at what he thinks proper, so it hinders the others from employing whom they think proper."
181. 118 U.S. 356 (1886). See *Barbier v. Connolly,* 113 U.S. 27 (1885); *Soon Hing* v. *Crowley,* 113 U.S. 703 (1885).
182. 118 U.S. at 374-
183. 239 U.S. 33 (1915).
184. *Id.* at 41.
185. *Id.*
186. 127 U.S. 678 (1888). See Chapter 8, notes 60 to 62.
187. This reasoning has been criticized as an "easy dismissal of the equal protection issue on the grounds that the law applies equally to all to whom it applies. . . . By the same token, a law applying to all red-haired makers of margarine would satisfy the requirements of equality" (Joseph Tussman and Jacobus tenBroek, *The Equal Protection of the Laws,* 37 Calif. L. Rev. 341, 345 [1949]).
188. 12.7 U.S. at 681.
189. Id. at 694 (Field, J., dissenting), citing *People v. Marx,* 99 N.Y. 377, 387 (1885).
190. *Connolly v. Union Sewer Pipe Co.,* 184 U.S. 540 (1902).
191. *Tigner v. Texas,* 310 U.S. 141 (1940).
192. 283 U.S. 553 (1931).

193. 297 U.S. 266 (1936).

194. 301 U.S. 459 (1937).

195. 354 U.S. 457 (1957).

196. *Id.* at 466.

197. *Id.* at 467.

198. 427 U.S. 297 (1976).

199. *Id.* at 303.

200. *Id.* at 304.

201. 278 U.S. 105 (1928).

202. *Id.* at 113-14.

203. 414 U.S. 156 (1973).

204. *Id.* at 164-67.

205. 330 U.S. 552. (1947).

206. *Id.* at 564.

207. *Id.* at 565.

208. 348 U.S. 483 (1955). See Chapter 8, notes 124-25.

209. 348 U.S. at 489. See Gunther, *supra* note 10, at 45-46.

210. See Geoffrey Miller, *The True Story of Carotene Products*, 1987 Sup. Ct. Rev. 397; Conant, *Systems Analysis in the Appellate Decisionmaking Process*, 24 Rutgers L. Rev. 293, 317-22 (1970).

211. *United States v. Carotene Products Corp.*, 304 U.S. 144 (1938).

212. *Id.* at 152, note 4.

213. 323 U.S. 32. (1944) affirming *State v. Sage Stores Co.*, 157 Kan. 404, 141 P. 2cl 655 (1943). The defendants contended unsuccessfully that the classification was arbitrary and in violation of the Equal Protection Clause in two aspects. First, they argued that it was arbitrary to control only this one combination of milk and oil or fat, other than milk fat, while other combinations of these same ingredients, such as evaporated milk with fish-oil vitamins, chocolate drink, infants' food, and margarines, were not subject to legislative control. Second, they urged that it was arbitrary to prohibit sale of these products when protection against possible deception in the sale of most other products was accomplished by adequate regulation of the selling. 323 U.S. 34-35.

214. "Apparently the objection under the equal protection clause is that the Kansas statute permits the sale of skimmed milk which has less calories and fewer vitamins than petitioners' compound and yet forbids the sale of the compound despite its higher nutritive value. Such an objection is governed by the same standards of legislation as objections under the due process clause. It is a matter of classification and the power of the legislature to classify is as broad as its power to prohibit. A violation of the Fourteenth Amendment in either case would depend upon whether there is any rational basis for the action of the legislature" (323 U.S. 34-35).

215. 232 Kan. 589, 659 P. 2d. 785 (1983).

216. *Id.* at 797.

217. *Milnot Co. v. Arkansas State Bd. of Health*, 388 F. Supp. 901 (E.D. Ark.1975).

218. 323 U.S. 18 (1944). For contrary views on the due process issue see *People v. Carotene Products Co.*, 345 Ill. 166, 177 N.E. 698 (1931); *Carotene Products Co. v. Thomson*, 2.76 Mich. 172., 267 N.W. 6o8 (1936); *Carotene Products Co. v. Banning*, 131 Neb. 42.9, 268 N.W. 313 (1936); *Coffee-Rich, Inc. v. Comm'r of Pub. Health*, 348 Mass. 414, 2.04 N.E.2d 281 (1965).

219. 32.3 U.S. 28-2.9.

220. *Milnot Company v. Richardson*, 350 F. Supp. 22.1 (1972).

221. 347 U.S. 497 (1954).

222. 335 U.S. 464 (1948). In more recent cases, the Court has invalidated most types of sex discrimination. *Orr v. Orr*, 440 U.S. 268 (1979); *Kirchberg v. Feenstra*, 450 U.S. 455 (1981).

223. 335 U.S. 467-68.

224. 336 U.S. 220 (1949).

225. *Family Security Life Ins. Co. v. Daniel*, 79 F. Supp. 62, 70 (E.D.S.C. 1948).

226. 372 U.S. 726 (1963). See Chapter 8, notes 171-172 and accompanying text.

227. 372. U.S. 72.7.

228. 368 U.S. 25 (1961).

229. Id. at 28 (Douglas, J., dissenting).

230. 458 U.S. 654 (1982). For condemnation of the earlier version of the statute that contained resale price maintenance, see *California Retail Liquor Dealers Assn. v. Midcal Aluminum, Inc.*, 445 U.S. 97, 100-2 (1980).

231. 458 U.S. at 659-70, citing *Continental T.V., Inc. v. GTE Sylvania Inc.*, 433 U.S. 36 (1977).

232. 458 U.S. 665.

233. On the distinction between the information function of selling activities and contrived product differentiation, see Edward Chamberlin, *The Theory of Monopolistic Competition*, ch. 5 (7th ed., Cambridge, MA: Harvard Univ. Press, 1956); Roger Sherman, *The Economics of Industry*, ch. 16 (Boston: Little Brown, 1974).

234. 472 U.S. 159 (1985).

235. *Id*. at 178.

Index of Cases

Subject Index